Very Special Places

VERY SPECIAL PLACES

REVISED AND UPDATED

by IAN KEOWN

with additional material by
Eleanor Berman, Sue Buck, Linda Burnham,
Susan Hannah, Alan Mooney,
Cynthia Proulx, and Bob Scanlon

Collier Books
A Division of Macmillan Publishing Co., Inc.
New York
Collier Macmillan Publishers
London

Macmillan Publishing Co., Inc.
866 Third Avenue, New York, N.Y. 10022
Collier Macmillan Canada, Ltd.

Library of Congress Cataloging in Publication Data
Keown, Ian.
   Very Special Places.

   1. Hotels, taverns, etc.—United States.
I. Title.
TX909.K46   1981   647'.9473   81–10098
ISBN 0–02–097820–0   AACR2

10 9 8 7 6 5 4 3 2 1

Printed in the United States of America

Contents

vi

Green Mountains, White Mountains

In and Around the Bosky Berkshires

From the Adirondacks to Bucks County

East Side, West Side

Around the Chesapeake Bay

Up Hill and Down Dale—the Shenandoah Valley and Blue Ridge Mountains

From the Carolinas to the Keys

From the Great Lakes to the Gulf

In and Around the Rockies

The Desert Resorts of the Great Southwest

Sunny Southern California

San Francisco and Its Neighbors

The Pacific Northwest

Hawaii

Added Attractions

The Rates— and How to Figure Them Out

Postscript

Preface

This is the largest edition yet of *Very Special Places*, with almost half as many more inns, hotels, and resorts as the previous editions. There are also completely new sections on Hawaii and New York. A few hotels have been dropped, others relegated to the Added Attractions chapter because they did not, for a variety of reasons, impress us this time around.

Several of the new entries are the result of readers sending in suggestions, with which we agreed once we had a chance to check out the properties. Your suggestions are most helpful. Likewise, those reports that bring us up to date on shortcomings, changes, improvements, and whatever are useful in keeping us abreast of what's going on, and we hope you'll keep them coming. The more details you can include, the better. My colleagues and I frequently pass your comments along to the innkeepers, and you'd be surprised how concerned most of them are to find satisfactory responses to the complaints.

Let me just remind you once more of two of the features that seem to set this guidebook apart from the others:

all inns, hotels, and resorts have been inspected in person by myself or one of my colleagues and

no one pays to be in Very Special Places—*it's completely independent.*

Thank-Yous

This guide could never have been produced without the help and encouragement of countless people—friends, readers, colleagues in the travel business, total strangers in chance encounters. I thank them all, and ask that they forgive me for not identifying them one by one.

I'd particularly like to thank the countless innkeepers, front office managers, housekeepers, and bellboys who took the time and trouble to guide me through rooms *they'd* seen a zillion times already. I suppose I should also thank various spouses and lovers who waited patiently (although not always uncomplainingly) while my colleagues traipsed through hotels and plodded through questionnaires.

A few people should be singled out for special mention, and I'll list them in alphabetical order: Marguerite Aumann Allen, Lynda Bernard, Myriam Bin, Doris Saatchi, Peter Verbeck, and Archer Ward.

A paragraph all to herself would seem to be in order in the case of Sheila Keenan, who addressed envelopes, licked stamps, made Xeroxes, kept files, checked rates, deciphered my handwriting, typed, collated, telephoned, edited, researched—yet, incredibly, remained cheerful and enthusiastic throughout, although she had her own literary efforts to consider at the same time.

Above all, a special thank-you to the colleagues identified throughout the guidebook by their initials:

E.B. ELEANOR BERMAN is the author of three books, the most recent of which is *Re-Entering*. Her career spans advertising, publishing, and public relations, and she has written articles for many magazines and newspapers, including *Newsday*, *Harper's Bazaar*, *Travel & Leisure*, and *Family Circle*.

S.B. SUE BUCK is a vice president in one of New York's top advertising agencies and author of several articles on sailing and sailboats.

L.E.B.   LINDA BURNHAM is the author of the *Arthur Frommer Guide to Amsterdam*. Her byline has also appeared in *Cosmopolitan, Travel & Leisure,* and other magazines.

C.P.   CYNTHIA PROULX was my co-author on *Guide to France for Loving Couples,* and has also written for *Saturday Review, Viva,* and *Travel & Leisure*. As a freelance copywriter she spends her time flying out to California on assignments.

S.H.   SUSAN HANNAH flies for PanAm on weekends, spends the rest of her time at Columbia University or in Kenya preparing for a Ph.D. in anthropology.

A.M.   ALAN MOONEY heads up the San Francisco branch of a leading international advertising agency. His idea of a vacation is to struggle with winches and spinnakers in the Newport to Bermuda Race.

R.E.S.   BOB SCANLON is a New Yorker by birth and inclination but currently living in Houston, Texas, where he writes advertising copy for Shell Oil, Houston Opera, and other clients.

Introduction

"O for a seat in some poetic nook,
Just hid with trees and sparkling with a brook."

This is a book of nice places.

Old inns. Hideaways. Resorts. Trysting places. Shangri-las. Places to nip off to for a few days to be together and alone.

These are special places for people who enjoy the finer things in life. Not necessarily expensive, just simple things—watching sandpipers at sunset, munching freshly picked apples, scrambling over rocks, sipping mulled cider in front of a log fire, bicycling through lanes of moss-covered oaks, trudging through the snow, listening to Mozart under the stars, riding desert trails among saguaro, cholla, and cottonwoods.

It's primarily for lovers—of all ages and inclinations. Man/woman, boy/girl, boy/woman, roué/Lolita, boy/boy, girl/girl, rich lovers, poor lovers. Couples whose children have grown up and fled the fold, and who now have an opportunity to enjoy each other once more.

The guide is most certainly *not* for swingers.

It's *not* for people who'd rather see a floor show than the moonlight, who'd rather hear the action at a crap table than the sound of surf in a rocky cove.

It's *not* for people who want heart-shaped bathtubs, or mirrors on the ceilings, walls, and headboards, or tiger-skin bedspreads and tiger-skin rugs in rooms with fountains dribbling down purple walls (don't snicker, these places exist). Swingers will be bored out of their bejoggled skulls by most of the places in this guide.

SETTING THE GROUND RULES. All the inns, resorts, and hotels in this guide have something special going for them. The something special could be antiquity (Longfellow's Wayside Inn in Massachusetts or the Wayside Inn in Virginia), location (Skyland Lodge in Virginia's Shenandoah National Park, Heritage House in California), charm (the Inn at Sawmill Farm in Vermont, Greyfield Inn on Cumberland Island), nostalgia (Wentworth-by-the-Sea in New Hampshire, La Valencia in California), unabashed luxury (The Stanford Court in San Francisco, the Boca Raton Hotel in Florida), seclusion (Sun-

xviiIntroduction

dance in Utah, Timberline in Oregon), sports facilities (Sun Valley Lodge in Idaho, Hilton Head Inn in South Carolina)—or more often than not, a combination of several of these special "somethings." A few are included mainly because they combine charm or unique location with relatively low prices.

They're places where you won't be embarrassed if you forget to write Mr. and Mrs. when you sign in, where bellhops won't wink if the initials on your luggage don't match, where chambermaids won't come barging in on you in the morning, where you won't have to sit down to breakfast with snoopy old ladies who'd just love to know what you were really doing up there. They're places where you can escape neon, piped music, television and jukeboxes, formula decor, conventions, coach-loads of tourists and irruptions of children. (Well, more or less, because the advantage to writing an independent guidebook is that you not only make your own rules; you can then break them. Some of the places listed in these pages *do* have piped music and television and conventions, but they're included because they have other qualities that compensate for these drawbacks.)

PET PEEVES. You'll notice occasional references throughout this guide to irritants like piped music and television. They're among my pet peeves, and even if I end up sounding like a curmudgeon, here's why. You go away for a quiet weekend together, and you deliberately pick out a spot where you think you'll be allowed to enjoy the blissful environment, so you do *not* want to sit down in the bar or dining room and have to listen to what someone else has decided you ought to listen to. It just doesn't make sense to search out a Colonial tavern in New England, order lobster or pumpkin pie, and have to listen to "Down Argentina Way" or some hack's orchestral arrangement of the love duet from *La Bohème* (I've had to listen to both during *one* piece of pumpkin pie). Likewise TV. You drive around country lanes, lapping up the scenery and the solitude, and you arrive full of the joys and glories of nature at a lovely old inn, go into the lounge expecting to find a welcoming fire, and instead find gunslingers going full tilt on the telly. (This is not to say that inns and hotels should not have any television sets for guests who want them; I just feel that TV should be in places where people can watch without interfering with other guests who *don't* want to watch.)

If you feel the same way about TV and piped music (and I'm delighted to discover from readers' letters that many of you do), ask the innkeepers to turn the bloody things off. Tell them you came to the country/beach/mountains to listen to the birds and crickets, not hectoring commercials or piped marshmallow music.

Live entertainment is another matter. You can't very well ask the innkeeper to send his musicians packing, so the best you can do here is to ask him to throttle back the amplification. In this guide, I've tried to alert you to places with live entertainment so that you will not be surprised when you get there; many of them are large enough to allow you to slip off to someplace where even the boomingest amplification can't penetrate.

Now, about children. They can be, at times, a combination of piped music, television, and amplification in a few tiny bodies. But not always. And it may not be the children who are the problem; more likely it's the parents, trying to have a vacation themselves, who allow family discipline to deteriorate to the point where order can be restored only by a public slanging match. This is no fun for other *parents* who are trying to get away from children for a few days, and quite shattering to people seeking a romantic atmosphere. A few of the smaller hotels in this guide flatly refuse to have children under, say, ten; many of the large resorts have separate play areas, dining rooms, and dining hours for children, which should help to keep them out of your hair. In a few of the hotels, children (and their transistor radios) are likely to be present during the vacation periods, which is only fair, and these hotels should be avoided at those times. (Some readers have, apparently, come to the conclusion that these comments indicate some form of kidophobia. Tsk, tsk. Some of my best friends are children, and I herewith apologize for any misunderstandings to Karen and Mandy, J-J and Susan, Jamie and Kate, and other young ladies and gentlemen who know how to eat with a knife and fork.)

CONVENTIONS. Throwing out hotels that hold conventions would mean eliminating every other hotel in the guide. However, there are conventions and there are conventions—groups, seminars, annual meetings, workshops, and a score of other assemblages. These days, any excuse to get away from the office is reason enough to hold a meeting in a hotel or, better still, resort; and even the smallest hotels rely on groups of some kind to keep themselves alive during the slow months. However, very very few of the hotels and resorts in this guide are able or willing to handle mob conventions of beer salesmen or placard-waving politicians; when they do host meetings, their groups usually consist of high-level executives, professors, governors, company directors, and others who can usually be relied upon to conduct themselves in an unobtrusive manner. Most of the larger hotels and resorts in this guide can be enjoyed by a loving twosome even when there's a group or seminar in the house (sometimes even more so, if the group in question is closeted all day in meetings, leaving you with the tennis courts and beaches all to yourselves). *However, to be on the safe side, when you make your reservation, ask if a large group is scheduled for that period.* Most hotels will understand your concern; indeed, some will warn you automatically without having to be asked. You can also do some preliminary research yourselves by reading the "P.S." category in the individual hotel listings, where you'll find a rough guide to the convention/group situation in each hotel.

CHECKING IN. In these liberated times, nobody seems to bother to check credentials. Even nice little old ladies at reception desks in Maine don't care (*unless* one of the partners looks very, very young, or one or both partners look downright disreputable). If you sign Mr. and Mrs., chances are no one will question it. If you balk at anything so specific, sign the accurate if unromantic "Mr. Blank and party." If both parties prefer to list individual names (for business reasons, for phone calls), most hotels will understand, especially since many *married* couples now check in by listing their individual names. The simplest solution, for guests and hotels, is the noncommittal M/M. Bear in mind that many hotels will add your name and address to their mailing list, for newsletters, brochures, and updated rates; if you're not supposed to be wherever you are, and you don't want anyone to find out months later, ask the manager to keep your name off his list.

SIGNING CHECKS. If, for some reason, you must check in under an assumed name (you are, say, a very famous film star), there's no point in flashing a credit card in your own name; in such cases, have a quiet word with the innkeeper or credit manager *before* you sign any checks in the bar or restaurant. Also, even if you have registered as Mr. and Mrs., the young lady, for example, may instinctively sign her own name, causing minor palpitations in the bookkeepers' cubicle; just remind each other occasionally who you are. Also, if the signing partner has a quaint name, like Keown, make sure the other knows how to spell it. And pronounce it.

RESERVATIONS. There's a lot to be said for just driving around in a pleasant carefree way, then stopping for the night where and when you like. But that's not always possible, and there's nothing more frustrating than being all ready to tumble into bed only to discover that there's no bed available in the inn where you wanted to tumble, nor in the other inn down the road, and you waste hours driving around looking for *something*, only to end up in an unromantic motel. Don't take chances: *always make a reservation in advance*, even if only a few hours in advance. (And always doublecheck the rate when you do so, just in case an innkeeper has had to jack up his rates since he first published his 1981 figures, quoted at the end of this guide.) Moreover, if you want to specify a particular room or type of bed, it's essential that you reserve as far in advance as possible.

Most inns, hotels, and resorts will hold your room until 6:00 P.M. If you plan to arrive later than that, ask them to hold the room (and to be sure they do, send a deposit). This is particularly important in small inns that cannot run the risk of having an empty room. Conversely, if you make a reservation and later decide to cancel, call the inn to tell them, so that another couple will not be turned away needlessly.

That's good advice for any hotel but doubly so in the case of most of those in this guide; because they *are* special, they may be the first to be booked, and in any case many of them have so few rooms that they are full most of the time. That's another point: don't count on the seasons anymore— even if it's a time of year when the hotel *should* be empty, it may still be full, simply because so many people seem to be on the move these days.

Above all, if you want a special room or a particular type of bed, it's essential that you reserve as far in advance as possible. Here and there throughout this guide we recommend rooms that we feel have particular attractions; innkeepers hate us for this, because it makes their lives complicated since everyone then wants the same rooms. All the more reason why you should reserve far in advance. Remember also that you have a better chance of getting the best rooms if you plan to stay several nights.

For adventurous lovers who're willing to risk last-minute go-as-you-please reservations, I've listed telephone numbers: call ahead early enough in the day so that you can still make alternative arrangements if your first choice is not available. For lovers who think ahead, here are the other ways of going about reservations:

1. *Travel agents*. The agent who books your flight, rental car, and train tickets can also arrange your hotel reservations, probably for no extra fee. Agents will also attend to the business of deposits and confirmations—which, be warned, can be pesky and time-consuming if you have to do it yourself for six or eight or a dozen hotels. However, travel agents may not be familiar with some of the smaller inns and hotels listed in these pages, and since they may be reluctant to send their clients to places they don't know, they may try to steer you to inns and hotels they *do* know. Stand firm. If necessary, show them this guidebook.

2. *Cables/Telex*. You can contact the hotel directly, using either a cable or telex address, which is listed, where available, under each hotel. Of the two, telex is faster because the message goes direct to the reservations office of the hotel and you can get a reply within minutes. It's also cheaper. Moreover, telex is more reliable than the telephone because both parties have the reservation and confirmation in writing. (You can send cables or telexes via Western Union, ITT, or RCA offices.)

Whichever method you choose, be sure your reservation is specific and clear. It should list the number of people in the party, date of arrival, time of arrival (especially if you are arriving late), flight number if you know it, twin beds or a double bed, bathtub or shower or both, upper floor or front or courtyard and so forth, whether you want your rate to be EP, CP, MAP, FAP. Finally, after all that, don't forget your name, return address, or telephone number or telex number.

RATES. Hotels have different ways, often unfathomable, of establishing their rates, and what you're going to pay may depend on such variables as twin beds versus double beds, with bath or without bath, lower floor or upper floor, ocean view or mountain view. And so on. I wish I could spell out all the variations for each hotel, but if I were to try, the seasons would be over before I managed to get halfway through. In any case, I assume that you like each other so much that tiresome trivia and a few dollars won't come between you.

Since the subject of rates is so complex and unpredictable, some guidebooks just don't give you any details. I think this is unfair to you: if you are paying for a guidebook, you deserve as much information as possible. Granted the published rates may not be 100 percent accurate, but at least they give you an opportunity to *compare* one hotel with another.

In this edition of *Very Special Places* detailed rates have been detached from the reports on individual hotels and collated in a listing at the end of the guide. In this way the rates can be brought up to date each time the guide is reprinted, without necessitating the costly process of resetting finicky figures within the body of the text. To compensate for that, I have added dollar signs to the ratings for each hotel, so that you can compare approximate rates hotel-by-hotel without having to refer to the back of the book each time. The signs are explained in detail in the following section on the ratings.

THE RATINGS. All the inns, hotels, and resorts in this guide are, in one way or another, *above average;* but some are obviously better than others, and to try to make life easier for you, I've rated the individual establishments. Unlike other guides, such as the Mobil guides which seem to rate hotels by a formula relying heavily on the number of elevators and coin-operated laundries, this guide's ratings are personal and subjective. Fortunately, the ratings seem to coincide with the views of most readers, too, judging from their letters and reports. Here's a short explanation of each rating.

Cupids represent *romantic* qualities—that is, personality or charm, decor and ambiance, the attitude of the staff, the setting, and what the hotel does with its environment. Please note: a cupid is not the equivalent of a star in other guides; it's more concerned with trees than elevators, with good taste than good plumbing. However, you *can* assume that every inn, hotel, and resort in this guide does have good plumbing (maybe not the most modern, but certainly functional), good beds, good housekeeping. That goes without saying.

Champagne bottles evaluate the wining and dining aspects of your stay; this includes the overall *attitude* to food and wine, and the competence of the staff, as well as the quality of the wine cellar and the food that's actually placed before you. It takes into consideration the ambiance of the dining facilities, the way a table is laid, the way a busboy removes empty dishes, the reception you get from a maître d', and so on. In other words, a hotel that rates only two champagne bottles might deserve three for the actual food but loses out because the waiters are sloppy and noisy.

Tennis rackets give you a guide to the availability (and accessibility) of diversions other than the one you really came for. The individual diversions are listed at the end of each hotel entry; wherever possible, I have tried to give you information on which facilities are *free* (usually the first listed).

$

    Use the dollar signs as a rough guide only, primarily for comparing one hotel with another. FOR DETAILED RATES, TURN TO THE SPECIAL CHAPTER AT THE END OF THE GUIDE.

    The $ symbols are based on peak-season rates for a double room only. Each $ represents approximately $50; where a hotel's rates overflow into several categories, the lowest category is shown, provided that a reasonable quota of rooms are available at this price.

Here are the ratings:

	For a one-night stand or stopover
	For a weekend
	For a week or longer
	Happily ever after
	Sustenance
	Good food
	Cuisine
	Haute cuisine
	A few diversions
	Real exercise

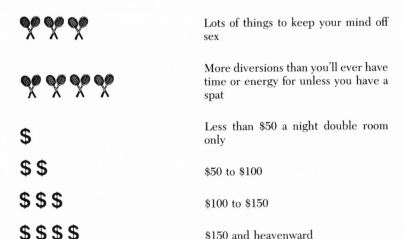

🎾🎾🎾	Lots of things to keep your mind off sex
🎾🎾🎾🎾	More diversions than you'll ever have time or energy for unless you have a spat
$	Less than $50 a night double room only
$ $	$50 to $100
$ $ $	$100 to $150
$ $ $ $	$150 and heavenward

(For details of specific rates for each hotel, please turn to the section on rates at the back of the guide.)

Remember, please: The cupids are an evaluation of "romantic" qualities, *not* of facilities or luxury; rates are, of course, subject to change, for reasons beyond the control of author or publisher.

DOUBLE OR SINGLE BEDS? Hotels nowadays have more twin beds than double beds. The reasons are that a surprising number of American couples prefer solitary slumbers; also, with so much convention and business traffic, hotels have to be able to accommodate a couple of executives in one room (apparently American corporate team spirit hasn't yet reached the point where executives want to bunk down in the same bed). However, most of the hotels, inns, and resorts in this guide have both twin and double beds. Always specify which you prefer when you make your reservation; if all the doubles have gone and you really must have one, most hotels will bully their maids or handymen into pushing the twins together and making a double. (This may not be true in smaller inns where the manpower situation is more critical.)

THE INN THING. You'll find many old-time inns listed in these pages. They are not everyone's cup of tea, and several innkeepers tell me they're concerned that people sometimes arrive on their doorsteps and are disappointed with what they find.

Here are some of the *nonfeatures* that may disappoint: you usually won't find a porter to carry your luggage; occasionally the innkeeper himself will help, but you should try to keep your luggage manageable because one of you may have to carry it up two or three flights of stairs.

You may not get room service in an inn. No breakfast in bed—unless one of you goes and fetches it. Also, don't expect the sort of service you'd get at the Beverly Hills Hotel or the Greenbrier; these places just don't have the staff to cope. They can offer you friendly personal service—but not night and day, and not in matters beyond the call of duty.

You may not find phones, radios, TV, or wall-to-wall carpet in your room. Or even a bathtub. The plumbing may be rebellious; the floors may creak; and if you get back late at night, you have to remember that other guests have come for peace and quiet. Tiptoe, please.

Also try not to *arrive* late at night, because the innkeeper is probably in bed, since he has to be up early the next morning; if you must arrive late, call ahead and say when you will get there.

Most of these inns are operated on precarious budgets, and survive on love rather than cash flow. We should all be grateful to all those innkeepers who get up at the crack of dawn to prepare breakfast, do the marketing, organize the staff, greet the guests, stick around the bar until after dinner, and probably get only a couple of weeks' vacation themselves in a year. Play the game. If you make a reservation, keep it; if you can't don't just shrug it off, but call the innkeeper or drop a line and cancel it, as far in advance as possible. One empty room in a twelve-room inn can be the difference between an inn's profit and its plot of land being bought up by a motel chain.

Who wants to stay in an inn, in that case? A lot of people—because inns offer other attractions that more than compensate for occasional drawbacks, as you'll see in the following pages.

The New England Coast and Long Island

One day I wrote her name upon the sand,
But came the waves and washed it away . . .

SPENSER

NEW HAMPSHIRE

ME.

Port

Kennebunkp

Portsmouth

MASSACHUSETTS

Boston

Springfield

CONNECTICUT

RHODE ISLAND

Hartford

Providence

New London

Newport

New Haven

Edgartown

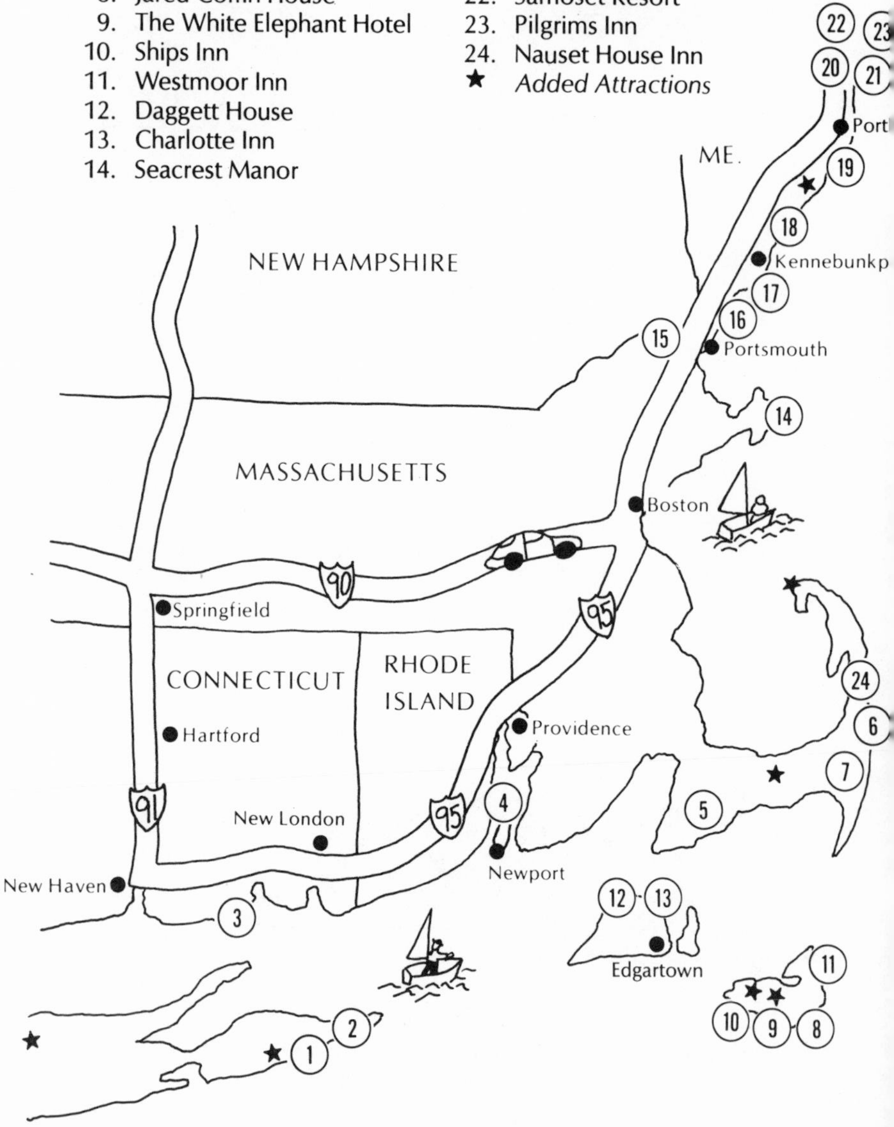

GURNEY'S INN
Montauk, N.Y.

$$$

You can't get much closer to the beach than this without living in a sand castle. And what a beach! Mile after mile of baby powder. You can jog on it from here to forever. It's almost the end of the world. The Atlantic comes rolling in on one side, hundred-foot-high hills shut out the world on the other, and 120 miles of Long Island separate you from New York.

The inn is actually a collection of cottages and motel-like units by the edge of the beach or up on the hill, spread comfortably over eleven acres, brightened with bushes, trees, and nooks of flowers.

It's an everything-or-nothing place. You can lie on the sand in front of the inn all day, or you can jog off together to a secluded corner of the dunes. You can drive over to Montauk and sniff around the fish market, or continue to Montauk Lighthouse and scramble among the rocks at the very tip of Long Island. In the evening, get involved with combos and dancing in the inn or go to the John Drew Theatre in East Hampton. Best of all, kick off your shoes and chase the moon along the beach.

Montauk is sensational in the fall and winter, when you have the beach to yourselves, and you have to huddle up in sweaters and scarves, and the spray comes whipping across the sand. Then after your walk you come back to a warm room, a warm shower, a warm bed. You can even have your dinner shipped over from the dining room—lobsters or roast beef or a thick steak.

You have quite a choice of accommodations at Gurney's. Make your days together a special event and have the inn's best love nest—the Crow's Nest (a self-contained cottage right by the edge of the beach, with a living room, fireplace, hostess pantry, patio, and bedroom), or a room in the Foredeck (a three-story lodge unit with pine-paneled walls, armchairs, individually controlled heat and air conditioning, telephone, television, tile bathrooms, his and her vanities, and a patio). Avoid the rooms on the hillside above the main lodge and the parking lot.

The new Forward Watch wing is totally out of synch with the rest of the resort, inside and out, and a new conference center and health spa hasn't helped matters from the point of view of lovers. More diners seem to be arriving from the surrounding resorts and highways, and much of the time there are too many banners, insignia and other impedimenta of business groups. Grrrrr, Gurney's!

But maybe you won't even notice if you spend all your days on the beach, your evenings in your room.

Name: Gurney's Inn

Owners/Managers: Joyce and Nick Monte

Address: Montauk, N.Y. 11954

Directions: Long Island Expressway to Exit 70, south to Route 27, then east to Old Montauk Highway. Transportation from local airports and train stations by arrangement with the inn.

Telephone: (516) 668–2345

Cables/Telex: None

Credit Cards: American Express, Diners, MasterCard, Visa

Rooms: 130, in 4 cottages and 6 wings.

Meals: Breakfast 7:30–10:00, lunch 12:00–3:00, dinner 6:00–10:00, jackets requested; room service; piped and live music in lounge and dining room.

Diversions: Health and Beauty Spa with saunas, steam rooms, Swiss showers, massage, big heated indoor seawater pool, exercise room; beaches.

Sightseeing: Montauk Point State Park, the fishing fleet.

P.S. Minimum stays on holidays; children under 18 not permitted in spa facilities; lots of business groups off-season (some of whom may take over the health spa and indoor pool for a day, leaving other guests out in the cold).

MONTAUK YACHT CLUB & INN
Star Island, Montauk, N.Y.

$$$

It's more inn than yacht club, in case you were about to reach for your blazer and white ducks. The original club was, in fact, "the first chartered yacht club in America," but the inn is a new cedar-shingle structure built around what remains of the old clubhouse and a sixty-foot-high lighthouse. Built, fitted out, and decorated very lavishly, too. The guest rooms have walls of barn-siding for a rustic-nautical look, but they're fitted out like the *QE2*—closets designed to hold steamer trunks, fitted dressing rooms with big fluffy towels and complimentary suntan lotion, coffee tables with marble tops, bedside hanging lamps with long cylindrical wool-tapestry shades. In winter, you can curl up on a king-size bed and watch color TV; in summer, you can lounge on your patio or balcony and watch the boats puttering around on the lake.

The public rooms are decorated with great care and taste. Corridors are hung with tapestries of wool and sisal; the dining room is dominated by an enormous stained-glass floating ceiling, vaguely whale-shaped; and the main Club Room focuses on a huge fireplace with a glove-leather sofa curving around the hearth. There are plants and fresh flowers everywhere, and "not a single artificial leaf anywhere—even in the health spa." Subdued, romantic lighting is supplied by an array of antique hurricane lamps and avant-garde spots that make the inn look almost like a museum of lighting.

In summer, you might find it a mite busy—what with people dropping in for lunch or dinner (inn guests have priority reservations for tables), and all the power yachts moored in the marina. In winter, it's exactly the kind of atmosphere you want for a snuggly escape: have a drink on the sofa before the fire, or in the softly lit circular lounge at the base of the lighthouse. Have a swim and a sauna in the indoor pool, a game of backgammon in the lounge; or muffle up in sweaters and scarves, drive to the Atlantic, and take a long tingly walk on the beach.

The inn is expensive (what do you expect with all that luxury?), but it has the advantage over hostelries in the neighborhood that you can stay there on the European Plan, and if you don't want to eat in the main dining room you can dine well, at moderate prices, in the Café Potpourri, among the blue tiles, natural woods, and potted plants.

Name: Montauk Yacht Club & Inn
Manager: Manuel Grau
Address: Star Island, Montauk, N.Y. 11954
Directions: On Lake Montauk. Drive through Montauk to West Lake Drive,

go left on the drive until you come to Star Island Causeway (on the right, beside the Coast Guard signs). Also by rail, seaplane, helicopter, or bus.

Telephone: (516) 668–3100: New York tie line 895–6446

Cables/Telex: None

Credit Cards: American Express, Carte Blanche, Diners, MasterCard, Visa

Rooms: 84.

Meals: Breakfast 7:00–11:30, lunch 12:00–3:00, dinner 6:00–11:00 (approx. $25 to $30 for 2), Café Potpourri open 7:00 A.M. to midnight; jackets suggested after 6:00 in the dining room; trio 6 nights a week in summer (in the dining room); pianist/singer nightly in summer.

Diversions: Immaculate indoor spa with pool, Jacuzzi, saunas, 16-foot-diameter whirlpool, table tennis, backgammon; heated outdoor fresh-water pool, small lakeside beach (for sunning, but you may not want to swim from it with so many powerboats glopping around), window permits for your own car for beach parking lots, tennis courts (free); golf, jet skis, water skiing, fishing boat charters, horseback riding ($10–$20 for rides along beaches and cliffs) all nearby.

P.S. Lots of business seminars; "The Inn functions primarily as an adult resort and has no facilities for infants or small children"; closed mid-November to mid-March.

THE GRISWOLD INN
Essex, Conn.

After dinner, stroll down to the boat jetty, perch on a bollard, and look across the still estuary. Sniff the night air. Listen to the clink of rigging on masts. Watch the moon shimmying across the water. It's the perfect public ending to a day at a sea-loving spot like the Griswold Inn.

The Griswold is the same age as the United States; in the eighteenth century they used to build ships across the street, and during the War of 1812, the British sneaked into the harbor and burned the Essex fleet. But not, praise be, the inn, and drinks and dinner at the Gris are still a tradition with yachtsmen on this

part of Long Island Sound. There's no reason why landlubbers shouldn't have some fun, too.

Essex is a lovely old Colonial seaport, its main street lined with houses that have weathered many a gale. The inn is three stories of white clapboard (with, oh dear, green plastic shutters) anchored to a two-story annex, the Hayden House. It has a small lobby-lounge with a large goblet full of jelly beans, and delightful new innkeepers. Until 1972, the Griswold had been in the same family for 140 years; now it's been taken over by a young couple, Bill and Vicky Winterer. Bill Winterer was once a Coast Guard officer, and then an investment banker, who also happens to be a gourmet cook and natural host. But he wanted to be near his 44-foot ketch, so now he has a two-hundred-year-old inn, with his ketch moored at the bottom of the street (across the lane from the Gris).

STEAMSHIP PRINTS, ANTIQUE PISTOLS. The dark-hued Tap Room (originally the first schoolhouse in Essex) is dominated by a girthy Franklin stove that once warmed the audience at the Goodspeed Opera House in East Haddam. Here you get your first introduction to the inn's unique collection of steamship prints and handbills, including a turn-of-the-century advertisement announcing sailings of the "State of New York (new and elegant steamer) leaving Hartford Wednesdays and Fridays and arriving in New York in time for early trains to the South and West."

The main collection is in the adjoining dining room, called the Covered Bridge Room, where the walls are awash in prints—some by Jacobson, others by Currier and Ives—and here and there a helpful if unheeded temperance poster (my favorite: "Large Streams from LITTLE Fountains Flow, GREAT SOTS from MODERATE Drinkers Grow"). Logs in the six-foot-wide fireplace crackle away during the winter months to cheer the landbound sailors waiting for the first glimmer of spring and a chance to unwrap their boats.

The recently restyled Library Room is a second restaurant, decorated with antique pistols, revolvers, flintlocks, carbines, and muskets; and off the main lobby there's a third dining room, the Steamboat Room. This one resembles a cabin of a posh yacht, looking aft; an illuminated painting of Old Essex, recessed into the wall, rocks gently to and fro to give you the idea you're at sea. (There's some speculation that this "motion" may be cutting down the bar sales.) That's a lot of eating and drinking space for one small inn, but in fact on summer weekends it takes all three rooms, with three sittings in each, to accommodate all the yachtsmen who come here. It's not because there's no other spot on the Sound, but because the menu is outstanding—Nantucket Bay scallops and broiled Cape bluefish from the list of local specialties; lamb pie and a brace of Canadian quail with Bulgar wheat are among the surprises. The wine list is short and to the point—enough to launch a meal if not a ship.

KNOTTY BEAMS, FOURPOSTER BEDS. The Gris's twenty-one rooms, fresh as a 10-knot wind, have all been renovated in the past few years, no mean feat when you consider that there is hardly a straight line in the place. Each one is different, each decked out with antiques or period furniture, decorated with prints chosen and framed with an artist's eye. A selection: room 1 has knotty beams, lopsided wardrobe, twin fourposter beds; room 4 has two giant magnificent mahogany fourposter beds and views of swaying masts in the boatyard, but at times may be afflicted with rumbling sounds from an exhaust fan outside the window; the new Governor Trumbull Suite has birdprint wallpaper, exposed brick walls, exposed beams, wooden shutters, and a cabin-sized sleeping alcove. My favorite is room 3, above the lobby, with beamed ceiling, barnboard paneling, and a big old bed with a list to starboard. All the rooms have air conditioning, seventeen have private bathrooms (although it should be pointed out that because these rooms were never intended to hold private johns, some of the bathrooms are tiny).

All in all, the Gris is still one of the best values in New England.

And Essex is still one of the prettiest towns. Even if you're not a sailor there's plenty to do in these parts. Take a trip upriver on the *River Queen*. Take in a musical or play at the Goodspeed Opera House or the Ivortown Theater. Drive over to Old Saybrook at the mouth of the river. Or just sit on a bollard and dream.

Name: The Griswold Inn
Owner/Manager: William G. Winterer
Address: Main Street, Essex, Conn. 06426

Directions: From the Connecticut Turnpike, either Exit 64 then north 5 miles to Essex, or Exit 69 to Route 9, then Exit 3 to Essex; by rail to Old Saybrook.

Telephone: (203) 767–0991

Cables/Telex: None

Credit Cards: American Express, MasterCard, Visa

Rooms: 21 (17 with private bath, 4 sharing baths) and 3 suites.

Meals: Breakfast 8:30–10:30, Hunt Breakfast on Sunday, lunch 12:00–2:00, dinner 6:00–9:00 weekdays, to 10:00 Friday and Saturday (approx. $14–$18 for 2); no room service; informal dress; banjo concerts Friday and Sunday evenings.

Diversions: Tennis (free town courts 1 mile from the Gris), golf, bicycles, horseback riding, ice skating on town pond, sailing and boating nearby.

Sightseeing: Essex village, the Connecticut Valley; Gillette Castle and State Park, Mystic Seaport, the Goodspeed Opera House all nearby.

P.S. No groups ever.

THE INN AT CASTLE HILL
Newport, R.I.

$$

Those millionaire mansions on Ocean Drive have nothing on this inn, at least in terms of the view.

Settle under one of Castle Hill's Cinzano umbrellas on the terrace for lunch or a drink, or sink into the big wooden chairs on the lawn, and you can enjoy an eye-enthralling, mind-blowing mosaic of sea and coastline and never-ending armadas of boats that could keep you hypnotized for hours.

The man to thank for your extraordinary perch is Alexander Agissiz, a noted naturalist whose expeditions form the basis for much of the modern science of oceanography. Agissiz was, happily, a millionaire as well as a talented scientist (he endowed Harvard's Museum of Comparative Biology) and when he wanted a summer place for the study of marine animals, he didn't think small—he bought the entire Ocean Drive peninsula known as Castle Hill. Then, after setting up his research laboratory (now a guesthouse on the grounds), he proceeded to build himself a real showplace on the top of the hill, a wandering shingled Victorian fantasy of turrets and towers, its enormous rooms filled with elaborate wooden paneling, Tiffany lamps, velvet upholstery, oriental art, and not-so-little touches like the remarkable inlaid woodwork of the sitting-room fireplace.

When new owner Paul McEnroe turned the house into an inn in 1975, he wisely chose to retain the character of the home and many original furnishings, while adding his own stamp—additions such as the handsome oak bar, the oriental motif grasscloth wallpaper in the halls, and the tasteful decorating throughout.

None of the rooms is more appealing than the oval dining room, done in sea colors with whole walls of windows to bring in the ocean view. There are also other dining rooms, each interesting, each different, some cozy crannies that hold just half a dozen tables, moods varying from plush velvet to blue and white nautical to stately red leather. The menu is uniform—sophisticated and French—and reservations are essential since Castle Inn has become one of chic Newport's favorite dining spots.

Better reserve early for rooms, too. There are only ten, very much one-of-a-kind, oversized, elegant, many with handsome paneled walls and all done full justice by their furnishings. The general feeling is Victorian, with oversized pieces and such niceties as skirted dressing tables, gilt mirrors, and daybeds. There's a green and white wicker aerie that's a favorite of many guests. And here's a place where even the bathrooms are memorable, some of them the largest bathrooms you've probably ever seen.

Castle Hill is busiest in summer, when Newport's beaches and harbor attract so many visitors, but the museum-mansions stay open all year, as do most of the shops in town, and the inn is a gracious retreat and a window to the sea any time of year. The fire glows brightly (but don't count on it) in the sitting-room fireplace to warm the blustery days, and up in your Victorian haven, with the waves crashing down below, romance is always in season.

                                                              E.B.

Name: The Inn at Castle Hill
Manager: Paul Goldblatt
Address: Ocean Drive, Newport, R.I. 02840

Directions: Follow signs for Ocean Drive from the center of town. Castle Hill
is on the right-hand side coming from town, clearly marked by a sign at
the entry road.

Telephone: (401) 849–3800

Cables/Telex: None

Credit Cards: MasterCard, Visa

Rooms: 10, 6 cottage rooms in Harbor House, summer only.

Meals: Breakfast 8:00–10:00, lunch 12:00–2:30, dinner 6:00–8:30 (approx.
$40 for 2); no room service; jacket preferred, no jeans at dinner; jazz on
Sunday night, Dixieland band for Sunday brunch.

Diversions: Small private beach; tennis, golf, horseback riding, water sports
nearby.

Sightseeing: Newport mansions, National Tennis Hall of Fame, 10 miles of
spectacular seascape on Ocean Drive.

P.S. Dining room closed except for breakfast January through Easter; no
lunch served November and December, bar open only Friday and
Saturday.

P.P.S. Our reports, at press time, are that the guest rooms are being
redecorated by Ione Williams, of the Inn at Sawmill Farm, which
should enhance the inn considerably. Also, innkeeper Paul McEnroe
recently opened his own inn (he's lessee at Castle Hill) in the heart of
Newport—THE INN-TOWNE, with 18 top drawer rooms, also styled
by Ione Williams. Rates are $84.80 to $95.40, with breakfast. Reservations: (401) 846–9200.

NEW SEABURY RESORT
New Seabury, Mass.

$$$

Start with a well-equipped country club—two golf courses, sixteen·
tennis courts, a spacious clubhouse. Now take a wooded seaside
setting, a 5-mile strand of beach along Nantucket Sound, and a host of
tasteful modern homes and condominium apartments. Put them
together and you have New Seabury, a kind of live-in country club by
the sea.

The owners refer to it as a "resort community," and it is one of
the most ambitious ever attempted in this part of the world. Located
halfway between Falmouth and Hyannis Port on the southern shore
of Cape Cod, the 2,700 acres were envisioned as a perfect, planned

community of vacation homes and apartments linked together by a variety of recreational facilities and a semiprivate club. The architecture was to be suited to its site, and the existing beaches, dunes, marshes, ponds, and forest were to be disturbed as little as possible.

The dream is about halfway there, and it's an attractive one— nine residential villages, two major dining rooms, beach and golf and sailing clubs and a marina, so far. If it sounds overwhelming, it needn't be. The houses are tucked away from everything and the stylishly furnished condominiums can be completely private if you snag a seafront location. No one's even going to care if you ignore all the activities and just take advantage of the quiet miles available for biking, walking, beaching, or birdwatching, something hard to come by in this congested part of the Cape.

But the overall ambiance here is definitely clubby, and you'll probably enjoy New Seabury best if that's your style. It's a golfer's heaven: the championship 7,715-yard Blue Course is listed by Golf Digest Magazine as one of America's one hundred best, and the Green Course, at 5,930, has its own challenges. Even the spacious dining room at New Seabury Inn, with sweeping views of golf course and Sound, seems to have been inspired by the game, with a velvety emerald expanse of carpet looking for all the world like a perfect putting green.

During the summer months you can switch to a beach club atmosphere—luncheons on the terrace, romantic outdoor dancing at the smaller Popponessett Inn directly on the shore to the east of the complex. There are no sleeping accommodations in either "inn" building; Popponesset's summer guests live in rustic cottages, less expensive but also much less elaborately decorated and furnished than the New Seabury "Tide Watch" condominiums.

New Seabury is a world to itself, with almost everything you'd want to do by day and plenty of activity at night as well. And if you don't want to join the club—well, there's always the beach or that oceanfront terrace waiting for the two of you.

E.B.

Name: New Seabury Inn
Manager: Robert Sullo
Address: P.O. Box B, New Seabury, Mass. 02649

Directions: Follow Route 28 east from Falmouth to Mashpee Rotary, turn
right and follow signs to New Seabury. Air service to Hyannis (New
Seabury is midway between Falmouth and Hyannis).

Telephone: (617) 477–9111

Cables/Telex: None

Credit Cards: "All major credit cards"

Rooms: 85, including 28 suites.

Meals: Breakfast 8:00–10:30, lunch 11:30–3:00, dinner 6:00–9:30 (approx.
$25 for 2), jacket required; no room service; entertainment Wednesday
through Saturday in season, piano bar nightly.

Diversions: Two 18-hole golf courses, 16 tennis courts, 5-mile private beach,
hiking; Sunfish for rent; riding, water sports, nearby.

Sightseeing: Cape Cod National Seashore, various historic mansions.

CHATHAM BARS INN
Chatham, Mass.

$$

They don't build them like this anymore.

Chatham Bars went up in 1914, the heyday of the grand hotel, a
sprawling brick-and-shingle structure situated on a superb spot on
high land overlooking Pleasant Bay and the spit of land called the
Outer Bar.

Mellons, DuPonts, John D. Rockefeller, and Queen Juliana all
visited the hotel once upon a time, enjoying the view from the long,
curving, columned porch. The guest list may be somewhat less
aristocratic today, but the McMullen family, who have been at the
helm since 1954, do their best to uphold some of the flavor of the
grand old days while providing facilities that are more in keeping
with the times.

If you still think there's something nice about a formal dining
room where gentlemen wear coats and ties, ladies show off their
pretty dresses, and there's cheek-to-cheek dancing on Saturday
night, you'll love it here. If you want to wear jeans to dinner and head
for a discotheque, better look elsewhere.

During the day, of course, you can be as informal as you like, even stay in your bathing suit all day having late breakfast, lunch, and cocktails at the Beach House Dining Pier. There's plenty to keep you busy—golf, tennis, boating, and a private beach. If you prefer ocean surf, you can take the hotel launch across the bay to the Bar, that deserted spit, right on the Atlantic. It's a perfect spot for a picnic for two; ask the night before and the hotel will gladly pack one for you.

Guests here are on the American Plan and the menu is an elaborate one that isn't going to help your form a bit. For starters there are things like clam chowder, gazpacho, minestrone, shrimp cocktail, or fruits; main dishes include roast rack of lamb, prime ribs, veal piccata, and all kinds of fresh seafood; dessert might be pecan pie, *profiteroles*, or chocolate mousse.

After dinner there will be drinks and dancing in the "Inner Bar" and sometimes special events in the cheerful wicker-furnished main lounge.

Rooms, public and private, are unusually large. In the main house you'll have an oversized bedroom in Colonial style, with private balconies on the third floor and sundecks for less lofty dwellers. Or choose an Early American room in a cottage sharing a private living room with the other guests in the house . . . or a rustic studio on the beachfront where you can almost literally roll out of bed onto the sand.

Chatham Bars can't be faulted on facilities. And it's one-of-a-kind on the Cape, an old-time gracious resort in an area that tends to run to inns or motel ticky-tack. It won't be everyone's cup of tea, but sitting on the porch or the balcony watching the moon over the bay, you may find this slightly sedate scene a refreshing—and even romantic—change of pace.

E.B.

Name: Chatham Bars Inn
Owner/Manager: E. R. McMullen
Address: Shore Road, Chatham, Mass. 02633
Directions: Take Mid-Cape Highway 6 to Exit 11, go east to Route 28 into
    Chatham, continue east to Shore Road.
Telephone: (617) 945–0096
Cables/Telex: None
Credit Cards: None

Rooms: 40 (plus 100 cottage rooms).

Meals: Breakfast 8:00–9:30, lunch 12:30–2:00 (late breakfast, lunch, snacks, drinks, served at Beach House Dining Pier), dinner 7:00–8:30 (approx. $32 for 2), jacket and tie required; full room service; live music and dancing in dining room Thursday and Saturday, in lounge nightly.

Diversions: 350-yard private beach, 5 tennis courts, 9-hole golf course, sailboats, private launch; horseback riding nearby.

Sightseeing: Chatham Light, Chatham Fish Pier, Chatham Railroad Museum, Grist Mill In Chase Park, Atwood House Historical Museum; Cape Cod National Seashore nearby.

P.S. Closed November to mid-May.

SHIP'S KNEES INN
E. Orleans, Cape Cod, Mass.

It's not a cutesy-pie title; a ship's knee is a block of wood that connects deck beams to the frames of sailboats, and when this shingle house was built 150 years ago it was held together by ship's knees. Now it has been charmed into the most decorative nautical hostelry on the Cape. Local antique stores were scoured for ship's trunks, old whaling prints, antique maps, Windsor chairs, duck decoys, and braided rugs; then the finds were sorted out in rooms designed in one of three basic colors, fitted with carpets, towels, bedspreads, and sheets in coordinated colors, making simple but delightful nooks for love affairs, fantastic or otherwise. The ship's knees hold together just ten rooms, four of them with private bathrooms and color television, and one (#3) with beamed ceilings and a fireplace. There's a small lounge where you help yourself to doughnuts and coffee for breakfast, and out in the garden you can toss a Frisbee, play tennis or volleyball, swim in the pool, or lounge in patio furniture till the stars come home. And that's it—quiet, unassuming, impeccable, escapist. The Ship's Knees sits at the junction of a couple of residential streets, under streams of telephone company spaghetti, just up the hill from the beach.

Just wait till you see *that!* Nauset Beach is part of the Cape Cod National Seashore, mile after unspoiled mile of sand and dunes, just a three-minute walk from and five-minute walk to the inn. This is paradise for off-season beach-lovers, a place to walk when the winds are churning the ocean and the seagulls are flying backwards, when the twilight comes early and eerily and turns the surfcasters into balloon-legged silhouettes; then, when your faces are all tingly, you can hurry up the hill to the color-coordinated warmth of the Ship's Knees' bedspreads and sheets.

Name: Ship's Knees Inn
Managers: Ken and Louise Pollard
Address: Beach Road, East Orleans, Cape Cod, Mass. 02643
Directions: Follow U.S. 6 to Orleans Exit, then go east on Mass. 28 to East
     Orleans and follow the signs for Nauset Beach; by air to Hyannis.
Telephone: (617) 255–1312
Cables/Telex: None
Credit Cards: None; personal checks accepted
Rooms: 19, plus 2 cottages, luxury apartment, housekeeping apartment.
Meals: Continental breakfast only (included in price, in season); coffee, toast,
     doughnuts year round; no liquor.
Diversions: Indoor games (checkers, chess, etc.), TV; heated outdoor pool,
     tennis court, badminton, croquet; golf, bicycles, hiking, horseback
     riding, sailing, waterskiing nearby.
Sightseeing: See "New Seabury Resort."
P.S. Busiest during summer, advance reservations a must.

NAUSET HOUSE INN
Orleans, Mass.

$

If you could have your own antique-filled Cape Cod home, chances are you'd want it to look like this one.

Like so many innkeepers, Jack and Lucille Schwarz left the city (in this case, New York) with the dream of owning a country inn. But this couple had something special going for them. Lucille is both a decorator and antique dealer, and here she was with a clapboard nineteenth-century home, not to mention a couple of outside buildings—living, dining, and fourteen sleeping rooms in all, just waiting to be fixed up and filled up with every intriguing thing she could find.

The result is a browsers' delight. Come into the all-white living room, cool and inviting even on the hottest summer day, and you'll find a bottle collection to admire in the window, a colorful antique drum serving as coffee table, an old demitasse set, figurines, paintings, flowers, plants in interesting containers, all artfully placed around on shelves, sills, walls, and tabletops.

She's managed to create a comfortable room at the same time, with pillowy couches and big wing chairs where you can curl up with one of the books or games piled high on the table and the shelves around the mantel.

You'd swear that the brick-floored dining room with its low beams and fireplace must be at least a century old, but it is actually a 1974 add-on, and it, too, is chock-a-block with nice things to look at—decoys and other wood carvings, mugs, old toys, a gleaming dark wood dining table, pewter candlesticks, pots, baskets, a ship's figurehead—you name it.

Looking is half the fun of staying at Nauset House and you're never sure just what you'll find because many of Lucille's finds are for sale, allowing her the fun of shopping for refills, and her guests some exceptional buys.

A gourmet breakfast is available daily, and setups for drinks later in the day. There's a little brick patio outside for sitting or sunning, gorgeous Nauset Beach just about a mile down the road, and if the day is less than beachy you can retreat to the wicker and plant-filled conservatory, a glass-enclosed marvel that was moved here piece by piece from an old Connecticut estate and reassembled on the spot.

As you might expect, the bedrooms in the main house and in an adjoining building are done with style and flair in attractive paisleys and prints with carved or canopied bedsteads, old trunks, antique chairs, and an assortment of offbeat pieces. Hallways are lined with old playbills, tools, and other collectibles. There's one pretty room dubbed "Honeymoon Suite" and a rustic studio set off by itself on the grounds.

Check the guest book at Nauset House and you'll find a far-flung clientele from all over this country and as far away as Germany and

Denmark. There's good reason. Even in an area with more than its share of inns, this one is exceptional.

E.B.

Name: Nauset House Inn
Owners/Managers: Lucille and Jack Schwarz
Address: Beach Road, Orleans, Mass. 02653
Directions: Follow U.S. 6 to Orleans Exit, then go east on Mass. 28 to East Orleans and follow the signs for Nauset Beach; by air, Air New England to Hyannis.
Telephone: (617) 255–2195
Cables/Telex: None
Credit Cards: MasterCard, Visa
Rooms: 14.
Meals: Breakfast only, on request, $3.75; no liquor license, but bring your own and the inn will supply setups.
Diversions: Terrace for sunning; Nauset Beach, tennis, boating, golf, water sports nearby.
Sightseeing: Cape Cod beaches and National Seashore, Museum of Orleans Historical Society, French Cable Station Museum.
P.S. Closed November 15 to April 1.

JARED COFFIN HOUSE
Nantucket, Mass.

Step inside the lobby and you're back in the days of the great whaling fleets of Nantucket. The public rooms are filled with Chippendale, Sheraton, Directoire, and American Federal furniture, antique oriental rugs, Chinese coffee tables, and Japanese lacquered cabinets; a sweeping stairway with a white balustrade leads you up to your guest room, which will be decorated with period furniture, authentic Colonial wallpapers, and traditional Nantucket curtains and bedspreads hand woven by local ladies. Jared Coffin, one of the wealthiest shipowners in Nantucket, built this red brick mansion on a street of mansions in 1845, and furnished it with treasures brought back from around the world by his ships. It still looks like a private home, although Coffin lived here for only one year before it was bought up by the Nantucket Steamboat Company and turned into a hotel in 1846; the Nantucket Historical Society took it over in 1961 and restored it to its original state. Since then it has been acquired by its longtime manager, Philip Read, who has continued with the program of restoration. He has also added half-a-dozen guest rooms in a former boardinghouse across the street, 54 Centre Street, each completely restored and modernized (private bathrooms, color television, thermostats). Here you step into an entrance hall with the original wide plank floors and mahogany stair rail, enhanced by gold-and-green tweed rugs and wooden side tables with hurricane lamps. Room 514, trimmed with Wedgwood Blue woodwork, is furnished with Colonial reproductions—a fourposter bed, Hitchcock rocker, wing chairs beside the fireplace; #515 has ecru walls with salmon-toned woodwork, the original fireplace, and a tester bed with a lace canopy; #516, biggest of all, was the original kitchen, and its Colonial charm is topped off with the original slate-hearth fireplace. The annex has its own back garden with lawn chairs, umbrellas, and tables.

The Jared Coffin House is the most famous and most popular inn on the island, which means that in summer its garden patio, Tap Room, and dining room are swarming with overnight visitors and day trippers; but it remains open throughout the year, which means you can visit Nantucket at its most Nantucketty. The islanders themselves rave about November in Nantucket, when the moors are a carpet of fall colors; but October is also a lovely month for hopping on a bike and riding along the clifftop roads, and May and June are great for tennis, golf, and playing leapfrog on the beach.

Just bring lots of sweaters to keep you warm on the moors and beach; the Nantucket embroidery will keep you warm in bed.

Name: Jared Coffin House
Owners/Managers: Philip Whitney Read and Margaret Read
Address: Nantucket Island, Mass. 02554
Directions: On the corner of Broad and Centre streets, near the top end of Main street; to get to Nantucket Island you take the ferry from Woods Hole or Hyannis, or fly Air New England from New York, Boston, Hyannis, and other points.
Telephone: (617) 228–2400

Cables/Telex: None

Credit Cards: American Express, Diners, MasterCard, Visa

Rooms: 41.

Meals: Breakfast 8:00–10:00, lunch 12:00–2:00, dinner 6:30–9:30 (approx.
 $15 to $25 for 2), limited food service in summer (2:00–6:00); room
 service for continental breakfast and drinks; jackets requested in spring,
 fall, and winter, casual (but neat) in summer; piano with dinner, live
 music in the Tap Room.

Diversions: Card room; heated outdoor pool, putting green, croquet,
 bicycles; tennis (9 courts, $10 per court per hour weekends, $8
 midweek); golf, horseback riding, sailing, boating, and beach nearby.

Sightseeing: The house itself, also in Edgartown: the Hadwen House–Satler
 Memorial (whaling museum), coastal scenery.

THE WHITE ELEPHANT HOTEL
Nantucket, Mass.

$$$

You wake up in the morning in a flower-covered cottage to see
seagulls preening themselves on the bollards and schooners riding at
anchor in the harbor. If it's sunny and warm you can slip into the pool
or wander over to the beach; if it's cool and misty, the way Nantucket
should be, you can hop on bicycles and ride across the moors of
Sargent juniper and Warminster broom. In the evening, wander
down to the wharf for a moonlight view of the harbor before you
return to your flower-covered saltbox cottage.

Nantucket is a nautical town, and the White Elephant is a
nautical hotel, right down on the waterfront, with its lawns ending up
in the harbor. It was built in 1963 by Walter Beinecke, Jr., of S&H
Green Stamps, who took over most of the Nantucket waterfront and
revitalized it (he's had his critics, but most people seem to feel he's
done a tasteful job, remodeling the place with a feel for its shingle-
saltbox heritage).

This elephant comes in six parts: the main two-story lodge with
spacious, modern rooms; the Spindrift cottages, on the lawn by the
water, with roses growing up the walls, neatly furnished living rooms
and bedrooms, and windows facing the harbor (which makes them

the most popular rooms in the hotel); and the Captain's Court, a
bunch of typical Nantucket homes the size of dollhouses, grouped
around a lawn with loungers spread out beneath the locust trees. The
suites in the Captain's Court cottages give you a chance to live in the
style of a Nantucket seafarer—pine walls, beamed ceilings, sturdy
furniture, fireplaces, and old prints and maps on the walls. The
remaining components are two more sets of cottages—Driftwood and
Pinegrove—and the new "The Breakers" wing, a few doors down the
street, also on the edge of the harbor, with twenty-six deluxe rooms.

March 15 -
too expensive

Name: The White Elephant Hotel
Manager: George Wingenfeld
Address: Nantucket Island, Mass. 02554
Directions: By ferry from Woods Hole or Hyannis; by Air New England from
    New York, Boston, or Hyannis.
Telephone: (617) 228–2500
Cables/Telex: None
Credit Cards: American Express, Diners, MasterCard, Visa
Rooms: 60 rooms and 22 cottages.
Meals: Breakfast 8:00–10:00, lunch 12:00–2:30 (served on outdoor patio),
    dinner 6:00–10:00 (approx. $20 to $30 for 2); room service 8:00–10:00 for
    breakfast, noon to 11:00 P.M. for drinks; informal dress; live music and
    dancing.
Diversions: Heated outdoor pool, putting green, croquet, bicycles, card
    room; tennis (9 courts), golf, horseback riding, sailing, and boating
    nearby.
Sightseeing: See "Jared Coffin House."
P.S. Closed Columbus Day to mid-May.

SHIPS INN
Nantucket, Mass.

The Ships Inn is to the Jared Coffin House what a ship captain is to a
shipowner. This clapboard house is a modest version of the Coffin
house, built in 1812 by Captain Obed Starbuck as a cozy place to
come home to after long voyages. It's now a cozy place where John

Krebs came to after a spell as a stockbroker in Baltimore in the heavy seas of the sixties. The period furniture is sturdy, the walls are lined with prints of whaling ships and flowers, the doorjambs are askew, the rooms are named for the ships Starbuck commanded, and all in all it has a salty Nantucket air about it. It's on a quiet street at the top of Main Street, away from the rabble, but still close enough to the wharf and bars and goings-on.

Downstairs, the Krebses have installed their own cocktail lounge—an unusual place where you can sit at a bar shaped like a whaling dory and have a drink while you're waiting for your place at the Captain's Table. Their restaurant has an interesting menu—beef, cheese, and seafood fondues, striped bass *à la Pesto, coquilles Parisiennes*—and prices are reasonable. It's a comfy little harbor to return to after days of exploring the island.

Name: Ships Inn
Owners/Managers: John and Bar Krebs
Address: Nantucket Island, Mass. 02554
Directions: On Fair Street, which runs off to the left at the top of Main Street.
Telephone: (617) 228–0040
Cables/Telex: None
Credit Cards: American Express, MasterCard
Rooms: 12.
Meals: Breakfast 8:00–10:30, no lunch, dinner 6:00–9:30 (approx. $27 to $32 for 2), for guests only; no room service; dress optional; taped jazz in the bar.
Diversions: Darts, backgammon, cribbage; tennis, bicycles, horseback riding, and water sports nearby.
Sightseeing: See "Jared Coffin House."

WESTMOOR INN

Nantucket, Mass.

$

The location is unusual for Nantucket (high on a private breeze-swept knoll, yet within a walk of town), and the house itself is unique. Built originally for a Vanderbilt, they say, which might explain its grand columned portico, formal wainscoting, and enormous rooms on an island better known for weathered cottages.

But once Nanci and Jerome Walker took over in 1976, Westmoor took on the warmth of its new owners. Now it's a friendly welcoming inn with rooms just the right side of cluttered. The big comfortable living room is chock-full of collectibles, plants, a grand piano, and plump sofas and chairs facing a fireplace, the kind of place where it's easy to feel at home. Breakfast is served on the sunniest of sun porches, done in blue and white with informal wooden tables and chairs, with lots of plants and fresh flowers everywhere.

Don't be surprised if you find yourself at some point joining other guests sitting out in the kitchen, laughing and chatting away with Nanci and her pretty daughters. The Walkers are longtime New Hampshire innkeepers transplanted to a warmer clime, and by now they have scores of friends from both locations who come back year after year and feel almost like one of the family. It's not an inn likely to attract children, but Nanci reports her few requests are often from parents who once honeymooned at the inn.

The nine upstairs bedrooms are worth coming back to, oversized and attractively furnished with all manner of interesting antiques. Whether you snuggle up under a canopy or in an old-fashioned carved bedstead, you'll have lace curtains at the windows, pretty touches like painted chests and wicker chairs, and louvered doors to catch that wonderful summer breeze.

What to do during the day? There are tennis courts next door, a riding stable nearby, Cliff Beach at the end of the road, and a secluded lawn at the inn for sunning. If you want to plan a day's outing or a bike trip, Nanci will gladly pack you a box lunch. At day's end, you can watch the sunset from the beach, take a walk into town for dinner, then wander back hand-in-hand to the moors. It's easy to see why Westmoor is a place that inspires return engagements.

E.B.

Name: Westmoor Inn
Owners/Managers: Jerome and Nanci Walker
Address: Cliff Road, Nantucket, Mass. 02554
Directions: From Main Street follow Centre Street or South Water Street north to North Water Street, which runs into Cliff Road. Inn is about 1 mile from center of town.
Telephone: (617) 228–0877

Cables/Telex: None
Credit Cards: None
Rooms: 9.
Meals: Breakfast or lunch on request, 8:30–9:30, 12:00–2:00.
Diversions: Walk to beach; tennis and riding adjacent; golf, water sports
    nearby.
Sightseeing: See "Jared Coffin House."
P.S. Closed January and February.

CHARLOTTE INN

Edgartown, Martha's Vineyard, Mass.

When Gery Conover left Philadelphia for Martha's Vineyard, he was
torn between two dreams—an art gallery and an inn. Eventually he
decided to do both at once, and the result is an elegant little Edgartown enclave that gets fan letters from guests all over America.

Enter this handsome white clapboard Colonial, right in the
historic heart of town, and you're standing in an art gallery. Works by
island artists hang side by side with canvases by nationally known
painters like Jamison, Ellis, and Wyeth. Behind the gallery, a tempt-
ing antique shop; and off to the right, an enclosed slate-floored,
plant-filled patio is the home of Chez Pierre and specialties such as
espadon maître d'hôtel and *chateaubriand bouquetière*.

But it's the guest rooms most visitors fall in love with here.
Whether in the main house or in the Captain Jared Jernigan House
next door, they're calculated to whisk you back to the aristocratic
eighteenth century. The decorating schemes differ, but all the furnishings are fine antique reproductions and all the rooms have chandeliers, formal draperies, and pieces such as wing chairs and fourposter beds. The extra touches are especially nice—fresh flowers and
plants, original prints on the walls, a cozy comforter on the bed.

Charlotte Inn, and Edgartown, are more likely to charm you if
you can plan a visit in the off-season, after the crowds of day trippers
have gone home. The inn is open all year so you can come to enjoy the
colorful fall.

Or better yet, reserve the Fireplace Suite, hop a quick Air New
England flight, and elope from winter. Island temperatures tend to

be milder than the mainland, and there's a special serenity about the harbor in its winter stillness. Bundle up and take a walk through the silent town, then hurry home to light the fire and curl up in that fourposter under your colonial comforter. You'll hardly remember what month it is.

E.B.

Name: Charlotte Inn
Manager: Gery D. Conover
Address: South Summer Street, Edgartown, Mass. 02539
Directions: Martha's Vineyard is about a 45-minute ferryboat ride from Woods Hole or Hyannis via Steamship Authority (make car reservations far in advance) or via Hyline from Hyannis (passengers only); 1 hour by air from Boston or New York via Air New England. (Cabs and car rentals available at ferry station or airport; bike rentals plentiful in Edgartown.) Summer Street is 1 block west of Watertown, Edgartown's major center; inn is between Main and Cook streets.
Telephone: (617) 627–4751
Cables/Telex: None
Credit Cards: MasterCard, Visa
Rooms: 14, 3 suites.
Meals: Continental breakfast 8:00–10:00, lunch 11:30–2:00, dinner 7:00–9:00 (approx. $50 for 2); jacket "suggested"; no room service.
Diversions: Beaches, tennis, golf, riding, water sports nearby.
Sightseeing: Dukes County Historical Society; cliffs at Gay Head; towns of Oak Bluffs and Vineyard Haven, Chappaquidick Island.
P.S. Far busier in summer, delightful off-season. And if budget allows, flying saves long drive, traffic, and ferryboat crowds.

DAGGETT HOUSE

Edgartown, Martha's Vineyard, Mass.

$

Snug's the word—a snug, tidy gray-shingled homestead that has been a part of Edgartown's Water Street since 1750.

Actually, part of Daggett House goes back even further. The first tavern on Martha's Vineyard was licensed to one John Daggett, who was fined back in the year 1660 for "suffering a disturbance" in his house. The public room of that old tavern was incorporated into the breakfast room of the present Daggett House and dubbed "The Old Chimney Room" because of the unique beehive construction of its big fireplace.

There's little disturbance here these days. In fact, it's a wonderfully peaceful little preserve with a private fenced garden extending right down to the waterfront. But you're somehow conscious that there's history in the house, and the owners will gladly give you an account of its many incarnations over the years from inn to store to sailor's boardinghouse to countinghouse, when it was owned by wealthy Captain Timothy Daggett during the town's most illustrious whaling days.

The rooms have been done to capture the flavor of those bygone days. Whether you are in the main house, across the street in Daggett House II (also the former home of a whaling captain), or in the garden cottage that was once a private school, you'll find attractive color-coordinated Early American decor, cloth headboards that match the chairs, pleated cloth lampshades, period chests, and here and there a brightening touch of wicker. Room 22 in Daggett II, an oversized all-white room all in wicker, is a little different and particularly pleasant.

The day gets off to an atmospheric start in the low-ceilinged breakfast room. Pour your own fruit juice, help yourself to coffee and home-baked goodies like grapenut bread or Irish soda bread, and while a pleasant young waitress whips up your breakfast to order, you can admire that big open hearth, the old wood cupboards, the pewter and china, old guns and other assorted memorabilia. Afterward, you're perfectly situated for strolling the town or taking the free island minibus to the beach, and you're right next door to the baby ferryboat that shuttles back and forth to Chappaquidick Island.

It's an ideal location, right on the main street yet a block removed from the shopping center—and the crowds. So it's serene. Sit in the garden and watch the boats go by. Or settle into one of the wing chairs or sofas pulled around the living-room fireplace.

Open all year, Daggett House is a snug port for all seasons.

E.B.

Name: Daggett House
Owners/Managers: Fred and Lucille Chirgwin
Address: North Water Street, Edgartown, Mass. 02539
Directions: See Charlotte Inn. Daggett House is at corner of North Water
     (main shopping street) and Daggett streets, 3 blocks north of Main
     Street.
Telephone: (617) 627–4600
Cables/Telex: None
Credit Cards: MasterCard, Visa
Rooms: 18.
Meals: Breakfast only, 8:00–10:00 A.M. No room service.
Diversions: Beaches, tennis, golf, riding, water sports nearby.
Sightseeing: See "Charlotte Inn."
P.S. July and August, 1-week stay minimum.

SEACREST MANOR
Rockport, Mass.

Rockport, on Cape Ann, is something of a shorebound Nantucket—
picturesque harbor just waiting to be painted, lobster pots and
fishnets hanging from weathered wooden shacks. On Bearskin Neck,
the stone jetty that has become the town's trademark, shingle-sided
sheds and houses have been converted into artists' studios, boutiques, and restaurants. Very pretty and, in summer, very crowded.
You can escape the crowds by checking into the Seacrest Manor,
located on a nontourist street on the edge of town, with a view of the
sea and the twin lighthouses of Thatcher Island. Walk to the end of
the street and the rocky shore beckons you to take a brisk, bracing
walk; on warmer days, settle into one of the shady bowers in the
Manor garden, beneath the red oak and maple and linden trees,
surrounded by beds of dahlias, begonias, and roses. For a view, or a
tan, climb the wooden steps to the second-floor sundeck.

     This turn-of-the-century manor, built for a former governor of
Massachusetts, was modulated into a refined and elegant guesthouse
in 1973: two large sitting rooms filled with antiques, paintings, and

family bric-a-brac; downstairs, there's one two-room suite, upstairs, four bright, cheerful and immaculate guest rooms, each with private bath, and two equally fine suites. The most expensive rooms have french doors leading to their own corners of the sundeck, but you'll probably be satisfied with any of the rooms (if you have time, and a choice, look around first and take your pick). Afternoon tea is served in the living room, breakfast in a breakfast room that has more character than *dining* rooms in most hotels. But then, breakfast is kind of special too at the Seacrest Manor: Miss Lillian's spiced Irish oatmeal with chopped dates, banana pancakes, and corn fritters. A complimentary newspaper brightens your morning (by order only on Sunday), and gentlemen may have their shoes shined simply by leaving them outside their doors at night. The governor himself could still be in residence.

Name: Seacrest Manor
Owners/Managers: Leighton T. Saville and Dwight B. McCormack, Jr.
Address: Marmion Way, Rockport, Mass. 01966
Directions: Rockport is 4 miles from the end of U.S. 128, northeast of Boston; the Manor is just off Highway 127A (Thatcher Road), where you'll see a small sign.
Telephone: (617) 546–2211
Cables/Telex: None
Credit Cards: None
Rooms: 8.
Meals: Breakfast 7:30–9:30, afternoon tea at 4:00. No liquor license, but the owners will supply mixers and ice.
Diversions: Reading, lounging, sunning, walking; bicycles for rent; golf, sailing, beaches, tennis, horseback riding, deep-sea fishing, boat rides nearby.
Sightseeing: Rockport, Bearskin Neck, art galleries and studios, the celebrated fish shack of "Motif Number One," Cape Ann Symphony Orchestra (summers); Gloucester, especially the Harbor area.
P.S. Rockport is a "dry" town, though spirits may be purchased in neighboring Gloucester. Closed during January.

WENTWORTH-BY-THE-SEA
near Portsmouth, N.H.

This is a veritable *Queen Mary* of resort hotels, a leviathan with elegant salons and hallways and dining roms, with balls and parties, dance bands, cabarets—even its own symphonietta. It rides the crest of one of the small islands at the mouth of Portsmouth Harbor, its gleaming white superstructure rising above an ocean of trees.

The Wentworth is an immense place (more than two hundred rooms), rather posh, but it sails into these pages because of location— and nostalgia. It's ironic that hotels of the Colonial era seem to be thriving more successfully than hotels of the Victorian era, that hotels built to cater to the stagecoach trade are doing better than hotels built for the carriage trade. The Wentworth is an exception.

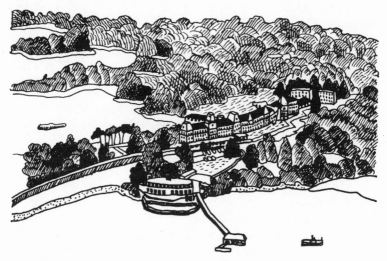

The first carriages started driving up to the Wentworth in the 1870s, and the hotel reached its pinnacle of fame in 1905, when it hosted the diplomats who signed the Russian-Japanese treaty. Ever since, it's been hosting the families of the well heeled as well as a sprinkling of celebs—Gloria Swanson, Richard Nixon, Sir John Gielgud, Ted Kennedy, Duke Ellington, Goodman Ace, Anthony Burgess, and Ogden Nash. A motley crew.

The hotel's rooms (or most of them) are big, with the gracious air of a country mansion. Each one is different but all, of course, have private baths, and the lanai suites also have enclosed porches with luxurious terrace furniture. But you don't have to stay with the crowd. The hotel has a few New England–style cottages scattered around the grounds, most of them across the street in the gardens above the sea.

PARKLIKE GROUNDS. Although the hotel is immense, you don't feel crowded because the grounds and the surroundings are so spacious. Walk across the street, through the gardens, around the pitch-and-putt course, and you come to a heated swimming pool of Olympic proportions, or the sandy beach. The hotel's private golf course, eighteen holes, skims alongside the shore half an island away, and there are first-class tennis courts out back. The cordial ever-present president-owner and his resident manager occasionally throw out a challenge to guests to a set of tennis or a round of golf; if they lose, the guest gets a free night's lodging. Don't dream—they gave away only two rooms last summer, even though the president is a shade older than, say, Bobby Riggs.

Name: Wentworth-by-the-Sea
Manager: James Barker Smith
Address: Portsmouth, N.H. 03801
Directions: From Interstate 95 northbound, take Exit 3, about an hour after
        Boston, then follow the signs to U.S. 1A where you'll pick up the signs
        for Wentworth and/or Newcastle; by air to Portsmouth.
Telephone: (603) 436–3100 (call Jim Smith person-to-person collect)
Cables/Telex: None
Credit Cards: None
Rooms: 240 rooms, 20 suites, 6 cottages.
Meals: Breakfast 8:00–9:30, lunch 12:00–1:30, coffee shop to 5:00 or 6:00,
        dinner 6:30–8:00; room service during dining hours; jacket at dinner;
        live music and dancing nightly, occasional floor shows.
Diversions: Movies, bingo, shuffleboard, table tennis; heated outdoor pool;
        tennis (7 courts, no lights, $5 doubles per hour in July and August only),

golf (18 holes, $10 weekdays, $12 per day weekends); horseback riding nearby.

Sightseeing: The Wentworth's collection of historic memorabilia; Portsmouth (the center, which is being restored, is much prettier than the outskirts of town): Prescott Park, the Theatre By The Sea, fish markets, walking tours, boat cruises, the Portsmouth Atheneum, Kittery Historical and Naval Museum, and Strawbery Banke, a 10-acre "outdoor museum" with 35 historic buildings—including 5 restored and furnished landmark homes, craft shops still in operation, a variety of exhibits, gardens, and restorations in progress.

P.S. July and August are the social season; during the group months "there are times when the guests will encounter a banquet meal and extra ebullience . . . call Jim Smith for group month appraisal."

P.P.S. The Wentworth has now been sold to a group of investors; Jim Smith is still there to ensure its character remains, but you should anticipate some changes.

STAGE NECK INN
York Harbor, Me.

$$

The name conjures up visions of sea-girt headlands and squawking seagulls and lobster pounds. And that's more or less what you find: a spit of land at the entrance to York Harbor, river on one side, beach on the other, ocean ahead, harbor astern. The inn was built (1973) to take full advantage of the site; all fifty-eight of its big, comfy rooms have a view (you pay less for the "harbor" view because it's half harbor, half parking lot), and the elegant blue-and-crystal dining room has picture windows on three sides. But then if you order one of their many seafood specialties, you won't have time for the view, so busy will you be plowing through a huge lobster or a delicate sole filet. Follow that, if you dare, with another specialty—deep-fried Camembert with strawberry jam. The inn's menu is not inexpensive, but the table d'hôte dinners at $8.95 are good values: melon and prosciutto or baked stuffed mushrooms, broiled swordfish, salad, dinner breads, and coffee or tea. And the dessert cart will throw anyone's diet to the wind. Not a bad way to spend an evening in the fall. Afterward you can sit in a plump sofa before the big fireplace in the lobby-lounge, surrounded by paintings by local artists and Chinese vases and needlepoint.

If this part of the inn looks and feels like a private home, it may be because most of the furnishings come from the Warracks' home in New Jersey, which they gave up when "Pud" Warrack quit his job as an investment banker to build an inn where he and his wife first met as children—among the headlands of York Harbor.

Name: Stage Neck Inn
Owner/Manager: Alexander Warrack
Address: York Harbor, Me. 03911
Directions: York is just across the state line from Massachusetts, ½ hours from Boston; Exit 1 on the Maine Turnpike (I–95) puts you within a few minutes of town, via U.S. 1A.
Telephone: (207) 363–3850
Cables/Telex: None
Credit Cards: American Express, Diners, MasterCard, Visa
Rooms: 58.
Meals: Breakfast 7:30–10:00 (Sundays 8:00–10:00), lunch 12:00–2:00, dinner 6:30–10:00 (approx. $20 to $25 for 2); room service for breakfast and bar; jacket required, tie requested in dining room; piano bar during week; quartet on Friday and Saturday, in the lounge.
Diversions: Heated saltwater pool, beach; tennis (2 clay courts, no lights, $3 per person per hour); golf nearby.
Sightseeing: York Beach and Harbor, Animal Forest Park.

DOCKSIDE GUEST QUARTERS
York Harbor, Me.

$$

The dock in question is opposite the neck of Stage Neck, where the York River makes a 90-degree turn and unwary skippers sometimes come to grief before the astonished eyes of the Quarters' guests rocking on the porch. It's an attractive location, although some guests may find the lobster fleet less than quaint as it putt-putts out of the harbor at six o'clock in the morning. This otherwise secluded seven-acre island complex lives up to its nautical name and location. The Maine House dates from the late eighties and retains the atmosphere of an old seadog's home, its lobby and lounge lined with model sailboats and paintings of clipper ships, cabinets filled with scrimshaw, walls lined with books on lighthouses and sailing. Guests in the five bedrooms here have a grandstand view of the river from wraparound verandas (these are also the least expensive rooms, all but one of them with private bath). The remaining rooms (the newest are only a couple of years old) are grouped in contemporary-style pine cottages along the shoreline, with rustic-nautical decor, blue-and-yellow towels like signal flags; all of them have decks with captain's chairs for lounging and thinking and watching the ducks and dories— or sailboats that run aground.

Name: Dockside Guest Quarters
Owners/Managers: David and Harriette Lusty
Address: Harris Island Road, York, Me. 03909
Directions: York is just across the Maine border from Massachusetts; once you leave Interstate 95, follow Routes 1, 1A, and 103 to York Harbor (not village), where you'll see signs for the Quarters.
Telephone: (207) 363–2868
Cables/Telex: None
Credit Cards: MasterCard, Visa
Rooms: 19 (5 in the Maine House, the remainder in shoreside cottages).
Meals: Continental breakfast (in Maine House or on veranda) 8:00–10:30; other meals in the adjoining restaurant, operated separately (lunch 12:00–2:30, dinner 5:30–8:30, except Mondays).
Diversions: Badminton, shuffleboard, parlor games, library; sailboats for rent; beach, tennis, golf nearby.
Sightseeing: See "Stage Neck Inn."
P.S. This is one inn where owners and regulars prefer guests to be married; if you're not, please act like you were. Closed mid-October to mid-May.

THE CAPTAIN LORD MANSION
Kennebunkport, Me.

$$

A *lord's* mansion, almost, rather than a captain's: Federalist styling with yellow clapboard walls and 160 bottle-green shutters, rising to an octagonal cupola, almost as high as the ancient elms in the yard. Inside, high-ceilinged corridors lead to elegant drawing rooms with tall windows and hand-sewn drapes, marble fireplaces, and furnishings of ornatest Victoriana. Captain Lord was a shipowner who couldn't abide to see his crew sitting around on their seafaring butts while the British blockaded Kennebunkport during the War of 1812; so he set them to work building the grandest mansion on the avenue, a masterpiece with all the hallmarks of the ship carpenter's craft—including a three-story unsupported elliptical stairway and mahogany doors with chunky brass locks. All the guest rooms are different, most of them larger than average, some with working fireplaces, some with fourposter beds, all spruced up in colonial colors. New owners, Bev Davis and Rick Litchfield, have added their own furniture, rugs, pillows, and color-coordinated floor to make the rooms more attractive than ever. There is no way we could decide which was most charming or comfortable or endearing. Suites obviously are more spacious, otherwise arrive early in the day, ask Bev or Rick to show you what's available, then take your pick.

Breakfast is served family style in the *House-and-Garden*ish kitchen (two sittings, each announced by chimes), with fresh juice, coffee, and just-baked muffin marvels (mincemeat, peach, blueberry, or date). Between them Bev and Rick manage to turn a normally bleary-eyed ritual into something between a picnic and a garden party. The remainder of the day you're on your own to explore the charms and crannies of coastal Maine; but round about sunset, buy a bottle of wine, return to the mansion, climb the steps to Captain Lord's crow's-nest cupola, settle down on the bench, and watch the twilight calm settle over the harbor.

Name: The Captain Lord Mansion
Owners/Managers: Bev Davis and Rick Litchfield
Address: P.O. Box 527, Kennebunkport, Me. 04046
Directions: Follow the Maine Turnpike to the Kennebunk signs (about 20–25
    miles north of the Massachusetts line), then follow route 9A or 35 into
    Kennebunkport; the mansion is one block inland from the waterfront,
    near the yacht club.
Telephone: (207) 967–3141
Cables/Telex: None
Credit Cards: American Express, Barclaycard, Carte Blanche, Diners,
    Eurocard, MasterCard, Visa
Rooms: 15, including 5 suites; most with private or semiprivate bathrooms.
Meals: Breakfast only, two sittings—8:00 or 9:00. There are plenty of dining
    spots in the area, and Bev or Rick will show you a selection of menus and
    make reservations.
Diversions: Snoozing in the lawn chairs, boat watching from the cupola;
    tennis, golf, boating, horseback riding, cross-country skiing, skating,
    theater nearby.
Sightseeing: Brick Store Museum, Seashore Trolley Museum, L. L. Bean,
    summer theater in Ogunquit.
P.S. No children under 12. Be forewarned—because the mansion is such a
    landmark, tours of the house are given 4 days a week in the summer.

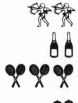

BLACK POINT INN
Prouts Neck, Me.

Stand at the front porch and there's Scarborough Beach stretching off
into the distance. Walk through the lobby to the lounge and lo!—
Sand Dollar Beach beckons. Both are white strands, both are uncrowded (access to them is only through private property) and this is
Maine. Black Point, then, is an ideal spot for joggers, beachcombers,
beach walkers, moon worshippers, sun worshippers. For the others,
there's plenty of choice—golf and tennis at the country club, bird
watching, day sailing at the yacht club, following the trail around the
rim of Prouts Neck to Winslow Homer's old studio. Somewhere
between the sea and the bird sanctuary, somewhere among the

scents of pine and balsam the whiff of barbecue tells you there are also a few private homes tucked away among the trees.

The inn itself is a silver-shingled three-story structure dating from the Twenties, kept shipshape all those years, and now under a new owner. Half the guest rooms are in the inn; half in shingle cottages between the inn and the beach. Either location, they're fancied up in country-inn style with lace curtains, American hard maple furniture, wallpapers that exude Colonial calm. They all have air conditioning and screens and you pay more for an ocean view. The dining room, walled with water-stained pine, looks out on the rose garden, the tables are carefully set, down to the sprays of fresh flowers and finger bowls. And to make sure that what goes on the table is top-drawer, owner Normand Dugas has called in Chef Walter Buettler, who winters at La Quinta in Palm Springs.

Summers are taken over by long-term regulars, spring and fall brings some groups and seminars (which either take over the entire property or stay in the inn, leaving the cottages for lovers and others; the staff will tell you if there are groups in the house when you make your reservation). Some people might find Black Point too gracious, too genteel, but if your fellow guests look like the bridge-and-jigsaw set, don't be dismayed—you'll have less competition for the courts, links, sailboats, and those two fine beaches.

Name: Black Point Inn
Owner/Manager: Normand Dugas
Address: Prouts Neck, Me. 04070
Directions: From the Maine Turnpike, follow signs for Scarborough (Exit 6A or 7), then Route 1 at Route 207; by air to Portland (Delta, Air New England, Bar Harbor Airlines).
Telephone: (207) 883–4311
Cables/Telex: None
Credit Cards: American Express, MasterCard, Visa
Rooms: 80, including 3 suites, and 19 rooms in 3 cottages.
Meals: Breakfast 8:00–9:30, poolside buffet luncheon 12:30–2:00, dinner 7:00–8:30 (approx. $30 to $35 for 2); room service at breakfast only; "quite dressy but not formal."
Diversions: Separate TV room, piano/combo in lounge and poolside; heated saltwater pool, 2 beaches, walking trails; bicycles at the inn, 18-hole golf course and 14 clay and all-weather tennis courts at the adjacent country club, day sailing at the yacht club; Scarborough Race track.

Sightseeing: Oldest lighthouse in the country (Portland Head), Bath Marine Museum, various historic mansions along the coast.

P.S. "Not recommended for children"; small groups off-season, but staff will alert you when you make your reservation; stays of 1 or 2 days can only be reserved 10 days in advance; closed mid-October through May.

THE SQUIRE TARBOX INN
Westport Island, Me.

$

This two-hundred-year-old retired farmhouse sits contentedly between the trees and a roadway that goes nowhere. Daisies grow in the parking lot, honeysuckle berries crowd the veranda, cedar waxwings flutter from honeysuckle to oak and back again. Guests come back again too: the young couple reading and drowsing on the veranda spent a night with the Squire on their way north and returned the following day because "it's just so peaceful here." Peaceful it is: eight rooms only, a few with private bathrooms, mostly period furnishings, with the quietest nooks in the former barn, above a rustic lounge with high ceilings and serendipitous decor. It's restful, too. The most energetic activity is croquet. Or you can take a walk through the woods to Squam Lake, but be back in plenty of time for the highlight of the day—dinner in the Colonial-style dining room, its plank floors and low beamed ceiling aglow in the light of candles and the logs in the brick-and-beam fireplace. Mississippians Elsie White and Anne McInvale have been here only a year (their first inn, too), but their cuisine has already earned a high reputation around the Boothbay region. Dinner at seven consists of four courses of "modified continental" cuisine—local flounder *meunière* or *boeuf en daube provençale*, fruit salad with poppyseed dressing, chocolate mint pie, and other interesting dishes that merit a drive along a road that goes nowhere.

Name: The Squire Tarbox Inn
Owners/Managers: Elsie White and Anne McInvale
Address: Route 2, Box 318, Wiscasset, Me. 04578

Directions: On Westport Island, between Bath and Wiscasset; from U.S. 1,
   follow the signs for State Highway 144, and then occasional signs for
   Squire Tarbox, about 8 miles from U.S. 1.
Telephone: (207) 882–7693
Cables/Telex: None
Credit Cards: None
Rooms: 8, some with private bath.
Meals: Breakfast 8:00–9:00, no lunch, dinner 7:00 (one sitting, approx. $30
   for 2 for 4 courses); informal.
Diversions: Croquet, darts, books, games, each other; tennis, golf, and so
   forth back on the mainland, wherever that is.
Sightseeing: Island scenery—enough in itself.
P.S. Open from Memorial Day weekend through Columbus Day weekend;
   closed remainder of the year.

SPRUCE POINT INN AND LODGES
Boothbay Harbor, Me.

The view is wall-to-wall harbor and islands, rocky headlands and
lighthouses, schooners and windjammers, and to make sure you can
enjoy the view to the full the Druces have installed a gazebo on the
embankment and wooden platforms with wooden armchairs at
strategic spots along the shore. The pool is beside the sea, and you
can fish off the dock, or, if you're feeling adventurous, hoist the flag
and one of the ferryboats plying the harbor will stop by and take you
into town. On Sundays guests board the ferry for a sunset cruise
through the harbor, fortified with hot chocolate and freshly baked
pastries; on Monday morning, there's a mariners' breakfast beside
the sea, on Tuesday a lobster bake. With all these opportunities for
enjoying the waterfront setting there's no need to insist on a room
with ocean view (although the suites in the lodge would be our first
choice); a room in a garden cottage fits the bill nicely (most of the
rooms are a deft combination of rustic charm and modern convenience, although you might want to avoid rooms with connecting
doors, *if* you're a light sleeper). The Spruce Point Inn has been
hosting many of America's leading families for forty years, but it has a

relaxed informal manner about it; it encourages families as families, but it's the sort of place where children are expected to behave like grown-ups at the appropriate times. In any case, you can always escape to the gazebo, or settle into a pair of wooden armchairs and watch the windjammers.

Name: Spruce Point Inn

Owners/Managers: John and Charlotte Druce

Address: Boothbay Harbor, Me. 04538 (in winter, 158 Prospect Street, West Boylston, Mass. 01583)

Directions: On a 100-acre wooded peninsula, about 5 minutes from the bustle of Boothbay proper, on Atlantic Avenue. The signs along U.S. 1 just north of Wiscasset will get you to Boothbay Harbor, about 100 miles north of the Massachusetts line.

Telephone: (207) 633–4152; winter (617) 835–3082

Cables/Telex: None

Credit Cards: American Express, MasterCard, Visa

Rooms: 60, including suites and villas, 13 with fireplaces, and 9 in the inn itself.

Meals: Breakfast 8:00–9:00, lunch 12:30–1:30, dinner 6:30–8:00, weekly lobster bakes, cookouts, etc.; no room service; jacket and tie for dinner.

Diversions: 2 pools (1 fresh, 1 salt), putting green, croquet, 3 all-weather tennis courts (no lights); golf, boating, sailing nearby.

Sightseeing: Excursion cruises out of the Harbor, the Boothbay Playhouse, art galleries, marinas, craft shops.

P.S. The social season absorbs July, August, and the first weeks of September; small groups appear in October, so your best bet here is likely to be the month of June or late September.

For detailed rate, turn to page 413.

SAMOSET RESORT
Rockport, Me.

$$

Tune out the piped music. Ignore the felt-covered table welcoming the Eastern Division Salesmen of Screw-and-Nut, Inc. Avert your eyes from the plethora of meeting rooms.

Focus, instead, on the setting. A windswept, rocky headland, pebble shore and offshore islands, a mile-long breakwater with an authentic lighthouse at its tip. Lobster boats and windjammers go by. Golfers play hide-and-seek in the mist. The setting sun gilds Penobscot Bay. Best of all you can enjoy this kind of Maine in the blustery months. There are only a few good places open in these parts in the scarves-and-sweaters months, and none where you can enjoy so much invigorating outdoor life and so much mollycoddling indoors. And where else on this coast will you find a hotel with indoor pool, sauna, and indoor tennis court?

When we first visited Samoset shortly after it opened (around 1975), there was much to admire but the place was chaotic. Now the owners and builders have taken over management themselves and you can appreciate the good points. Start with the main building. It's constructed almost entirely from the southern hard pine of one turn-of-the-century granary—even to the polished wood-block floor, the custom-designed chairs and tables and headboards. The split-level lobby is dominated by acres of picture window and a huge fieldstone fireplace that rises 175 feet to the peak of the cathedral ceiling. The restaurant downstairs treads a fine line between rustic timbers and the sophistication of chrome and copper (the food is so-so, the service attentive, although the homemade fish chowder seems more Idaho than Penobscot). Guest rooms, certainly the best of them (the others are being upgraded), make good use of the granary timbers as highlights against shag carpeting and summery fabrics. There's even color television for the hours when the mists roll in and you can't admire the view. The top-floor suites are particularly spacious, with big terraces (equipped with tables, chairs, loungers) notched into the roof line. But we'd plump for what management calls "end rooms," that is, those at the ends of the three wings, facing directly to the sea, each with balcony or patio and queen-size bed. If there's a group of Eastern Division Salesmen in the house, stay put in your end room; if not, Samoset could be a wonderful place for a cuddly weekend in winter.

Name: Samoset Resort
Manager: Marcel Lacasse
Address: Rockport, Me. 04856
Directions: Closer to Rock*land* than Rock*port*. Just off Route 1 Coastal, an hour north of Portland; 3 miles north of Rockland look for Baptist Church and small Samoset signs directing you along Walds Avenue; scheduled ½-hour flights by Bar Harbor Airlines between Boston and Rockland (free pickup from airport).
Telephone: (207) 594–2511
Cables/Telex: None
Credit Cards: American Express, Carte Blanche, Diners, MasterCard, Visa
Rooms: 150, including 18 suites.
Meals: Breakfast 6:30–11:00, lunch 11:30–2:00, snack bar at clubhouse to 6:00, dinner 6:00–10:00 (approx. $25 to $30 for 2); informal dress; full room service during dining-room hours.
Diversions: Lounge with big screen TV for sports events, live music and taped music in lounge and dining room; indoor and outdoor pools, sauna and exercise room; walking trails; tennis (3 courts, indoors), golf (18 holes), skating, cross-country skiing (rentals); nearby—sailing and skiing. Also occasional day trips on windjammers.
Sightseeing: The harbors and windjammers of Rockport and Camden, boat trips to offshore islands.
P.S. Lots of tour groups and meetings (including weekends).

PILGRIM'S INN
Deer Isle, Me.

$$

The "Moveable Feast," Tuesdays in summer, finds all the guests driving to a nearby fishing village. There a lobsterman boils his catch on the jetty and serves it up in his garden. This is just one of the likable ideas introduced by George Pavloff, a former clergyman and psychologist in Washington, D.C., who retired to this lovely old inn with the aim of offering his guests "an atmosphere that's recreating and refreshing." The setting alone fulfills the promise.

Deer Isle is a paddle of land. One narrow road running down the middle, linking an artist's landscape of coves and islets, of rocks and seaweed and sailboats bobbing. Pilgrim's is a large plum-colored, gambrel-roofed inn. Two towering chestnut trees stand like sentries on each side of the front porch. On one side, Northwest Harbor almost laps at the chestnut trees; at the rear, a placid millpond, with a few rustic armchairs waiting invitingly at the edge of the lawn. Built over a hundred years ago as the Down East home of a shipowner, the inn is now on the National Register of Historic Places. The Pavloffs have lovingly restored their landmark. Guest rooms are properly decked out with Victoriana, some brass beds, quilts, rag rugs; but what sets them apart from other restorations is Eleanor Pavloff's deft use of colors for the woodwork and the lively contrast of contemporary paintings and prints. Each room is warmed by wood-burning stoves, each couple by electric bed warmers and colorful comforters. That should compensate for the fact that you have to trot across the hall to the bathroom (one for every two rooms), which themselves are bright, colorful oases, with little extras like Neutrogena Soap.

The paneled parlors and lounges are decorated with a sort of back-to-basics sophistication, and the Common Room, adjoining the garden, is a low-beamed nook with huge brick fireplace and twin Dutch ovens. At six every evening, classical music purrs quietly in the background, the fire crackles with maple or birch, guests gather for cocktails and complimentary hors d'ouevres. At seven on the dot they all retire to the barn-sided dining room for home-cooked, garden-fresh meals.

Unless, that is, it's summer and Tuesday—and everyone drives off for the Moveable Feast.

Name: Pilgrim's Inn
Managers: George and Eleanor Pavloff
Address: Deer Isle, Me. 04627
Directions: By car, take Interstate 95 to Brunswick, U.S. 1 to Bucksport, then Route 15 south to Deer Isle (follow signs for Stonington); by air to Bangor (Delta).

Telephone: (207) 348–6615
Cables/Telex: None
Credit Cards: MasterCard, Visa
Rooms: 12, sharing 6 bathrooms.
Meals: Breakfast 8:00–9:00, no lunch, cocktails at 6:00, dinner at 7:00 (Tuesdays in summer, outdoors); informal dress; dinner for nonguests by reservation only; no room service.
Diversions: Taped background music in lounge (mostly classical); rowing on millpond, clamming; golf and tennis at country club 5 minutes away; mailboat excursions to Isle-au-Haut or Eagle Island.
Sightseeing: Stonington (picturesque fishing harbor), and Blue Hill (villages), studios of artists and craftsmen, theater and chamber-music recitals in summer.
P.S. "To preserve the spirit of harmony within the Inn we remind parents that they are responsible for the conduct and safety of their children." Closed November through May 15; minimum stay of 4 days in August.
P.P.S. At the time of writing, the inn had been bought by a geologist from Connecticut, but the Pavloffs would continue to run it and maintain their style of innkeeping. Meantime, the Pavloffs have bought *Goose Cove*, a tucked-away resort on a quiet cove a few miles down the road; they're currently renovating, face-lifting, and upgrading, and when they've rid themselves of the Naugahyde and added a few more rustic touches, this could prove to be a dream getaway—if you can snare one of the dozen rooms.

For more suggestions in this area
turn to Added Attractions, page 375.

Green Mountains, White Mountains

No, make me mistress to the man I love
If there be yet another name more free
More fond than mistress, make me that to thee!

POPE

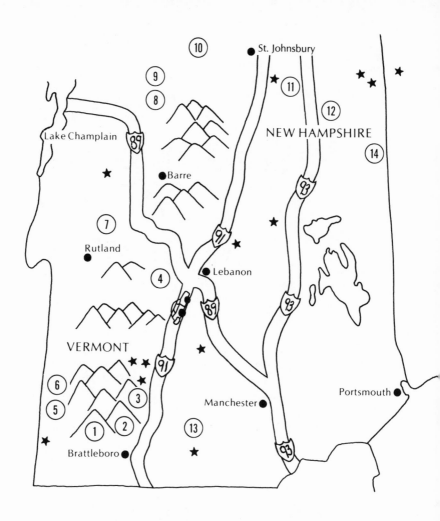

1. The Inn at Sawmill Farm
2. The Four Columns Inn
3. The Old Tavern at Grafton
4. Woodstock Inn
5. Reluctant Panther Inn
6. Barrows House
7. Hawk Mountain
8. Topnotch at Stowe
9. Stowehof Inn
10. The Inn on the Common
11. Lovett's Inn
12. Snowy Owl Inn
13. The John Hancock Inn
14. Stafford's-in-the-Field
★ *Added Attractions*

THE INN AT SAWMILL FARM
West Dover, Vt.

$$$

The old stable is now an airy lounge with a wall of window looking onto swamp maple and tamarack trees. The former stalls are bedrooms and the haymows are sleeping lofts. The cupola-crowned sugar house, where the farmer used to render the maple syrup, is now a summer card room by the edge of the swimming pool. The chess table in the bar was once a hand-cranked washing machine, and the planter on the dining room wall used to be a South Jersey cranberry rake.

Many people have converted barns; few of them have succeeded as nobly as Rodney and Ione Williams. What the Williamses have wrought is not so much a conversion as a metamorphosis. But then they started out with several advantages. Rodney Williams was, until a few years ago, an Atlantic City architect; Ione Williams was an interior decorator. The remainder of the family contributed muscle or encouragement during the transformation period, and they still play an enthusiastic part in running the inn (son Brill is head chef), which is now virtually a small village on its own, complete with trout pond.

AROMATIC WELCOME. The inn gets its name from a sawmill that was erected here sometime in the late 1700s, where a branch of the Deerfield River funnels through a narrow rocky gully. You drive across this gully and up the hill a few yards, step out of your car and immediately you notice the scent of apple trees and the whiff of a wood fire. Welcome to the Sawmill.

The inn's foyer is decked out like a farm shed, with yokes and harnesses, forks and hoes, and all the impedimenta of a working farm. Go upstairs, and it's nothing like a farm. Nor a hotel, for that matter. It looks more like a classy antique store—an antique store where you can lounge and eat and drink and play.

The basic structure of the eighty-year-old barn is still intact. All the hard-hewn weathered beams and barnboards are original; ditto the mellowed brick and textured fieldstone. None of the original timbers were discarded; when they weren't needed in their original position, they were salvaged and used elsewhere. There's nothing phony about the Sawmill. Look up, for example, to the ceiling of the stable-lounge. Those hefty timbers are real. Note the balustrade along the library balcony—it's made from the stall dividers that once separated the cows from the bulls. There's a lot to admire in this lounge: the nonagenarian Elliot grandfather clock, the dainty Davenport desk, the copper-covered coffee table, the bronze telescope, the honest-to-goodness pans, pots, spoons, tongs, and candleholders surrounding the big brick fire. All the colors of Vermont are here— from spring's celery-tinted walls and the lime-green upholstery to the russet and copper of autumn.

FLAGSTONE FLOORS AND BARN-SIDING. Beyond the lounge you have a pair of dining rooms. The first is a formal jacket-and-tie sort of place, with overhead fans, walls lined with American primitives of young girls and old ladies, and chairs that are far too slender and elegant for a public dining room. The more popular dining room is a glass-enclosed patio overlooking the apple trees and the pool, a rustic room with flagstone floors, dark-brown barn-siding, and directors' chairs to match. People drive for miles, through spring muds and winter snows, just for the pleasure of dining here: avocado stuffed with hot crabmeat, *escargots bourguignonne*, roast duckling with green peppercorns, rack of baby lamb *persille*, backfin crabmeat *au gratin* (the crab by special delivery direct from Crisfield, Maryland). The one-hundred-bin cellar, put together over the years with the same care and refinement as everything else at Sawmill, includes many esteemed California wines, including a Sauvignon Blanc from the Joseph Phelps Vineyard to sip with your backfin crabmeat.

OLD CIDER HOUSE. The Sawmill has only twenty rooms, eight of which have fireplaces. The ten rooms in the main building are in various styles—Early American, Georgian, Victorian, Vermontian— all with color-coordinated papers and fabrics, all with the finest Fieldcrest towels and linens, each with delicate touches, like, say, washbasins recessed in copper-topped vanity tables. The suites, each with refrigerator, club chairs, sofas, king-size beds, are probably the

classiest accommodations in Vermont. Take your pick—Cider House
or Spring House, overlooking the pool or overlooking the pond—
they're all exquisite. But, if you have the wherewithal, the choice
spot is the Old Wood Shed, beside the pond: cathedral ceiling,
fireplace, daybed in front of the fire, champagne in the refrigerator;
even the bathroom is special, with floor-to-ceiling windows looking
out on a secret Japanese rock garden.

SEASONAL PLEASURES. West Dover is one of the oldest villages in
Vermont, mostly white clapboard houses and a white church with a
tall spire hidden behind a grotesquely ornate telephone pole. A quick
walk along the main street and you've more or less seen West Dover,
but there are plenty of activities in the neighborhood, at any season of
the year. There are miles and miles of walking trails, the nearby
Marlboro Music Festival in summer, the foliage in fall; but maybe the
region comes into its own in winter, when you have a choice of
downhill skiing at Mt. Snow, a mile and half to the north, skating on
the inn pond (bring your own skates), cross-country skiing on four-
hour trials (the Williamses will make up a picnic lunch with wine), or
snowshoeing through the forest. Let others shiver, however; we'll be
sitting on the big sofa in the lounge with afternoon tea, feet propped
up on the copper-topped table, watching the snow fall on the tama-
racks and maples—a panorama of white on white.

Name: The Inn at Sawmill Farm
Owners/Managers: Rodney Williams and Family
Address: Route 100, Box 367, West Dover, Vt. 05356
Directions: On Vt. 100, 6 miles north of Wilmington, halfway between
     Brattleboro and Bennington, and 10 miles from the Marlboro Music
     Festival.
Telephone: (802) 464–8131
Cables/Telex: None
Credit Cards: None
Rooms: 20, including 8 suites with fireplaces.
Meals: Breakfast 8:00–9:30, no lunch, dinner 6:00–9:30; room service during
     meal hours; jackets at dinner.
Diversions: Indoors—TV lounge, library, chess, Scrabble; outdoors—pool
     and 2½-acre spring-fed pond for swimming, tennis (1 court, no charge
     for house guests), hiking trails, canoes, fishing; golf, rental bicycles,
     horseback riding, sailing, and Wilderness Lake nearby; in winter, ice

skating, snowshoeing, cross-country skiing, downhill skiing (1½ miles away).

Sightseeing: West Dover, Marlboro Music Festival (summer), Mt. Snow and nature abound.

P.S. Busiest in foliage and snow seasons, quietest in *summer*. Two-night minimum stay on weekends.

THE FOUR COLUMNS INN
Newfane, Vt.

At some point on your trip, probably close to lunch or dinner, you may decide how marvelous it would be if Vermont had one of those great little inns like they have in France.

It does. *Voilà.* The Four Columns.

Poke your head into the restaurant here and you might think you're in Burgundy. Have dinner here and you may still think you're in Burgundy. The reason is, of course, that René Chardain, *le patron*, comes from France (from Champagne, rather than Burgundy), and

Anne Chardain from French Canada. What they've created is an almost-typical French *auberge* in Vermont.

The France-in-Vermont ambiance runs all the way through. None of the twelve rooms are alike, and though the antique and not-so-antique furniture comes from auctions around Vermont, the print wallpapers, the curtains, and the bedspreads collectively have a look of France about them. All the rooms have private baths, and most of them have air conditioning.

The name comes from the four white columns decorating the slightly pompous facade of Kemball Hall, a house built for a Mr. Marshall Kemball back in 1830. It sits well off the main road, behind the Newfane Inn, the village green, and the county courthouse. It's in two parts—the old white house at the front, and a red barn at the rear—the two connected with a sheltered patio where you can drink and dine in summer. The restaurant, bar, and half the rooms are in the barn. At the rear, a footbridge leads across a pond, with a flock of cantankerous geese, to a trail leading up to the hill (affectionately known as Mont Chardain) behind the inn.

PHEASANT AND CANDLELIGHT. This is no grab-a-snack joint. It's a place where you dawdle until the last drop of Burgundy is sipped, where you plot an entire evening that begins with a *kir* and ends with a kiss. The dining room greets you with a huge fireplace, a wall with subdued splashes of roses, a pheasant on the mantelpiece, a stag's head on the wall; the gentle lighting comes from sconces and candles; and copper pieces hanging from the dark, beamed ceiling glitter in the candles' glow. It's a mellow atmosphere. And *très intime*. No rush, no bustle.

The portions, *hélas*, are mountainous, and, doubly *hélas*, delectable to the last morsel. M. Chardain's specialties are duckling *Bigarade flambée*, rack of lamb, *filet mignon poivre vert flambée*, lobster with crabmeat stuffing, trout (live from the tank or the pond), pheasant from their own farm, filet Wellington. A meal here is expensive, but that's the way French food is. The question is, is it worth it? That depends on who's with you.

M. Chardain's skills have been highly praised in *Life*, *Holiday*, *Vogue*, and *Esquire* (in each case when he was running the Newfane Inn across the green). However, a recent visit revealed some lapses in service. A table which was reserved for eight would be, we were

informed, ready in five minutes. "Meantime, m'sieur, why don't you
have a drink in the bar?" The five minutes turned out to be forty, in a
bar which is a poor second to a stroll around the village green. To
compound matters, we were seated near a table on which was piled a
reserve supply of appetizing-looking *tarte aux fraises*; but by the
time we were finally seated and served, the tantalizing *tartes* were
"all finished, m'sieur." Boo!

Name: The Four Columns Inn
Owner/Manager: René Chardain
Address: 230 West Street, Newfane, Vt. 05345
Directions: Off State Highway 30, 15 miles northwest of the Brattleboro Exit
    on Interstate 91.
Telephone: (802) 365–7713
Cables/Telex: None
Credit Cards: American Express, MasterCard, Visa
Rooms: 12, 1 suite.
Meals: Breakfast 8:00–9:30, no lunch, dinner 6:00–9:00 (approx. $35 to $50
    for 2); no room service; jacket requested in the dining room; piped
    music.
Diversions: Eating.
Sightseeing: Scenery; also see "The Inn at Sawmill Farm."
P.S. Closed Mondays, and for 1 month in spring (call ahead for dates).
P.P.S. Rumor has it, at press time, that the Four Columns may be changing
    owners—check before you go.

THE OLD TAVERN AT GRAFTON
Grafton, Vt.

This may well be the ultimate New England inn.

It's historic (it opened its doors in 1801), and it had a distinguished clientele (Daniel Webster, Nathaniel Hawthorne, Ralph
Waldo Emerson, Ulysses S. Grant, Teddy Roosevelt, and Rudyard
Kipling, who stayed here so long one of the rooms is named after
him). But historic inns often look their age, because it takes so much
money just to keep them from falling down. Not the Old Tavern at

Grafton, thanks to the Windham Foundation, which has restored
many of the old Colonial homes in the village, and particularly this
proud old hostelry. Now it's virtually a brand-new 180-year-old inn,
with modern heating, a fire detection system, sprinklers, and an
elevator. Kipling and Co. never had it so good.

When The Old Tavern first opened its doors, it was a much
simpler structure than today's three-storied whitewashed building
with twin verandas, a bar in the old barn, and across the street a
couple of old homes (also dating from the 1800s). The proprietors call
this the "most elegant little inn in all New England." They're not
exaggerating.

Step through the main door and you're in the drawing room of a
well-to-do squire—except that it's really the lobby and reception
area. To the left is the Kipling Library, a blue parlor with shelves of
books flanking an open fire, writing desks for dashing off *billets-doux*,
and comfy sofas to settle back in with a volume of Kipling or Emerson
or Hawthorne.

Upstairs in the guest rooms, you'll find the same impeccable
taste. All the rooms are different in detail, but they're all decorated

with antiques and drapes and hooked rugs, some with tester beds—mini fourposters with cute embroidered canopies. The inn has thirty-five rooms spread over three buildings—fourteen in the old inn itself, the remainder in the Homestead and the Windham Cottage opposite. Normally, the words "across the street" might throw you into a tizzy. How dare they shunt you off to the annex! In this case, go. The rooms are delightful there, too. Karen's Room is all pinks and pastels, with bay windows and armchairs; Addie's Room, green and white, has a chaise longue where you can stretch out and watch the action down by the inn's swimming hole. In the inn proper, the prime rooms are #9 (alias the Aunt Pauline Fiske Room), and #8 (similar to #9, a corner room, but in this case facing Main Street); but the best buys are #10 and #3, for less than $30 because, in each case, the private bathroom is across the hall.

One of the most convivial rooms in the inn is one Kipling and his cohorts never saw. It's the Tavern Bar, an unadorned corner of the barn, so snug you can't avoid clinking glasses before you drink. On the other side of the bar's fireplace is the barn proper, with an even larger fireplace, puffy chairs, and sofas; above it, the haymow has become a games room, with a TV set tucked away in a corner. An attractive new "conservatory" in the rear patio brings the total number of dining rooms to three, which means perhaps more outsiders dropping for dinner than you'd like, but that's the price you may have to pay for staying in a landmark.

QUIET CORNERS, COVERED BRIDGES. The Old Tavern at Grafton is one of those places where you'll want to spend more than a single night. Just sampling all the quiet corners in the inn takes time: one morning writing postcards in the Kipling Library, an afternoon taking advantage of your tester bed, cocktail hour in the Tavern Bar, an after-dinner drink in the Barn Lounge. Next day, a dip in the inn's private swimming pool in the meadow behind the Homestead. After lunch, a game of tennis. Or croquet. Or sit and rock on the porch, watching the automobiles go by every half hour or so. Or take a walk down the village street, past the antique shops, the art gallery, the general store, and the lovely old homes, across one of Grafton's kissing bridges, and wander up the leafy lane on the side of the mountain. It's so peaceful you can almost hear the butterflies flap their wings.

Name: The Old Tavern at Grafton
Manager: Lois Copping
Address: Grafton, Vt. 05146
Directions: On State Highway 121, about 10 miles west of Bellows Falls and
    Interstate 91.
Telephone: (802) 843–2375
Cables/Telex: None
Credit Cards: None
Rooms: 37.
Meals: Breakfast 8:00–9:30, lunch 12:00–2:00, dinner 6:30–8:30 (approx. $25
    to $30 for 2); no room service; jacket at dinner only.
Diversions: Pool, Ping-Pong, skittles; outdoor pool, tennis (2 clay courts,
    free), bicycles, cross-country skiing (fully equipped ski shop just down
    the street), ice skating, horse and carriage rides, croquet (summer
    only); hiking, golf, horseback riding, skiing nearby.
Sightseeing: Scenery—everywhere.
P.S. Closed for the month of April, and on Christmas Eve and Christmas
    Day.

WOODSTOCK INN
Woodstock, Vt.

$$

What the world needs is more Laurance Rockefellers, conservation-
ists who have the wherewithal to put their money where their hearts
are, men who'll put up beautiful inns like this one and then spend $3
million of their own money to bury telephone poles around the
village green. Even before the poles went under, Woodstock was one
of "the five most beautiful villages in America." It has an elliptical
village green ringed with Colonial homes, four sets of Paul Revere
bells in its church steeples, and a brand-new kissing bridge across the
Ottauquechee River. The green, the bells, the bridge, and the river
are circled by a protective bowl of hills where people ski in winter and
hike in summer.

There's been an inn on this same spot on the village green since
1793, but all that remains of the earlier hostelries is the great hand-

carved eagle above the portico of the 1969 inn—guardian of the inn's tradition of two hundred years of New England hospitality. Someone really cared about the details in the Woodstock Inn: handmade quilts, brass hinges on the doors, photographs on the walls, custom-designed oak furniture and bedside table with concealed AM/FM radio (the TV, alas, is not so discreet). The prime rooms are on the third floor, the most interesting ones have private steam baths.

You spend your public hours in equally tasteful, restful sur-roundings, with ten-foot stone fireplaces, weathered Vermont tim-bers, a neat coffee shop, a cocktail lounge/piano bar. In the rear there's a broad terrace where you can dine beneath the awnings or sit in a rocker and admire the garden while readying your appetite for dinner, but take your time over the decision because it's so pleasant rocking, listening to the birds twittering their evensong and the Paul Revere bells chiming the hour, as the shadows lengthen across the lawn. In any case, if you miss your dinner reservation it's no great loss. The dining room is elegant but perhaps overambitious for the abilities of the staff. And you may not want to fill the gaps between courses listening to a stolid duo, piano and fiddle, playing a stolid arrangement of Beethoven's variations on Mozart's "Ein Mädchen oder Weibchen." Try the coffee shop. Or one of the country res-taurants in and around the village.

ADDER'S TONGUE, DUTCHMAN'S BREECHES. Woodstock is a nice place to be any time of the year, but every lover has his favorite season. Come here in the spring and you can follow woodland trails, stepping lightly through the wild flowers—adder's tongue, Dutchman's breeches, cowslip, bloodroot, and jack-in-the-pulpit; in fall, you're sitting inside a golden bowl, or you can take a horse-drawn wagon up Mt. Tom to survey the valley and village from on high. In winter you can go jingling through the streets in a one-horse open sleigh. Spring, summer, and fall you can swim in the garden pool (but no diving, it's only four feet deep); or play tennis and golf at the country club (one of the oldest courses in the country); or rent a bike ($4 a day) and go riding off down the backroads. Mr. Rockefeller, apparently, doesn't want his guests to be bored.

Name: Woodstock Inn
Manager: Michael E. Neary

Address: Woodstock, Vt. 05091

Directions: By car, from New York, take Interstate 91 to the White River
   Junction Exit, then go 14 miles west on Vt. 12 (driving time 5 hours);
   from Boston, follow Interstates 93 and 89 to U.S. 4, then go west 10
   miles (driving time 2 ½ hours); by air, scheduled flights to Lebanon,
   N.H. (a $12 per-couple cab ride from Woodstock).

Telephone: (802) 457–1100

Cables/Telex: None

Credit Cards: American Express, MasterCard, Visa

Rooms: 121 (including deluxe rooms with steam baths); 2 suites.

Meals: Breakfast 7:00–11:00, lunch 12:00–2:00, dinner 6:00–9:00 (approx.
   $18 to $30 for 2), coffee shop open all afternoon; room service during
   breakfast and lunch; dress informal in winter, jacket required in dining
   room in summer; duo (piano and violin) in the dining room; piano and/or
   live music in the bar.

Diversions: Heated outdoor pool, paddle tennis (2 lighted courts), marked
   hiking trails (maintained by the inn), ice skating; tennis (10 courts, $10
   per court per 1 ½ hours, pro, ball machines, clinics), golf (18 holes, $12
   per round), cross-country skiing trails, downhill skiing, sleigh rides,
   horseback riding; sailing and bicycles for rent nearby.

Sightseeing: The village green, covered bridges, countryside, antiques and
   craft shops, local museums, historic homesteads.

P.S. Small top-echelon groups most of the year, but the meeting rooms are all
   downstairs and you may never know there's a group in the house.
   Sports, honeymoon, and "serenity season" plans available.

RELUCTANT PANTHER INN
Manchester Village, Vt.

$

Like the name, there's a touch of whimsy in the exterior (an un-
Vermontlike muted mauve) and eclectic interior decor—Chinoiser-
ie, Victoriana, an antique desk clerk's clock, hanging lanterns and
planters in one of the two snug dining rooms. Most guests come here
for the Panther's inventive cuisine (Greek *avgolemone* soup, *crêpes*
Rangoon, breast of chicken stuffed with almond-and-apple dressing),
but people who really know the place call ahead and book a room as
well as a table. If it's fall, they'll specify one of the four rooms with

wood-burning fireplaces. Like everything else in this 150-year-old
house, the guest rooms will come as a surprise: some have carpets
that continue halfway up the wall, the color schemes are unorthodox,
but they all have modern bathrooms and cable TV. It all may sound
rather odd, but in fact it's done with great flair, and you needn't be
reluctant to spend a night or two with the Panther.

Name: Reluctant Panther Inn
Owners/Managers: Wood and Joan Cornell
Address: Box 678, Manchester, Vt. 05254
Directions: In Manchester *Village*, at the intersection of Route 7, West Road,
     and Seminary Road.
Telephone: (802) 362–2568
Cables/Telex: None
Credit Cards: American Express
Rooms: 7.
Meals: Breakfast 8:00–9:00, no lunch, dinner 6:00–9:00 (approx. $26 to $34
     for 2); room-service breakfasts; informal dress.
Diversions: Bicycles, hiking trails, tennis, golf, horseback riding nearby.
Sightseeing: Manchester Village and surrounding countryside.
P.S. No children or pets.

BARROWS HOUSE
Dorset, Vt.

$$

It's almost a village within a village, eight houses on as many acres—
Hemlock House, Truffle House, the Carriage House, the Field
House and Stable, the Birds' Nest, a cottage named Schubert
(Charles, not Franz), and Barrows House itself, a big white mansion
built back in 1784 by one of the first preachers in Vermont. The guest
rooms are New England traditional (floral wallpapers, dust ruffles,
patchwork comforters, pillows and sheets—all matching), except for
a few rooms, in the Stable, which are more luxurious. Since 1972 the
inn has been owned, managed, and cherished by Charles and
Marilyn Schubert, an energetic and congenial couple who have laid
on plenty of diversions for their guests (see below), and who'll be

happy to direct you to local activities like barn sales and summer theater. But they won't be too upset if you just lounge around and enjoy the peacefulness of their garden, beside a quiet tree-lined street in the kind of Vermont village where everyone seems to be at church listening to the preacher.

Name: Barrows House
Owners/Managers: Charles and Marilyn Schubert
Address: Dorset, Vt. 05251
Directions: Drive north or south along U.S. 7, then from Manchester north-east along State Highway 30; the Schuberts are right on 30, 6 miles from Manchester.
Telephone: None
Credit Cards: None
Rooms: 22, with 4 suites.
Meals: Breakfast 7:30–9:00, lunch 12:00–1:30, dinner 6:00–9:00 (approx. $30 to $35 for 2); room service; jacket preferred at dinner.
Diversions: Sauna, game room, backgammon, chess, TV in Tap Room; heated outdoor pool, 2 tennis courts; bicycles for rent in summer, cross-country skiing in winter (the inn's facilities include 60 sets of skis and gear, and there are 20 miles of trails in a nearby forest); golf ("oldest course in the country"), hiking, horseback riding nearby, as well as downhill skiing and ice skating.
Sightseeing: Green Mountain National Forest, Dorset Playhouse.
P.S. 1-night reservations require payment in advance. Closed November 1 through 20.

HAWK MOUNTAIN
Pittsfield, Vt.

Turtledove Mountain would be more like it, because there's a love affair going on up here, a love affair between people and trees. "The nice thing about Vermont," as one young Vermonter once remarked, "is that the trees are close together and the people are far apart." And that's the way it is on Hawk Mountain. You have complete, unruffled seclusion (you rent homes, not rooms) among the pines, spruce, and maple trees, where kingbirds and tree swallows swoop and sing as if they're happy to be here. You'll have a terrace among the branches of the spruce and maple, and if you're here in warm weather you may find yourself spending most of your time there: brunching on the terrace, snoozing on the terrace, reading on the terrace, sunbathing on the terrace, sundowners on the terrace, dinner on the terrace, love on the terrace with the moonlight of Vermont filtering through the leaves.

Hawk Mountain is a place for two people who are happy just being with each other. There's no "action" (plenty of it, though, in Killington). You enjoy simple pleasures here—a swim in the spring-fed pond, a walk to the top of the mountain for stunning views of wave after wave of green-clad slopes (you're surrounded on three sides by the Green Mountain National Forest); walks around the common grounds in fall to pick armfuls of apples, blackberries, or raspberries.

TIMBER HOUSES, FIELDSTONE FIRES. Hawk Mountain is neither a resort nor a hotel in the usual sense, and to say it's a housing development is like calling Yehudi Menuhin a fiddler. At Hawk Mountain people buy lots, build vacation homes, and put them into a rental pool when they're not in use. You're the big winner—because for a few nights or a few weeks you have all the advantages of living in a smart vacation home in the forest without owning it. They're hardly run-of-the-mill vacation homes either: they're all screened from each other (and from the driveways) by trees, they're built of timber and finished with stain only (no paint), and even the "garbage houses" have to match the homes. A few have two bedrooms, most of them have three or four (the rates are not much different once you check into them). Decor varies from owner to owner, but most of them are summer townhouse modern; all of them have complete kitchens, terraces, fieldstone fireplaces, stacks of firewood, electric heating, picture windows filled with treescapes. The newer homes have washers, dryers, and compactors, a few have private saunas. You can request maid service or you can do without it, if you don't want to see any living creatures except the kingbirds and swallows.

Hawk Mountain (with its cousins, Great Hawk and Timber Hawk) is the brainchild of a Harvard-graduated architect, Robert Carl Williams, and a doctor, Hugh Kopald, who grew up together in the Great Smokies of Tennessee, discovered they shared the same concern for man and nature, and found the perfect spot for turning their ideas into reality along Route 100 in Vermont.

Route 100 is known as the "Skiway," because of Killington and a dozen other ski slopes. Which brings you to two of the advantages of the three Hawks—they're year-round hideaways, and if you do decide to rejoin the world for a few hours, you'll find golf, tennis, riding, fishing, sailing, hiking, dining, and dancing within a short drive of your terrace. You'll also find no gas stations, no junkyards, and no traffic.

It's nicer up on the mountain. Stay there, and enjoy your love affair with the trees.

Name: Hawk Mountain
Manager: Gary Gaskill
Address: Route 100, Pittsfield, Vt. 05762
Directions: 260 miles from New York, 155 miles from Boston, 18 from Rutland; from Interstate 89N take Bethel Exit (#3) to Vt. 107 west to its intersection with Vt. 100, then south on 100 to Pittsfield; from Interstate 87N, take Exit 20 to N.Y. 149, follow U.S. 4 east through Rutland to Vt. 100. By air, to Rutland, Lebanon, Montpelier, Burlington; by Amtrak to Whitehall or White River Junction.
Telephone: (802) 746–8911, toll free (800) 451–4109
Rooms: 85 homes.
Meals: Annabelle's at Hawk Center serves lunch and dinner in a quaint, New England setting; live entertainment on weekends.
Diversions: Spring-fed ponds, exercise rooms, hiking trails, tennis (2 courts, no lights, $5 per court per hour), squash and racquetball ($6 per court per hour); cross-country skiing (rentals), sleigh rides, ice skating, skiing nearby; golf, canoeing, trout fishing, paddle tennis also nearby.
Sightseeing: Green Mountain National Forest.
P.S. Open all year, busiest during ski weekends, during July and August, during foliage season (but what is "busy" at a place like Hawk?).

For detailed rate, turn to page 413.

TOPNOTCH AT STOWE
Stowe, Vt.

$$

And topnotch it is, too.

The reception desk looks more like a small library, all books and antiques. The receptionist is more of a concierge than a mere greeter. The living room, one step down, is all fieldstone and glass, with a big open fire in the center, topped by a Heath Robinsonesque copper chimney. The decor is contemporary but the accents are antique, and everywhere you walk some new detail entrances the eye. Small lounges beckon in unlikely corners, for couples who want stylish seclusion. Turn a corner and there's a big ship's breakfront decorated with a ship of the line; turn another and you come face to face with a contemporary painting or lithograph or an old Vermont cheese press. In the Buttertub Bar, antique pewter and copperware line the walls, the fixtures are old barnsiding, and a conversation bench with big cushions encircles another wood-burning fire. From the dining room you look out on trees and rock gardens, and lawns highlighted with Debre sculptures, and beyond the sculptures, tennis courts nestle among the trees. Evidently a healthy clientele checks in at Topnotch, because the inn publishes a folder mapping out five jogging routes through the 120-acre maple-and-pine estate—from a gentle workout to a vigorous 8.4-mile challenge.

Manager and part-owner Bill Kiesler is a Rockresort alumni so you'll find a meticulous attention to detail à la Caneel Bay or Little Dix Bay: bath gelée, shoe horns, glycerine soap, shampoos, shoe polish, sewing kits, hand lotion, variable spray showers, heat lamps, magnifying mirrors, terry cloth bathrobes. Each room has a small private library, ice is delivered each afternoon, and if you check into one of the suites you'll find a refrigerator disguised as an armoire.

Even the boutique here is exceptional—Godiva chocolates and Cartier jewelry.

All very topnotch.

Name: Topnotch at Stowe
Owner/Manager: Lewis Kiesler
Address: Stowe, Vt. 05672
Directions: On Mountain Road, or Route 108, a few miles northwest of Stowe—that is, about 3 hours from Boston, 2 from Montreal. Nearest airports—Burlington or Montpelier (hotel limo by arrangement, $24 each way per couple).
Telephone: (802) 253–8585
Cables/Telex: None
Credit Cards: American Express, Barclaycard, Carte Blanche, Diners, Eurocard, MasterCard, Visa
Rooms: 76, including 8 suites (plus 6 townhouses with 1-bedroom and 2-bedroom apartments).
Meals: Breakfast 8:00–11:00, lunch 12:00–2:00, Sunday brunch in winter 10:30–2:00, afternoon tea, dinner 6:30–9:00 (approx. $35 for 2); room service for breakfast only; jacket requested at dinner; taped classical music in dining room, combo in Buttertub Bar.
Diversions: Game room, whirlpool bath, sauna, exercise room; swimming pool, badminton, walking and jogging trails, putting green, tennis (11 outdoor, 4 indoor courts, resident pro and All-American Sports clinics), horseback riding (18 horses), cross-country ski center, ice skating; downhill skiing and golf 5 minutes away.
Sightseeing: Stowe Tennis Grand Prix (at Topnotch, third week in August), Stowe Performing Arts Festival, antiquing, scenery, Shelburne Museum (40 minutes away).
P.S. Some small tour groups, some seminars in quieter months—April, May, November, early December; ask for a room facing the pool, to avoid the parking lot.

STOWEHOF INN
Stowe, Vt.

$$

You're up in the mountains here, among pine and birch and beech. Indian paintbrush and mayflowers bloom in the spring. Vermont spreads out before your eyes in rolling hills and distant farms. Fortunately, Stowehof is designed to make the most of the view—from guest rooms (most of them, anyway), terrace pool, panoramic lounge and dining room (where the windows are angled and guests sit, not beside, but *in* the window).

But what first strikes you as you drive up the hill is Stowehof's dramatic lounge—half chalet, half ship's prow, all glass and timber thrusting from the hillside. Once inside, it's equally stunning: the bald, sculptured trunks of three large maple trees support the roof; a conversation pit surrounds a fieldstone fireplace; afternoon tea is set out on the sideboard; walls are lined with antique clocks and prints. And beyond the tree trunks, a few steps up, the main lounge fans out to its backdrop—those huge windows and the splendid view. A great place to congregate at any time, it's especially attractive on a chilly day in fall or winter to watch the sunset or a snowfall.

You could also spend a happy hour puttering around admiring the antiques. In the lobby, a Norwegian church bench with carvings depicting the saga of Samson and Delilah. In the Tap Room downstairs, the cider barrels hand-painted by the original owner, Larry Hess, once a colleague of industrial designer Raymond Loewe.

Decor in the rooms is, to say the least, eclectic. No two are alike. Rooms 43 and 44, for example, are up in the peak of the chalet roof, above the lounge, each with high ceilings, armchairs, sofas, acres of pile carpeting and windows (but beware, the balcony outside your window goes all the way around the building so keep the drapes drawn or bathrobes handy). Of the four "fireplace suites," #30 has no view but makes up for it with a king-size mirror behind a king-size bed. For the record, standard rooms can overlook either the "park" (driveway and trees) or the valley; superior suites overlook the park, deluxe rooms overlook the valley. Opt for the valley view.

But even without the view, Stowehof is a pleasant experience. The staff is friendly and attentive, and Christi Ruschp is one of the most decorative innkeepers in the country.

Name: Stowehof Inn
Manager: Christina Ruschp
Address: Stowe, Vt. 05672
Directions: On Edson Hill Road, 3 ½ miles from Stowe on the way to Mt. Mansfield ski center, along Route 108.
Telephone: (802) 253–8500
Cables/Telex: None

Credit Cards: American Express, Carte Blanche, MasterCard, Visa

Rooms: 47, including 7 suites.

Meals: Breakfast 8:00–9:30 (continental 9:30–10:00), lunch 12:00–2:00 (poolside in summer), dinner 6:30 and 8:30 (approx. $30 to $38 for 2); jacket "requested"; room service during dining-room hours.

Diversions: Occasional live music in dining room or Tap Room; games room with pool table, Ping-Pong, TV; 4 tennis courts, swimming pool, sauna, walking trails; cross-country skiing (inn trails connect with 50 miles of trails in and around Stowe), ice skating; indoor tennis, golf, downhill skiing, horseback riding nearby.

Sightseeing: See "Topnotch at Stowe."

P.S. Some small tour groups in quiet months (i.e., spring and late fall).

THE INN ON THE COMMON
Craftsbury Common, Vt.

The beds snuggle under the kind of custom quilts some art galleries hang on their walls. Wallpapers are color-coordinated with the quilts and accented by original paintings and woodcuts. Rooms and hallways are lined with antiques, the dining table is set with Tiffany china and heirloom silverware. This is not, in other words, a run-of-the-mill inn.

The Schmitts wouldn't have it any other way. They quit their New York treadmills (Penny, ad agency V.P., Michael, investment banker) when they discovered this 1800 house begging to be transformed into an inn. In the seven years since, they've attracted a loyal clientele (diplomats, lawyers, doctors, theater people) and expanded to the Federal-style house across the street. They don't plan to expand farther since their silver-and-Tiffany dining room can't accommodate any more guests. And dinner is the big event of the day: cocktails at 6:30 in the lounge, dinner at 8:00 ("jackets requested, and *no* blue jeans"). The Schmitts join their guests at table ("the best kind of quality control—we eat the same food"), and the fixed menu, with complimentary wines, may include scaloppine piccatta or Penny Schmitt's special paillard of veal. Not that dinner is the *only* event of the day. Breakfast is "an absolute orgy of food"—

seven types of omelette including the "Everything Omelette," sticky buns, coffee cake, whole-wheat or dark raisin bread. Between orgies, guests putter around in book-lined lounges, playing chess or backgammon. At the rear of the main house, the two acres of garden have quiet corners for snoozing, croquet, tennis; and beyond the post-and-rail fence, mile after unspoiled mile of beautiful Vermont countryside. Across the street, behind the Federal house, guests can sunbathe on rustic loungers or take a dip in an unusual, solar-heated swimming pool.

The fourteen guest rooms are all different, varying not only in decor but also in size and amenities. Some are small, some share bathrooms. But the pick of the crop are in the Federal house—corner rooms with Jotul wood-burning stoves, or #12, a ground-floor suite with kitchen facilities. Regular guests are happy to have whatever is available, some even choosing a favorite because of its custom quilt.

Name: The Inn on The Common
Owners/Managers: Penny and Michael Schmitt
Address: Craftsbury Common, Vt. 05827
Directions: It's way up there, about 35 miles from Canada. By car, take I–91 to Exit 21, St. Johnsbury; from there, go west on U.S. 2 to West Danville, north on Route 15 to Hardwick, then north on Route 14 until you see the sign for Craftsbury, East Craftsbury, and Craftsbury *Common*. Nearest airports, Burlington or Montpelier.
Telephone: (802) 586–9619
Cables/Telex: None
Credit Cards: MasterCard, Visa
Rooms: 14, most sharing bathroom.
Meals: Breakfast 8:00–9:00, no lunch (but guests can use the kitchen in the annex for making light snacks), dinner at 8:00; no outside reservations; jacket requested ("definitely not casual, no blue jeans"); no room service.
Diversions: TV in sitting rooms; tennis, solar-heated pool; "unlimited hiking opportunities"; guests have access to the Craftsbury Sports Center or Big Hosmer Lake (swimming, kayaking, canoeing) and the Craftsbury Nordic Ski Center (25 miles of groomed trails, no trail fees for inn guests); moonlight horse-drawn sleigh rides by arrangement.
Sightseeing: Surrounding countryside, Big Lake Hosmer, fiddle and banjo festivals.
P.S. Closed mid-October to mid-December, mid-March to mid-May; "children eat separately an hour earlier"; 2-day minimum stay.

LOVETT'S INN
Franconia, N.H.

Down a steep, winding country road you go, between cliffs of spruce and pine and birch, until the scenery opens out into a meadow and you cross a brook and into Lovett's. Guests in the cottages often spot deer and foxes and bears padding across the meadow, but even if you don't spot any wildlife the surrounding White Mountain scenery is exhilarating.

The main house here goes back 170 years, and it's been run continuously by two generations of Lovetts. They've filled it with appropriate antiques and collectibles to preserve its stone-wall beamed-ceiling personality, yet they've managed to add a few contemporary cottages (each with picture windows and terrace, some with fireplace) in the garden at the rear without spoiling the setting. Most important for some guests, though, the family has managed to tack on a kitchen that wouldn't look out of place in an inn twice the size. Lovett's is famed for miles around for home cooking, which, even with all the fresh herbs and vegetables from the garden, is more cosmopolitan than country: a typical dinner here might consist of black bean soup with Demerara rum, pan-broiled chicken in brandy, or curried young lamb with Franconia chutney, topped off with fudge rum pie or macaroon crumble.

Obviously, the Lovetts expect their guests to turn up in the dining room with farmers' appetites primed by fresh air and exercise, and there's certainly plenty of both in these parts: walking, hiking, trips up mountains on aerial tramways or cog railways, to say nothing of horse shows, auctions, flower shows, and country fairs. Or just sitting in the fresh air in the garden, waiting for a fox or deer to appear.

Name: Lovett's Inn
Owner/Manager: Charles J. Lovett, Jr.
Address: Profile Road, Franconia, N.H. 03580

Directions: Near Exit 38 of Interstate 93, just after it leaves the White
    Mountain National Forest.
Telephone: (603) 823–7761
Cables/Telex: None
Credit Cards: American Express, MasterCard, Visa
Rooms: 22 (8 in the inn sharing 5 bathrooms, the remainder, with private
    baths, in cottages, some with fireplaces).
Meals: Breakfast 8:00–9:00, no lunch, dinner 6:30–7:45 (approx. $24 to $28
    for 2); no room service; jacket and tie at dinner.
Diversions: Pool, table tennis; heated outdoor pool, hiking trails, lawn
    games; cross-country skiing (rentals at the inn); tennis, golf, horseback
    riding, winter sports nearby.
Sightseeing: White Mountains, Robert Frost's home in Ripton, aerial moun-
    tain tramways.
P.S. The inn is open *only* from the last Friday in June to the Monday of
    Columbus Day weekend and from December 26 to April 1.

SNOWY OWL INN
Waterville Valley, N.H.

The valley first. The Mad River shoulders its way through a gap
between three mountains—Tecumseh, Snow, and Osceola—and the
surrounding peaks rise above forests of spruce and pine to a height of
four thousand feet or more. The scenery is, well, magnificent, and
you could spend days walking and hiking here without passing the
same tree twice. Even with the year-round resort that has taken root
here in the past few years, this is still very much nature's own
country, partly because the only way in is winding Route 49 and the
only way out is back along the same winding 49. Here and there
among this extravaganza of trees and mountains and streams you
come upon the enclaves of the Waterville Valley resort—lodges,
condominiums, restaurants, and a few shops, all in tune with the
setting. Of the valley's four inns, the Snowy Owl is the wise choice.

It has been described by a leading ski magazine as "the best
designed lodge in U.S. mountain resorts," which may be overstating
the case, but it is certainly *one* of the most beautiful lodges in the

country: weathered pine facade and a veranda lined with antique wicker chairs; a lobby rising to three stories around a massive fieldstone fireplace; rustic-modern decor highlighted with a few well-chosen antiques and owls in all forms—macramé owls, oil owls, photographic owls, carved wooden owls. One level down, there's a conversation pit in front of the big fire, then a terrace and stone steps leading down to Snow's Brook, which ripples along like something out of Schubert *lieder*. *"Bachlein, so munter rauschend zumal/Wollen hinunter silbern ins Tal."*

Right up top, up a wrought-iron spiral stairway, there's a small cupola with a bench and heater, where you can take your morning coffee (or late-night wine) and look at the treetops, the birds, the sunset, or the stars, far from the madding crowds and the Mad River.

Name: Snowy Owl Inn
Owners/Managers: Tish and Roger Hamblin
Address: Waterville Valley, N.H. 03223
Directions: Take Interstate 93 to Exit 28 and follow the signs; the valley is about 1 hour by car north of Concord.
Telephone: (603) 236–8383
Cables/Telex: None
Credit Cards: American Express, MasterCard, Visa
Rooms: 37.
Meals: Complimentary coffee all day, continental breakfast in winter only. The inn has no dining facilities; the Fourways Restaurant (a 2-minute walk through the trees) serves all meals including dinner from 6:00 to 9:00 (approx. $20–$25 for 2). Dress is informal. Fourways is also the site of the local discotheque, the Rusty Nail.
Diversions: Whirlpool, sauna, heated outdoor pool; hiking trails; tennis (18 courts, no lights, $4 an hour per court), golf (9 holes, clubs for rent; easy drive to 18-hole course), fishing, ice skating, 30 miles of cross-country ski trails (6 full-time instructors), 32 downhill slopes; beach area nearby.
P.S. Rates slightly higher 10 days at Christmas, and 10 days in February ("President's Week"). Special packages available. N.H. law precludes a full service bar, so for cocktail hour or nightcaps, BYOB. If Snowy Owl is full, try the Hamblins' Silver Squirrel or the Valley Inn (which has an indoor-outdoor pool, platform tennis, and a few rooms with terraces).

STAFFORD'S-IN-THE-FIELD
Chocorua, N.H.

$$

It tops a knoll above a gravelly back road, a tall, mellowed farmhouse with a big old barn alongside, in a meadow somewhere between a village, a lake, a forest, and a mountain. If it looks like a farm outside, it feels more like a home inside. It's very much a family affair: Fred Stafford, genial and laconic, is your host, his wife Ramona is cook (usually the first words you hear about the inn are "the food is terrific"); daughter Momo, in her early twenties and pretty as spring, is the pastry chef/baker and a stickler for natural ingredients; sons Fritz and Hansel help out with the hard labor, odd jobs, and running the place. They all trekked east from San Diego a decade ago because they hankered after "something old and New England." They found the old here, in a house that dates from 1784 and took in its first paying guests in 1894, and added an extra dash of New England with a collection of milk churns, butter washers, boudoir desks, and a blacksmith's bellows that's finding its second wind as a coffee table. Charming is an overused word in describing old inns (this guide is as guilty as any), but here *charming* is the word. The Staffords have only seven rooms in the main house (more in the cottages at the rear, but you'll probably prefer one of these seven), and they've decorated them the way you hope a country inn will be decorated—with cheery wallpapers, braided rugs, and some tasteful family bric-a-brac. Three of the rooms have double beds, only two have private bathrooms (the others share four baths and toilets, a manageable ratio). The dainty rooms on the top floor have corner windows looking straight into the leafy limbs of maples—you feel like you're waking up in a tree house.

A HAPPENING EVERY NIGHT. The focal point of the inn is the antique-filled dining room, and the highlight of the day is dinner. It's served at a rural 6:30, which may seem early, but most guests actually start congregating long before. (The inn has no liquor license, but Fred provides setups and ice and you just help yourselves.) This is the time to sit in a rocker on the porch to watch evening settle over the gentle countryside; it's a time, too, to greet your fellow guests, and you may find yourselves rocking beside a musician or writer, corporate lawyer, or museum curator. Bringing people together is what Fred Stafford enjoys most about innkeeping, and since the evening meal is served dinner-party style, with Fred at the head of the table, "every evening becomes a happening . . . people react beautifully." Good food helps, of course, as much as good conversation—four courses of wholesome home cooking, with vegetables and berries fresh from the garden, bread warm from the oven, and entrées that range from New England to India to France to California/Mexico, depending on how Ramona sizes up that day's guests. By the time you've sipped your coffee you appreciate the wisdom of the 6:30 start, because even after four courses of "terrific food" you have time for a nightcap on the porch (or, as the bugs sometimes insist, indoors among the serendipitous antiques in the parlor) and *still* get to bed ahead of your usual schedule.

Name: Stafford's-in-the-Field
Owners/Managers: Fred and Ramona Stafford
Address: Chocorua, N.H. 03817
Directions: Chocorua is on N.H. 16, between Lake Winnipesaukee and the White Mountain National Forest, about 10 miles from Conway; the inn itself is a few miles from the village, on N.H. 113.
Telephone: (603) 323–7766
Cables/Telex: None
Credit Cards: None
Rooms: 23, including 7 in the inn itself.
Meals: Breakfast 8:30–9:30, no lunch, dinner 6:30, served family style; no room service; informal dress; occasional musical events in the big barn, without intruding on the peacefulness of the inn; no liquor, bring your own (setups provided).
Diversions: Walking, swimming in the lake, canoeing, climbing Mt. Chocorua; tennis, golf, summer theater; cross-country skiing on the grounds (skis for rent), downhill skiing nearby.
Sightseeing: Lake Winnipesaukee, White Mountain National Forest.
P.S. Open all year, except for the period between late October and December 26; busiest in summer and foliage season.

THE JOHN HANCOCK INN
Hancock, N.H.

Hancock is reputed to be, quote unquote, one of the six prettiest towns in New Hampshire. That's one reason for going there. The other is the local hostelry, which has been luring travelers off the highway long before anyone ever thought of such things as prettiest villages.

The John Hancock Inn has been standing tall and stately since 1789, on a street of fine Colonial buildings, a few yards from the village green and a meetinghouse with bells forged by Paul Revere. Hancock himself never actually saw the place; apparently the Declaration of Independence wasn't the only document Hancock signed—he was also a land-speculator and put his quill to a title deed buying up several hundred acres of property in this neighborhood. Some of his local admirers voted to name the village after him (when he turned down an invitation shortly afterward to visit the town, the snubbed villagers tried to have the name changed).

If Hancock never dined here, Daniel Webster did, and over the generations a host of notables have walked through the heavy hospitable red door of the inn—Peter, Paul, and Mary; Nelson Rockefeller; Ted Williams; and Tony Bennett among them.

Much of the inn's decor is authentic, some of it dating from the days of John Hancock, Esquire. The ten rooms (all with private bath) are decked out with braided rugs, wide floorboards, fireplaces (but no fires), washstands, half tester beds, pencil post beds, slatback chairs with footstools, travel trunks, patchwork quilts. The most unusual room in the inn (in fact, one of the most unusual anywhere) has "primitive" murals depicting a blue-green lake-and-forest setting, painted by an itinerant artist, Rufus Porter.

The Hancock's Carriage Lounge is the snug sort of room you look forward to finding in a country inn: the seats are tufted leather benches from old buggies, the tables blacksmiths' bellows, and there's a big roaring brick fireplace in one corner. Businessmen drive from miles around to have lunch here, but most diners continue through to the rear and one of three pleasant dining rooms. One is an enclosed patio overlooking the garden at the rear, another is a quiet blue-hued den with only four tables. The Hancock's cuisine is basically New England country fare, with an occasional bow to continental cuisine. The New England seafood casserole in sherry sauce is as tasty a way as any to wind up an evening.

Name: The John Hancock Inn
Owners/Managers: Glynn and Pat Wells
Address: Main Street, Hancock, N.H. 03449
Directions: On N.H. 137, a few miles from U.S. 202 (between Hillsborough and Peterborough) and about 20 miles from Keene; nearest airport, Keene.
Telephone: (603) 525–3318
Cables/Telex: None
Credit Cards: MasterCard, Visa
Rooms: 10.
Meals: Breakfast 8:00–9:30, lunch 12:00–2:00, dinner 6:00–9:00 (approx. $18 to $23 for 2, including tax), Sundays 5:00–8:00; no room service; dress optional "but in good taste."
Diversions: Chess, checkers, and conversation at the inn; swimming in town lake, free tennis on 3 town courts, lots of hiking trails in neighborhood, ice skating on town rink; antiquing, theater, concerts, golf, and skiing nearby.
Sightseeing: Hancock Village Green, scenery, covered bridges, antiquing, Brookstone's store in Peterborough, Franklin Pierce Homestead at Hillsboro, Antique Carriage and Sleigh Museum in Chesterfield; chamber music recitals in nearby villages by Apple Hill Players.

For more suggestions in this area
turn to Added Attractions, page 375.

In and Around the Bosky Berkshires

O, my Luve is like a red, red rose
That's newly sprung in June;
O, my Luve is like the melodie
That's sweetly play'd in tune . . .

BURNS

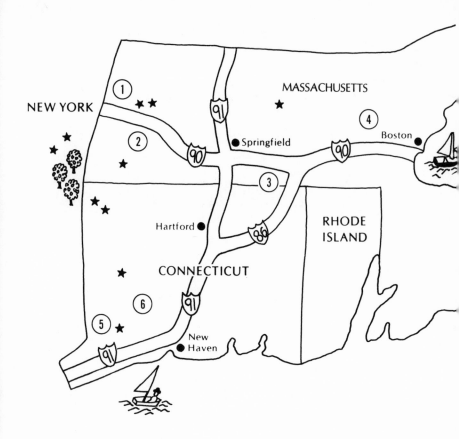

1. Wheatleigh
2. The Red Lion Inn
3. The Publick House
4. Longfellow's Wayside Inn
5. West Lane Inn
6. Harrison Inn and Conference Center
★ *Added Attractions*

WHEATLEIGH

Lenox, Mass.

$$$

There must be a St. Lenox up there somewhere watching over this charmed village. First there's all that beautiful Berkshire hill-dale-and-forest scenery; then the Tanglewood Music Festival with its magical evenings of lawns, stars, and the Boston Symphony; and now when you go there you can stay in a Florentine villa, once the home of a contessa.

Wheatleigh was built in 1893 or thereabouts, bequeathed by an American tycoon to his daughter and her Spanish count. It's very Italianate, a piccolo palazzo: circular courtyard with large fountain, glass-and-iron Belle Epoque marquee above the main door, great hall with chandeliers and polished oak floors, grand stairway illumined by stained-glass windows. The twenty-two acres of gardens are decorated with terraces and statuary, a secluded swimming pool in a grassy glade, and what looks like a campanile but is really a water tower. A couple of years ago Wheatleigh was acquired and restored by David Weisgal, a youngish New York fund raiser, and now he and his wife run the inn on the lines of house parties in a gracious country home. Weisgal himself rustles up pancakes and bacon-and-eggs for his guests; and either he or Ms. Brooks-Dunway are on hand to greet new arrivals and show them to their rooms, with a casual request to remember to sign the register at some point.

This being a private home, the bedrooms are all different: half of them are deluxe (almost mini-suites, some with terraces and ten with fireplaces), a few are quite cramped (but they're several dollars less expensive, so don't scoff at them). Furnishings are mostly antiques and period pieces, including some beds with white frilly half-canopies. Rooms 2I and 2D, on the corner, have both terraces and fireplaces. But the most romantic of the lot is the Aviary Suite, in a separate wing connected to the main house by an ivy-covered galleria; it's on two levels, sitting room downstairs, with iron steps spiraling up to a second-floor nest with fluffy carpets and twin beds. It really was an aviary at one time; and it's now popular with musicians (Leonard Bernstein and my favorite pianist, Claudio Arrau, among them) because they can just squeeze a piano into the sitting room. If privacy is a consideration, the Aviary also has its own entrance from the courtyard. Cocktails are served on the terrace, by the pool, or in the library, dinner in the cozy candlelit dining room or in the enclosed porch at the rear. The menu is restricted to three entrées each evening, one of them Italian, in keeping with the villa's heritage.

Bravo, St. Lenox!

Name: Wheatleigh
Owners/Managers: A. David Weisgal and Florence Brooks-Dunway
Address: P.O. Box 824, Lenox, Mass. 02140
Directions: For Lenox, take the Mass. Pike to the Lee Exit, then follow the signs for Lenox; in town, go left at the Curtis Hotel onto Stockbridge Road, turn right at the bottom of the hill, and continue for about 1½ miles to the Wheatleigh driveway.
Telephone: (413) 637–0610
Cables/Telex: None
Credit Cards: American Express, MasterCard, Visa
Rooms: 17, including 10 deluxe and 2 suites (16 rooms and suites in winter).
Meals: Breakfast 8:00–9:30, lunch 12:30–2:00, dinner 6:00–9:00 (daily except Monday and Wednesday in July and August: approx. $22 to $25 for 2). September to June: breakfast remains the same, but no lunch, and dinner on Fridays, Saturdays, and Sundays only; informal dress (but stylish); pianist in lounge on weekends.
Diversions: Pool, walking, tennis (1 court, free), sailboat and rowboat (free) on Stockbridge Lake, cross-country skiing; golf, horseback riding, trout fishing, downhill skiing nearby.
Sightseeing: Berkshire Music Center at Tanglewood, South Mountain Concerts, Music Inn, Berkshire Playhouse, Williamstown Playhouse, and of course the Berkshires.

THE RED LION INN
Stockbridge, Mass.

$$

Stockbridge has one of the prettiest main streets in America, ending at one of the country's most famous inns. The original Red Lion was built in 1773 to serve the stagecoaches between Boston and Albany, and rebuilt more or less in its present form in 1897, with its classic long veranda dotted with a dozen wicker rocking chairs. Through the years it has hosted "everyone from Hawthorne and Longfellow and Roosevelts to Aaron Copland, Bob Dylan, and Gene Shalit."

When it was bought in 1968 by Jack and Jane Fitzpatrick, a Stockbridge couple who run Country Curtains (a mail order company that ships all over the world), the inn was renovated from top to bottom, spruced up with period wallpapers specially produced by an old mill in northern Massachusetts, and, of course, with curtains. Curtains in all their variety—muslin, gingham, organdy, with ruffles, tiebacks, and knotted fringes. No two rooms are identical, but they all have air conditioning and room phones, two-thirds of them have private baths, and one-third of them (the thirty-odd rooms that stay open in winter) have television. Rooms 240 and 230 are big, bright corner chambers—one with rose-patterned wallpaper and matching upholstery, wicker headboards, marble-topped coffee table; the other with pink paper, floral carpets, twin beds, rockers, and wing chairs. More recently the big house round the corner was bought up by the inn and converted into four fairly luxurious suites. But the suites and half the rooms face Main Street, which is also Route 7, and you may have your slumbers disturbed by lumbering trucks changing gears to get around the corner. If not the trucks, maybe the wheezy radiators in chilly months. Come in winter to admire the Christmas-card setting (like something from an old *Saturday Evening Post* cover, which it was, since Norman Rockwell had lived around the corner for years and painted this venerable centenarian many times). Go walking in the frost or snow, wrap your arms around each other to keep warm, then hurry back to the Red Lion for a drink in the wood-paneled warmth of Widow Bingham's Tavern.

Name: The Red Lion Inn
Manager: Betsy Holtzinger
Address: Stockbridge, Mass. 01262
Directions: 5 miles southwest of Exit 2 on the Mass. Pike, at the junction of U.S. 7 and Mass. 102.
Telephone: (413) 298–5545
Cables/Telex: None
Credit Cards: American Express, Diners, MasterCard, Visa
Rooms: 96, 4 suites, some rooms sharing bath.
Meals: Breakfast 7:30–11:30, lunch 12:00–2:30, dinner 6:00–9:30 (approx. $15 to $20 for 2), sandwiches to 1:00 A.M.; informal dress in courtyard and tavern, jacket and tie in main dining room; live music in Lion's Den Bar downstairs.
Diversions: Small heated outdoor pool, bicycles, hiking; tennis, golf, horseback riding, white water and lake canoeing, winter sports nearby.
Sightseeing: Tanglewood, The Berkshire Playhouse, Nathaniel Hawthorne's "Little Red House," Chesterwood (home of the artist who sculpted the Lincoln statue in D.C.), Naumkeag (mansion and gardens), Norman Rockwell Museum.
P.S. Crowded on weekends in summer (especially Tanglewood season) and during the fall foliage (when reservations are essential for the inn *and* dining room). Two-night minimum required on weekends in July and August.
P.P.S. Senator and Mrs. Fitzpatrick have now taken over Blantyre, a lovely old mansion-into-inn in Lenox, which, at the time of writing, is being renovated (the tennis courts already are). It will be a more luxurious version of The Red Lion—worth looking into.

THE PUBLICK HOUSE
Sturbridge, Mass.

$$

Lafayette once warmed his *derrière* before the huge open fireplace in the taproom. The taproom is now the dining room and you can feast yourself before the same fire—on onion popovers, baked lobster pie or prime ribs, cranberry bread or pumpkin muffins.

The Publick House was first established as a coaching tavern in 1771, by Colonel Ebenezer Crafts, a legendary innkeeper who could lift a barrel of cider and drink from the bunghole. He also equipped and drilled a company of cavalry on the common opposite the inn, and marched them off to help Lafayette in some of his skirmishes. The tavern did a hefty business because of its location at one of the busiest crossroads in the Colonies. "The old fordway at Tantiusque" was the route taken by the Indians when they carried corn to the Pilgrims in Plymouth; in turn, the first white settlers traipsed over the same route on their first ventures westward. Later, the Old Colonial Post Road ran through Sturbridge. Ben Franklin traveled along it when he was deputy postmaster of the thirteen Colonies and made a field trip to most of his post offices.

This is the era you still breathe when you step beneath the lantern and through the door of the Publick House.

APPLES BY THE BEDSIDE. If Lafayette had stayed the night he would have slept in a room that hasn't changed much to this day. He might not recognize the wallpaper on the landing but it's so jolly and patriotic it would probably have sent him off to bed with his heart as

warm as his *derrière*. The period furniture and lurching floors have been joined by discreet concessions to the twentieth century—like tiled bathrooms, cuddly towels, telephones, air conditioning, and a sprinkler system. In addition to the bright-and-breezy rooms in the inn itself, there are now a few suites in the white clapboard Chamberlain House next door; decor here is in keeping with the Colonial surroundings but augmented by plush carpeting, Schumacher fabrics, air conditioning, TV, and AM/FM radios. A mile away, on a hilltop dotted with posh homes, there are ten more suites and rooms in an eighteenth-century house. Here's one case where you shouldn't fuss if the receptionist shunts you off to an annex—in fact, we're almost tempted to advise you to ask for the Colonel Ebenezer Crafts Inn, as it's called, especially at those times when the dining rooms are likely to be overrun with day trippers. The rooms here are attractive, quiet (suite 10, in a separate wing with a separate entrance, is particularly apt for trysts), and Madame Bibeau, who runs the place, bakes chocolate chip cookies for her guests, serves afternoon tea with cranberry bread or crumpets, turns down the bed at night and leaves cookies or candies on the bedside table. All the rooms welcome you with a bowl of apples on the bedside table. But don't spoil your appetite. Your innkeeper has some tasty dishes waiting downstairs.

The taproom, with its big fire and curtained windows, is a pleasant enough spot, but lovers will probably prefer the inn's Barn Restaurant, where the hand-hewn beams and timber stalls make quiet nooks for diners who want to look into each other's eyes while dipping into their lobster pies. For special occasions, alone or with a few friends, you can also call ahead and reserve a private parlor for prearranged dinner, with your waiter appearing to serve or remove only when you ring the bell.

SUGARING-OFF PARTIES. If you're here on a Yankee Winter Weekend (January through March) the inn will also entertain you with hot buttered rum, roast chestnuts, roast venison, and mincemeat pie, square dancing, sleigh rides through Old Sturbridge Village, and sugaring-off parties; then wake you next morning with the aromas of an openhearth breakfast—hickory-smoked bacon, porridge with maple syrup, and hot apple pan dowdy.

In spring, the county's orchards are fluffy with apple blossom; in the fall, you can visit the orchards, pick your own McIntoshes, and

then wander off, hand-in-hand, away from the village and the highways, and find yourselves a leafy glade for an afternoon of munching,
drowsing, and daydreaming.

Or you can visit Old Sturbridge Village. It may sound like a
corny, touristy sort of thing to do, but do it anyway if there aren't too
many people around. If you go in summer, you'll be surrounded by
crowds (it's very popular), but at other times you may be all alone in
Colonial New England and it can be very romantic. Old Sturbridge
Village is a 200-acre re-creation of a New England country town of the
late eighteenth and early nineteenth centuries—forty fully furnished
homes, shops, a meetinghouse, and costumed hosts and hostesses to
show you around and demonstrate how your ancestors used to spin,
weave, make pottery and brooms, and grow herbs. Hop on the
horse-drawn carry-all wagon for a jaunt around the village, and buy
your sweetheart old-fashioned penny candies at the General Store.

Name: The Publick House
Owner/Manager: Buddy Adler
Address: On the Common, Sturbridge, Mass. 01566
Directions: Take Exit 3 from Interstate 86, Exit 9 from the Mass. Pike, and
   follow the signs.
Telephone: (617) 347-3313
Cables/Telex: None
Credit Cards: American Express, Carte Blanche, Diners, MasterCard, Visa.
Rooms: 27, with 3 suites.
Meals: Breakfast 7:30–11:00, lunch 12:00–4:00, dinner 4:00–8:30 Sunday
   through Thursday, 5:00–9:00 Friday and Saturday (approx. $14 to $18
   for 2), supper till 11:30; room service 8:00 A.M. to 8:30 P.M.; informal
   dress; live music and dancing in the cocktail lounge (downstairs).
Diversions: None at the inn, but plenty of sightseeing, tennis, golf, horse-
   back riding, skiing, and sleigh rides nearby.
Sightseeing: Countryside, Old Sturbridge Village (also see "Longfellow's
   Wayside Inn").

For detailed rate, turn to page 413.

LONGFELLOW'S WAYSIDE INN
South Sudbury, Mass.

"As Ancient is this Hostelry/As any in the Land may be . . . " So rhymed, precariously, Henry Wadsworth Longfellow.

He wrote and set his *Tales of a Wayside Inn* in this very hostelry. Alas, this makes it superhistoric, and a place that many Americans feel they ought to see, even if they've never managed to get beyond "Listen, my children, and you shall hear/Of the midnight ride of Paul Revere." They come out from Boston by the coachload. This puts you, the guests, almost in the category of exhibits in a museum, not much fun for most lovers unless they're the kind that fancies an audience.

Still, the Wayside Inn is such a delightful old place it's worth bucking the busloads; in any case, during the offseason (October through June) there's only a scattering of day trippers. Then you have the place practically to yourself because there are only ten guest rooms to begin with (it must have been a tight squeeze when King Ibn Saud and his retinue dropped in). They're not the most elegant in Massachusetts, but they're charmingly furnished with period pieces, and they all have phones, air conditioning, and private baths. Most of them were tacked on a long time after Longfellow rhymed, but two of them are authentically ancient: room 9, with its plank floors, pine walls, low beamed ceiling, sconces, sideboards, and armchairs; and room 10, which is smaller, with tiny windows, red curtains, and antique tables (but no phone).

PATRIOTS, POETASTERS, AND TEAMSTERS. This inn is so old it goes back to the days *before* stagecoaches. The original two rooms were built in 1686—the date that led Longfellow to rhyme his lines claiming it as the oldest inn in the country. In those days guests came galloping up on horseback or lumbering up by oxcart; they warmed themselves in the taproom and then retired upstairs to a sort of dormitory, now known as the Drovers' Room, where there were five beds for the teamsters. The inn was built by a David Howe and called the Howe Tavern, but by the time of the Revolution it had become the Red Horse. It was still owned by a Howe, Colonel Ezekiel, who gathered a group of Sudbury farmers in his taproom before marching them off to the field at Concord. When the fracas got properly under way, the colonel dined here with George Washington, who was on his way to Boston to take command of the army. The inn got its present name, of course, from Longfellow, who actually spent only two weekends here.

The inn stayed in the Howe family until the turn of the century, when it started to decay. Henry Ford bought it in 1920 and fixed it up (some say *over*fixed). He stayed there many times, and often invited his friends over for a few days—Edison, Firestone, the Prince of Wales. In 1953, the inn caught fire, but fortunately on a freezing morning; when the firemen poured on water it turned to ice and froze the fire. Otherwise, the entire inn might have been destroyed. It was restored in 1958 with a grant from the Ford Foundation, and the inn is now run by its own foundation dedicated to preserving it as an historical and literary shrine. It's nonprofit; any money you spend there goes to keeping the place in tiptop condition.

You can tell the money isn't wasted the minute you set eyes on its neat, russet-colored clapboard exterior, rather like the shape of a haystack, and the trim lawn guarded by two tall oaks. It's set back a hundred yards from the main road on a twisting country lane, or as Longfellow put it, "A region of repose it seems/A place of slumber and of dreams/Remote among wooded hills."

On your right when you go through the door is the Old Bar Room—an austere, timbered room with the original settle, pewter sconces, hutch tables, and chairs. Across the hall is the Longfellow Parlor, one of the rooms where Longfellow supposedly wrote and recited some of his tales. It's still furnished with authentic period items, including "the first spinet in Sudbury," and other items mentioned in the poem. The Longfellow Bedroom upstairs is preserved as an example of the sort of room people used to stay in back in the eighteenth century, with pencil post bed, Spanish-foot chairs, and a 1710 highboy.

Most of the trippers who visit the inn stop off for lunch or dinner in the big Colonial-style dining room at the rear, but the Red Horse Room is cozier, a publike sort of place with hovering beams, slat-backed chairs, and wooden tables. The menu is basically New England, but with something for everyone—Yankee beef broth with barley, roast Massachusetts duckling, baked fresh scrod, ribs of beef, filet mignon. You've read of many inns that bake their own bread, but the Wayside Inn goes one better—its rolls and muffins are made from flour and meal stone-ground at the inn's own grist mill, down the road.

Name: Longfellow's Wayside Inn
Manager: Francis J. Koppeis
Address: South Sudbury, Mass. 01776
Directions: On U.S. 20, the old stagecoach route, midway between Boston and Worcester, and an easy drive to places like Concord, Lexington, and Sturbridge.
Telephone: (617) 443–8846
Cables/Telex: None
Credit Cards: American Express, Carte Blanche, Diners, MasterCard, Visa.
Rooms: 10.
Meals: Breakfast 7:00–9:30, lunch 11:30–3:00, dinner 5:30–9:00 weekdays, 12:00–8:00 Sundays (approx. $20 to $25 for 2, reservations essential); no room service, except breakfast if you make arrangements with the front desk the night before; jackets requested in the evening.
Diversions: No pool, no sports, just lovely countryside; Patriot's Day is April 19, and the first Saturday in October is Minuteman Day, to be seen or avoided depending on your tastes.
Sightseeing: South Sudbury, Lincoln, Walden Pond, Lexington (Lexington Green, Hancock-Clarke House), Concord (National Minuteman Historic Park, re-creation of Thoreau's Cabin, Concord Bridge, Antiquarian Museum, Emerson House, Louisa May Alcott House), Old Sturbridge Village.
P.S. Given the kind of monument this is, the inn's trustees and so on are concerned about the image, so please act like a properly married couple.

HARRISON INN AND
CONFERENCE CENTER
Southbury, Conn.

$$

Put this down as a possibility for a windy, wintry weekend. You can curl up in snug rooms that look like pages from a California homes-and-gardens magazine: cedar walls, rattan chairs, handwoven wall hangings and blowups of photographs, custom-designed wood-block closets, a bath-and-a-half, and stereo and TV. Without ever venturing beyond the inn's cedar-sided walls you can soak in a sauna, work out in an exercise room, play pool, listen to Big Band sounds, attend plays; shop in one of the most unusual bazaars this side of Ghirardelli Square, and dine in a pubby restaurant.

If you come on a mellow day you can swim in the heated pool, or sit in the gazebo and look at the gardens and listen to the stream. There are a pair of all-weather tennis courts, a golf course on the other side of the stream, and bikes and horses to take you through the countryside.

All this sounds like a pleasant country inn, and that's how Harrison Inn promotes itself, but it's really nothing like a traditional New England country inn. It's located in a residential community, and it's part of the Harrison Conference Center, geared to seminars and groups of executives from all those corporations proliferating around Hartford and in Westchester. That doesn't sound too romantic, but the truth is that the inhabitants seem to keep to themselves and the executives all go home on weekends, when the inn is taken over by a youngish, moderately swinging clientele. And it is an interesting inn, warm, snug, and comfortable in winter.

Name: Harrison Inn and Conference Center
Manager: Ted McCallum
Address: Heritage Village, Southbury, Conn. 06488
Directions: Take Interstate 84 to Exit 15, then drive to Conn. 67 and follow the Harrison signs. Limousine service from La Guardia and Kennedy airports.

Telephone: (203) 264–8255
Cables/Telex: None
Credit Cards: American Express, Diners, MasterCard, Visa
Rooms: 121, 9 suites.
Meals: Breakfast 7:00–9:00 (continental only 9:00–10:00), lunch 12:00–2:00,
    Sunday brunch 11:00–2:30, dinner 6:00–9:00, 10:00 on Saturday
    (approx. $25 to $50 for 2); no room service; jacket required Friday and
    Saturday; live music and dancing.
Diversions: Outdoor pool, sauna, therapy pool, exercise room, game room,
    bicycles, billiards, ice skating, skiing, tennis, free of charge (2 courts,
    lights until midnight); golf (9 holes, $10 per round), hiking trails,
    horseback riding nearby.
Sightseeing: Heritage Village Bazaar; Danbury State Fair (July).
P.S. A variety of special packages available at different times of the year.

WEST LANE INN

Ridgefield, Conn.

$$

A Japanese maple shades the bow-fronted veranda where white
rattan chairs and tables are set up for breakfast. A white rattan
swing-for-two dangles from the veranda roof, and a pair of bikes wait
for lovers ready to take a spin through the tree-lined streets of the
village. Indoors, the spacious hall is paneled in mahogany, a show-
piece of the Victorian craftsman's art. Throughout, Victoriana sets
the tone, but owner Maureen Mayer has lightened the ambiance
with her deft decorating flair, and there's an element of plushness
you don't normally find in small inns of this sort. Expensive designer
fabrics on beds and windows. Working fireplaces in four rooms.
Cuddly towels, variable spray shower heads, and scales in every
bathroom; color TV, FM radio, and individual air conditioning in
every room. Of the fourteen rooms, #206 and #201 have bow
windows looking out on the trees, and three of the more romantic
nests—#301, #302, #303—are up in the eaves with attic ceilings
and tiny windows.

    For the benefit of the rest of the world, Ridgefield is a well-
entrenched, well-heeled community, a one-hour dash from Manhat-

tan. It's noted for its restaurants (including the Stonehenge, listed under Added Attractions), but until recently, places to spend the night were less than satisfactory. Now there's the West Lane Inn. And if you decide to dash off on the spur of the moment to sample its comforts, the inn has spare toothbrushes and hair dryers at the front desk.

Name: West Lane Inn
Owner/Manager: Maureen Mayer
Address: 22 West Lane, Ridgefield, Ct. 06877
Directions: On Route 35, just south of the village center. From Interstate 684, take the Katonah Exit then head for Cross River and South Salem; from Interstate 95 or the Merriott Parkway, take the exit for U.S. 7 and head north toward Danbury, turning west on Route 103 at Branchville.
Telephone: (203) 438–7323
Cables/Telex: None
Credit Cards: American Express, MasterCard, Visa
Rooms: 14, 4 with fireplaces (and an additional 8 rooms to follow in a garden wing).
Meals: Breakfast only, 7:00–9:30, 8:00–11:00 weekends, served on the veranda in summer; coffee, tea, soft drinks, snacks all day. (The Ridgefield Inn across the lawn is not connected with West Lane, but the two have a good working arrangement, if you want to make a dinner reservation.)
Diversions: Tennis, golf, horseback riding nearby (and the inn may have its own pool by 1982).
Sightseeing: In Ridgefield, Aldrich Museum of Contemporary Art, Keiler Tavern; nearby, Hammond Museum and Japanese Garden in South Salem, Caramoor Festival in Katonah.

For more suggestions in this area
turn to Added Attractions, page 375.

From the Adirondacks to Bucks County

How silver-sweet sound lovers' tongues by night,
Like softest music to attending ears! . . .

SHAKESPEARE

1. The Point
2. Mohonk Mountain House
3. Auberge des Quatre Saisons
4. The Springside Inn
5. Brae Loch View Inn
6. Sherwood Inn
7. 1740 House
8. The Sign of the Sorrel Horse
★ *Added Attractions*

THE POINT
Upper Saranac Lake, N.Y.

$$$$

As any well-heeled world traveler knows, it's always possible—with the right credentials and the right travel agent—to move in with an earl or a duke for a week of Holbeins, history lessons, and feeling more or less as if you owned the castle yourself. But the good news is, now you can do it in the Adirondacks instead of the Loire. With minor but welcome differences.

But before getting right to the Point, let me explain about the Adirondacks in case you had the same idea of them I did. For these are no northern cousins of the lowly Catskills, studded with billboards and Bagel Hamlets. In fact, Wyoming would be hard put to match so much wilderness so fiercely conserved.

Conservation is such a religion here that even black bears and rattlesnakes have been allowed to make a discreet comeback. The only endangered species are ticky-tacky cabins and roadside stands, for virtually all of the northern Adirondacks—thank heaven and Wall Street—are the property of either the state or the unconscionably rich. And of the latter, all one sees from the road are mailboxes that read like the membership of the New York Stock Exchange, circa 1928.

Now, picture in the most exclusive enclave of the most exclusive lake (*Upper* Saranac, of course) what local historians deem "unquestionably the most lavish of the privately owned camps." That's the Point. Don't, however think of it as the Wilderness-Sheraton. Or as a hotel at all.

The grand seigneur of the Point is a dashing forty-year-old named Ted Carter, who has made, lost, and remade so many fortunes he doesn't seem to keep count. After living in thirty-two different countries in half as many years, he returned to the scene of his boyhood summers where his grandfather had owned an Adirondack camp. Carter took one look at the Point, said, "I have to have it," and it was his. He'd just treated himself to nine perfect acres—seven on land, two under water—graced with a complex of lodges, cabins, and boathouses so magnificent the word *rustic* may never recover.

As one of the precious few survivors of an age without income taxes and the FTC, the Point could never be duplicated today—even by the Rockefellers, who built it half a century ago. When no pine trees could be found in the Adirondacks big enough to form the massive roof trusses their architect envisioned for the main lodge, they sent to Canada for the superlogs that now lord it over the thirty-by-fifty living room. At either end, native boulders the size of small glaciers house the walk-in fireplaces that blaze year round. In what was Mr. Rockefeller's favorite bath hangs a shower head as big as a basketball net. Everywhere, fittings and fixtures are made of the solid copper and chromium you'd expect to find on a very royal yacht—all of it in the same gleaming, shipshape condition of fifty years ago.

In spite of its grand scale, the Point's new owner never meant to become an innkeeper. He simply wanted a home, and that's how he's furnished every nook and cranny of it. With antique rugs and chests and leather-bound books from his grandfather's nearby estate—and with the dash and daring of owning houses all over the world himself.

But from having a few personal friends to keep him company, it became a small—and natural—step to invite a few paying guests, never more than a dozen at a time so far, often far fewer. You can have the library in the main lodge, cozily furnished as a guest room and paneled in oak and the latest best-sellers. Or quarters in a separate-but-equal three-room lodge with its own fireplaces and terraces looking out on the lake. Or anywhere else in either lodge, boathouse, or guidehouse. Mr. Carter will even move out of his room and do it up for you if you fancy it.

What you get with every room is the feeling you really belong. Not just because you usually have the beach, the boats, the main room of the lodge, all to yourself, but because your host loves having you there. How does he avoid having people he *doesn't* like? "Only nice people want to come to the Adirondacks," he answers. There has been one exception: an Italian princess who pouted for days because there was no disco.

Mr. Carter presides over every meal except breakfast, with lunch tending to run on into the cocktail hour (or, more accurately, *hours*), which runs on into dinner at nine or ten, which ends with the last cognac at one or two. He has a small but devoted house staff augmented on special weekends by a noted cook-caterer from New York. The food is always good (leg of lamb, standing rib roast, etc.) and on the famous-cook weekends superb. All drinks, including the world's best Bloody Marys and excellent wines and after-dinner drinks, are there for the taking all the time. (Your bill is the same no matter how much of a pig you've been.)

Warning: Although children are allowed (so are well-behaved pets), it takes a special sort of nonadult to weather the serenity and sophistication of the place. So the little Jennifers and Adams of the world might be just as happy left at home.

There are, however, plenty of games for adults to play. Keeping in mind that spring comes late to the Adirondacks and autumn early, in warm weather there's: swimming in the mountain-fresh lake that surrounds the Point on three sides, waterskiing, skimming across it in a spectacular speedboat called *Diamond Lil'*, midnight sails on a motor launch complete with bar, canoe trips to the Saginaw Bay nature preserve, cookouts, picnics. In chillier times 600 miles of prepared cross-country trails start right at the Point's front door; there are good downhill courses nearby, moonlight skating on the lake, hayrides, a snowmobile, trips to Lake Placid.

But before you get there, have a chat with Mr. Carter and tell him what *you* like to do. Short of moving the Olympic bobsled run from Lake Placid to your front door, he'll do just about anything that will make you happy.

Of course, nobody can promise that all of this will last forever. The call of the wild may have lured him here—but it may not always *keep* him here. So if this sounds like your cup of tea, now's the time to sip it.

C.P.

Name: The Point
Owner/Manager: Edward G. L. (Ted) Carter
Address: Star Route, Saranac Lake, N.Y. 12983
Directions: From Manhattan: take N.Y. Thruway to Adirondack Northway, Exit 23, then Route 28 to Blue Mt. Lake, Route 30 to Trading Post, 10 miles north of Tupper Lake, second turn right after Gulf station; also, 18 miles northwest of Saranac Lake, 26 miles from Lake Placid.
Telephone: (518) 891–5674

Cables/Telex: None

Credit Cards: None

Rooms: 8, plus boathouse apartment, divided among three buildings.

Meals: Breakfast served all morning, lunch 1:30, dinner 8:30; informal; full room service during dining room hours; occasional dancing in boathouse.

Diversions: Tennis (1 court), beach, walking trails, swimming, sailing, speedboats, waterskiing, canoes, rowboats, skiing, ice skating, cross-country skiing, snowshoeing; golf, horseback riding nearby.

Sightseeing: Adirondack Museum, Lake Placid, Ausable Chasm, John Brown's Grave, Indian reservations, bird sanctuary, mountains for miles.

P.S. May be closed March and April, check for specific dates.

THE SPRINGSIDE INN
Auburn, N.Y.

Whoever wrote, "Across the river and through the trees to Grandmother's," must have really been thinking of Owasco Lake and Springside. A big, comfortable barn-red house with a long and shady front porch and a lawn that lazes down to a duck pond, this is a fine place to stop and admire the Finger Lakes. It's right on one of them and an easy drive to several others, including Cayuga and Skaneateles.

Built as private boys' school by a Dutch Reformed parson in the nineteenth century, its original purpose was to "avoid the evils necessarily attendant upon large and promiscuous assemblages of the young." Which may be why the young mostly steer clear of it even today. Quiet and still blessedly nineteenth century, Springside is run by a woman who grew up there and her husband, who is the chef. Their affection for the place shows in spotlessly kept guest rooms furnished in authentic Upstate antiques and freshly repainted, papered, and carpeted every three or four years.

But the pleasantest surprise is on the menu. Good food of the sort that might just give back *homemade* its good name. Steak, roast beef, and all the other usual meat-and-potatoes dishes at remarkably low prices, served in a big, cheery room with beamed ceiling and blazing fire. Springside's weekend special includes lodging (specify if you prefer shower or tub) plus a hot toddy to greet you and followed by Friday- and Saturday-night dinner, a breakfast, a brunch—and a jar of homemade salad dressing to take home. Price: $125.

The Finger Lakes may be a long way to go for peace, quiet, and a bargain, but of course there's also the view.

C.P.

Name: The Springside Inn
Managers: William and Barbara Dove
Address: 41 West Lake Road, Auburn, N.Y. 13021
Directions: N.Y. Thruway Exit 40 to Route 34S, then to Route 38S. The inn is on Route 38S, ¼ mile down along the west shore of Owasco Lake.
Telephone: (315) 252–7247
Cables/Telex: SPRINGSIDE
Credit Cards: MasterCard, Visa
Rooms: 7.
Meals: Continental breakfast, Sunday brunch 10:30–12:30, no lunch, dinner 5:00–10:00, Sundays 1:00–6:00 (approx. $10 for 2); informal; no room service; taped music in lobby, lounge, and dining room; piano music on weekends in dining room.
Diversions: Beach, swimming, walking trails; tennis, golf, horseback riding, water sports, roller skating, cross-country skiing, ice skating, snow-shoeing nearby.
Sightseeing: Finger Lakes, wineries, Filmore Glen, state fairs, dinner cruises.
P.S. Special weekend packages available.

MOHONK MOUNTAIN HOUSE
Mohonk Lake, N.Y.

It's eye-boggling. A rambling, gabled, turreted, eighth-of-a-mile-long Victorian château, 1,250 feet up in the mountains, with a lake at its doorstep and miles of wilderness all around. From a distance it looks like medieval Nuremberg, from close up like a Disney fantasy

elongated for Cinemascope. Inside it's even more stunning: walls and balustrades of intricately carved birch, square columns with carved capitals, leaded and textured glass, pierced-wood screens, "Sultan's Corners" with plush banquettes, bentwood settees, velvet-covered love seats, a pair of five-foot Japanese cloisonné vases flanking a parlor organ and a Steinway concert grand.

"FOREVER WILD." The whole massive anachronism is the cherished preserve of a family called Smiley. The first Smileys started it all back in 1869, when they built a summer house for their friends; hence the word *house* rather than *hotel*, because the fourth generation of Smileys still like to think of it as a private country house (some country house, with 305 rooms and 150 fireplaces), and love to show guests around the gardens or entertain them with a recital on the Steinway. They're Quakers, and you have to put up with a few eccentricities: no smoking in the dining room or main parlor; no drinking in public places except during dinner (you can tipple in your room if you like, alcoholic beverages may be purchased for *private consumption* at the Guest Services Desk, and the hotel will supply you with setups); you may not play the piano in the lounge between two and five in the afternoons; you'll find room phones, but no TV in the uncompromisingly Victorian, somewhat stodgy rooms; but you can forgive these trivia when you see what else the family has done for you. A few years ago they turned over 60 percent of their land (a tidy

$10 to $15 million worth of real estate) to the Mohonk Trust to ensure that the mountain wilderness will be "forever wild."

Forever wild, and forever enjoyed, because the Smileys have set things up so that you can fill your days with unpolluted pleasures. Sun yourself on the sandy beaches (that's right, sand even at 1,250 feet). Paddle a canoe across the lake. Put a dime in a dispenser for a handful of fish food to feed the trout. Ride horses along forty-five miles of woodland trail lined by spruce, birch, and beech. Wander hand-in-hand through the formal gardens of red salvia, snapdragons, asters, and zinnias; sniff the mignonette, heliotrope, and shrub roses. All over the gardens and up the side of the mountain, the Smileys have built tiny gazebos (about 150 of them) of weathered hemlock with thatched roofs where you can rest, kiss, and admire the view across the Shawangunk Mountains and Rondout Valley to six states. You can go sightseeing by horse-drawn carriage, play golf or tennis, or sit on a veranda and rock the hours away to dinnertime; in winter you can go cross-country skiing, snowshoeing, sleigh riding, or skating.

Outdoors, there's something for almost everyone, but the hotel itself may not be everyone's cup of afternoon tea. The rooms, for example, are not as large, stylish, or comfortable as the rates might lead you to expect (be sure to pack slippers, because some well-trodden carpeting has still to be replaced); but for those who enjoy something unique, a keepsake of bygone gracious days, Mohonk offers magnificent surroundings and crystal-clear air—and hour after hour, mile after mile of Quaker quiet.

Name: Mohonk Mountain House
Owners/Managers: Ben H. Matteson (vice president), Frank A. Hamilton (hotel manager), the Smiley family (owners).
Address: New Paltz, N.Y. 12561
Directions: The hotel is 6 miles west of New Paltz, about 90 from New York City; by car, take the N.Y. Thruway to Exit 18, then follow New Paltz's Main Street until you come to the bridge over the Wallkill River, then turn right and follow the signs for Mohonk; by bus from Port Authority, N.Y.C., to New Paltz, where the Mohonk car will pick up guests for a small fee; or by rail to Poughkeepsie, where you can arrange to have a car meet you; airport shuttle limousines from all major N.Y.C. airports stop at New Paltz.

Telephone: (914) 255–1000; N.Y.C. tie line (212) 233–2244

Cables/Telex: None

Credit Cards: MasterCard, Visa

Rooms: 305, with 21 tower rooms and 8 cottages (which can accommodate 2–6 people, available from mid-May to mid-October); almost half the rooms have fireplaces; a few have running water but no bathrooms. Particularly noteworthy are the spacious tower rooms, arranged à la Victorian sitting rooms complemented by fireplaces, lovely antique fixtures in the bathrooms, and balconies where you can step out into another world.

Meals: Breakfast 8:00–9:30, lunch 12:30–2:00, dinner 6:30–8:00; room service during meal hours; jacket required in dining room; dancing Saturday nights May to October.

Diversions: Bridge, chess, Ping-Pong, TV rooms indoors. Spring-fed lake half-mile long with bathing area and beach, hiking trails, boating, winter sports, trout fishing, shuffleboard, croquet, lawn bowling, sleigh rides, carriage rides, platform tennis; tennis (6 courts, $6 per court per hour, pro facilities), golf ($3.50 per round Friday-Sunday, holidays, $2 Monday through Thursday), horseback riding ($9 per hour), cross-country skiing (rentals)—all on the premises.

Sightseeing: Surrounding gardens, woodlands, and mountains.

P.S. Busiest in summer, small groups remainder of year. Special seminar/ events and sports packages available. Check with hotel for dates of special events.

AUBERGE DES QUATRE SAISONS
Shandaken, N. Y.

$

Lie on the lawn, with the birds singing and the brook chuckling, and let the cooking smells that wisp past your noses lull you to Burgundy. Walk into the dining room and everything confirms that you're in a small French provincial inn—the pine walls, the checkered tablecloths with white napkins; the French accents, the way the wine appears on the table before the food. Even the new chalet wing wouldn't look out of place in the Haute Savoie. Your map tells you you're in the Catskills, but a long way from the Catskills in spirit. This is France, from the aperitif on the porch to the first sip of Beaujolais, from the *soupe à l'oignon* to the deliciously gooey *profiteroles*. You come here to eat, and between meals you can frolic in the pool, sun yourselves on the lawn, play volleyball, Ping-Pong, or tennis—all within sniffing distance of the kitchen. You can take long lonely walks through sixty-five acres of woods behind the hotel, or just sit on the porch and watch the big white cat chase a chipmunk.

The Auberge is a mile or so from busy Route 28 on unbusy Route 42, a dark-shingled lodge on a tiny hill surrounded by a hillside of trees. Its rooms, too, are more Burgundian than Catskill—piney walls, lino floors with skimpy rugs, and so small you have to embrace every time you turn around. Most of the rooms in the lodge don't have private baths; if you want that kind of extravagance, and room to move around without getting into a clinch, take a room in the chalet. Twice the space, but half the charm.

As if it weren't enough to have the birds, the trees, the brook, the tennis, the Frenchness, and the *profiteroles*, the Auberge keeps its most endearing quality when it presents your bill—what you'd normally pay for just a room in most inns buys you room *and* breakfast *and* dinner at the Auberge.

Name: Auberge des Quatre Saisons
Owners/Innkeepers: Edouard and Annie Labeille
Address: Route 42, Shandaken, N.Y. 12480
Directions: About 120 miles or 2 hours and 15 minutes from New York by N.Y. Thruway to Exit 19 (at Kingston), then by U.S. 28 to N.Y. 42; or by Palisades Parkway to Thruway Entrance 9, then to Exit 19.
Telephone: (914) 688–2223
Cables/Telex: None
Credit Cards: None
Rooms: 37, including 1 suite.
Meals: Breakfast 8:00–9:30, no lunch, dinner 6:30–9:30, no room service, informal dress.
Diversions: Pool, volleyball, lawn games, tennis court (free); fishing, hunting, golf, horseback riding, summer stock theater nearby.
Sightseeing: Seasonal antique shows and country fairs.

BRAE LOCH VIEW INN
Cazenovia, N.Y.

This is one of upstate New York's most charming old towns. Its antebellum architecture is still intact, and its picture-book lake is still clear and swimmable. Some people stop here for the antique-hunting, others just to get one last glimpse of unspoiled nature before pushing on to Syracuse, Rochester, or Buffalo.

The Brae Loch is a marvelously preserved relic of Gothic Victoriana—Cazenovia's past in aspic. The inn began life in 1802 as an unassuming little cottage in a town famous for its uppity mansions and lakeside estates. And nothing much has changed, including Brae Loch.

Stained-glass windows, old steamer trunks, and rag rugs give the guest rooms a touch of Victorian class, in spite of their glossily up-to-the-minute conveniences. Number 2 (of eight rooms and an apartment) gives you a tiled fireplace, and a sunny bay window with a view of lake and park. Numbers 7 and 8 are the most private—in their own wing with their own staircase.

Not Scottish in name alone, the inn is done up in tartans from front door to back bar. And a pretty little shop in the sun porch is stocked with everything from bolts of authentic tartans to sporrans, tams, and bagpipes.

The food at dinner is straightforward but well-prepared steak-and-lobster-tails fare. But Sunday brunch here is unusually good in country where they haven't quite got used to putting vodka in their tomato juice and champagne in their orange juice.

C.P.

Name: Brae Loch View Inn
Manager: James R. Longo, Jr.
Address: 5 Albany Street, Cazenovia, N.Y. 13035
Directions: Centrally located in the village of Cazenovia on U.S. Route 20.
Telephone: (315) 655–3431

Cables/Telex: None
Credit Cards: American Express, MasterCard, Visa
Rooms: 9.
Meals: Dinner only, 5:00–10:00, Sunday noon–10:00, (approx. $11 to $15 for 2); informal; flexible room service; taped music in lounge and dining room.
Diversions: None on premises; beach privileges at Cazenovia Lake, golf (18 holes, $7 per round) nearby; several ski centers in the area (downhill and cross-county), ice skating nearby.
Sightseeing: Chittenango State Park, Chittenango Falls.

SHERWOOD INN
Skaneateles, N.Y.

The Sherwood Inn is a find. First for Joy and Bill Eberhardt, who bought it six years ago and now are busily—and faithfully—restoring the 170-year-old rooms. Next for a travel writer in search of hotels that *haven't* answered the clarion call of the Howard Johnsons. Finally for the two of you in search of a room with a view in a pleasant little town in the Finger Lakes.

Skaneateles is the kind of town you can relax in and enjoy. No sights that *must* be seen or dressy events to attend, but great old houses to walk or ride a bike past, tidy shops to poke around in, and fun things to do, like dinner on the mailboat while it makes its rounds, or a polo match on Sunday afternoon, or a sailing regatta on the lake. Which neatly brings us to the subject of how nicely the Sherwood Inn is situated. Skaneateles caps the north end of long-and-skinny Skaneateles Lake. Now, guess what hotel sits right at the tip of the lake with the best view in town. And if it's that view you're after, ask for the Bridal Suite, room 21; it's big and bright and papered in blue flowers that confirm the Eberhardts' good taste and their intention to blot out a World War II era "refurbishing" by reinstating furnishings in keeping with the hotel's beginnings, in 1807, as a stagecoach stop.

But before taking the Bridal Suite, have a look at the suite at the

end of the hall. The Garden Suite (room 24) is nice, isn't it? All those
windows and the array of hanging plants shading you from view. You
could lie in bed tonight, bathed in the freshness of this greenery, with
the lake sparkling outside your window and moonlit shadows flicker-
ing across the garden room floor, listening to the chirping of the
crickets.

L.E.B.

Name: The Sherwood Inn
Owners/Managers: Joy and Bill Eberhardt
Address: 26 West Genesee Street, Skaneateles, N.Y. 13152
Directions: Skaneateles is on U.S. 20 (the old stagecoach road), 17 miles
    southwest of Syracuse (or Exit 40 on the New York Thruway), and the
    inn is just west of the town square.
Telephone: (315) 685–3405
Cables/Telex: None
Credit Cards: American Express, Carte Blanche, MasterCard, Visa
Rooms: 13.
Meals: Breakfast 6:00–11:00, Sunday brunch 10:00–2:00 in summer, lunch
    11:30–4:00 weekdays and Saturday, dinner 5:00–10:00 weekdays, 5:00–
    11:00 Saturday, 3:00–9:00 Sundays (summer), 12:00–8:00 Sundays
    (winter), approx. $15 to $26 for 2; no room service; informal dress; piano
    in the bar Friday and Saturday.
Diversions: None at the inn, but the village has lighted public tennis courts;
    golf, hiking, swimming, waterskiing, boating, canoeing, indoor skating,
    downhill and cross-country skiing nearby.
Sightseeing: Skaneateles Lake, Finger Lakes, winery tours in Hammond-
    sport, Naples and Penn Yan, Sonnenberg Gardens, Genesee Country
    Village.

1740 HOUSE
Lumberville, Pa.

Lumberville slumberville—this small village drowses alongside the
Delaware River and the Pennsylvania Canal, about three miles up-
stream from the Stockton Bridge. This is the place where Harry and

Janet Nessler decided to build their dream inn when they gave up the real estate business in New York a few years back.

The 1740 House is a warm, friendly place, right on the edge of the canal and surrounded by sycamores, pines, oaks, and boxwood, and banks of asters, roses, and rhododendron. River Road runs by on the other side, almost as silently as the canal. This is what peace is all about. "The folks who feel insecure without color TV in the room and a piano bar in the cocktail lounge should stay away," says Harry Nessler. "They'll hate it here." In fact, not only is there no TV or piano, there's no bar either. The 1740 part of the 1740 House is an old stable, but most of the inn is a modern cedar-sided structure, blissfully at one with the surrounding trees. You wake to nature, you dine with nature, you play in nature. The inn has acres of windows; each of its twenty-four rooms overlooks a panorama of river and woods and canal, and if that's not enough step out onto your own patio and take in the whole depth of the scene—the greenery, the scent of the forest, the chirping of birds, the swish of a canoe along the canal.

Breakfast is served in a small dining room filled with ivy, a lemon tree, gardenias, and begonias, overlooking the river. It's buffet style—great pitchers of orange juice, pots of coffee, a pewter pot filled with boiled eggs, heaps of freshly baked croissants, rolls, and cold cereals.

After breakfast, tiptoe down the rickety steps with English ivy growing all over them that look as though they've been there since 1740, untie one of the two canoes or the rowboat, and go for an expedition along the canal. You won't have to worry about rapids and white water here—the most ruffled the water gets is when a mosquito flits down for a drink. The inn has its own small pool, and there are golf, tennis, and fishing in the neighborhood. In winter, someone lowers the level of the water in the canal so that you can go ice skating or ice boating. The rooms, in fact the entire inn, are handsomely highlighted with antiques. (Bucks County is a region of fine old family homes and when someone dies the antiques often go up for auction; a lot of them have ended up here.) The reading table that holds the register, for example, is a copy of one found in the governor's palace in Williamsburg. Two of the rooms are in the old part of the structure—room 2, with thick stone walls and beamed ceilings, was once this stable; and room 23, with a cathedral ceiling and wide oak beams, was once the hayloft, both adjoining the pool. Otherwise, all the rooms are new, with wall-to-wall carpeting, individually control-led central heating and air conditioning, and sparkling bathrooms with tubs and showers. The original house, which was formerly an antique store, is now the sitting room. Here you'll find lurching floors and old ceiling boards, with comfortable antiques and a big wing chair as well as Mariah, a Labrador retriever, and Molly, a longhaired dachshund, in front of the log fire. The Nesslers' motto is, "If you can't be a houseguest in Bucks County, be ours." Be theirs.

Name: 1740 House
Owner/Manager: Harry Nessler
Address: River Road, Lumberville, Pa. 18933
Directions: On State Highway 32, about 7 miles north of New Hope and the exit from U.S. 202, or about 50 miles from Philadelphia.
Telephone: (215) 297–5661
Cables/Telex: None
Credit Cards: None
Rooms: 24.
Meals: Buffet breakfast 8:30–10:00, no lunch, dinner 7:00–7:30 (approx. $26–$36 for 2); no room service, no liquor license, but the inn has ice and setups if you want to bring your own; jackets suggested for dinner.
Diversions: Small pool, canoes, walking; tennis and golf, fishing, ice skating, sledding, some skiing nearby.
Sightseeing: Delaware River.

THE SIGN OF THE SORREL HORSE
Quakertown, Pa.

Beethoven with breakfast. Fresh fruit and flowers in your room. A crystal carafe of sherry waiting for you in the upstairs lounge.

It took two years before Ron Strauss and Fred Cresson found just the right 1700s stone house, but once they discovered this tiny charmer off the tourist paths (on the old Colonial road between Philadelphia and Bethlehem) they proceeded to transform it into one of Bucks County's most delightful small inns.

Not that it was easy. The two men, who had become friends

when both were enmeshed in the Washington bureaucracy, spent months chipping off the plaster that had "modernized" the mellow stone walls inside and out. They divided the downstairs into two intimate dining rooms and a dim cozy bar. The latest project is enclosing the side porch into a glass-walled atrium to hold the resident doves, cockatoos, and lovebirds and the lush array of flourishing plants that are Fred's forte.

Plants line the windowsills of the bedrooms as well, nicely filling the deep niches resulting from those thick stone walls. The tall carved headboards, Victorian chests and mirrored commodes, quilts, and oriental rugs were lovingly collected at local auctions. Small private bathrooms were installed for four of the six rooms, and more bathrooms are in the works. The old wall paneling and wide floorboards, fortunately, couldn't be improved upon.

Besides learning quite a bit about paint and plaster and plumbing, Fred went to bartending school while Ron enrolled in the Philadelphia Restaurant School. So well did the fledgling chef learn his lessons that the restaurant is booked solid for Saturday nights at least a month in advance. Ron's eclectic menus are light on meats, heavy on game, poultry, veal, and seafood. Among the house specialties are Cornish hen with ground pork and fresh fennel stuffing, chicken with pecans in mustard sauce, and poached salmon in season. He's also devised an eight-course harvest dinner, served up with four kinds of wines, and a regal multicourse New Year's Eve dinner that are rapidly becoming legends in the area.

Bucks County can teem with tourists in season, but you'd never know it here in your historic Pennsylvania stone house in the country. Take your breakfast on the patio, where morning newspapers are served up with the flaky croissants. Bring the paper with you and relax by the pool. Take a walk in the countryside. Later you can come back for a nip of sherry, pull back the patchwork quilt for an afternoon siesta—and then descend the steep spirally Colonial stairs for one of Ron's elegant dinners, with candlelight and classical music. William Penn never had it so good.

                                                                    E.B.

Name: The Sign of the Sorrel Horse
Owners/Managers: Ronald Strauss and Fred Cresson
Address: Old Bethlehem Road, Quakertown, Pa.

Telephone: (215) 536–4651

Directions: Follow PA 313 to 563, then north 2 miles to Old Bethlehem Road, turn left, and watch for the inn on the left.

Cables/Telex: None

Credit Cards: MasterCard, Visa

Meals: Breakfast 8:00–9:30, dinner 6:00–9:30 weekends, until 9:00 during the week (approx. $28 for 2), Sunday brunch 12:00–2:30; no room service; dress optional.

Diversions: Swimming pool; Lake Nochamixon nearby with bike paths, fishing, sailboats for rent, cross-country skiing.

Sightseeing: Mercer Museum and Fonthill; Peddler's Village shops in Lehaska; New Hope shopping and Bucks County Playhouse about 25 minutes away.

P.S. Great idea for a quiet New Year's weekend with elegant dining: closed after New Year's to early March.

P.P.S. Remember to make your Saturday-night dinner reservation when you reserve your room!

For more suggestions in this area
turn to Added Attractions, page 375.

East Side, West Side

There are three things that can never be hidden—love, a mountain, and one riding on a camel.

ARAB PROVERB

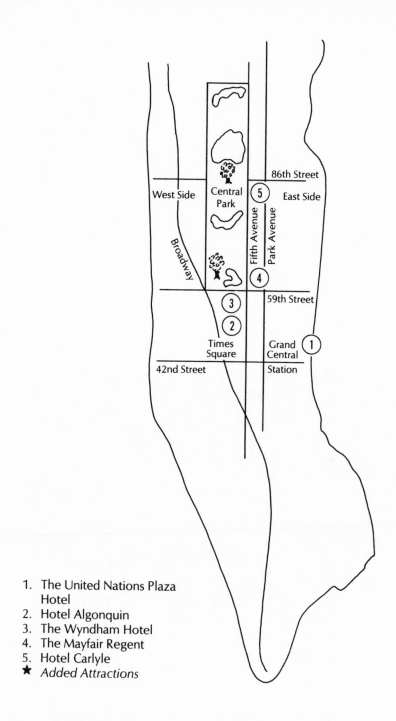

86th Street

West Side

Central
Park

⑤ East Side

Fifth Avenue

Park Avenue

Broadway

④

③ 59th Street

②

Times
Square

Grand
Central
①

42nd Street

Station

1. The United Nations Plaza
   Hotel
2. Hotel Algonquin
3. The Wyndham Hotel
4. The Mayfair Regent
5. Hotel Carlyle
★ Added Attractions

New York City is a law unto itself. You go there for reasons entirely different from those that motivate a trip to the sea or the mountains—or even to San Francisco or New Orleans. Since different yardsticks apply we have not rated the hotels for anything but $. The main attraction that these hotels have in common is that you will not be swamped by conventioneers or tour groups.

THE UNITED NATIONS PLAZA HOTEL

$ $ $ $

What a pity that this glorious hotel be so misunderstood. It seems firmly positioned in people's minds as *the* place to put up corporate heavies and other starched-collar dignitaries.

Don't fall for this pursed-lip propriety otherwise something beautiful is going to waste here.

Where else can you fling open the sheers and gaze at a wall-to-wall, floor-to-ceiling view of New York's blinking skyscrapers? From *bed*, that is. Where else can you slip into terry robes and skip downstairs for a midnight sauna or swim (*also* with skyline views)?

The U.N. Plaza is a forty-story tower with hotel rooms only on the twenty-seventh to thirty-ninth floors. It is close to the East River so views are unobstructed on all sides. The decor is as sleek and contemporary as you'll see anywhere in the world. Hard-edge surfaces everywhere: mirror, glass, chrome, polished steel, black or white Lucite, softened with sudden voluptuous touches in a bedspread or in a wall hanging. To achieve this superb design, *total* design, architects Kevin Roche and John Dinkeloo held absolute control over all interiors and furnishings throughout this handsome building. There's no disparity of concept anywhere, inside or out.

You expect to pay dearly for luxury as lavish as this and sure enough you do. If you can't afford to go the whole hog, plan your visit for a weekend when you can get special package rates (*only* by asking for them).

R.E.S.

Name: United Nations Plaza Hotel
Manager: Bruno Brunner
Address: One United Nations Plaza, New York, N.Y. 10017
Telephone: (212) 355-3400 direct, or reserve through the Hyatt system: (800) 228-9000
Cable/Telex: UNPLAZATEL, answer: HHCHUNA-NYK./126803
Credit Cards: American Express, Carte Blanche, Diners, Eurocard, Master-Card, Visa
Rooms: 289 units, some are suites, some are duplex suites (living room downstairs, spiral staircase to upstairs bedrooms).
Meals: Breakfast 7:00–10:00, lunch 12:00–3:00, dinner 5:30–10:00 (approx. $30 to $50 for 2); dress mostly jacket and tie; room service 7:00 A.M. to midnight.
Diversions: Year-round swimming, sauna, exercise gym, indoor tennis courts.
Sightseeing: Directly across the street from the U.N. General Assembly building (the hotel is always fully booked when the General Assembly is in session); easy crosstown cab ride to Broadway theater district.

HOTEL ALGONQUIN

$$

The legend lives on.

Somehow, there's still a mysterious sense of *presence* that lingers in the public rooms of this marvelous old landmark hotel. And you can't pass it off solely to nostalgia. The legendary Algonquin wits had their day and have long since gone. Dorothy Parker's *not haunting* the place.

No, the presence is real. Palpable. And it just seems to come naturally from the exhilaration of the people who gather here to be sociable over tea or cocktails or after-theater supper. But what triggers all the merriment when the cast of characters is changing all the time? That's the secret of the Algonquin's ongoing popularity.

What you have here is a very clubby atmosphere. The lobby is like an outsized sitting room. Tables and chairs are grouped and regrouped as parties come and go. The air is charged with electricity. And everyone but everyone is chatting up a storm.

Stay here if you love the theater and want to be close to it. Stay here if you enjoy being a celebrity spotter—the Algonquin is a home-away-from-home for actors, playwrights, authors, publishers. Stay here if you revel in tradition, rather than luxury.

The Algonquin is family-owned and family-managed. Quite obviously, they love the place. That accounts, perhaps, for the hominess of the rooms, the comfortable settees and easy chairs. It also accounts for the *esprit* of the place. If there are any churls on the Algonquin staff, we didn't cross their paths. (Be sure to make the acquaintance of Harry; officially he runs the Algonquin newsstand, but he's also a theater buff par excellence and a ticket broker to boot.)

R.E.S.

Name: Hotel Algonquin
Manager: Andrew A. Anspach
Address: 59 West 44th Street, New York, N.Y. 10036
Telephone: (212) 840–6800
Cables/Telex: ALGONQUIN NEW YORK/66532
Credit Cards: American Express, Barclaycard, Carte Blanche, Diners, Eurocard, MasterCard, Visa
Rooms: 140, 20 suites.
Meals: Breakfast, 7:30 A.M. to 10:30 P.M., lunch noon–3:00, tea 3:00–5:00, dinner 5:30–9:30 (approx. $40 to $60 for 2), after-theater buffet supper 9:30 P.M. to 12:30 A.M.; jacket and tie; room service 7:00 A.M. to 10:00 P.M.; bar open daily until 2:00 A.M.
Sightseeing: All New York is at your door; walk to all Broadway theaters; bus, subway, or cab to Lincoln Center.
P.S. Ask for a side or back room if you're light sleepers; New York City garbage trucks make noisy collections on the street in early-morning hours.

THE WYNDHAM HOTEL

$ $

If you caught the 1980 Dick Cavett interview with Sir Laurence Olivier and Joan Plowright, you know what a suite at this gem of a hotel looks like. (The show was taped in Suite 1001. Actually, the

Oliviers were ensconsed in 1401 at the time and didn't want a band of TV technicians swarming through their living quarters.)

Here is a hotel that never takes groups, never advertises, yet it stays full or very close to full most of the time. Why is that?

The Wyndham is a standout because the people who own it are on hand front and center every day to keep it spinning like a top. John and Suzanne Mados are the live-in bonifaces. They've been sole owners since 1976. (They were part owners for ten years before that.) Quite obviously, the Wyndham is a labor of love for both of them.

John learned all the snares and all the solutions for running a quality hotel during his early days at the Park Lane and the St. Moritz. Suzanne is the decorator. What she has created is some 130 different living environments. No two rooms are alike. The overall effect is one of elegance and tradition. Yet there's nothing standoffish or haughty about this decor: the rooms are at once quite striking, yet somehow warm, homey, and personal. You feel you're being put up in a good friend's apartment, not a hotel room.

There's no New York riffraff milling about the lobby. The door to the street is always locked. There's an elevator man on duty twenty-four hours a day.

Clientele is heavy with theater personalities (Jean Stapleton, Henry Fonda, Peter Falk, Ginger Rogers, Ian McKellan, Hume Cronyn, and Jessica Tandy—working actors can walk to their theaters from the Wyndham).

Them that has, *keeps*. The Wyndham is easily one of the best values you'll find anywhere in New York City.

R.E.S.

Name: The Wyndham Hotel
Owners: John and Suzanne Mados
Address: 42 West 58th Street, New York, N.Y. 10019
Telephone: (212) 753–3500
Cables/Telex: None
Credit Cards: American Express, Carte Blanche, Diners, Eurocard, Master-Card, Visa
Rooms: 64, 70 suits with pantries.
Meals: The Wyndham does not maintain its own restaurant; however there's a direct lobby entrance to an adjacent restaurant, Jonathan's, which is open for breakfast, lunch, and dinner; no room service.

Sightseeing: This location between Fifth Avenue and the Avenue of the Americas puts you close to New York's best shopping, close to Carnegie Hall, to Central Park, to excellent resturants; let the working actors walk to their plays on Broadway, you'll be happier in a cab.

P.S. Ask doorman Miguel to point out some nearby shortcuts, particularly if it's raining; you can nip through to 57th Street via the lobby of the Avon Building next door; there's also a quick, dry route to Central Park South; just ask.

THE MAYFAIR REGENT

$$$

The name may not ring a bell because it's new to New York. This used to be known as Mayfair House, a residence hotel composed mainly of lavish suites leased to corporations. There are still some long-lease suites, but since 1978, when it was taken over (by Regent International), renamed, and renovated, the Mayfair Regent has been a discreet, *intime* hotel catering to individual travelers from all over the world.

The omens are all good as you case the wood-paneled lobby of this quiet, dignified hotel. Highly attentive staff. Huge pots of Shasta daisies. Coffered wood ceiling. Good-looking guests, expensive luggage. Your instincts tell you that you're in for a round of the good life—and so you are.

Beyond the lobby and the elevators (with attendants!) the newly refurbished lounge is now a gathering spot for well-heeled shoppers and gallery-goers at tea-time; just off the lobby is one of New York's toniest restaurants, Le Cirque; and there's round-the-clock room service, if you prefer the privacy of your suite. What's nice about the rooms here is their size—high ceilings, pre-war spaciousness, with no attempt to carve them up into cubicles. The hotel is still undergoing redecorating: undone rooms are just a shade above frowsy, so be sure to ask for one of the refurbished rooms.

The Mayfair Regent (not to be confused, by the way, with its near neighbor, the Regency) is living proof that a good manager attracts a devoted following. The present helmsman is from Venice, so wealthy Italians always want to "stay with Dario" when they're passing through New York. Signor Mariotti's predecessor hailed from London's Connaught, so the hotel is also a way station for visiting Britons and other international nabobs. This gives the place its cosmopolitan, multilingual ambiance.

R.E.S.

Name: Mayfair Regent Hotel
Manager: Dario Mariotti
Address: 610 Park Avenue, New York, N.Y. 10021
Directions: At Park and 65th, entrance on 65th
Telephone: (212) 288–0800
Cables/Telex: 236257 MAYREGE
Credit Cards: American Express, Carte Blanche, Diners, MasterCard, Visa
Rooms: 150, including 51 suites and 16 junior suites.
Meals: Breakfast anytime; 24-hour room service.
Sightseeing: Close to the Metropolitan, Frick, and Whitney museums, to
   Bloomingdale's, Bergdorf Goodman, and Tiffany's.
P.S. Special weekend packages available.

HOTEL CARLYLE

$$$$

If your list of New York "must-sees" includes a handful of good museums, art galleries, and chic little shops, there's no better place to stay than the Carlyle. You'll be in a prime residential area of the Upper East Side, surrounded in elegance.

Two U.S. presidents have maintained *pieds-à-terre* at the Carlyle. Three superstars of stage and screen keep apartments here now. So do captains of industry from this country and from abroad.

Only half the Carlyle's space is taken by hotel rooms. The other half has been converted to pricey co-op apartments. And everything's intermixed. None of that "equal but separate" stuff.

Despite all its celebrity, the place stays very low key. The management will not divulge guests' names for publication, but keep your eyes open when you're having a buffet breakfast or when you pop into the lounge to listen to Bobby Short.

All rooms are furnished differently, but the look is traditional throughout the house. And the favorite color appears to be a creamy beige. Try for a room on an upper floor, if you yearn for a skyline view. If you plan to entertain, better splurge on a suite (#1407–08 is a beauty with a thirty-foot living room; $350 per day).

You pay rather dearly to stay at the Carlyle, but it's worth every penny.

R.E.S.

Name: Hotel Carlyle
Manager: Frank Bowling
Address: Madison Avenue at 76th Street, New York, N.Y. 10021
Telephone: (212) 744–1600
Cable/Telex: 620692
Credit Cards: American Express, Carte Blanche, Visa
Rooms: 190 units, more than half of these are suites.
Meals: Breakfast 7:00–10:30, lunch noon–3:00, tea 3:00–5:00, dinner 5:30–9:30 (approx. $60 for 2); jacket and tie; room service 24 hours a day; bar open daily 11:00 A.M. to 1:00 A.M.
Sightseeing: Directly across Madison Avenue from Sotheby Parke-Bernet, 1 block from Whitney Museum, 6 blocks from Frick Museum, 7 from the Metropolitan Museum of Art; 1 block from Central Park; beyond these immediate pleasures, there's your pick of all New York.

For detailed rate, turn to page 413.

Around
the
Chesapeake
Bay

Omnia vincit Amor: et nos cedamus Amori. . .

VIRGIL

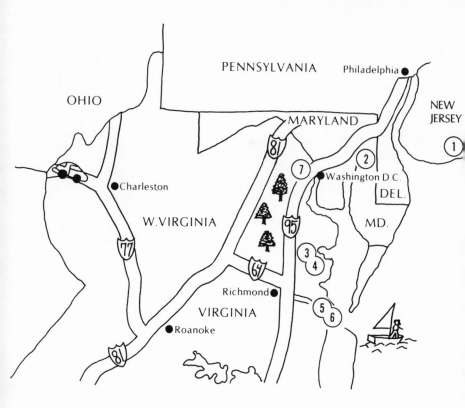

1. The Mainstay Inn
2. Robert Morris Inn
3. The Tides Inn
4. The Tides Lodge
5. Colonial Houses
6. Williamsburg Inn
7. Fairfax Hotel
★   *Added Attractions*

ROBERT MORRIS INN
Oxford, Md.

Robert Morris was a prominent English merchant who met a curious-
ly unheroic end in the Colonies when he was fatally wounded by the
wadding from a gun firing a salute in his honor. The Robert Morris
you might have heard of was his son—a close friend of George
Washington and fund raiser for the Continental Army.

The inn was built as a private home in the earliest days of the
eighteenth century by ship's carpenters using the techniques of
shipbuilding—wooden pegged paneling, fourteen-inch square
beams and pilasters fastened with handhewn oak pegs, that sort of
thing. The house was purchased for Robert Morris Senior in 1730 and
first became an inn at the time of the Civil War. It sits by the edge of
the Tred Avon River, just by the boarding point for a ferry that's been
in operation continuously for two hundred years and hauls half-a-
dozen cars at a time across the estuary. It's still very much a Colonial-
style inn. Four of the rooms have the original handmade wall paneling; the fireplaces were built of brick made in England and used as
ballast in sailing ships; the mural panels in the dining room were
made from wallpaper samples printed 125 years ago on a screw-type
press using woodcuts carved from orangewood.

The inn has twenty-two rooms, all with air conditioning, but
otherwise they're very basic—no phones, no TV, and only seven of
them have private bathrooms. Your best bets are room 1, which has
both a bath and a view, and #15, which has a pencil post bed so high
you need a set of steps to get up to it. There are ten more rooms
(seven have private bathrooms) in the Lodge—a big Victorian house a
few yards along the bank of the river, with spacious lawns and
verandas overlooking the Tred Avon traffic. And right next to the
Lodge is the River House, recently renovated and boasting two
waterfront rooms with baths and large bay windows.

The public rooms at the inn are plusher—the delightful River-

view Lounge with the original wood-pegged wall panels, one of the
old brick fireplaces, and an antique grandfather clock. The dining
room is decked out with silk drapes, chandeliers, and Hitchcock
chairs; and the beamy Tap Room, where you can sip a hot toddy or
buttered rum before a big brick fire, is all wooden and nautical. The
menu's *pièce de résistance* is a glutton's Special Seafood Platter—
chilled gulf shrimp and lump crabmeat, deep-fried crab cake,
shrimp, clams, stuffed shrimp, and broiled crab imperial and filet of
rockfish. Too much? Then try the crab and shrimp Norfolk, another
local dish. Ask Maître d' John Miller (from Oxford, England, to
Oxford, Maryland, by way of Claridge's in London and Luchow's in
New York) to recommend a wine from his well-stocked cellar.

MUNGING AND JOUSTING. The Robert Morris Inn sets the atmosphere
nicely for Colonial Oxford and its surroundings, and it's a perfect base
for discovering the oddities of Chesapeake Bay—Baymen "munging"
for terrapin; "gunkholes," or creeks, with names like Canoe Neck or
Ape Hole or Antipoison; the skipjacks and bugeyes—the last working
fleet of sailing vessels in the entire country; the jousting tournaments
over in Talbot County. In summer there are several regattas. When
you hear a starting gun go off—duck. The wadding can be dangerous,
remember?

Name: Robert Morris Inn
Owners/Managers: Wendy and Ken Gibson
Address: P.O. Box 70, Oxford, Md. 21654
Directions: From the Delaware Memorial Bridge, take Route 13 South to
     Route 301 South to Route 213; turn left to Route 50 East to Easton; then
     turn right to Route 322; then right to Route 33 to Oxford. From the
     Chesapeake Bay Bridge, follow Routes 50, 301, and 50 to Easton; from
     the Chesapeake Bay Bridge Tunnel, take U.S. 13 north to Route 50, go
     west to Easton, then take Route 333 to Oxford. By boat, follow the
     Choptank River to the Tred Avon River and tie up at the protected
     anchorage at Town Creek.
Telephone: (301) 226–5111
Cables/Telex: None
Credit Cards: American Express, MasterCard, Visa
Rooms: 32; 2 cottages; 1 apartment.
Meals: Breakfast (served daily, times vary), lunch 11:30–4:00, dinner 5:00–
     9:00, Sunday 1:00–8:00 (approx. $18 to $25 for 2); no room service;
     jacket required in dining room, dress informal in taproom and tavern.
Diversions: Swimming in the river (from early spring); bicycles, sailing,
     boating, tennis, golf; goose and duck hunting (November–January)
     nearby.
Sightseeing: The village of Oxford, Oxford-Bellevue Ferry.
P.S. Weekend reservations at any time of the year require *2 to 3 months
     advance notice*.

THE MAINSTAY INN
Cape May, N. J.

$

"Innkeeping is a lot easier than teaching English to a bunch of
high-school kids," according to ex-schoolma'am Sue Carroll; which
doesn't speak very highly of school kids since innkeeping for the
Carrolls has involved four solid winters of scraping and painting
fifteen-foot-high ceilings, making lace curtains for twenty-four very
tall windows, and tacking lace trim to sheets and pillowcases for every
room of their pride and joy. But this stalwart pillared mansion has
probably never looked better since it was built in the Victorian

heyday of Cape May, a gambling club for southern gentlemen who quit their Mississippi plantations to spend their summers by nothern shores. Now Tom and Sue Carroll have refurbished its twelve rooms with Victoriana—massive beds and wardrobes to match the proportions of the main rooms, smaller pieces for the half-dozen nooks in the former maids' quarters. Except for two of the smaller rooms, which somehow manage to incorporate private facilities, guests share two bathrooms (though by spring 1981 seven of the rooms will have private baths), one of them with its original copper bathtub encased in walnut paneling. There are touches of a comfortable home everywhere—patchwork quilts, braided rugs, potted plants (even in the cupola)—and staying here would be like visiting a favorite aunt if it weren't for the youthful, affable Carrolls. Despite all the work that has to go into keeping the mansion shipshape, they still seem to consider their Mainstay as a means of entertaining—friends, guests, neighbors, everyone. It's a relaxed, informal place ("we seem to use a lot of first names in introductions around here"), and a blessing if you have an urge to visit Cape May. The town is noted for its Victorian buildings (more than six hundred of them, some of them restored, some of them tottering), a couple of streets with gaslight, an Atlantic beach, and the wildness of Cape May National Seashore. But if I were going back to Cape May the attraction would be to spend a couple of relaxing days at The Mainstay: breakfast on the porch, idle chitchat with fellow guests, a game or two of croquet on the unpredictable lawn, until it's time for afternoon tea in the ornately Victorian parlor, beside the big fireplace, the ten-foot gilt mirror, and the shelves of Thackeray. Then I'd climb the steps to the daintily decorated cupola to watch the sun go down on Cape May's gingerbread.

Name: The Mainstay Inn
Owners/Managers: Tom and Sue Carroll
Address: 635 Columbia Avenue, Cape May, N.J. 08204
Directions: By car, to the south end of the Garden State Parkway or via the Lewes–Cape May ferry.
Telephone: (609) 884–8690
Cables/Telex: None
Credit Cards: None; personal checks accepted
Rooms: 12.
Meals: Breakfast 8:00–9:30, afternoon tea 4:30; no room service.

Diversions: Croquet, Monopoly; beach 3 blocks away, National Seashore a
few miles away; bicycles for rent nearby; tennis (indoor and outdoor),
golf, horseback riding a few miles away.
Sightseeing: Cape May National Seashore, Victorian Village.

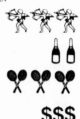

THE TIDES INN

Irvington, Va.

$$$

Some inns treat you to hayrides or sleigh rides, but the Tides Inn
welcomes you with cruises aboard its yachts—the "whiskey run" at
sunset, or a dinner cruise by moonlight, from Carter's Creek into the
Rappahannock River and then out to the Chesapeake Bay, on the
Stephens family's private yachts—which range from forty-six feet to
the stately hundred-footer *Miss Ann.*

Everywhere you turn here, you see water. The creek surrounds
the inn on three sides; lounges, terraces, dining rooms, and most of
the guest rooms look out over water; lunch is served in a gazebo
above the water; there's a seaside heated pool, and a tiny beach with
swivel-and-tilt wicker sunchairs; the inn's second "parking lot" is a
marina where waterborne guests tie up for the summer.

The Tides Inn sits on a low hill overlooking the creek, sur-
rounded by twenty-five acres of lawns, Virginia pine, and crepe
myrtle, with the Virginia scents of magnolia and azalea competing
with the salty tang of the water.

The setting, in other words, is superb; and the hotel itself is not
far behind. A bit stuffy maybe (you can't set foot in the lobby after
6:30 without a tie), but its other blessings more than make up for that:
the 110 rooms range from elegant and simple (in the four-story lodge)
to elegant and luxurious (the semi-suites in Lancaster House and
Windsor House); and there's plenty of pleasant activity to keep you
going until it's time for the whiskey run.

BY FERRY TO THE GOLF COURSE. You can rent pedalos and sailboats,
play tennis; and if you want to play golf, you walk down to the water,
board the *Gondola,* and cross the creek to The Tides Lodge (see next

listing) or take the shuttle bus to the new Golden Eagle course. Most of the staff, like Curtis Sampson, has been with the inn since it opened thirty-four years ago, and they all perform with the friendly, dignified service you expect in Virginia. Even in the Northern Neck of Virginia. Irvington is on that patch between the Rappahannock and the Potomac, a relatively uncrowded but historic corner of the state: Route 3, which takes you to the inn, is known in these parts as Historyland Highway because George Washington, Robert E. Lee, and President Monroe were born nearby, just in case you get bored with all that water.

Name: The Tides Inn
Manager: Bob Lee Stephens
Address: Irvington, Va. 22480
Directions: By car from the north, take U.S. 301 south from Baltimore to Va. 3 (a few miles after you cross the Potomac) and follow it east for about an hour to Irvington; from Richmond, take Interstate 64 and Va. 33 to West Point and Saluda, then turn right to the Rappahannock River Bridge and The Tides Inn.
Telephone: (804) 438–5000
Cables/Telex: None
Credit Cards: MasterCard, Visa
Rooms: 110, with 4 suites.
Meals: Breakfast 8:00–9:30, lunch 12:00–4:00, dinner 7:00–9:00; room service during meal hours; jacket and tie at dinner; live music and dancing.
Diversions: Outdoor pool, bicycles, sailing/boating, waterskiing; two 18-hole golf courses, one 9-hole course ($12 per day), 4 tennis courts ($1 per person per hour).
Sightseeing: Historyland Highway (Route 3) passes by the birthplaces of Washington, Monroe, Lee, and other points of interest.
P.S. Special package rates are available; holiday weekends require a 4-night minimum stay. The inn may be closed for a few weeks in the winter.

THE TIDES LODGE
Irvington, Va.

The Lodge is known as a golf resort, but toss the word golf into the creek and you're left with a secluded location, up a creek, miles from anywhere, on a peninsula surrounded on three sides with water and on the fourth with a golf course; a modern two-story lodge with edge-grained fir siding hemmed in by mountain laurel and wildflowers, where you can breakfast on a private balcony and watch the morning mists rise and the early birds swooping for the early fish. Even if you never set foot on the first tee, you can fill your days with sailing and outboard boating, tennis, putting, swimming in a heated pool, fishing, lounging in hammocks strung out among the trees, or cruising in the lodge's sixty-five-foot yacht.

The Tides Lodge is kid brother (it was opened in 1969) to the Tides Inn, above; it's owned by the same family and shares most of the other's facilities, but it's operated as a separate entity and has a personality all its own—amiable, relaxed, and less formal than the inn. The lodge's forty rooms all have balconies with views of the water, color TV, room phones, and so much tartan decor that going to bed here is almost like cuddling under a kilt.

The tartan is in honor of Sir Guy Campbell, the revered golf course architect from St. Andrews, who helped design the lodge's links; he also has a tartan-splashed lounge named in his honor, where you can drink a toast to his memory before dinner. The pubby dining room features local delicacies—Rappahannock soft shell crabs, Chesapeake Bay shad roe, or roast Urbanna duckling. If you're ever up the creek, this is as nice a way as any to go.

Name: The Tides Lodge
Manager: E. A. Stephens, Jr.
Address: Irvington, Va. 22480
Directions: Same as for The Tides Inn, but branch off a few miles farther west from Va. 3.
Telephone: (804) 438–6000, or toll free (800) 446–5660 (East)
Cables/Telex: None
Credit Cards: MasterCard, Visa
Rooms: 48, 1 villa.
Meals: Breakfast 8:00–10:00, lunch 12:00–3:00, dinner 4:00–10:00 in Binnacle II, 7:00–9:00 in dining room (approx. $28 for 2); room service 8:00 A.M. to 10:00 A.M.; jacket at dinner; live music, dancing ("soft" disco).
Diversions: Pool, sauna, shuffleboard, horseshoes; tennis (3 courts, 1 lighted, $4 per hour per court), golf (two 18-hole courses, $10 per day), bicycles, canoes, sailboats, paddleboats, rowboats for rent; yacht cruises by arrangement.

Sightseeing: See "The Tides Inn."

P.S. Spring is the busiest season; occasional small groups at other periods.

WILLIAMSBURG INN
Colonial Williamsburg, Va.

$$

Resort is hardly the word that springs to mind when someone mentions Williamsburg, but that's just what you'll find here—one of the most attractive resorts between Maine and Florida. Step through the inn's french doors into the garden and see what you find: two golf courses disappearing into the loblolly pine and magnolia trees, half a dozen tennis courts, two lawn bowling courts (and a lawn bowling *pro*), croquet, putting green, driving range, and a pair of outdoor pools screened from the rubbernecking hordes. All of them right on the doorstep of an inn fit for a queen, an emperor, several presidents, sheiks, and other grand panjandrums on state visits to the U.S.A., who arrive every few months at the inn's imposing facade of arches and columns, framed by trees and set off by a curving driveway lined

with an honor guard of flowers. Indoors, it looks like a mini-White House—Regency lounge with twin fireplaces, chandeliers, fresh-cut flowers, Kittering reproduction furniture, and velvet drapes that are changed with the seasons. All very gracious, very *Virginia*. Likewise the spacious guest rooms (with the exception of a contemporary garden wing called Providence Hall).

Likewise the dining room, a spacious candles-and-chandeliers salon that transforms the dinner hour into an event. (Even children have to dress up in their best bibs-and-tuckers to dine here.) This is an inn that takes its clarets and cuisine seriously: an authentic sommelier will guide you through an extensive wine list, the *chef de cuisine* (from Belgium, via Washington's swank Jockey Club) beckons you to the realm of the epicure with dishes like braised quail with tournedos Rossini. You're only one block from all the wonders of Colonial Williamsburg, yet dining here, staying here, playing here, you're insulated from the masses of day trippers.

COLONIAL HOUSES
Colonial Williamsburg, Va.

$$$

Wake up in a canopy bed. Throw open the shutters, push aside the honeysuckle and dahlias, listen to the birds singing in the mulberry trees. Beyond the trim white picket fence and holly hedge is Virginia's Colonial capital. In the evening, you can sip salmagundi and juleps in taverns where Washington and Patrick Henry dined, and Jefferson wooed his fair Belinda; afterward, stroll arm in arm along cobbled streets uncluttered by cars or crowds. There you have the magic of these Colonial cottages: when the crowds have gone trudging off to pseudo-Colonial cells in nearby motels, you can give your chunky latch key a twist and step into the real thing.

This is a world of brass andirons and rag rugs, wing chairs and pewter sconces; some have fireplaces, most have kitchens. The majority of these dozen-odd Colonial Houses were actually the homes of eighteenth-century Virginians, and the remainder were Colonial-style kitchens and laundries, now converted into some of the most captivating lodgings in the country. They've been restored and furnished to the last detail in the style of their periods; but without detracting from their ambiance they somehow manage to incorporate air conditioning, private bathrooms with adjustable spray showers, and other contrivances even Franklin and Jefferson never imagined. (From the outside, incidentally, they're so authentic looking many tourists think they're exhibits and try to come in. Or in some cases peep through the windows. Be prepared.) The Colonial Houses are operated by the Williamsburg Inn (see previous listing), and their guests enjoy all the services of the inn, including room service; but the Houses get a category all to themselves here because they are *so* special. Where else can you have dinner for two served on a mahogany dining table lighted by silver candelabra, in a private heavy-beamed dining room? Then settle back in a Chippendale sofa before a log-burning fire, there to sip a glass of port before climbing the stairs to a dormer bedroom and your canopy bed?

Name: Williamsburg Inn and Colonial Houses

Owner/Manager: James E. Baldridge

Address: Colonial Williamsburg, Va. 23185

Directions: By car, take Interstate 64 to Route 60, follow 60 to York Street, Francis Street, and the inn; by air to Newport News, then 20 miles by limousine or taxi to the inn; by Amtrak to Williamsburg.

Telephone: (804) 229–1000

Cables/Telex: None

Credit Cards: None

Rooms: 145 in inn, 79 in Colonial Houses, including 22 suites.

Meals: Breakfast 7:30–10:00, lunch 12:00–2:00, dinner 6:30–11:00 (approx. $35 to $45 for 2); room service 7:30 A.M. to 11:00 P.M. (including Colonial Houses); jacket and tie in Regency Dining Room at dinner, no shorts at any time; dancing to a live orchestra Friday and Saturday in Regency Dining Room, piano or harp nightly in Regency Lounge, recitals Sundays in East Lounge.

Diversions: Two heated outdoor pools, croquet, putting green, shuffleboard, chess, checkers, etc., lawn bowling and lawn bowling pro; bicycles for rent, tennis (6 courts, no lights, $3 per person per hour, pro shop, ball machines, clinics), golf (two 18-hole courses, $15 per day); horseback riding nearby ($5 an hour).

Sightseeing: Colonial Williamsburg, Busch Gardens, Abby Aldrich Rockefeller Folk Art Center.

P.S. Open all year, crowded in July and August and on holiday weekends,
      best times spring and fall, and a pleasant hideaway in winter (especially
      in a Colonial House); some conventions, but they tend to be confined to
      the adjacent Providence Wing.

THE FAIRFAX HOTEL
Washington, D.C.

If you were spending a gala weekend in the capital and wanted to dine
at one of the best restaurants in town, you'd probably head for the
Jockey Club. Check into the Fairfax and you won't have to go farther
than the lobby. And if you don't feel like rubbing shoulders with the
bigwigs just dial 2 and have the Jockey Club send up, say, rockfish
braisé diable or crabmeat imperial. But don't order an after-dinner
liqueur. The chambermaid will put a miniature of Courvoisier on
your bedside table, alongside a Godiva chocolate, when she turns
down your bed for the night.

The Fairfax has commanded a corner site on Embassy Row since
the Twenties, serving as a residential hotel until it was transformed in
1979 into its present $7 million deluxe state by Chicago entrepreneur
John Coleman, who was "brought up lunching at places like the Ritz
Carlton" (and who now, incidentally, owns two other hotels in this
guide—the Whitehall and Tremont in Chicago).

The Fairfax has two hundred rooms, a substantial house, but
you'd never suspect anything so large when you step into its intimate
lobby, all Carrara marble and hand-carved pilasters, Federal furnishings, and brass chandeliers. (There's so much brass—the metal-
lic kind—around that the hotel employs a full-time polisher.) Beyond
the lobby are two small interconnected lounges with cozy booths to
offer the kind of whispery privacy one needs in D.C. so that you-
know-who can mingle unobtrusively with isn't-that-so-and-so. Banquettes covered with batik, leather club chairs, open fireplaces, and
the owner's collection of seascapes give the place a clubby look. The
second lounge, the Potomac Room, doubles as a piano bar in the
evening.

Guest rooms vary in size and accoutrements, but they all include grace notes like extension phones in the bathroom, quiet air conditioning, double glazing, Fieldcrest linen, TV, radio, color-coordinated bedspreads and draperies, upholstery of French and Belgian cotton prints in soft earth tones. The furniture, American Reproduction, is by Baker, fabrics by Braunschweig & Fils.

Owner Coleman's aim was to emulate the finest small hotels in Europe, so you will have at your disposal night butler service for pressing clothes and polishing shoes, a lady concierge to rustle up a limo to take you to the Kennedy Center, fresh rose and crisp linen on your breakfast tray.

During the week, the Fairfax rooms fill up with politicos and celebrities, but weekends are for lovers. July and August are the quietest months of all. And if you decide after all that you don't want to dine at the Jockey Club, the Fairfax will fit you out with a picnic basket (smoked trout, that sort of thing) and you can slip off to a secret corner of Rock Creek Park.

Name: Fairfax Hotel
Manager: Michael Harmon
Address: 2100 Massachusetts Avenue, N.W., Washington, D.C. 20008
Directions: On Embassy Row, between Dupont Circle at Sheridan Circle, 2 blocks from Metro.
Telephone: (202) 293–2100, toll free (800) 424–8008
Cables/Telex: FAIRFAX WASH DC 7108229228
Credit Cards: "All major cards"
Rooms: 200, including 18 suites.
Meals: Breakfast 6:30–noon, lunch noon–12:30, brunch Saturday and Sunday, dinner 6:00–11:00 (approx. $60 for 2); jacket and tie, reservations advisable; room service around the clock.
Diversions: Piano bar; talent spotting.
Sightseeing: All of Washington.
P.S. Seminars up to 50, no name tags. Special weekend packages.

For more suggestions in this area
turn to Added Attractions, page 375.

Up Hill and Down Dale— the Shenandoah Valley and Blue Ridge Mountains

We'll gently walk, and sweetly talk,
Till the silent moon shine clearly . . .

BURNS

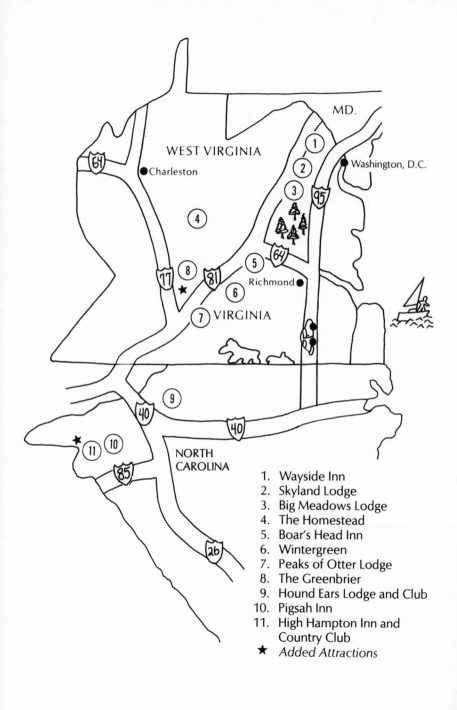

1. Wayside Inn
2. Skyland Lodge
3. Big Meadows Lodge
4. The Homestead
5. Boar's Head Inn
6. Wintergreen
7. Peaks of Otter Lodge
8. The Greenbrier
9. Hound Ears Lodge and Club
10. Pigsah Inn
11. High Hampton Inn and Country Club
★ *Added Attractions*

WAYSIDE INN
Middletown, Va.

The Wayside Inn has known the sighs of lovers for 175 years but it still greets you with the charm and low-ceiling, lopsided elegance of those early days when Virginia dandies rode up in their coaches with sweet southern belles. The inn is owned by a D.C. banker and avid collector of Americana, who drove past the inn one day, liked what he saw, and bought it within an hour. (If that isn't avid collecting, what is?) Since then he has decked it out with close to a million dollars' worth of Americana and, here and there, Britannica: the two lounges alone are almost museums—with George Washington looking down from above the fireplace on a Beau Brummel commode, an early Blickensdorfer portable typewriter, an English coin sorter, a petit-point chair, and leather scroll footrest. The owner's great hero is George Washington and you can't go anywhere in the Wayside without G.W.'s beady eyes looking down on you from an engraving, painting or statuette—sometimes alone, sometimes with Martha.

You'll find them upstairs in the guest rooms, too. Especially in room 16, a big green room with a pair of canopied double beds, a tallboy, chest of drawers, and half a dozen prints of G.W. Room 1 has a canopied double bed, fireplace, circular commode, and a few steps leading down to a real bathroom (all of the inn's rooms have private bathrooms and air conditioning, but no TV); room 10 is a flamboyant nest with red velvet bedspreads and drapes, twin mahogany beds with gilt embellishments, and a hefty curlicued dresser—since the room is at the rear, it's quieter than its decor. All twenty-one rooms are different, and your preference will probably depend on your taste in antiques.

So many people want to dine here that the Wayside has had to expand to six dining rooms (the most romantic being the candlelit Slave Kitchen or the Lord Fairfax Dining Room, which only seats two or four guests). Don't get caught up in the bustle. Grab a couple of the seven white rockers out on the veranda and listen to the birds in

the bushes until the throngs have gobbled their ham and trotted off to the theater.

A few yards down Main Street you come to the 259-seat, air-conditioned Wayside Theater where you can see professional productions of plays, musicals, and revues in summer; in winter, the theater hosts festivals of historic and unusual movies. Beyond Main Street, all the pastoral prettiness of the Shenandoah Valley is at your pleasure. Try some of the quiet back roads that wind up into the Shenandoah Mountains—they haven't changed much since the days of Virginian dandies and southern belles.

Name: Wayside Inn
Manager: Margie Alcarese
Address: 7783 Main Street, Middletown, Va. 22645
Directions: Take Interstate 81 to Exit 77, drive west a mile to U.S. 11, then go left into Middletown's Main Street.
Telephone: (703) 869–1797
Cables/Telex: None
Credit Cards: American Express, MasterCard, Visa
Rooms: 21, with 7 suites.

Meals: Breakfast 7:30–11:30, lunch 11:30–3:00 Monday-Saturday, dinner 5:00–9:00, 12:00–9:00 on Sundays (approx. $16 to $30 for 2); no room service; informal dress.

Diversions: Beach, swimming, hiking, fishing, boating, skiing, and golf nearby.

Sightseeing: Shenandoah Valley; Wayside Theater, Belle Grove, Wayside Wonderland recreational park, George Washington's Headquarters, Crystal Caverns, Skyline Drive; Apple Blossom Festival and antique fairs.

SKYLAND LODGE
Shenandoah National Park, Va.

Chase a white-tailed deer through the hickory and pignut. Take a deep breath and sing "O Shenandoah, I long to hear you" into the wind. Scramble over the rocks for a picnic beside a waterfall. Lie on the grass and tickle each other's ears with columbine, while you read Spenser: "Bring hither the Pink and purple Columbine/With Gilly-flowers/Bring Coronation and Sops in wine/Worn of Paramours/Strew me the ground with Daffadowndillies . . . " All around you are 300 square miles of wildlife preserve, rustling with deer, black bear, woodchuck, and gray fox; meadowlarks and indigo buntings skim through the staghorn sumac and chokecherry; and in spring, louse-wort, bebb's zizzia, and columbine paint the meadows.

The location is close to beatific—the highest point on the Skyline Drive, that marvelous ambling highway that snakes along the spine of the Blue Ridge Mountains. Skyland's 160 rooms are spread out among lodges and cottages with names like Bushytop, Raven's Nest, Hemlock, Wildwood, scattered among the pines and hemlocks, and all on different levels so that every room seems to have a view across the shimmying Shenandoah. The rooms are so-so, but at least they're piney and rustic; they all have private bathrooms, but no room phones. And no TV, so you'll just have to look at the stars.

BIG MEADOWS LODGE
Shenandoah National Park, Va.

A ninety-two-room, stone-and-timber brother of Skyland Lodge, also operated by the Virginia Sky-Line Company. Like Skyland, its main attraction is its peaceful, nature-loving location on top of the Blue Ridge Mountains, screened from the traffic by pine and hemlock and lawns. Big Meadows is nine miles south of Skyland; all the information below applies to both, except where indicated.

Name: Skyland Lodge
Manager: David F. Emswiler
Name: Big Meadows Lodge
Manager: Bruce Fears
Address for Both: P.O. Box 727, Luray, Va. 22835
Directions: Both are on the Skyline Drive—Skyland, 9 miles south of the intersection with U.S. 211; Big Meadows, 19 miles south of U.S. 211.
Telephones: (703) 999–2211 for Skyland, (703) 999–2221 for Big Meadows
Cables/Telex: None
Credit Cards: American Express, MasterCard, Visa
Rooms: 158 and 6 suites in Skyland, 92 and 6 suites in Big Meadows.
Meals: Breakfast 7:30–10:00, lunch 12:00–3:00, dinner 5:30–9:00 (approx. $12 and up for 2), winter hours at Big Meadows 7:00 A.M. to 6:00 P.M. (7:00 on Friday and Saturday); no room service; informal dress; live music.
Diversions: Bicycle rentals at Big Meadows, game room at Skyland; hiking trails; horseback riding ($4 per hour, not available in winter).
Sightseeing: Shenandoah National Park, Mountain Craft Shop.
P.S. Conference facilities for groups up to 150 are available; children have their own playground area. Try to avoid weekends and holidays, and especially weekends at fall foliage time; make a reservation well in advance, and always before you go up onto the highway, because with a 35 mph speed limit it takes a long time to get back down.

WINTERGREEN
Wintergreen, Va.

$$

Like the lodges above, Wintergreen sets you down in the middle of nature, among pines and balsams, flowered hedgerows and mountain laurel. But here you'll be enjoying comfort and style unmatched in these parts.

Wintergreen is just ten minutes from the Reed's Gap exit of the Blue Ridge Parkway, a few feet below the crest of the mountains—and the Wintergreen golf course, the highest in Virginia. The estate's thirteen thousand acres include ski runs, cross-country ski trails, lakes for swimming and boating, waterfalls, and so many hiking trails Wintergreen publishes a twelve-page guide of treks to Black Rock and Logger's Alley, Shamokin Creek, and Rockfish Valley. Condominium townhouses are tucked in among the trees, their cedar shake roofs and rough-sawn cedar siding blending gently with the surroundings. The best views are from apartments in the Highlands wing, above tree level, but some of the most attractive bedroom suites are in Three Ridges—contemporary-rustic wood furniture, chunky fabrics, planter and rattan, contemporary prints and lithographs. All the apartments have kitchens, some have Jacuzzis in the bathroom, some have fireplaces. Most of them have verandas or balconies for surveying raccoons and squirrels and admiring the pink and white mountain laurel.

There's a small, well-stocked market on the premises, but the resort's dining room, designed around an open fire with a copper canopy, offers a varied menu including deep-fried brie, fettucini, and veal marsala. The staff is pleasant, young, and efficient, and the hostess actually lets *you* decide where you'd like to sit.

Name: Wintergreen
Manager: Gunther Muller
Address: Wintergreen, Va. 22938
Directions: From the north, take Interstate 64 to the Crozet/Route 250 Exit,

then go west on 250 to 6E, then follow the Wintergreen signs; from the south take Route 29 to Route 151N and Route 664; from the Blue Ridge Parkway, take the Reed's Gap Exit.

Telephone: (804) 361–2200

Cables/Telex: None

Credit Cards: American Express, MasterCard, Visa

Rooms: 300 in condominiums and private houses, of which 30 are studios and 100 are 1-bedroom suites.

Meals: Restaurant open from breakfast to 9:30 P.M. (bar to midnight); dinner for 2 approx. $30; casual dress; no room service. (There's also a less-expensive restaurant, Rodes Farm Inn, down in the valley, and a snack bar at the golf course.)

Diversions: Live music ("low-key") in the lounge on weekends in summer, nightly in winter; swimming pools (one for children), walking trails; tennis (12 courts, 2 with lights), golf (18 holes, par 72—if you plan to play a lot, take the golf package with free golf), horseback riding; own ski slopes.

Sightseeing: The Blue Ridge Mountains; Jefferson's home at Monticello is less than an hour away.

P.S. As the guide was going to press, the Wintergreen opened a new 48-room Mountain Inn; since Wintergreen is a private community, you must have an advance reservation; expect some groups (200 maximum) in the off-season.

PEAKS OF OTTER LODGE
near Bedford, Va.

Here's another dreamy location—by the edge of Otter Lake across from Sharp Top, Flat Top, and Harkening Hill, in the Shenandoah National Park. In spring the meadows are jubilant with merrybells, trillium, and columbine; in fall with joepyeweed, goldenrod, and bottled gentian. You can follow mile after mile of hug-and-cuddle trails through sweet birch, black cherry, pignut, pine, and oak; or find a quiet spot to watch for a meadowlark, chickadee, or white-breasted nuthatch. In the evening, elk and white-tailed deer sometimes wander down to the lake for a sundowner. This is strictly a place for basking in nature and love. There's no swimming pool, no tennis court. Just unspoiled, unhurried nature.

And the Virginia Peaks of Otter Company has taken the trouble to erect a rustic lodge that harmonizes with the surroundings— rough-hewn pine walls, slate-topped dressers and tables, cane- backed chairs, acres of glass for admiring the views, acres of lawn for lounging by the lake, and all rooms with balconies or patios facing the lake. The main lodge has an open veranda and a glass-enclosed lounge facing the lake, a downstairs bar, and a raftered dining room with tables for twosomes by the window. You can dawdle over Allegheny Mountain trout or barbecued pig ribs while you watch the sun set over Flat Top and the moon slip past Sharp Top. (Meals here are a bargain, by the way—two people can dine for around $15.)

Get to bed early, but leave the balcony door open and you can be awakened by the meadowlarks and chickadees.

Name: Peaks of Otter Lodge
Managers: Shelby Carter and Carolyn Woods
Address: P.O. Box 489, Bedford, Va. 24523
Directions: On the Blue Ridge Parkway at the junction with Va. 43 (or Mile 86, if you begin at the beginning), 10 miles northwest of Bedford, about 20 miles north of Roanoke.
Telephone: (703) 586–1081
Cables/Telex: None
Credit Cards: MasterCard, Visa
Rooms: 58.
Meals: Breakfast 7:30–10:30, lunch 11:30–2:30, dinner 5:00–8:30 (approx. $10 to $24 for 2); no room service; dress optional.
Sightseeing: Blue Ridge Mountains, Shenandoah National Park, Great Smoky Mountain National Park.
P.S. Busy with families in summer; book far ahead for the fall foliage weeks.

For detailed rate, turn to page 413.

THE HOMESTEAD
Hot Springs, Va.

$$$

Back in the unhurried, unruffled days before the Civil War, Virginian high society whiled away its summers on a grand tour of the mineral springs in the Allegheny Mountains—from Warm in the north, southward to Hot to Sweet to White. A week here, a week there. Nowadays they head straight for Hot Springs and the magnificent Homestead.

The Homestead sweeps you up into a mountain world where sixteen thousand acres of forests and streams and meadows blot out the humdrum and the mediocre. You can go riding here day after day, mile after mile, and never trample the same soil twice; you can take leisurely strolls through the gardens, or rugged hikes that will leave you massaging thighs for therapeutic rather than aphrodisiac reasons; you can relax in mineral baths or saunas, take buckboard rides, play a set or two of tennis on a dozen courts, or a round of golf on three beautiful pine-lined courses; you can float in an outdoor or an indoor pool—and how many mountain resorts treat you to a sandy beach for sunning yourselves?

CHAMBER MUSIC, AFTERNOON TEA. The Homestead is one of America's great classic resorts, built on a scale you don't see too often these days—a towering château of 615 rooms that looms over the forest and rooftops of Hot Springs. When you enter The Homestead, you find yourselves in the Great Hall—a nave of sixteen pillars and fourteen chandeliers, great log-burning fireplaces, a solarium, and a string orchestra playing chamber music during afternoon tea. That's just the Great Hall—you've still to visit the lobbies and lounges and shopping arcade. Everything at The Homestead is on the grand scale, and if you start to wonder how a hotel like this manages to survive in this day and age, wander down to the lower level of the new $8 million South Wing, where you'll see suites of meeting rooms to house the conventions that keep those 615 rooms busy throughout the year. The Homestead is now one of the nation's classic convention hotels—a description which should instantly eliminate it from this guide; but the truth is that even with half a dozen conventions and seminars in the house, there's no overcrowding, and no hint of strained service.

The Homestead was geared to mollycoddle the mollycoddled, and the emphasis is still on service that takes everything in its well-ordered stride even if they no longer have waiters who dance with stacked trays on their heads. In return, it expects a little class from its guests, and the hotel's brochure reminds you that "gentlemen must always wear coats when dining"; and even with "young ladies can wear contemporary bathing suits" this is clearly no place for people who like to spend their vacations lounging around in stained jeans. You come to The Homestead to show off a beautiful woman in beautiful gowns, to make an entrance in the dining room, to command attentive service from maître d', head waiter, waiter, wine steward, and busboy.

On the other hand, if you don't want to go through the fuss of dressing up every night, slip into a robe and order up room service. The Homestead has the right kind of rooms for casual, bathrobe evenings, with soothing pastel colors and comfortable furniture. The

most coveted rooms have parlors and big screened porches high above the gardens; the quietest rooms are in the eleven white clapboard cottages in the garden; and the plushest rooms are the penthouse duplexes in the new South Wing, with spiral stairs leading to bedroom balconies. Up in that cozy love nest you're light miles from the conventions and the fol-de-rol.

Name: The Homestead

Owners/Managers: Thomas J. Lennon (president), W. Dan Reichartz (vice-president)

Address: Hot Springs, Va. 24445

Directions: On U.S. 220, 80 miles north of Roanoke, 15 miles north of Interstate 64; by air, to Ingalls Field 17 miles away (daily scheduled air taxi flights); or by Chessie System to Covington, where you'll be met by limousine.

Telephone: (703) 839–5500

Cables/Telex: None

Credit Cards: None, but personal checks accepted

Rooms: 590, plus 78 parlor suites.

Meals: Breakfast 7:30–10:00, lunch 12:30–2:00, afternoon tea 4:00, dinner 7:00–8:30; room service during meal hours; jacket and tie at dinner; live music, dancing nightly.

Diversions: Outdoor heated pool, therapy pool, sauna, exercise rooms, health spa, movies, hiking trails, lawn bowling, carriage rides, sleigh rides, ice skating, skeet and trap shooting, fishing, skiing; tennis (19 courts, 1 all-weather, no lights, $3 per person per hour, pro shop), golf (three 18-hole courses, 1 of them rated among the nation's top 30 by *Golf Digest*, $12 per day), horseback riding ($8 first hour, $6 thereafter).

Sightseeing: Mountains, forests, gardens, etc.

P.S. Special packages available. Winter rates slightly higher over Christmas, New Year's, Washington's Birthday. If you'd like to enjoy all these facilities but stay in more modest surroundings, make a reservation at the nearby Cascades Inn (703-839–5355), in the hamlet of Healing Springs.

BOAR'S HEAD INN
Charlottesville, Va.

This part of Virginia is America's Sussex—rolling meadowlands, forests and streams, spic-and-span farms, a peaceful land where the landed gentry of yesterday (Thomas Jefferson and James Madison among them) built country estates, and where the landed and unlanded gentry of our day still ride to hounds. Appropriately, the best inn for miles around gets its name from Shakespeare.

The Boar's Head is a complex of well-proportioned buildings in Colonial style tacked onto an old grist mill. It's part of a new housing estate with landscaped grounds, a pair of lakes with ducks and trout, gardens of magnolia and boxwood, and eighteenth-century calm.

The grist mill is over a hundred years old, but it had to be taken to pieces beam by beam and moved to this site; its great forty-three-foot beams now house the Old Mill Room restaurant on the ground floor with some of the inn's hundred-odd guest rooms upstairs. The original fifty-four guest rooms are the most interesting, some with dormer windows and log-burning fireplaces, some with pine-paneled walls and set-in beds. (The new rooms are first-rate—but motelly.)

The lobby is decorated with oak paneling and authentic dark oak antique furniture. The whole place is very decorative, but somehow contrived, somehow closer in spirit to Norman Rockwell than William Shakespeare. Or Thomas Jefferson for that matter.

Besides the tennis courts, swimming pool, and sauna, there's a Boar's Head Sports Club with more tennis courts (including indoor), platform tennis courts, and a squash court. Inn guests can join the club for $6 a day.

On the whole, the Boar's Head is a pleasant enough relaxing inn, but it is less a resort than a base for exploring the attractions of this part of Virginia—Jefferson's exquisite and fascinating Monticello, his elegant campus for the University of Virginia.

These are places to savor, so avoid weekends and holidays. And that advice applies equally to the Old Mill Room at the Boar's Head.

It gets crowded on weekends, and you have to make a reservation for dinner even if you're a guest. The restaurant's menu lists items like "escargots à la Provincial," whatever that is, but when the chef sticks to tavernlike dishes such as roast beef, he does well. But remember to make a reservation.

Name: Boar's Head Inn
Manager: Jeffrey G. S. Houdret
Address: Ednam Forest, Route 250, West Charlottesville, Va. 22905
Directions: Follow the U.S. 250 bypass, 2 miles beyond the intersection with U.S. 29; or by air, scheduled service, to Charlottesville.
Telephone: (804) 296–2181
Cables/Telex: None
Credit Cards: American Express, Diners, MasterCard, Visa
Rooms: 178, 9 suites.
Meals: Breakfast 7:00–10:30, lunch 12:00–2:00, dinner 6:00–9:30 (approx. $24 to $30 for 2); room service 7:00 A.M. to 9:00 P.M.; jacket and tie in dining room; live music and dancing (except Sunday).
Diversions: Outdoor pool, sauna, bicycles, hiking; tennis (sports club, daily membership fee $6, 14 outdoor courts with lights, 3 indoor courts, pro and clinics); horseback riding, skiing, ice skating nearby.
Sightseeing: Jefferson's Monticello; the University of Virginia.
P.S. Special packages available.

THE GREENBRIER
White Sulphur Springs, W. Va.

$$$

There's a touch of *Last Year at Marienbad* about The Greenbrier: a string trio plays for afternoon tea, chandeliered corridors lead you to more chandeliered corridors, couples stroll arm in arm across acres of lawns. Occasionally, someone sips a glass of the mineral water from the sulphur spring, and some of the old-timers may be reminiscing about the day the Prince of Wales sat in with the orchestra during a gala ball.

More likely the guests are trying to recall names and faces not from last year's spa, but from last year at the insurance executives'

conference, or the convention of ad biggies; because The Greenbrier is another classic resort, like The Homestead, that now keeps its aristocratic head above water by filling most of its rooms with conventioneers. They haven't taken over completely, because fortunately a lot of people still recognize that The Greenbrier is a great spot to vacation.

CHAMPAGNE AND WATERMELON. The Greenbrier owes its fame and fortune to a spring with water that tastes and smells something like a hard-boiled egg that's been lying in the bottom of a rucksack for a week. The Indians knew of its curative powers; then a Mrs. John Anderson came along in 1778 and from that point on White Sulphur Springs became one of America's great spas. Robert E. Lee spent a lot of time here, riding Traveler around the estate and admiring the gaggles of south'n belles and the budding beaux who regaled them with champagne and watermelon. They've been followed through the years and social upheavals by tycoons, dukes, lords, princes, shahs, sheiks—and now conventioneers. The Greenbrier is one of the largest resort hotels in the world, and there are a lot of well-heeled and well-traveled types who'll tell you it's one of the best.

Marienbad would probably have to look a long way back in its memory book to match the present opulence of The Greenbrier.

Its palatial facade gleams in the clear mountain air, white and massive against the dense green of the pine-clad mountains all around. Across the parklike garden, the hilltop Presidents' Cottage reminds you that no fewer than nineteen U.S. presidents have visited White Sulphur Springs, and the rows of piazza-fronted cottages running from either side take you back to the days of Robert E. Lee. (One of the rows actually houses an artists' colony, where you can buy handwoven tweeds or handmade pottery.)

The Chesapeake & Ohio Railroad, which built it, didn't stint on The Greenbrier: the hotel has 650 rooms, and no two are alike; the ashtrays at the entrance are antique Chinese rice bowls (and every time they're cleaned out the porter imprints the sand with The Greenbrier's special script-type logo); it has its own fire department, and every room is linked directly with a warning control panel in the firehouse; sixty-three gardeners and groundsmen tend the lawns and the fifty-four fairways; thirty-three chefs whip up everything from scrambled eggs to *tête de veau tortue*.

LOVER'S LEAP. Don't let all this abundance turn you off. The Greenbrier is so big you can easily escape to quiet corners. Take a walk, for example: you have a choice of thirteen trails, from a quarter mile to 10 miles (one of them ominously named Lover's Leap). You're not going to find too many conventioneers up there; in fact, you're not going to find too many anythings up there except shagbark hickory, big tooth aspen, Virginia pine, and staghorn sumac. If you decide to go riding on some of the hotel's 200 miles of private trails, you don't even have to go to the stables to pick up your mounts; the groom will deliver them "at the appointed hour" in the riding circle by the north entrance.

When you get back from your ride, stop off in the clubhouse terrace overlooking the golf courses and sample the sumptuous buffet lunch. You have something like ninety dishes to nibble from.

You can pamper yourself silly in a place like this, and you can leave feeling like a million. Of course, it helps if you *arrive* with a million. Elegance doesn't come cheaply these days.

Name: The Greenbrier

Manager: William C. Pitt III (vice-president & managing director)

Address: White Sulphur Springs, W. Va. 24986

Directions: By car, take Interstate 64 to the White Sulphur Springs Exit, then U.S. 60 one-half mile west of town; by train, daily Amtrak service practically to the doorstep; by air, daily scheduled flights by Piedmont to Greenbrier Valley Airport.

Telephone: (304) 536–1110, or toll free (800) 624-6070

Cables/Telex: None

Credit Cards: American Express, MasterCard, Visa

Rooms: 650 rooms, 68 suites, 28 villas.

Meals: Breakfast 7:30–9:45; á la carte lunch served April–October in The Grille Room, Coffee Shoppe, and Golf Club Buffet, November–March, only in the Coffee Shoppe; dinner 6:30–8:30, jacket and tie required; room service 7:00 A.M. to 12:30 A.M.; live music and dancing.

Diversions: Heated outdoor and indoor pools, sauna, exercise room, indoor bowling, billiards, backgammon; platform tennis, hiking trails, trap and skeet shooting, fishing; bicycles for rent, tennis (20 outdoor, $10 per person per hour; 5 indoor, $16 per court per hour; pro shop, ball machines), golf (three 18-hole courses, $15 per round), horseback riding ($14 per hour); winter sports—ice skating, cross-country skiing.

Sightseeing: Creative Arts Colony, the Presidents' Cottage Museum; woodland trails, the Allegheny Mountains.

P.S. Busiest seasons are summer and fall, with some conventions all year, but think of winter—indoor pool, indoor tennis, sumptuous dining, long walks in untrampled snow.

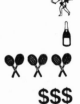

HOUND EARS LODGE AND CLUB

Blowing Rock, N.C.

$$$

More country club than resort, Hound Ears is certainly one of the most comfortable spots along the Blue Ridge. A seven-hundred-acre, bowl-shaped estate, three thousand feet up in the mountains, is haven for some very exclusive private homes, with a chaletlike clubhouse and guest lodge on the fringe of the eighteen-hole golf course.

Lodge rooms have deep pile carpeting, air conditioning, color television, and big windows and balconies overlook the fairways. On cool evenings guests and members gather around the big open fire in the lounge. The dining room also boasts fireplaces, two of them, but you have to tuck into your meal to the accompaniment of an electronic organ. The most romantic feature of Hound Ears (the name, by the way, comes from the configuration of the mountains) is a unique swimming pool carved from the rock, in a secluded dell five minutes from the clubhouse.

Name: Hound Ears Lodge and Club
Manager: Bill Jeffcote
Address: P.O. Box 188, Blowing Rock, N.C. 28605
Directions: In the Blue Ridge Mountains, on Route 105 between Boone and Linville; by private plane to Beech Mountain Airport, 20 minutes away.
Telephone: (704) 963–4321
Cables/Telex: None
Credit Cards: American Express, MasterCard, Visa
Rooms: 22 in lodge, 5 suites in clubhouse.
Meals: Breakfast 7:30–10:00, lunch 12:00–2:30, snack bar 10:30–4:00, dinner 7:00–9:30 (approx. $25 to $30 for 2); jacket and tie after 7:00 (except in winter, "when ski attire is acceptable"); room service for ice and setups only; *bring your own wine.*
Diversions: Live music/electronic organ in lounge and dining room; heated outdoor pool; tennis (4 courts), golf (18 holes); horseback riding, walking trails, skiing, cross-country skiing nearby.
Sightseeing: The Blue Ridge Parkway and Mountains, Grandfather Mountain Highland games.
P.S. Some small seminars (up to 100) in off-season.

PISGAH INN
Canton, N.C.

The Cherokee called the mountain "Elseetoss" and the ridge "Warwasseeta." This was their exclusive domain—to hunt, but not to own. Then the settlers came. They wanted it too—to own. In 1776, General Griffith Rutherford led an expedition against the Cherokee, and by 1808, "Warwasseeta" was renamed "Mount Pisgah," for the ridge east of Jordan from which Moses looked down to see the "Promised Lands" (Deuteronomy, fourth chapter, remember?).

The analogy is as apt today as it was then. As far as the eye can see, in a 360-degree sweep, are rugged virgin forests—in fall, a pointilist canvas of red, yellow, and green, in spring, bursts or rhododendrum, azalea, and mountain laurel. Deer, bear, fox, mink, and other forest creatures frolic freely.

The Mount Pisgah area has been a popular retreat for generations. Shortly after the U.S. Forest Service bought up Vanderbilt acres to found the Pisgah National Forest, Thomas Weston opened the doors of the Old Pisgah Inn, the large, eighteen-room American chestnut building standing near the present inn's dining room. Those were the days when the only telephone was at the foot of the mountain and traffic went in only one direction, down in the morning and up in the evening.

With the opening of the Blue Ridge Parkway in the 1960s, a new Pisgah Inn was built to accommodate today's hustle-and-bustle travelers. It's not one of those nostalgic old mountain hunting lodges with a dolorous moose head staring down at you from above a crackling fire. It is, however, a chain of attractive, unobtrusive birchwood cabins overlooking the valley. Although blandly decorated, it caters to today's comforts (modern conveniences, *two* double beds). But no television and no telephone in the rooms! The view is the attraction here, and all the cabins have a private porch with old-fashioned rockers where you can while away the hours gazing into the misty valleys below, or off into the gently rounded ridges of the Blue Ridge Mountains. Guests in the Pisgah Suite also enjoy the intimacy of a beautiful stone fireplace (complete with complimentary wood). Wraparound, floor-to-ceiling windows offer you the same splendid panoramic views elsewhere in the inn—in the dining room and gift shop (all sorts of mountain-crafted gifts, like dried-apple dolls, hooked rugs, stained-glass window hangings, and frog rocks).

How to spend your days? Just like old Thomas Weston's times, in welcome, quiet peace. Up here in Pisgah, you wake to the singing of birds. Watch the sunrise—from your bed if you like. Feast on hearty specialties—country ham, red-eye gravy, grits, fresh mountain trout caught every day half-way down the mountain, by local fisherman. Take walks along Buckspring and Weston trails, picking berries and wild flowers. Or climb to the peak of Mount Pisgah itself. At night, head for the Old Pisgah Inn to hear about visitors of bygone days, like the man from Charleston who came every summer, for the season—with his piano. Learn about the mountain people through their songs and music. Or simply slip into bed and dream about the pleasures of this promised land.

S.H.

Name: Pisgah Inn
Managers: Phyllis and Tom O'Connell
Address: P.O. Drawer 749, Waynesville, N.C. 28786
Directions: On the Blue Ridge Parkway at Route 2, Canton, N.C., 26 miles southeast of Asheville.
Telephone: (704) 235–8228
Rooms: 51 double, 1 suite with fireplace.
Meals: Breakfast, 7:30–10:00, lunch 12:00–12:30, dinner 6:00–8:30, snack bar, 10:00–6:00; room service available on request; no liquor license, but the inn will provide setups and chill your beer and wine, if you want to "brown bag" your own.
Diversions: Walking trails.
Sightseeing: Pisgah National Forest; in Asheville: Thomas Wolfe Playhouse, Colburn Memorial Mineral Museum, the Mountain Dance and Folk Festival (August), the Vanderbilt mansion "Biltmore."
P.S. No pets; fewest children May, June, October; best to book 2 months in advance, especially for fall foliage (first 3 weeks in October); closed November 10 through early spring.

HIGH HAMPTON INN
AND COUNTRY CLUB

Cashiers, N.C.

Nature lovers rejoice! Two thousand acres of private woodlands. Mountain laurel, dogwoods, hemlocks, and white pines to wander among. Waterfalls you can walk under or picnic beside. Rocky ridges you can climb or just look at (Whiteside Mountain is the highest sheer precipice in eastern America, rising 1,800 feet above the evergreen countryside). Forty acres of lakes for swimming, boating, and fishing. Nothing seems to change here but the seasons. Even the inn. It's all mountain rustic with chestnut-bark exterior and pine-paneled interior. Its enormous four-sided stone fireplace, hooked rugs, and family protraits probably look much as they did when the lodge was built almost a century ago as the private summer hunting and fishing retreat of General Wade Hampton, of Civil War fame.

Its hospitality is still warm and southern, and the eager-to-please staff often outnumber guests two to one. But High Hampton's backwoods simplicity is not for everyone. Some folk expect something posher—they arrive, take one look, and leave without bothering to unpack. "If we can just get them to stay for one night," notes one member of the staff, "they are still around two days later and come back next year, bringin' someone with them. It just kinda gets in your blood."

In fact, half the guests are repeat visitors, and they want "their" cottage just the way it has always been—even if the beds may list, the curtains sag, and the mountain-crafted furniture doesn't match. This camplike ambiance seems to be part of the High Hampton charm. Many of the rooms share a sitting room with fireplace (the inn supplies the firewood), but a few like #147 in the Lewis Cottage or the secluded one-roomed Log Cabin have fireplaces right in the bedroom. All rooms have views of mountain greenery—golf course, forest, lake, or mountain.

Probably the main reservation about High Hampton is not the rustic feeling but the fact that the hotel makes a point of catering to children, priding itself on one of the most comprehensive children's programs anywhere. This may sound ominous if you've come to the mountains for peace and quiet, but in fact the hayrides, cookouts, leathercrafting and games keep the kiddies occupied. They even have their own beach and swimming area. In any case, there are all those thousands of acres of unspoiled nature to escape to.

S.H.

Name: High Hampton Inn and Country Club
Manager: Bill McKee
Address: Cashiers, N.C. 28717
Directions: By car (rentals available) from Asheville Airport, south on Fanning Bridge Road to NC 191, turn east (2 miles) to NC 280. Go south 14

miles to Brevard and bear right onto U.S. 64. Continue south on U.S. 64, 29 miles to Cashiers, another 1½ miles to the inn. Limousine service by arrangement with inn ($35 one way).

Telephone: (704) 743–2411

Cables/Telex: None

Credit Cards: None

Rooms: 35 in inn, 95 in cottages.

Meals: Breakfast 8:00–9:30, lunch 12:30–1:30, dinner 7:00–8:30 (all meals buffet-style), afternoon tea served in lounge 4:00–5:00, soup traditionally served in lounge before dinner, no liquor in dining room, but happy hour in Rocky Mountain Tavern 6:00–7:45, setups and locker for your liquor provided ($1), snack bar, picnic lunches on request; no room service; jacket and tie in dining room in evening.

Diversions: Movies, bingo, horseracing, square dancing in lounge/lobby, club room for teen-agers downstairs, horseshoes, shuffleboard, croquet, archery, Italian lawn bowling, badminton, birdwatching (150 species), 3 lakes (40 acres), swimming, separate beach and swimming area for children, mountain climbing, walking trails (with or without guide); kayaks, canoes, rowboats ($1.20 per hour, $5 per day), pedal boats ($2.25 per hour), sailboats (Sunfish $4 per hour, prams $1.25 per hour), fishing (bass lake free, $2.50 per half day for trout, bream), skeet and trap shooting, tennis (8 courts, $2 per person per hour, videotape, pro shop), horseback riding (with instructions $5.50 per hour, guided trail riding $5.50 per hour), golf (2 putting greens, practice range, 18-hole, 71-par course designed by George W. Cobb, $8 per day, golf carts extra); nearby: ruby mining, antique shops, square dancing, snow skiing, Nanahalla river rafting, waterskiing.

Sightseeing: Whiteside Mountain, the Nanahalla River and scenery, scenery, scenery.

P.S. Busiest in summer, especially with children; best for fall foliage second week in October, but book ahead.

P.P.S. Names of guests are posted daily; if you don't want anyone to know you're there, or who you are, better let the manager know as soon as you arrive.

For more suggestions in this area
turn to Added Attractions, page 375.

From the Carolinas to the Keys

What men call gallantry, and gods adultery,
Is much more common where the climate's sultry . . .

BYRON

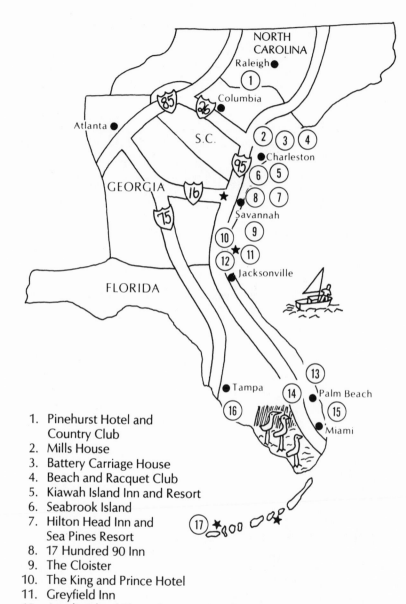

1. Pinehurst Hotel and
   Country Club
2. Mills House
3. Battery Carriage House
4. Beach and Racquet Club
5. Kiawah Island Inn and Resort
6. Seabrook Island
7. Hilton Head Inn and
   Sea Pines Resort
8. 17 Hundred 90 Inn
9. The Cloister
10. The King and Prince Hotel
11. Greyfield Inn
12. Amelia Island Plantation
13. The Breakers
14. Palm Beach Polo and
    Country Club

15. Boca Raton Hotel and Club
16. Far Horizons
17. Pier House
★ *Added Attractions*

PINEHURST HOTEL AND COUNTRY CLUB
Pinehurst, N.C.

$$

Smack in the middle of the Tar Heel State there's this little New England village, where azaleas, dogwoods, and camellias bloom amid holly and long-needle pines, where well-heeled young sports enthusiasts bound out of bed in the crisp clear morning air to play golf, swim, sail, play more golf, shoot skeet, fish, then play more golf. Or tennis.

Pinehurst is a hotel, cuddled into a town, surrounded by a country club, in the middle of a forest, on top of a hill, in the heart of North Carolina farm country. It's an enclave first developed more than eighty years ago by a Boston soda-fountain manufacturer named Tufts, as a place for the idle rich to while away their time when it was too late for New Hampshire, too early for Palm Beach. Tufts's frail health responded well to the balmy climate of the Carolina Sandhills, particularly when he found he could buy five thousand acres for about $5000. He called in the firm of Frederick Law Olmsted (the same Olmsted who laid out New York's Central Park and Washington's Mall) and together they laid out the land and planted their trees exactly where they wanted them to be; then Tufts called in a Scot named Donald Ross to design a golf course or two, and he laid out four—all teeing off from and chipping back to the same sprawling clubhouse. If you've heard of Pinehurst, chances are it was a golf nut who told you about it.

New owners plan to go a stage, maybe two stages, further: more condominiums, more golf, more tennis. They've refurbished the spacious, stately old hotel (formerly the Carolina, now the Pinehurst), and installed a complete health club with masseur-masseuse team to keep you trim. The gun club, which once boasted Annie Oakley, of *Annie Get Your Gun* fame, as an instructor now hosts a dozen skeet and trap tournaments every year. The result is one of the liveliest, friendliest, snappiest resorts on the East Coast, doing booming business in golf packages and videotape tennis clinics with Aussie pros.

But is it romantic? Not exactly, but it is peaceful, stylish, *invigorating;* and even with all the activity, Pinehurst has lots of quiet spots hidden away on its thirteen thousand acres of pine and sycamore, where you can escape, hand-in-hand or bike-by-bike, among the azaleas and dogwoods and camellias.

L.E.B.

Name: Pinehurst Hotel and Country Club
Manager: Marcus Fields
Address: P.O. Box 400, Pinehurst, N.C. 28374
Directions: By car, from U.S. 1 west on State Highway 2 at Southern Pines; by air, Piedmont can fly you to Fayetteville (the closest major airport), Greensboro, or Raleigh/Durham, with connecting flights (Mid-South Airlines) to Moore County Airport, 5 miles from the hotel, or by limousine, a drive of approximately 1 hour. By Amtrak to Southern Pines.
Telephone: (919) 295–6811, toll free (800) 334–9560
Cable /Telex: None
Credit Cards: American Express, Diners, MasterCard, Visa
Rooms: 260 in the hotel, plus more than 250 golf-course villas.
Meals: Breakfast, lunch, and dinner (approx. $18 to $24 for 2) served, dining hours vary according to season; room service, more or less dining-room hours; jacket for dinner; live music and dinner dancing nightly.
Diversions: Outdoor and indoor pools, therapy pool, sauna, exercise rooms; archery, jogging, hiking, bicycling, trap and skeet shooting; tennis (20 courts, 4 lighted, $4 per hour, pro shop, clinics), golf (*six* 18-hole courses, $18–$25 per round), horseback riding ($10 per hour), sailing and canoeing ($5 per hour).
Sightseeing: Surrounding woodlands, the World Golf Hall of Fame.

HOLIDAY INN MILLS HOUSE
Charleston, S.C.

"Bathing rooms for gentlemen are fitted up in good style, convenient to the barber's pole . . . " wrote a local newspaper on the opening of Mills House in 1853; and it was probably such style and convenience that persuaded Robert E. Lee to establish his quarters there when he commanded the Charleston garrison. Now, 128 years and a $6-million facelift later, there are private bathing rooms for gentlemen *and* their ladies, fitted up in tiled and gleaming style, and hop-and-skip convenient to the canopied beds. What you have at the Mills House, in fact, is something unique—one of the oldest hotels in the country looking as if it were built yesterday. Which is more or less what happened.

A group of Charlestonians who were proud of their heritage (and few people are prouder of their heritage than Charlestonians) got together to buy the venerable but rather dilapidated Mills House. They planned to spend half a million dollars repainting it and install-ing private bathrooms. But the local fire department, proud of *its* heritage, said nix, it's a fire hazard. So the gallant group then decided to raze the innards and rebuild virtually from the ground up. The bill came to something like $6 million. But it was worth it—at least from the point of view of guests. Since 1979, Mills House has been, if you can believe it, part of the Holiday Inn chain. Still, if Robert E. Lee came clattering down Meeting Street today he'd recognize the old place—wrought-iron balconies, gas lamps, the elegant tripartite doors, a mansionlike lobby with a sweeping double staircase, a garden patio with a three-tiered fountain. He'd feel at home in the interior but he might not recognize the individual decorations—a Regency-styled zebra-wood table, Chinese Ming portraits, French clocks, Empire candleholders, a black lacquered Dutch bombe chest, and a pair of mirrors from a Viennese hunting lodge, all from the early nineteenth century. You even sign in on a marble-and-brass inkstand on a marble registration desk.

The room you check into is furnished in a style that suggests rather than re-creates the 1800s—canopied (but squeaky) beds in fabrics that match the drapes, leather Queen Anne wing chairs, footstools, silver and copper table lamps, and such modern touches as princess telephones, individual temperature controls, and color TV. All 240 rooms are attractive, but the eight pool-side rooms have french doors leading to little wrought-iron porches next to the pool. If you want the best in the house, ask for the Mary Boykin Chestnut Suite (if you can't remember that mouthful, it's the one on the fourth floor).

There are many beautiful things in the Mills House and one of the most beautiful is the Barbados Room, a forty-table dining room with small alcoves in mirrored arches just big enough for two, fresh flowers on the table, candles in brass candlesticks, pewter plates, ceiling fans, rattan chairs, and an overall atomosphere redolent of the Caribbean island that gives the room its name (another touch of heritage—many of the first settlers in Charleston came up from the islands). Even breakfast can be something special here: papaya lightly flavored with fresh lime juice, shrimp *pâté* and grits, waffles with creamed chicken, beaten biscuits, honey and muscadine jelly. The menu will introduce you to some of the dishes that distinguish Carolina cooking: oyster pie, Myrtlebank lump she-crabmeat cocktail, Charleston she-crab soup, *langouste* Calhoun (lobster, mushrooms, in cream and sherry sauce, served in the shell), roast duckling Carolina (with peaches and baked apple), Huguenot torte and strawberries Mills House (marinated in Grand Marnier and served with ice cream, cognac, and *crème* chantilly).

They've really created one of the country's prettiest restaurants here, which is hard luck on the staff because in a less beguiling setting the service probably wouldn't remind you of Joe's Corner Café. There is, for example, a surprisingly good wine list, but if you have any respect for good wine you'll order a humble Beaujolais rather than watch a superb burgundy being whirled and twirled and juggled like a drum major's baton. Fortunately, the Beaujolais happens to be rather good for the price.

CANDLELIGHT, WINE, MUSIC. Don't let the few failings in service put you off coming here. The Mills House would be worth visiting even in Gary, Indiana. As it is, it happens to be in one of the loveliest cities in the South—one of those places that people always want to call "a grand old lady." There's still enough of the aristocratic Charleston left to let you savor the atmosphere of the antebellum South. The promenade down by the waterfront, lined by more stately townhouses than you could raise a top hat to, is one of the most handsome cityscapes in America—particularly when the mist comes rolling in from Fort Sumter like candy floss. The Mills House will rent you a map and cassette recorder if you want to take a walking tour past the homes, Catfish Row (the one that inspired *Porgy and Bess*), and the restored Market. Around Easter you can take a tour through the interiors of half a dozen of these historic homes and gardens; some evenings also feature galas in the houses, with candlelight, wine, chamber music, or concerts of spirituals. Dinner in the Barbados Room, chamber music in the Nathaniel Russell House, love in the

Mary Boykin Chestnut Suite—that's not such a bad way to spend an evening anywhere.

Name: Holiday Inn Mills House Hotel
Manager: Charles Bridges
Address: Meeting and Queen streets, Charleston, S.C. 29401
Directions: By car, take the Meeting Street/Downtown Exit from Interstate 26, then follow Meeting to Queen; also, by scheduled air and Amtrak services to Charleston.
Telephone: (803) 577–2400
Cables/Telex: None
Credit Cards: American Express, Carte Blanche, Diners, Eurocard, Master-Card, Visa
Rooms: 215, 15 petite suites.
Meals: Breakfast 7:00–11:00, lunch 12:00–3:00, sandwiches 3:00–5:00, dinner 6:00–11:00 (approx. $50 for 2); room service 7:00 A.M. to 11:00 P.M.; jacket and tie at dinner; piano or combo in lounge, harp in dining room on selected evenings each week.
Diversions: Outdoor pool; harbor trips, bikes, horseback riding, boating nearby.
Sightseeing: Charleston: historic houses, Charleston Museum, The Confederate Museum, old Powder Museum, old Slave Mart Museum and Galleries, Hunley Museum, Charles Towne Landing Exposition, Middleton Place, Hampton Park, Cypress and Magnolia Gardens, the Dock Street Theater, the History Trail (walking tour), beaches, fishing piers, amusement parks.
P.S. Busiest months are March through May (that is, around Easter and when the gardens bloom and homes are open for tours), and now also during the Spoleto Festival.

BATTERY CARRIAGE HOUSE
Charleston, S.C.

$$

You're welcomed with a glass of sherry from a cut-glass decanter; you cuddle up in a canopy bed; breakfast is served, on a silver tray, in the wisteria arbor. Here's your chance to savor something of the gracious life-style of Old Charleston.

One of the glories of this city, hinted at in the paragraphs on the

Mills House, is the parade of imposing mansions and walled gardens facing the waterfront, and there can be few visitors without a secret longing to stay in one of them. Now you can. Well, almost. Frank Gay and his family live in hundred-year-old Battery Mansion, four floors of verandas, columns, and shutters rising to a mansard roof; the two-story Carriage House, in the quiet walled garden at the rear, has now been converted into an elegant guesthouse. Each of the ten rooms is decorated with historic Charleston wallpapers and draperies; furnished with Madison dressers, gilt mirrors, canopy beds, and other period pieces; then inducted into the twentieth century with dial-a-massage shower heads, FM radios, color TV, alarm clocks, room phones, air conditioning, concealed pullman kitchenettes, and refrigerators with complimentary soft drinks and wine. These are very elegant snuggeries—maybe too snug for some people, but then the intention is not to spend all your time indoors. Explore Charleston. Grab a pair of the "beaten-up old bikes" and go riding off through narrow alleys and streets to the historic sights. Frank Gay or one of his colleagues is always on hand with advice on what to see and where to dine.

On the other hand, after breakfast in the wisteria arbor, with the birds chirruping in the trees, the farthest you'll travel may be across the garden to the hammock slung between a pair of palm trees. That's gracious living, too.

Name: Battery Carriage House
Owner/Manager: Frank Gay
Address: 20 South Battery, Charleston, S.C. 29401
Directions: By car, take the Meeting Street/Downtown Exit from Interstate 26, then follow Meeting to the waterfront.
Telephone: (803) 723–9881
Cables/Telex: None
Credit Cards: American Express, MasterCard, Visa
Rooms: 10.
Diversions: Bicycles, tiny pool, walking.
Sightseeing: See "Mills House."
P.S. Busiest March through May and during Spoleto Festival.

KIAWAH ISLAND INN AND RESORT
Kiawah Island, S.C.

In a place with so many delights, where do you begin? With the Sandbar, maybe. It's a wall-less bar on top of the dunes, but it's been given a separate observation deck by the edge of the beach, and (a small point, but somehow typical of the care that has gone into Kiawah) an unusual countertop crafted ingeniously from driftwood, its crevasses filled with hundreds of tiny seashells and then covered with peekaboo plastic, at once practical and appropriate to the setting.

And what a setting! Kiawah Island is ten miles of virtually private beach, low sand dunes on the Atlantic side and low-lying marshland on the creek side, secluded, unspoiled, subtropical, the habitat of wild ponies and white-tailed deer, alligators and river otters. Since 1976, the alligators and otters have shared their swamps with eagles and birdies—on eighteen fairways of championship caliber, designed by Gary Player; its lagoons and dunes are now dotted with villas and townhouses, all in contemporary cedar-and-cypress styling, set among live oaks and palmettos.

The people who designed Kiawah (a company called Wallace, McHarg, Roberts & Todd) had a chance to polish and refine their concepts at Sea Pines and Amelia, a pair of plantations farther south, with the result that their third try, Kiawah, is one of the most beautiful resorts in the country. Its felicities of design seem to have been created not so much in harmony as in a spirit of camaraderie with its surroundings. The inn itself has deep porches front and rear, each with its quota of wicker rockers, and even the second-floor Topside Lounge has an open deck for guests who want to observe the dunes and ocean as they sip their juleps. The two dining rooms compete with each other in the charm of their decor: in the Jasmine Porch, bamboo shades, wood-bladed fans, hanging plants, and cane-back chairs with leaf-patterned cushions; the Charleston Gallery is an intimate candlelit salon, half a dozen tables for seven-course dinners.

Service and cuisine match the surroundings (the minted noisette of lamb was superb).

The guest rooms, in two three-story cedar-and-cypress wings, are spacious, restful, carefully color-coordinated, and decorated with framed charts of Charleston harbor and pen-and-ink drawings of Charleston landmarks or something equally appropriate. One flaw, though. You really have no alternative to the air conditioning—no louvers, no screens, no ventilators (I have the same reservation about the Jasmine Porch, a Caribbean-style room just crying out for a trade wind, and already equipped with fans and louvered screens). The solution may be to stay in one of the handsome villas or townhouses with screened porches (the Beach Townhouses are particularly attractive, but pricey); or come to Kiawah in fall or winter when you probably won't need air conditioning. But come anyway. Here's a place worth visiting.

Kiawah is Kuwaiti-owned, but the only hint of its ownership is a volume on Islamic culture, tucked away on a library shelf in the Topside Lounge, between Evelyn Waugh and Charles C. Colson; if this is what petrodollars can do, the average resort developer should be made to pump gasoline.

Name: Kiawah Island Inn and Resort
Manager: Henry A. Hickox
Address: Kiawah Island, S.C. 29455
Directions: Kiawah is 24 miles southeast of Charleston. By car, take Interstate 26 to U.S. 17S (about 7 miles), go left on State Highway 20, and follow the signs for 17 miles to Kiawah Island. By air, scheduled services to Charleston Airport (50 miles by limousine, $30 per couple each way); by Amtrak to Charleston.
Telephone: (803) 768–2121
Cables/Telex: 57–6422
Credit Cards: American Express, Carte Blanche, MasterCard, Visa
Rooms: 300, including 150 in the inn, the remainder in townhouses and villas.
Meals: Complimentary coffee in your room on request, breakfast 7:00–10:00, lunch 11:30–2:00, Sunday brunch 11:30–2:30, poolside lunches and snacks, dinner 6:00–10:30 (approx. $34 for 2 in the Jasmine Porch, $55 per couple for the 7-course dinner in the Charleston Gallery); room service; jacket required at dinner in the Jasmine Porch, jacket and tie in the Charleston Gallery; piano (quiet) in the dining room, combo (noisy) and dancing in the lounge upstairs; no liquor on Sundays.

Diversions: Freshwater pool, therapy pool, sauna, bridge, and backgammon; oceanfront pool (adults only); tennis (14 courts, 2 lighted, 2 all-weather, $8 per court per hour, pro shop, clinics), golf (18 holes designed by Gary Player, $10 a round, driving range, putting green), bicycles ($1.75 per hour). Hobie cats, Jeep safaris through maritime forests ($5–$10); horseback riding nearby.

Sightseeing: Kiawah Island beaches; seasonal events include the Antiques Symposium, The Great Kiawah Island Horse Race, and the Kiawah Cup tennis tournament; also see "Mills House."

P.S. Golf and tennis year round, with the best months late September to November (still warm enough to swim in October) and early March through April; some conventions. Special sports and honeymoon packages available.

SEABROOK ISLAND
Seabrook Island, S.C.

$$

You could almost jump across the creek that separates Kiawah from Seabrook (the islands), but the resorts are isolated from each other, hints of rooftops on a distant beach. At Seabrook, you register at the Reception Center, beside the paddock, before you check in, then through the main gates; there's no inn here, only a variety of condominiums and private homes, ensconced in lush semitropical foliage. It's quiet, secluded, very private. The best values for couples are the High Hammock Villas and Shadowwood Townhouses, clusters of two-story townhouses adjoining the golf course, where luxurious one-bedroom suites (equipped down to the very ironing board) cost $70 a night. Since they sleep four people, you could enjoy even better value if you took along a compatible couple. Villas H, I, L, O, and P of this group are close to boardwalk decks on top of the dunes—perfect spot for sunset watching. For $100 a day you get a dreamhouse—a Beach Club Villa, handsomely designed, handsomely furnished, handsomely located on the quietest part of Seabrook's 3½-mile beach, facing the North Edisto River and the shrimp boats. These Beach Club Villas have one to *three* bedrooms; if you wanted a bargain in this case you'd have to round up *two* compatible couples, but make sure *you* get the upstairs bedroom with the private sun-deck.

Seabrook is strictly a place for enjoying the open air—crabbing, searching for sand dollars, birdwatching, swimming, and turtle watching (Seabrook is the nesting ground of the great loggerhead turtle). The hub for socializing is the brand-new Island House, with cocktail lounge, grille, and elegant dining room ruled over by a chef who's a stickler for freshness, so you can never be quite sure what's on the menu; but chances are you'll be able to sample the local seafood hauled ashore on the boats you see going up and down the North Edisto River.

Name: Seabrook Island

Manager: (not available)

Address: P.O. Box 32099, Charleston, S.C. 29407

Directions: 23 miles southeast of Charleston; by car, Interstate 26 to U.S. 17, then follow the signs along State Highway 20; to U.S. 17, then follow the signs along State Highway 20; by Amtrak or air to Charleston ($20 per couple one-way by limousine).

Telephone: (803) 768–1000; out-of-state toll free (800) 845–5531

Cables/Telex: None

Credit Cards: American Express, Carte Blanche, Diners, MasterCard, Visa

Rooms: 275 in various formats in villas, townhouses, and beach houses.

Meals: Breakfast 7:00–11:00, lunch 12:00–2:00, dinner 7:00, 8:00, 9:00 (approx. $20 to $25 for 2); no room service; jackets in the evening; piped music in the dining room, occasional live music.

Diversions: Freshwater pool, walking trails, crabbing (gear available); tennis (7 fast-dry courts, $2.50 per person per hour, pro shop, ball machines, practice areas, clinics), golf (18 holes, $10 per round), bicycles ($1 per hour, $5 per day), Hobie monocats for rent, horseback riding (trail rides $7, sunset rides, sunrise rides, jump trails available but only with proper garb).

Sightseeing: See "Kiawah Island Inn and Resort and Holiday Inn Mills House."

P.S. Some honeymoon and sports packages available, check with hotel for details.

BEACH AND RACQUET CLUB
Isle of Palms, S.C.

$$

This is the newest of the barrier island resort communities, opened in 1978 and still abuilding (although you probably won't suffer any inconvenience). The Isle of Palms is located just 15 miles northeast of Charleston, in the opposite direction from Kiawah and Seabrook (above). The Club is smaller than either, less commercial than Hilton Head, and, being the newest, has managed to avoid most of the pitfalls of the others. It covers an area of 1,500 acres, natural land-scapes of unspoiled marshlands and lagoons, interspersed with live oak and loblolly pine, and fringed by 2½ miles of dune and sand.

There are no crowds here, but if the sight of even another couple is an intrusion, simply walk north along the beach to the tip of the island, where you and the seagulls have the world all to yourselves. Well, almost to yourselves. You may spot a golfer or two, because owners Henry and Raymon Finch set aside some of the most valuable acreage to fashion two of the most beautiful oceanside fairways in golfdom. The Wild Dunes, as the course is known, is distinguished by many holes that look and play like a Scottish seaside links. But the climate is better.

In addition to golf, the Club's sports facilities include a palm-encircled pool and sundeck and sauna. A complex of tennis courts is arranged in clusters of two, private among the trees. You can go riding off on rental bikes along nature trails, or across the hard-packed sand, if you want to give your thighs a real work-out.

Accommodations are in condominium cottages and villas, all tastefully decorated and equipped for elegantly casual living—king-size beds, full kitchen with washer and dryer, balcony, television, and louvers and screens to take advantage of the Atlantic breezes. Fabrics are muted earth tones and subtle pastels, furniture is wicker and rattan, the feel is deluxe. There are rooms and suites among the woods and facing marsh, lagoons, or fairways, but the most romantic are probably the Sea Grove Villas, among the dunes, just a few steps from the beach. Ask for the top floor. You'll see more of the ocean.

The Club's new restaurant was still under construction during our inspection tour, but the cuisine served in the interim dining room could hold its own with the finest restaurants in Charleston. Service throughout the resort was relaxed, friendly, and efficient—maybe because the owners themselves live on the estate. Presumably to be closer to their Wild Dunes fairways. After all, if you're going to use the best plots for fairways rather than income you might as well take advantage of them as often as possible.

Name: Beach and Racquet Club
Manager: Wallace Street
Address: P.O. Box Y, Isle of Palms, S.C. 29451
Directions: 12 miles northeast of Charleston, via Sullivans Island.
Telephone: (803) 886–6000 or toll free (800) 845–8880
Cables/Telex: None
Credit Cards: American Express, Diners, MasterCard, Visa
Rooms: 150, in groups of villas and cottages.
Meals: Breakfast 8:30–10:30, lunch 11:30–2:30, dinner 6:00–9:00 (approx. $30 for two); no room service; informal, jackets optional in the evening
Diversions: Beach, 25-meter pool, surfcasting, crabbing, shrimping; tennis (14 courts, some lighted, pro shop), golf (18 holes), bicycles, fishing, boat trips, sauna.
Sightseeing: See "Mills House."
P.S. Least crowded in the fall and winter; some seminars (up to 120) but housed and assembled in a separate part of the estate.

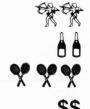

HILTON HEAD INN AND SEA PINES RESORT
Hilton Head Island, S.C.

$$

Not Conrad—William. William Hilton was the English sea captain who discovered the island back in the 1600s. At one time it was all plantations, forty-five square miles of rice and cotton and loblolly pines; now Hilton Head is pine-to-pine resort, with golf courses by the dozen and tennis courts by the score.

The Sea Pines Plantation company started the fashion a decade ago, and the most popular corner of the island is still this 5,200-acre

resort community, the entire southern tip of Hilton Head, surrounded by four miles of white beach, crisscrossed by marshes and
lagoons, looking and feeling appropriately semitropical under palmetto and bamboo and live oaks with mossy whiskers. There are
hammocks under the trees, boardwalks across the marshes, environ-
mental beach walks and a 572-acre forest preserve that's home to a
gallimaufry of winged creatures—hawks, eagles, quail, dove, and
ibis.

SPORTS GALORE. Jack Nicklaus designed one of the plantation's three
courses, Arnold Palmer designed another, and the Harbour Town
links has been called "one of the ten greatest tests of golfing skill in
the world" by a leading golf magazine. There are more than four
dozen tennis courts within the plantation alone and a local resident,
Stan Smith, is the touring pro. You can go riding, hiking, swimming,
crabbing, shrimping, or sailing, and there are no fewer than four
hundred bikes available for rent. Not many resorts can offer you such
an abundance of facilities, but probably even fewer dangle so many
types of accommodations before your eyes.

First, the inn. The Hilton Head was the first hotel on the island
(in the early sixties), but it's been enlarged and remodeled in recent
years; some of the two-story brick-and-cypress wings have sprouted
an extra story, and the main lodge has a new Crow's Nest Lounge
with crow's-nest views of the beach and ocean. The inn's 204 guest
rooms (new and original) have been decked out with beachy colors
and contemporary paintings and prints, but they also have several
practical attractions. For a start, they're more spacious than normal,
with separate dressing areas and bathrooms, a balcony or patio with
chairs and occasional table for breakfast alfresco; other features include coffee makers, wet bars, and in most cases refrigerators. Add a
sitting room to these standard features and you have a Cottage Suite,
most of them secluded among the foliage, a shade more private than
the regular rooms. The inn is right at the entrance to the plantation
proper, a short ride by bike or free shuttle bus from the main
plantation activities.

If you prefer to be closer to these activities, rent a room, suite,
townhouse, or villa inside the plantation. There are a thousand or
more options, all built within the past decade, finished in cedar and
cypress to blend with their surroundings, most of them equipped

with kitchens, wet bars, refrigerators, television, the larger suites and villas with dishwashers, dryers, and other frills. Probably the most romantic of the plantation accommodations are the circular "tree houses" among the pine trees. Tennis players seem to prefer the Heritage Villas, adjoining the Racquet Club (the courts where, apparently, everyone wants to play, although they are the most expensive on the resort). If you're looking for a lively pseudo-Portofino atmosphere, check into an apartment at Harbour Town, a circular harbor inspired by Mediterranean fishing villages, with half a dozen restaurants, outdoor cafés, and boutiques in chic colors— ivory, taupe, and salmon, to name a few.

Our preference would be the section known as South Beach, a secluded self-contained nouveau hamlet at the very tip of the island, Calibogue Sound and beaches on one side, a placid cove on the other with marina, dockside Italian restaurant and a tavern in Nantucket style. All rather confusing, isn't it? Then just check into the inn (you have access to all the other facilities, and you can charge bills to your room), or write to Sea Pines Plantation for the brochure describing all the types of accommodations—sixteen categories in the plantation, five in the inn alone. Even Hilton can't beat that—Conrad, not William.

Name: Hilton Head Inn and Sea Pines Resort
Manager: (Not available)
Address: Sea Pines Resort, Hilton Head Island, S.C. 29928
Directions: The inn is 31 miles from Savannah, 95 from Charleston. By car, take U.S. 278, then go east and follow the Hilton Head signs (once you cross the bridge you still have another 10 miles to go); continue to Sea Pines Circle, go left to Coligny Circle, then go right; by air, scheduled service to Savannah, then limousine or air taxi service to the Island Airport; by Amtrak to Savannah.
Telephone: (803) 785–5111, toll free (800) 845–6131, in S. C. (800) 922–7042
Cables/Telex: 804737
Credit Cards: American Express, Barclaycard, Carte Blanche, Diners, MasterCard, Visa
Rooms: 202, including 28 cottage suites (and the thousand-plus rooms, studios, and villas at Sea Pines Plantation).
Meals: Breakfast 7:00–11:00, lunch 12:00–2:00, dinner 6:30–11:00 (approx. $25 to $30 for 2), sandwiches during the day in the Crow's Nest Lounge, other restaurants in Sea Pines Plantation; room service 7:00 A.M. to 10

P.M.; jackets required in main dining room (reservations necessary), combo and dancing in 2 lounges; no liquor on Sundays.

Diversions: Three outdoor and indoor freshwater pools, putting green at inn; in the Plantation: sauna and exercise rooms, horseback riding, hiking trails, sailing school (spring through fall); tennis (72 courts at several locations, some lighted, $10–$12 per court per hour, pros, ball machines, videotape, clinics), golf (3 18-hole courses, $18 to $22 per round, additional surcharge for play on famous Harbour Town Golf Links), 400 bicycles for rent.

Sightseeing: Savannah.

P.S. Open all year, busiest Easter, July, and August, but you can play golf, tennis, and other sports at any time of the year; check for conventions.

17 HUNDRED 90 INN
Savannah, Ga.

$$

That was the year the foundations were laid, and it's right in the heart of Savannah's revitalized historical district, but as an inn it's only a few years old. Its clapboard-and-brick walls rise three stories above the brick sidewalk and its outside staircases, in the style of Old Savannah, lead you up to a plant-filled second-floor hall. No formal lobby here—it's more like the entry to an elegant home. It all fits in nicely with German owner Chris Jurgensen's aim: southern hospitality with European flair. Hence the little extras. Fresh flowers, a bottle of wine, wineglasses (and corkscrew) await your arrival, and when you switch on your room light the gas fireplace comes on automatically for a twice-cozy welcome; while you're having dinner, the chambermaid turns down your bed and places mints on your pillows; in the morning, a white-jacketed waiter serves you breakfast (and a newspaper) in bed. And if you let the owner know in advance when you're arriving he'll even send his limousine to the airport to sweep you into town. It all adds up to something close to grand hotel service in a country inn ambiance. There are only fourteen rooms, decorated in the style of a specific salon in a historic Savannah home—mostly in Federal or Regency style, with appropriate antiques and fabrics or wallpapers from the Scalamandre Savannah Collection. Television sets (nineteen-inch, cablevision) are tucked away in armoires, and the big brass beds are polished only once a month so that they don't look *too* glossy and new. All the rooms are air conditioned and bathrooms come equipped with shower-head massagers. If you have a choice, opt for one of the corner rooms. Ten of the guest rooms are located over the restaurant, which in this case is unlikely to be a problem since you'll most likely be dining there yourselves. It's considered to be one of the finest in the city, and its original beams and skylights and hanging planters make an elegant backdrop for sipping Bordeaux and tucking away some of chef Gregor Kummer's specialties: poached flounder Tybee (with herbs, local shrimp, and oysters), perhaps, or filet of red snapper Parisienne (dipped in egg batter and lightly sautéed). With so much cosseting you may forget to get out and see the historic sights of nineteenth-century Savannah.

Name: 17 Hundred 90 Inn
Owner/Manager: Chris Jurgensen; Jim Cavanagh, innkeeper
Address: 307 East President Street, Savannah, Ga. 31405.
Directions: By car, U.S. 80 will take you to President Street from Interstate 95, while I–16 from the west will drop you off a few blocks away; by air to Savannah Airport, 8 miles from the town center.
Telephone: (912) 236–7122
Cables/Telex: None
Credit Cards: American Express, Carte Blanche, Diners, MasterCard, Visa
Rooms: 14, plus 3 suites in an adjoining building.
Meals: Breakfast 7:30–9:30 (on the house, served in your room), lunch 12:00–2:00 weekdays, dinner 6:00–11:00, except Sunday (approx. $30 for 2); jackets requested; limited room service; Sunday dry day (at least officially); background music in lounge and dining room.
Diversions: None on the premises; tennis, golf, beach, horseback riding, water sports nearby.
Sightseeing: Savannah's Historic District, right on the doorstep—early nineteenth-century homes, museums, forts, shops, restaurants.
P.S. Children not encouraged in inn, not allowed in dining room; some tour groups (maximum 30).

THE CLOISTER

Sea Island, Ga.

$$$

You should really arrive at the Cloister in a shiny surrey topped by a tasseled fringe and pulled by a pair of frisky white horses. This is the quintessential plantation South, a dreamy other-worldly Eden where the Spanish moss dangling from the live oaks sets the pace for the whole island. The relaxed atmosphere begins at the main lodge, with its patios and plashing fountains, and wafts across manicured lawns to the five miles of superb private beach and twelve thousand acres of unspoiled dunes, forests, and marshes. If you're on your first visit you'll be welcomed as someone they'd like to see back again; and the thousands who do come back year after year are welcomed with an enthusiasm that goes beyond fine old southern hospitality. There's a very special ambiance about The Cloister, closer to a country club than a hotel, closer to a country home than a club; credit the old-fashioned ideas of the owners.

KEEPING BEHIND WITH THE JONESES. A remarkable family with an unremarkable name, Jones, has owned The Cloister since 1928. They're a bit behind the times: they plow all their profits back into the hotel; they've expanded slowly because they never build an additional room until they have the cash in the kitty, and until they've had a chance to train extra staff and inculcate them with the special Cloister brand of service; and while other resorts point merrily to their new rooms and condominiums, the Joneses haven't cluttered their plantation with subdivisions. It may sound like a funny way to run a hotel these days, but what the Joneses and their staff have created is one of the three or four finest resorts along the Atlantic Coast. Maybe *the* finest.

In many ways The Cloister is a perfect resort: it's detached from the everyday world, yet it's accessible; it basks in a delightful climate the year round; it's immaculate (the staff takes tremendous pride in the place—like old family retainers rather than employees); it's well-

groomed outside (the hotel employs fifteen gardeners and a hundred groundsmen, and even the lamps that light the trees at night are disguised as lily pads); because of its unspoiled acres you have a marvelous sense of freedom, of quiet spaces where you can wander off and do your own thing; it's restrained and soft-spoken, but far from stuffy (when New Year's Eve in 1972 fell on a Sunday, a day on which Georgia law forbids the sale of liquor, The Cloister celebrated the Hong Kong New Year, twenty-four hours early, and then topped off the shindig with a pantry raid in the wee dry hours of Sunday morning).

DINING IN, OUT, ON THE BEACH. The Cloister mollycoddles you when it comes to dining. Where would you like to have breakfast? On your patio (with linen tablecloth), in the dining room, at the beach club— or a late breakfast in the Solarium with its two huge cages of parakeets and finches? Lunch? Dining room, beach club, golf clubs—or a picnic in a quiet grove screened by Spanish moss. Afternoon tea? In the Solarium. For dinner you can choose the dining room and the serenading of a string orchestra (it's a huge Y-shaped dining room so the music won't overwhelm the meal), or you can join an oyster roast on the beach. Best of all, call room service and have the waiter bring your dinner over by bicycle; then, if you're staying in a beachfront villa, you can finish your bottle of Pouilly-Fuisse on the balcony, the air soft and balmy, the palms riffling in the breeze and a full moon shimmering on the surf.

The beachfront villas are the first rooms to be filled (the other seventy-two rooms are in cottages or the main building), but spend a few days at The Cloister even if you have to take a chauffeur's room. And even if you have to arrive in a newfangled horseless carriage.

Name: The Cloister

Owner/Manager: Ted Wright

Address: Sea Island, Ga. 31561

Directions: By car, via Interstate 95 and U.S. 17 from the north or south, via U.S. 25/84/341 from the west, then join the causeway at Brunswick (about 10 miles from Sea Island). By air, scheduled services to Brunswick, Savannah, or Jacksonville (75 miles); by Amtrak to Jesup (49 miles); limousine service from airports or station.

Telephone: (912) 638–3611; out of state toll free (800) 841–3223; in Georgia (800) 342–6874

Cables/Telex: None

Credit Cards: None

Rooms: 264, 100 suites in a dozen buildings (plus luxurious private homes, available for rent by the week).

Meals: Breakfast 8:00–9:30 (to 10:00 Sundays), lunch 12:00–2:00 (to 4:00 at golf club), dinner 7:00–8:30; room service during meal hours; jacket for breakfast and lunch, jacket and tie for dinner (in the dining room); combo and dancing in the dining room, harp concerts and other recitals.

Diversions: 2 outdoor pools, beach club, hiking trails, skeet, miniature golf, lawn bowling; tennis (18 courts, no lights, $10 per court per hour, pro shop, clinics), golf (three 18-hole courses, $14 per day), horseback riding ($6.50 first hour), bicycles, windsurfers, and sailboats for rent (April to November).

Sightseeing: 12,000 acres of island splendor.

P.S. Peak seasons are spring and fall, quietest is winter (except for Christmas and New Year); some conventions in winter. Special packages available.

THE KING AND PRINCE HOTEL
St. Simons Island, Ga.

$$

This Spanish *palacio*, by the edge of a splendid beach on the largest of Georgia's Golden Isles, opened its doors in a classic feat of bad timing, on July 4, 1941. It didn't get into its stride until after the war, when it became one of the traditional spots for vacations in these parts; now it seems to be holding its own under yet another round of new ownership and management. Most of the gracious atmosphere has been retained (in some cases by popular demand—when central heating and air conditioning were installed, regular guests insisted that the old blade fans be retained, which they have, even if some of them no longer work). The Sidney Lanier Room is still a sunny, elegant lounge with Queen Anne and Chinese Chippendale furniture, the patios have been replanted with oleanders and azaleas; the dining room would still be a pleasant experience surrounded by the stained glass of the Delagal Room, were it not for nightly performances by an electronic keyboard contraption. A covered walkway has been converted into eight cabana suites with sunken living rooms and entrances directly onto the beach. These are the most attractive (and expensive) accommodations. The remaining eighty-odd rooms are spread over three floors, all with private bathrooms, air conditioning, room phones, color TV, and those operative or inoperative ceiling fans. There's an unusual Bridal Tower (room 300), a pink-and-green circular room at the top of a spiral stairway, with a semiprivate entrance to the beach and an almost-360-degree panoramic view of the ocean. Even so, a prince and count rather than king and prince.

Name: The King and Prince Hotel
Manager: Richard Tucker
Address: 201 Arnold Road, St. Simons, Ga. 31522
Directions: By car, follow U.S. 17 or U.S. 341 to Brunswick, then the causeway to the island, then the tiny signs to the K&P; by air, to Brunswick (scheduled flights) or to McKinnon Field on the island.
Telephone: (912) 638-3631

Cables/Telex: None
Credit Cards: American Express, Diners, MasterCard
Rooms: 94, 4 suites (but you don't want to stay in a wing called Oglethorpe
    House).
Meals: Breakfast 8:00–10:00, lunch 12:00–2:00, dinner 6:30–9:30 (approx.
    $20 for 2); room service during dining-room hours; appropriate informal
    dress ("no jeans or tennis shoes"); piped music or live music in the
    Frederica Tavern and dining room. No liquor on Sunday.
Diversions: Outdoor freshwater pool, beach; tennis (3 courts, no lights); golf,
    horseback riding nearby.
Sightseeing: Fort Frederica National Monument, Retreat Plantation, St.
    Simons Lighthouse and Museum, Christ Church, and beaches all
    around.
P.S. Open all year and a welcome break in winter if there are no conventions
    in the house. May through August are the busy months.

GREYFIELD INN
Cumberland Island, Ga.

$$$

Cumberland Island is not of this world. It exists somewhere between
Atlantis, Bali Hai, and the Garden of Eden, eighteen miles of wilder-
ness, of sea oats, marsh grass, forests of wizened live oaks, and
beaches a couple of hundred yards wide. Alligators wallow in the
marshes, wild boars snuffle around among the trees, and wild horses
canter through the fields, their manes flowing in the wind, like
pent-up poodles let off the leash in the park. The island's human
population is twelve; you can walk a hundred yards here, pick out a
sheltered dune, and slip out of your swimsuits without having to
crane your necks every five minutes. This is pure escapism. You can
reach Cumberland only by ferry or chartered plane. Fly over and
you'll get a bird's-eye view of the gray-green, gray-white island as you
come in to land. Your pilot circles the inn to alert the innkeeper that a
guest is arriving; you approach the vague landing strip, and hope the
boars will get out of the way before you land. A few minutes later,
Janet Ferguson comes jouncing along in a beat-up Jeep and jounces
you back along overgrown lanes, and across the dunes to the inn.
    If Greyfield didn't exist, Tennessee Williams or Somerset

Maugham would have invented it: a slightly decaying, peeling, three-story plantation mansion in a grove of live oaks, with a flight of stairs rising from the hitching posts up to the veranda. There's a spooky quality to the garden, and inside, the inn is creaky and ancestral.

Guests are welcomed in a parlor brimming with family clutter—ivory-inlaid chairs, rolltop desks, a shell collection, silver candlesticks, bulky scrapbooks with yellowed curling pages. But these are no ordinary family heirlooms: it's a Carnegie silver pot your tea is poured from, and it's a Carnegie sofa you're sitting on.

Greyfield was built in 1902 for Margaret Carnegie Ricketson, daughter of Thomas Carnegie, brother and partner of Andrew, and it's been in the family ever since. In 1966, Lucy Ferguson, the current head of the clan and granddaughter of Thomas (you may meet her, and she has some tales to tell), decided to invite paying guests from their wide circle of friends. It's still pretty much a family affair, but they now take in a few guests from beyond their immediate circle. In fact, you may be asked to send references with your reservation. Send them; Greyfield is worth a ten-page résumé. There's nothing like this anywhere else along the entire coast.

Only one of the rooms has a private bath. There's no television, no pool, no tennis court, no golf. Not even a bartender; when you want a drink you go and mix it yourself, and pay for it on the honor system.

You dine family style off the Carnegie mahogany table. The meals don't try to be gourmet; the kitchen makes do with what's around the island—oysters, clams, mullet, flounder, shrimp, occasionally roast lamb or roast beef. Before dinner, retire to the snug library and skim through a volume from the collected works of Abraham Lincoln; after dinner, sip a nightcap out on the veranda beneath the moon.

It's strictly a back-to-nature existence on Cumberland Island. Digging for clams. Building sand castles. Kicking the surf at each other. Swimming, sunning, shelling, surfing. Riding in a one-horse shay. But on an island as serene as this, lovers don't need prompting; they know what to do, and they have all the time in the world to do it.

Maybe.

"Cumberland Island is the nation's foremost example of an

unspoiled wilderness island," said Georgia's governor, with the best of intentions. All the property on the island is owned by only a few families, and when one landowner tried to sell off some lots, the state stepped in and had the island declared a National Seashore. Now 75 percent of Cumberland Island is owned by the National Parks Service, which plans to preserve the nation's foremost example of an unspoiled wilderness island by introducing ferry services for an anticipated ten thousand beer-can-tossing trippers *a day* ("currently three hundred a day and that's bad enough," sigh Cumberland Island fans). The only people allowed to stay overnight on the island will be campers, and Greyfield, as an inn, may join the other Carnegies as a pleasant memory. Hurry.

Name: Greyfield Inn
Manager: Peggy Nix
Address: Drawer B, Fernandina Beach,Fla. 32034
Directions: On Cumberland Island, Ga., a few miles offshore; get there by catching the Greyfield ferry, The R. W. Ferguson, at Fernandina Beach, Fla.; by private boat to private dock (inn guests only; $25 fee); by charter plane or helicopter from Golden Isles Aviation, St. Simons Island; or Jax Helicopter service in Jacksonville, Fla.
Telephone: (904) 261-6408
Cables/Telex: None
Credit Cards: MasterCard, Visa
Rooms: 9 plus 1 cottage.
Meals: Breakfast 8:30–9:30, picnic-style lunch, hors d'oeuvres (at the bar, on the house) 6:00, dinner at 8:00; no room service; dress at dinner "from sports coats to jacket and tie, dresses for ladies, but no blue jeans."
Diversions: Beach, dunes, croquet, shelling, tours of mansions and graveyards, fishing, biking, hiking.
Sightseeing: Cumberland Island.
P.S. Spring and fall are the best times to be there.

For detailed rate, turn to page 413.

AMELIA ISLAND PLANTATION
Amelia Island, Fla.

The plan here is to check into a Pool Villa. In the morning, you step from bed, tiptoe across the wall-to-wall, push aside the glass doors, and plop into a private pool. Forget about swimsuits; palmettos and sabal screen you from the marsh and the wild ducks and ospreys. After your wake-up dip, you can breakfast *au naturel* on your private screened patio; there's no room service here, but you have a complete kitchen at your disposal. If you'd prefer to wake up to glistening vistas of dunes and ocean, check into one of the inn rooms. These would be attractive love nests even if they were looking into the parking lot: contemporary colors and paintings, stylish resort furniture, four-bladed ceiling fans (and air conditioning), wet bar and refrigerator, separate dressing area and a bathroom *and* toilet, *plus* a sundeck or balcony with live seascapes beyond. You could also choose from hundreds of townhouses and villa suites, because Amelia Island Plantation, in case you haven't already guessed, is another of those planned communities that make an honorable effort to respect and enhance the environment. Wooden walkways weave through a sunken forest of live oak and laurel oak; observation decks stand watch at strategic locations so that you can admire the wildlife (half of the nine-hundred-acre plantation has been set aside for conservation). Step across the walkways to the beach and you can walk a mile or two in either direction without passing a building higher than the trees. (Unfortunately, not everyone in these parts has the same respect for the environment; the county allows motor vehicles on the beach, so you may share your morning jog with a camper truck or beat-up old Chevy. Fortunately, when the tide's out it's a wide, wide beach.)

BEAUTIFUL RACQUET PARK. One of the outstanding features of Amelia (its *raison d'être*, even, if you happen to be tennis players) is the beautiful Racquet Park run by All-American Sports and home to the Annual Women's Tennis Association Championships in April. Its nineteen composition courts are spaced in clusters of two or three among a grove of oak trees; the sunken center court with timber bleachers avoids the usual eyesore of tubular scaffolding; the club-house is designed in the contemporary cedar-and-cypress vogue, and it's all so pleasant you may just sit on its verandas all afternoon, watching the sun filter through the foliage. If you're here between September and May, you can polish up your game at one of the highly praised All-American clinics (one pro to every four students, working on each individual's existing game). There are special three-day programs for people who don't want to dedicate their annual vaca-tions to tennis, and court time is free, when available, for players enrolled in the clincs. *If* you're here from September through May, a word of warning: don't put in a hard day on the courts and then rush back to your Pool Villa before checking to see whether your pool is *heated*. Brrr.

Name: Amelia Island Plantation

Manager: James M. Rester

Address: Amelia Island, Fla. 32034

Directions: Take Interstate 95 to Ferandina Beach/Callahan Exit, go east on A1A and Amelia Island Parkway, a distance of 29 miles from Jackson-ville; by air to Jacksonville, where you can rent a National car and drop it off at the plantation without a drop charge (which works out less than limousine service).

Telephone: (904) 261–6161; toll-free outside Florida (800) 874–6878; in Flor-ida, (800) 342–6841

Cables/Telex: None

Credit Cards: American Express, Diners, MasterCard, Visa

Rooms: 24 in inn; plus 340 villas and townhouses.

Meals: Breakfast 7:00–11:00, lunch 11:30–2:30, dinner 6:30–10:30 (approx. $25 to $30 for 2), snacks at beach club, tennis centers, fast foods restaurant, golf clubhouse; room service in inn rooms only; jackets in the dining room in the evening; live music in the dining room, inn lobby, and lounge.

Diversions: Outdoor freshwater pool at beach club (plus a dozen other pools on plantation), sauna, steam, exercise room, therapy pool, 5 miles of walking trails (mostly boardwalk, including a sunken forest), hayrides, fishing in lagoon; bicycles ($1.50 per hour); tennis (19 composition, 3 lighted, $4 per person per hour, pro shop, videotape, ball machines, clinics run by All-American Sports Tennis Academy), golf (27 holes, Pete Dye design, $12 per round), horseback riding ($10 per hour, on trails or beach).

Sightseeing: Amelia Island.

P.S. Open all year, busiest in spring, rainiest in July; some groups at other times of the year. Special packages available.

THE BREAKERS
Palm Beach, Fla.

$$$

Walking into The Breakers' lobby you get something of the soul-soaring lift opera buffs get when they walk into the Met. All that marble. All those frescoes. All that gilt. All those glistening, glittering, scintillant chandeliers. It's enough to make you launch into a duet from *Tosca*.

Oddly enough, Tosca and Cavaradossi and other lovers from the realm of opera might feel at home here, because the architect commissioned to design The Breakers way back in the twenties got so carried away with its oceanside location that he decided that the only thing to do it justice would be an Italian palazzo. But what he finally put together was a pastiche of Italian palazzi: the twin towers and arches of the exterior were inspired by the Villa Medici in Rome (which is rather like saying the Washington Monument was inspired by the Campanile in the Piazza San Marco); the ornate ceiling in the Gold Room was copied from the Palazzo Ducale in Venice; the frescoes in the lobby are based on those in the Palazzo Carega in Genoa; and so on, marble column after marble gilt column and frescoed ceiling after frescoed gilt ceiling. It may not add up to a true palazzo but it certainly is quite a place to show off your latest Puccis.

FROM MANSE TO MANSION. The Breakers is, in fact, a memorial, built by the trustees of the Flagler estate and dedicated to the creator of the Flagler millions. Henry Morrison Flagler was a poor boy who figured there had to be a better way of life than his minister father could offer in Hopewell, New York; so at fourteen he left the family manse, went into business, and after a series of ups and downs joined forces with a man called John D. Rockefeller; together they formed a company that went on to prosper as the Standard Oil Company of

New Jersey. Many years and many, many millions later, Flagler built
railroads to the South that ultimately brought him to Palm Beach,
and with remarkable vision was able to foresee that that expanse of
swampland could become America's answer to Europe's Riviera.
Everywhere his railway went, Flagler built a hotel; in Palm Beach he
built two, both of which disappeared, but to commemorate the great
man, the Flaglers built The Breakers in 1926. It's still owned and
operated by the family.

How do you pass the charmed hours in surroundings of such
opulence? Slip into your beach Pucci and shuffle down to the small
but private beach. Or sample the hotel's beach club: sauna, massage,
and your choice of pools—outdoor saltwater, indoor freshwater.

In the evening, dress up and treat yourselves to a slap-up dinner
in the Rotunda—a great circular dining room reaching for the
heavens in a dome of glass above a gigantic Venetian chandelier, and
surrounded by mirrors, crystal, and frescoes that make most other
dining rooms look like pizza parlors. Unfortunately, it also makes
your guest room look barely one notch above a Howard Johnson, so
unless you are lucky enough to snare a room in the new five-story

wing at the rear, with sliding doors and small balconies overlooking the sea and the real breakers below, you may find yourselves spending most of your time parading through the public spaces, amidst all that marble, all those frescoes.

Name: The Breakers
Manager: Stayton D. Addison
Address: South County Road, Palm Beach, Fla. 33480
Directions: From Interstate 95 or U.S. 1 go east on Palm Beach Lakes Boulevard or Okeechobee Road; by air to Palm Beach (30 minutes away by limousine).
Telephone: (305) 655–6611
Cables/Telex: 80–3414
Credit Cards: Eurocard, MasterCard, Visa
Rooms: 600, including 42 suites.
Meals: Breakfast 7:00–10:00, continental breakfast 10:00–11:00, lunch 11:30–3:00, dinner 6:00 and 8:30 (expensive); room service 7:00 A.M. to 10:00 P.M.; jacket and tie at dinner; live music in Alcazar Lounge, dancing in the dining room.
Diversions: Indoor (freshwater) and outdoor (salt) pools, beach club, walking trails, lawn bowling, putting green, bicycles, movies, bingo, bridge, backgammon; tennis (14 courts, $4 per person per hour), golf (two 18-hole courses, 1 in the front garden, $15 per round, carts extra).
Sightseeing: The tony shops, the tony mansions, the Henry Morrison Flagler Museum, concerts, recitals and plays, jai alai, horse racing.
P.S. Open all year, a beehive of millionaires in winter, an even busier hive of name-tagged conventioneers (up to 900 at a time) in summer and fall; try to be there when you won't be outtipped or elbowed out.

PALM BEACH POLO
AND COUNTRY CLUB
West Palm Beach, Fla.

Sounds formidable, perhaps? Posh Palm Beach. The sport of maharajahs. Country club atmosphere. Yet the welcome here can be as friendly and personal as in a country inn.

The PBPCC is, of course, far from being a country inn. What it is, in fact, is another subdivision, with expensive condominiums and

homes spread over 1,650 acres; but what sets this one apart from all
the others is the charisma of polo. You've probably been to resorts
with *one* polo ground. Maybe even two. But here there are *nine*. Plus
stables for three hundred horses and quarters for their grooms. Plus a
grandstand *en fête* with flags and banners. Plus a handsome clubhouse in Spanish grandee style. Those stylish, tanned, well-heeled
couples at the next table own polo ponies by the stringful, play the
sport of princes and maharajahs (frequently bloodied and bandaged
princes and maharajahs) and come here from all over—Argentina,
Mexico, and the stately homes of England.

But even if you don't know a chukkar from a chappati you won't
be out of place here. Polo is only part of it. You can rent horses and go
cantering off into the estate's 120-acre cypress preserve. Plop into
one of the half-dozen swimming pools. Serve aces on any of fifteen
tennis courts (or, if the aces aren't there, take lessons from the
resident John Gardiner/Ken Rosewall pro). Play golf on eighteen
George Fazio fairways. Jog along miles of trails. Or drive into Palm
Beach for lunch at the Café de l'Europe.

The club is still in a relatively early stage of development (it
opened in 1980) and that may be why rates are so reasonable. You can
rent a studio here, with full kitchen, for the price of an average room
in an average hotel elsewhere; or for the price you'd pay for a regular
room at The Breakers, the club will give you a one-bedroom suite.
Ponies extra.

Name: Palm Beach Polo and Country Club
Manager: Richard Reichel
Address: 13198 Forest Hill Boulevard, Wellington, West Palm Beach, Fla.
   33411
Directions: It's 10 miles west of *West* Palm Beach, 15 west of Palm Beach and
   the ocean. By car, take Forest Hill Boulevard Exit from I–95, Florida's
   Turnpike or U.S. 441; by air, to Palm Beach.
Telephone: (305) 793–1113, toll free (800) 327–4204
Cables/Telex: 803489
Credit Cards: American Express, MasterCard, Visa
Rooms: 250, including studios and suites, in two "villages."
Meals: Breakfast 7:30–10:30, lunch 11:30–2:30, dinner 6:00–10:00 (any price
   range from $25 to $50 for 2); jackets for men; no room service (but the
   club can prestock the room refrigerators); live music and dancing in
   lounge or dining room on weekends.
Diversions: 6 heated swimming pools, whirlpool bath, walking and jogging

trails, croquet; tennis (15 Har-Tru courts, John Gardiner tennis clinics, pro shop, 9 lighted), golf (18 holes), horseback riding, sailing on 150-acre lake, hardball, racquetball, squash, and, of course, polo; water sports 15 miles away at Palm Beach.

P.S. January through April is polo season, for which reservations must be made far in advance; but the most attractive months are reputed to be May, June, October, November. Few conferences, never more than 80 participants.

BOCA RATON HOTEL AND CLUB
Boca Raton, Fla.

$$$$

The *Saturday Evening Post* once called this "Florida's flossiest hotel," and Frank Lloyd Wright called its architect "little more than a scenic designer." Both critics have gone, but the Boca Raton keeps getting bigger and bigger.

The original 1926 hotel had a hundred guest rooms built in the style of a cloister around formal gardens; in 1928 the inn was bought by a tycoon named Clarence H. Giest, who had a penchant for wandering through the lobby in his bathrobe, and who added three hundred more rooms; more recently another 257 rooms have been tacked on, in a twenty-six-story tower just east of the original cloister, on the edge of Lake Boca Raton, overlooking the Intracoastal Waterway; and now, winter 1980, a stunning new two hundred-room hotel, the Boca Beach Club, on the ocean (more about it later). The hotel is no longer a quiet little hideaway, flossy or otherwise, but it's still true to the original affluent concept.

Many of the original antiques are still there—priceless then, more priceless than ever now: the wooden beams and carved wall brackets from the University of Seville, a spendid refectory table, a massive seventeenth-century credenza and gold-embossed mirror from Spain, countless artifacts from country churches in Guatemala.

If its architect was little more than a scenic designer, the story of its creation was downright horse opera. Addison Mizner had come to Palm Beach in 1918 in failing health, planning to spend his few remaining weeks or months on earth in one of earth's balmier corners; there he encountered another invalid ready to breathe his last, Paris Singer, the son of the Singer who invented sewing machines. Singer was not only prepared to breathe his last but also to spend his last, and together they concocted plans for the ultimate pleasure domes. Since neither of them died as soon as expected, they went on to build some of their dream palaces and Mizner became the most demanded architect in Florida. The Boca Raton is one of the offshoots of this strange partnership. It was originally called the Cloister Inn, and when it opened on February 6, 1926, there was such a dazzling array of tycoons, movie stars, and royalty on the doorstep that the hotel still keeps the guest register of that auspicious evening under glass in the main lobby.

But never in their wildest dying dreams did Singer and Mizner conceive something like the present-day Boca Raton Hotel. When you come here to please yourselves in this pleasure dome, you'll find a thousand acres of semitropical paradise with secret places among the angel trumpet, creeping gif, gumbo limbo trees, monkey apple, golden dewdrop, Spanish bayonet, screw pine, and shaving-brush trees. This being a millionaires' resort, you have everything at your fingertips. Tennis? Twenty-two courts. Golf? Fifty-four holes. Sunning? A mile of beach and a cabana club. Bikes? Bikes. Fishing? Boats and tackle and bait. Polo? Every Sunday afternoon from January through April. Yachts? Several, from 16 feet to 102 feet. Restaurants? Eleven. Two of them are located in the newest unit of the Boca estate—the stunning new Boca Beach Club, beside the beach, across the waterway, and so special it really merits a listing its own.

THE NEW BOCA BEACH CLUB. You can cruise over to the new hotel aboard a gleaming mahogany-hulled launch called *Mizner's Dream*, tying up at a dock beside a columned and pillared extravaganza that looks like a set for a superspectacular *Aida*. Twenty-two million dollars went into its seven stories and two hundred rooms, and no expense or effort is being spared to make it the grandest hotel along the coast. Guests are preregistered, greeted by name at driveway level, escorted up to the lobby, offered a glass of champagne; meantime, their luggage is whisked up to the room and not until the bellboy calls down and says everything is in order are the guests escorted upstairs. Everything here is on a lavish scale: not one but two authentic Clefs d'Or concierges are available for guests' requests; in the oak-paneled library, even the card tables are leather-bound; terry robes hang in every bathroom; even the roofs of the lower levels are planted with flowers so that guests won't be obliged to look down on unsightly concrete.

So that you won't have to trot up and down to your room when you plan a day at the beach, the Boca people have installed 125 cabinettes, some with wet bars (the fact that they cost almost as much to rent as some of us want to spend on a room is beside the point). And since the hotel will be operated strictly as a club (local members and hotel guests only) you will never feel crowded.

The Club is definitely the place to stay in Boca Raton, even if you'll be paying the highest tab in the entire hotel; and you might as well go whole hog and check into one of the garden-level rooms with private lanais and direct access to the beach.

If you decide to stay in the "mainland" parts of the Boca, the Tower Twins and Tower Suites are quietest (but you're sealed into air-conditioned rooms). The most romantic guest chambers over here are the cloister rooms looking out on the flowers and fountains— anything numbered 201 to 217, 220 to 223, 226 to 228, 230 to 236. They have the authentic feel of the Boca Raton of the Twenties.

Name: Boca Raton Hotel and Club
Manager: R. Scott Morrison
Address: Boca Raton, Fla. 33432
Directions: On the Inland Waterway, 45 miles north of Miami, between Ocean Highway (A1A) and U.S. 1, and between Palmetto Park Road and Camino Real; by scheduled air service to Palm Beach or Fort Lauderdale, or by private/charter flight to Boca Raton Airport; limousine from Palm Beach or Fort Lauderdale by arrangement, $58 for up to 4 people.
Telephone: (305) 395–3000, toll free (800) 327–0101
Cables/Telex: 803936 BOCACLUB
Credit Cards: American Express, Barclaycard, Eurocard, MasterCard, Visa
Rooms: 900, including 46 suites and 60 apartments in 4 buildings.
Meals: Breakfast 7:00–11:00, lunch 11:30–2:30, dinner 6:45–10:30, room service to 2:00 A.M.; jackets for dinner (depending on which of 11 rooms); piano bar, 3 orchestras every night.
Diversions: Beach, 3 pools, therapy pool, sauna, exercise rooms, parcours jogging track, putting green, fishing, skeet shooting, bicycles; tennis (22 clay courts, 6 lighted, $5 per person per day, pro), golf (three

18-hole courses, $12 per day), cabana club on Atlantic (5 minutes from hotel) with ½-mile private beach, sailing, power yachts; additional tennis courts and golf courses at Boca West, a sister resort 20 minutes away.

Sightseeing: Everglades, jai alai, trotters, thoroughbred racing, dog racing, plus all the attractions of Palm Beach, Fort Lauderdale, and Miami.

P.S. Peak season from January 3 through Memorial Day, lots of conventions at other times in main hotel—no groups ever at new Boca Beach Club.

PIER HOUSE
Key West, Fla.

It's more or less on the spot where the old Havana ferry used to set sail for Cuba (some of the old dockside bollards can be spotted in the grounds), which places the Pier House right at the end of the Overseas Highway, in the heart of Old Key West, a shuffle away from Sloppy Joe's and other Hemingway haunts. The inn has just resurfaced after a $3 million overhaul, with new owners, new decor, new furnishings, new dining rooms and kitchens, and new plantings on its five end-of-the-line acres. The old spirit is still there—only more so.

The core of the inn is "the most unusual motel design in America," a sort of habitatlike structure of staggered rooflines, balconies, and "deckhouses," designed by famed Greek architect Yannis Antoniadis. Additional rooms are located around the patio and pool, but the prime nests are those right on the water, especially the suites on the upper floors—one of the duplexes, say, or, if you're lucky, the penthouse with sundecks fore and aft. The new decor is fresh as the hibiscus and bougainvillaea that tumble from every garden in town, and each room comes with refrigerator and color TV. Even if you can't snare one of the waterfront cabins, check in here anyway, because in a town like this—America's answer to the Grenadines— you're likely to be out and about, sightseeing and frolicking by day, socializing by night. Young ladies have been known to go topless on the inn's patch of relatively private beach, while other guests go whizzing off in Sunfishes or diving among the angelfish and coral. Old

Key West itself is a town worth trotting around in, but you can also whistle up a bicycle-rickshaw and do the town in style. (There's also a Disney-like Conch Train for hardcore sightseeing, if you can stomach the commentary.)

But no matter what you do by day, the first hint of sunset will probably find you back on the broad deck of the inn's Old Havana Dock Bar, sipping a rum concoction, watching the shrimp boats and sailboats, while the sun dips behind the offshore keys. It's the big event of the day in Old Key West.

Name: Pier House and Beach Club

Manager: (not available)

Address: One Duval Street, Key West, Fla. 33040

Directions: By car, keep driving until you run out of America; by air, from various points in Florida via Air Florida and Boston & Providence Airlines.

Telephone: (305) 294–9541, toll free (800) 327–8340, in Florida (800) 432–3414

Cables/Telex: None

Credit Cards: American Express, MasterCard, Visa

Rooms: 101 in 3 buildings.

Meals: Breakfast 7:00–11:00, lunch 11:00–5:00 (indoors and outdoors), dinner 7:00–11:00 (indoors/outdoors, approx. $30 to $35 for 2), informal; room service; live entertainment every night, in the Beach Bar or in the lounge.

Diversions: Small private beach, freshwater pool; nearby—tennis, water sports (living coral reef 2 miles offshore), sailing, parasailing.

Sightseeing: Old Town (Audubon House, Gingerbread House, Hemingway House, etc.), museums, shopping, offshore islands.

P.S. Pier House is as much a gathering place for the Conches (residents of Key West) as it is for visitors, so you must expect some hustle and bustle; and a walk-through during the renovation showed hints of amplified music-making indoors and out.

For more suggestions in this area
turn to Added Attractions, page 375.

FAR HORIZONS
Longboat Key, Fla.

$$$

The sign on the door says "Enter/Entrée," the manager comes from Paris. It's the only hotel in America serving Coteaux Champenois wines from the Champagne country of France, and one of the few resorts in America associated with France's prestigious Relais-Chateaux organization. In other words, Far Horizons is not a run-of-the-mill Florida resort. But you might never suspect this when you see its metallic blue-and-white awning and uninspired architecture. But step through that *entrée* and you'll notice the difference: the peppy tropical colors are accented with antiques—a *bureau de changier* here, an *escabot* there, *secretaires* and *commodes*, eighteenth-century Parisian clocks on the wall. In the chrome-and-wicker lounge, one entire wall is covered by a Sid Solomon triptych. Beyond the circular Miami-style bar, a pleasant terrace shaded by palms and banyan trees invites you to linger over lunch as you sip your Coteaux Champenois.

Most of the guest rooms are in bungalows dotted throughout the palm-and-sea grape beachside garden. Square and squat on the outside, the bungalows are bright and cheerful inside, each fitted out with kitchen, separate bedroom, pile carpeting, splashing fabrics, color TV, and air conditioning as well as jalousies and screens. The housekeeping is meticulous (when did you last see a chambermaid pick up a chair to dust the bottom of the legs?).

The most desirable accommodations are the Sunset Suites, on a pair of two-story wings right on the beach, with the surf curling around the base and balconies overhanging the sand—numbers 155/7, 255/7, 159/61, and 259/61, all corner locations. Of these, the crème de la crème is 155/7. It's a complete surprise in a location like this: wraparound windows and terrace, glass-and-chrome dining ensemble, separate contemporary-styled bedroom—and vitrines filled with authentic Aztec figurines. This suite is considered a sort of "owner's cabin." He's the reason for this somewhat hybrid hideaway (part fishing camp, part Caribbean resort, part *auberge*), a French industrialist, head of a conglomerate involved in everything from phosphates to champagne; when business took him and his executives to Tampa they used to stay at this resort (built in the fifties, one of the first on the Key). In the end, they decided just to buy the place and add some French accents.

Now, sitting on the terrace at lunch or on your own patio, you could easily think you're on a French island. Guadeloupe, maybe. Except when you look up at the high-rise condos on either side. Then it's more like San Juan. But, if you can ignore the high-rises, Far Horizons is probably the most interesting spot to stay on the Gulf Coast—for comfortable rooms, friendly service, fine dining, and a *soupçon* of *la belle France*.

Name: Far Horizons Beach Resort

Manager: Jean-Pierre Ledoux

Address: 2401 Gulf of Mexico Drive, Longboat Key, Fla. 33548

Directions: By car, take U.S. 41 to Sarasota, then Route 790 to Longboat Key (Far Horizons is near the southern end); by air, to Sarasota (limousine by arrangement).

Telephone: (813) 383–2441

Cables/Telex: 810–864–4361

Credit Cards: American Express, Barclaycard, Carte Blanche, Diners, Eurocard, MasterCard, Visa

Rooms: 61, including 8 suites, in main lodge and garden and beachside bungalows.

Meals: Breakfast 7:30–10:30, lunch 12:00–2:30, dinner 6:30–10:00 (approx. $30 to $35 for 2); jackets; room service during dining room hours; taped music in lobby/lounge, dinner-dancing on Friday.

Diversions: Beach (by the mile), heated spring-fed pool, tennis (2 courts, lighted); snorkeling, sailing (Sunfishes); golf 3 miles away.

Sightseeing: Sarasota (Ringling Mansion and Museum, Circus Museum, Asolo Theater, concerts, opera, recital, plays).

P.S. Best months—May, June, October, November; some seminars ("small, and no name tags").

From the Great Lakes to the Gulf

And when Love speaks, the voice of all the gods
Makes heaven drowsy with the harmony . . .
SHAKESPEARE

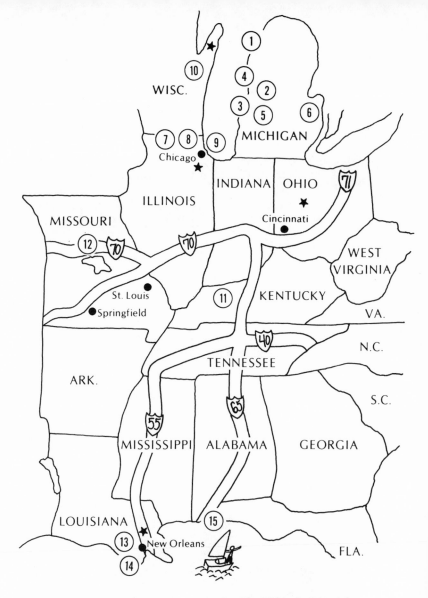

1. Grand Hotel (Mackinac Island)
2. Hilton Shanty Creek
3. The Homestead
4. Stafford's Bay View Inn
5. National House
6. Dearborn Inn Colonial Homes and Motor Houses
7. The Ritz Carlton
8. The Whitehall Hotel
9. The Tremont Hotel
10. The Pioneer Inn
11. The Inn at Pleasant Hill
12. Lodge of the Four Seasons
13. Hotel Maison de Ville and Audubon Cottage
14. The Saint Louis Hotel
15. Grand Hotel (Point Clear)
★   *Added Attractions*

GRAND HOTEL
Mackinac Island, Mich.

$$$

The Grand is grand in every way. It's the world's largest summer-only hotel, with the world's longest veranda overlooking one of the world's longest suspension bridges. It flies more than a dozen rippling flags, is bedecked with boxes and boxes of marigolds and geraniums, and is surrounded by more than twenty-five thousand flowering plants and groves of cedar. You can sleep beneath a teardrop chandelier in an outrageously spacious room, dine lavishly in a 250-foot mirrored ballroom with a view of the sparkling clear waters of Lake Huron, and enjoy the sort of service your great-aunt swore had disappeared.

Mackinac (pronounced Mackin-*aw* despite the final C) is America's Bermuda. A sparkling summer island ("open" mid-May to mid-October only), it's lush and hilly, dotted with bright white eighteenth- and nineteenth-century homes, a Revolutionary War fort, and remnants of John Jacob Astor's fur-trading operations.

It's accessible only by ferry or private plane, and transportation on Mackinac is *exclusively* by horse-drawn carriage or self-powered bicycle. When you arrive at the island you'll see your bags, and ten or twelve others, piled high on a bicycle basket to be skillfully pedaled up the hill to the hotel by a bright-eyed college student while you board a waiting phaeton to be driven there by a gallant top-hatted coachman. By day Mackinac is chock-a-block with day trippers buying moccasins and chocolate fudge (which seems to be the island's principal export item), taking pictures of the world's longest porch, and counting their traveler's checks to see if they can afford the Grand's magnificent ten-table buffet lunch. But come evening, when the hotel sends one of its liveried doormen halfway down the hill to enforce the "after six" dress rules, it's then the grandeur of the Grand emerges. The sun takes a long time to set on this little island at 46 degrees North Latitude, where evening breezes are cool and laden with the scent of flowers. You join the after-dinner strollers on the

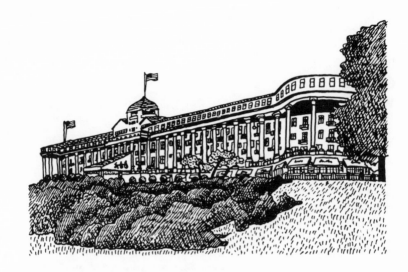

porch as violins and a delicate piano invite you to dance in the Terrace
Room. A carriage waits to take you on a sunset ride through the now
quiet village, or you may choose to travel in a Palm Beach rolling
chair or simply to sit and watch the stars come out from one of the
little benches on the sloping lawn. Later, you'll wander to the gaze-
bolike Grand Stand bar near the golf course, drawn there by the scent
of fresh-brewed espresso and the possibility of sampling a liqueur-
laced Grand Café. But there's no hurry as you stroll along, hand in
hand; you pause a moment to greet the spirit of Isabel Archer
returning from her evening walk with Phileas Fogg.

L.E.B.

Name: Grand Hotel
Manager: John M. Hulett III
Address: Mackinac Island, Mich. 49757 (from October to April, 222 Wiscon-
 sin Avenue, Lake Forest, Ill. 60045)
Directions: By ferry, as many as 70 a day in midsummer, between Mackinaw
 City and the island; private and charter flights can land at Mackinac
 Island Airport, but the nearest commercial airfield is at Pellston, Mich.,
 and from there you can take a limousine to connect with the ferries at
 Mackinaw City.
Telephone: (906) 847–3331; or (312) 234–6540 from October to April

Cables/Telex: None
Credit Cards: None
Rooms: 262, including 2 large suites, the Governor's and the President's.
Meals: Breakfast 8:00–9:45, buffet lunch 12:00–2:00, dinner 7:00–8:45; room service during meal hours, with snacks to 1:00 A.M.; "In accordance with Grand Hotel traditions, guests are requested to observe the following customs of dress: after six in the evening ladies are dressed in their loveliest for the enjoyment of many social activities; for gentlemen, sportswear and shirts with collars are most acceptable in all hotel areas during the daytime; after six in the evening neckties and jackets are required in all areas of the hotel. Leisure suits are permitted after six, but ties must be worn with such attire." Other entertainment besides dressing up includes piano bar, combos, dinner-dance orchestra, and occasional cabaret acts.
Diversions: Heated serpentine pool, sauna, bicycles; tennis (4 courts, $10 per court per hour), golf (9 holes, $6 per day) hiking, sailing, waterskiing, horseback riding, fishing nearby.
Sightseeing: Fort Mackinac, beaches, cliffs, summer homes.
P.S. Special "Fall Fling" packages available during October. Closed late October to mid-May.

HILTON SHANTY CREEK
Bellaire, Mich.

$$

Shanty Creek is sports. Golf, tennis, fishing, swimming, waterskiing, sailing, snowmobiling, canoeing, hunting, hiking, riding, boating, cycling, skeet shooting, mushroom hunting in the spring, berry picking in the summer, bowling, roller skating, badminton, croquet, horseshoes, volleyball and—some romance at last—dinner-dancing, sleigh rides, and saunas. You might call it a Caribbean resort and a Colorado ski area keeping company on a mountaintop in northern Michigan. And since the Hilton people took over a couple of years ago, it's all better than ever. They've invested millions in improving the grounds, adding golf clubhouses at the ninth and eighteenth greens, adding a downhill lift and new cross-country ski trails, and building an indoor swimming pool and whirlpool facilities.

Originally, in the 1950s, Shanty Creek and its 1,200-plus acres were paced off with the idea of creating a private club, an exclusive sports retreat for a select group of one hundred members. But inflation barked at the heels of the project; club became hotel and now chunks of the land are being sold as woodland home sites (with the result that suburban bungalows and pseudo-chalets are popping up like those spring mushrooms around the golf course and along the road to the trout pond).

As for the lodge itself, it's a handsome building with soaring cathedral ceilings and big picture windows that look out over the countryside. The rooms, unfortunately, are not exactly what you would call romantic. Spacious, yes, and newly and tastefully redecorated as part of the general refurbishing of the place, but sad to say the big sliding door picture windows and private balconies face the front drive or the swimming pool or a phalanx of rooms on the wing directly opposite or even the stares of curious day trippers on the ski lifts. You can always draw the drapes, of course. Better yet, opt for one of the rustic supermodern condominium units that will let you look out on the golf course or the ski slopes in privacy. The deluxe condominiums come with big private fireplaces, skylights upstairs over sunken bathtub and bedroom. Order in your meals from room service and you may never know there's anyone else around at all.

Even the standard rooms are quiet enough at night, when the skiers have all gone home and the entertainers have sung their last set in the lounge. With the moon coming over the mountain and the two of you in your perch nearly a thousand feet above Torch Lake, Shanty Creek turns romantic. It's time for sports again.

L.E.B.

Name: Hilton Shanty Creek
Manager: John Meeske
Address: Bellaire, Mich. 49615
Directions: Off Mich. 88, between Bellaire and Mancelona, and well signposted; from Interstate 75 take Grayling Exit and travel west on Mich. 72, north on County 571 to Mancelona (or, if arriving from the north, exit at Gaylord and follow County 42 west to 131 south to Mancelona); from Traverse City Airport, U.S. 31 northeast to Mich. 72, east to County 593, north along Torch Lake to County 620, east to Bellaire and from there south on 88 to the hotel. Phew!
Telephone: (616) 533–8621, toll free in Michigan (800) 632–7118

Cables/Telex: None
Credit Cards: American Express, Diners, MasterCard, Visa
Rooms: 123, including 17 lodge suites, 32 double rooms in the Windcliff
    Lodges.
Meals: Breakfast 7:30–11:00 (to 10:30 on Sunday), lunch 12:00–2:30 (to 3:00
    for Sunday brunch) dinner 6:00–9:00 weekdays, 6:00–10:00 Friday and
    Saturday (approx. $12 to $20 for 2); room service during meal hours,
    beverages and sandwiches available "most of the time"; "at the evening
    meal jackets for gentlemen are not required but are desired, dresses
    and pant suits are the desired attire for ladies"; live music and dancing
    nightly except Sunday in summer, mostly weekends in winter.
Diversions: Indoor swimming pool, whirlpool; beach or pool swimming,
    hiking; tennis (2 courts, $1 per person per hour), golf (9- and 18-hole
    courses, $10 per round), skeet shooting, bicycles; in winter, downhill
    and cross-country skiing, iceskating, snowmobiling, ice fishing.
Sightseeing: Scenic spots, occasional local events.

DEARBORN INN COLONIAL HOMES
AND MOTOR HOUSES
Dearborn, Mich.

$$

Rabbits hop round the corners of tidy Colonial cottages, gentlemen
read *The Wall Street Journal* in wing chairs in the lobby, and children
are dressed in starched pinafores and school blazers. The doors are
solid mahogany and the hand-painted wallpapers and bargellolike
carpets have lasted—and stayed bright—for more than forty years.
This is a gracious inn, created by a remarkable man.

Henry Ford I built the Dearborn Inn in 1931 for the conve-
nience of executives and dignitaries visiting Ford Motor Company.
Here he expressed his love for the elegance of Early American
Georgian architecture and decoration and, by reproducing the Colo-
nial homes of five famous Americans as additional accommodation
space, found another outlet for his penchant to preserve America's
historic buildings (best exemplified by his Greenfield Village across
from the inn).

But a hotel is only as good as its management, and Adrian de
Vogel (or "Dutch" as he is known to some) is a manager in the best

European tradition, having served with several of the world's finest hotels and passenger liners, prior to his twenty years at Dearborn. He's the one who *maintains* the graciousness and efficiency of the Dearborn Inn, who personally supervises the blending of every Colonial hue used in repainting and the subtle lighting that highlights the gracious decor. His menus are so American—in fact, so Michigan—you'd think the man in the front office came from Ann Arbor instead of Amsterdam.

Take any room available at Dearborn Inn (except those in the uninteresting Motor Houses), but try your darnedest to get one of the thirty-three rooms in the five Colonial Homes. They're charmers. You'll have a latch key to the front door and your room will be your own Colonial sitting room, with a mantelpiece, perhaps, a sofa or set of wing chairs and a reproduction of Oliver Wolcott's nightstand, Barbara Fritchie's fourposter, or a writing table like Edgar Allan Poe's. Unfortunately, you'll have a color TV anachronistically staring you in the face, but you'll have much more fun if you watch the frisky rabbits and squirrels out on the lawn.

L.E.B.

Name: Dearborn Inn Colonial Homes and Motor Houses
Manager: Adrian A. de Vogel
Address: 20301 Oakwood Boulevard, Dearborn, Mich. 48123
Directions: Dearborn is a suburb southwest of Detroit, halfway between downtown and Metropolitan Airport; once you reach Detroit area, follow signs for Greenfield Village, the inn's neighbor on Oakwood Boulevard.
Telephone: (313) 271-2700
Cables/Telex: None
Credit Cards: American Express, Diners, MasterCard, Visa
Rooms: 181, including 6 suites and 33 rooms in five Colonial Homes.
Meals: Breakfast 6:00–11:30 (7:00–12:00 Sunday), lunch 11:30–2:00 (Sunday brunch 10:30–6:00), dinner 5:00–10:00 weekdays, 5:00–11:00 Friday and Saturday (from $7 to $35 for 2); room service during dining-room hours; informal dress; piano in the dining room weeknights, combo for dinner-dancing Friday and Saturday.
Diversions: Heated pool, shuffleboard, 2 free tennis courts; public golf course nearby.
Sightseeing: Henry Ford Museum and Greenfield Village; Detroit Institute of Arts, Detroit Historical Museum, the Symphony Orchestra (Henry

and Edsel Ford Auditorium); excursion boats down the Detroit River to
Bob Lo Island (Woodward Avenue pier).

P.S. Special packages are available upon inquiry. Children have separate
play yard.

NATIONAL HOUSE INN
Marshall, Mich.

The National House would be a gem even in the heart of New
England. In a location just off the busy highway between Chicago and
Detroit, both the inn and its historic hometown may strike you as a
minor miracle.

You see, the settlers who headed west to Marshall weren't out to
make their fortune on the new frontier—they brought the fortunes
with them. These were wealthy easterners who expected to grow
even more prosperous by getting the inside track on land and business in the town rumored to be the sure choice for the capital of the
new state. By the time the newcomers learned that Marshall had
been bypassed in favor of Lansing, they had already reproduced the
handsome post-Colonial homes they had left behind back East, now
among the best examples of nineteenth-century architecture in the
country. These homes have been carefully preserved. There are
thirty-seven of them on the town walking tour (including the "governor's mansion" that never housed a governor), an array so unique in
the area that the annual open house each fall draws some ten
thousand visitors.

National House had been the most prestigious building in town
when it was a major stagecoach stop, but later had come upon sad
days as a rundown apartment house before it was rescued in 1976 by
two Detroit couples, the Kinneys and the Minicks. Using old photos
as a guide, they painstakingly restored the gracious original exterior,
unbricking windows and pressure-cleaning layers and layers of paint
in the process. The old bricks were used to build a floor-to-ceiling
fireplace in the lobby, and beams from a period house were rescued
to re-create the warmth of earlier times.

It took a full year to track down appropriate furnishings for the rooms, the brass and iron and carved wooden antique beds, ceiling-high commodes, rockers, trunks, mirrors, and prints that fill fifteen American Country or Victorian bedrooms. Three antique marble sinks found at a wrecking company were copied for the bathrooms, lighting fixtures were inspired by original oil lamps.

By the time the rooms were done with authentic wallpaper patterns reproduced by the Henry Ford Museum in Dearborn and coordinated with bedspreads, drapes, carpeting, and complementary sheets, they were such showplaces that the doors are left open when guests are not in residence so that everyone can enjoy a tour. Each room is named for one of Marshall's original settlers, and a brief history of the honoree is printed at the door. You'll learn that Charles Gorham of Danbury, Connecticut, who opened a general store when he came to Marshall, went on to become a founder of the Republican Party and eventually an assistant secretary of the interior. Then you can admire the Gorham Room, a Victorian vision with eyelet-trimmed canopy beds, a velvet settee, blue carpet and drapes, petit-point chairs, and lace curtains. Samuel Hill of Lyme, New Hampshire, is the name on the door of a delightful country-style retreat with an old iron bedstead, patchwork bedspreads, and a desk made from an old sewing machine.

The cozy dining room where guests are served homebaked goodies for breakfast, has authenticated salmon-colored woodwork, antique oak tables and chairs, and a remarkable reproduction of a nineteenth-century folk-art rug on the floor. Upstairs, there's a homey lounge with a fireplace, where handmade cabinets conceal some latter-day conveniences such as an ice machine and a color television set.

National House is a romantic fling with America's past—and an ideal place for a fling or two of your own.

E.B.

Name: National House Inn
Manager: Steven W. Poole
Address: 102 South Parkview, Marshall, Mich. 40968
Directions: Exit off route 94, just east of Battle Creek, Michigan; about 2½ hours from Chicago or Detroit.
Telephone: (616) 781–7374

Cables/Telex: None
Credit Cards: MasterCard, Visa
Rooms: 13.
Meals: Breakfast 7:30–9:30 weekdays, 8:30–10:30 weekends; no room service.
Sightseeing: Walking tour of nineteenth-century village homes, town antique shops.
P.S. The breakfast dining room is *sometimes* used for parties and dinners.

STAFFORD'S BAY VIEW INN
Petoskey, Mich.

When Stafford Smith and Janice Johnson were college students working for the summer at the Bay View Inn back in 1960, they fell in love twice—with the place and with each other.

So in spring 1961, Stafford bought the inn, making him, as he tells it, "the youngest and most inexperienced hotel owner in western Michigan." Then in June he married Janice and together they began the loving restoration and expansion that still continues today, taking care all the way to maintain the Victorian flavor that had won them over in the first place.

The original three-story 1887 "rooming house" front with its green mansard roof remains, likewise the many-sided tower that was added in 1895. Some of the furnishings, including the French clock on the fireplace mantel and the antique oak chairs in the dining room, also date from the 1890s.

But there have been many additions over these years to make things even nicer for guests, the inviting wicker-filled Sun Room, and the Garden Room, a nostalgic mix of wicker, latticework, hanging plants, and Tiffany-type lamps, where you dine with a view of the bay. The inside dining rooms have been expanded twice, the old-fashioned front porch restored, the kitchen completely rebuilt, and private baths added to each of the twenty-two guest rooms.

The latest redecorating of the rooms was just completed in 1980, each room done in a different distinctive period paper, ruffled curtains hung at the windows, and interesting Victorian pieces used throughout, like the huge fourposter, rocker, and brass-trimmed chest in room 9 or the painted furniture in room 21.

One thing that needed no improvement was the inn's location—within a few hundred feet of Little Traverse Bay and in the midst of the delightful Bay View community of Victorian summer cottages, where lectures, concerts, and classes go on all summer. Not far away is the "gaslight district," named for its atmospheric light fixtures, and lined with the kinds of posh resort shops that list branches in places like Palm Beach and Southampton.

Recently, the state of Michigan recognized the inn's near-century of continuous operation by conferring the official status of Historic Site, but the Smiths have saved more than the outer shell of the inn. Taking in the view from your rocker on the front porch or taking tea in the afternoon in the Garden Room, you can feel the carefully preserved ambiance of a peaceful past.

E.B.

Name: Stafford's Bay View Inn
Owner/Manager: Stafford Smith
Address: Box 3, Petoskey, Mich. 49770
Directions: Follow Route 31 or 131 north just past Petoskey into Bay View, the inn is right on the road on the left, within sight of the bay.
Telephone: (616) 347-2771
Cables/Telex: None
Credit Cards: American Express, MasterCard, Visa
Rooms: 22.
Meals: Breakfast 8:30–10:00, lunch 11:30–2:00, dinner 6:00–9:00 (approx. $18 for 2), Sunday brunch 10:00–2:00, Sunday dinner 6:00–8:30, afternoon tea 3:00–5:00, no room service.
Diversions: Nearby canoeing, golf, tennis, sailing, swimming, riding, boat charters, fall foliage, scenic lakeside drives.
Sightseeing: Mackinac Island ferry; Little Traverse Historic Festival in June offers concerts and special events; Bay View Association offers lectures, concerts, travelogues, movies, music classes in summer.
P.S. No liquor license, but guests are invited to bring their own wine to dinner. Inn open weekends only from January to mid-March; closed mid-October to Christmas, mid-March to May 23.

THE HOMESTEAD
Glen Arbor, Mich.

$$

Here's a seashore resort with spectacular dune views—yet you're almost a thousand miles from the ocean.

Actually, The Homestead is a handsome four-season vacation community of condominiums set on more than two hundred wooded acres. But it's that mile of sandy shore along Lake Michigan's Sleeping Bear Bay that sets this place apart. That and the view of the Sleeping Bear Dunes National Lakeshore, a glacier-created natural wonder that has been carefully preserved by the U.S. Park Service, soon will be the featured attraction of a *new* seventy-thousand-acre national park and already there's a paved drive along the shore, the Stocking Nature Trail, that presents absolutely breathtaking lakeside vistas at every turn.

Back at The Homestead, many of the attractive modern condominiums are set on a high ridge to take in that lake-dune seascape. Some are right on the shore, still others front the peaceful Crystal River that runs through the resort property down to the lake. Wherever you are, you'll have a private balcony to enjoy the scenery, and since you'll be staying in a luxury privately owned vacation home, you can be sure of tasteful, comfortable surroundings.

Summer days here can be blissfully lazed away on the beach, and the owners have thoughtfully provided a café at beachside so you needn't stir or change all day long. Should you want something a little more active, you can play tennis or paddle tennis, or rent a sailboat, canoe, or a couple of bikes.

Come dinner there's a choice of formal dining in the tall rustic weathered timber inn, or a more relaxed rough-sawn wood-and-fieldstone setting at the Racquet Club, where there is also entertainment on the weekends.

Sunday brunch at the inn is a real production, dozens of dishes from homemade Danish and scrambled eggs to quiche or roast beef. You may need a brisk walk when it's all over.

As a matter of fact, a walk hand-in-hand through the woods and along the shore is a good idea anytime. One of the nicest things here is The Homestead's care to keep the land unspoiled and make the most of their dramatic setting. Gazing at the dunes and watching the waves whip up on the water, you'll swear you're walking the seashore.

E.B.

Name: The Homestead
Manager: (Not available)
Address: Glen Arbor, Mich. 49636
Directions: Take 75 or 31 north to Traverse City, then Route 72 21 miles west to Empire and Route 22 8 miles north to Glen Arbor. The entrance is on Route 22, about 2 miles north of Glen Arbor.
Telephone: (616) 334–3041
Cables/Telex: None
Credit Cards: American Express, MasterCard, Visa
Rooms: 200.
Meals: Breakfast 8:00–10:00, lunch 11:30–2:00, dinner 6:00–10:00, (approx. $40 at the inn, $30 at the Racquet Club for 2), Sunday brunch 9:30–2:00, jackets requested at the Inn; no room service; entertainment weekends at the Racquet Club.
Diversions: Beach, outdoor pool, hiking, tennis (charge for courts), platform tennis (charge for courts), Sunfish, canoes, bicycles for rent; golf, cross-country ski trails nearby.
Sightseeing: Sleeping Bear Dunes National Lakeshore; Interlochen Arts Academy concerts, Cherry County Playhouse in Traverse City.
P.S. Some meetings in inn building, lots of family groups.

THE RITZ CARLTON HOTEL
Chicago, Ill.

$$$

So what if winds are howling in the Windy City? It's perennial springtime in this elegant aerie, from the moment you step off the twelfth-floor elevator into the nineteen-foot-high lobby, lit by a giant skylight and filled with flowers and greenery.

It's quite a place, that twelfth floor—a two-acre expanse that tops the lower portion of Water Tower Place, Chicago's stylish atrium shopping and entertainment complex. Straight ahead of you, beyond a trickling fountain, is The Greenhouse, a foliage-filled setting for lunch or drinks amidst wide window walls with views unlimited. From the formal French dining room, you look out on an indoor garden, complete with miniature waterfall. Then there is The Cafe, open for informal meals around the clock, The Bar for drinking and dancing at night, conference rooms, an extravagant ballroom (peek in to see the chandeliers, dangling some 400,000 tiny cut-lead crystals), and The Promenade, a walkway of showcases featuring choice baubles from the city's best shops.

Guest rooms at the Ritz Carlton begin on the fifteenth floor and go up to thirty-one, guaranteeing a memorable view whether you face the lake or Chicago's spectacular skyline. The higher the floor, of course, the better. The rooms themselves are just what you'd expect at a Ritz—big, traditional, sumptuously furnished in pastel shades, closets with lights that go on when you open the door, a maid to turn down your bed at night, an invisible manservant who whisks your shoes away for a shine overnight. Suites? Plump for the Anniversary Suite which has a sunken bathtub built for two.

For a real dunking, take the elevator down to the eleventh floor and a big indoor pool beneath a skylight. Then luxuriate in a spa complete with saunas and tanning chambers.

Another elevator ride away is Water Tower Place, where Marshall Field, Lord and Taylor, more than one hundred other fine shops and boutiques, four movie houses, the Drury Lane Theater, and eleven restaurants are waiting for you.

Outside the door is the heart of Chicago's Gold Coast, but you may never choose to step out that door. You've got the best of the city right here, view and all, all wrapped in greenery.

E.B.

Name: The Ritz Carlton Hotel
Manager: Charles Ferraro
Address: 160 East Pearson Street, Chicago, Ill. 60611
Directions: Just off North Michigan Avenue on the Near North Side.
Telephone: (312) 266–1000, toll free (800) 828–1188, in New York state (800) 462–1150
Cables/Telex: 20–6014
Credit Cards: "All major credit cards"

Rooms: 450.

Meals: Breakfast anytime, lunch 12:00–2:30, dinner 6:00–10:30 (approx. $80 for 2); appropriate dress, cafe open 24 hours; room service 24 hours; dancing in The Bar every evening.

Diversions: Indoor pool, spa.

Sightseeing: Water Tower Place, Chicago.

P.S. Seminars and meetings are held in private rooms, and normally do not disrupt hotel facilities.

THE WHITEHALL HOTEL
Chicago, Ill.

$ $ $

It's the little things you'll remember about the Whitehall. The doorman who greets you by name. The little refrigerator in the room to keep your champagne chilled. The pretty ruffled shower cap and the three kinds of soap in the bathroom. There's a concierge on call all day to help with your plans, a room-service waiter at your service around the clock, a chambermaid to turn down your bed at night or appear at your summons with an iron should you somehow rumple your clothes.

These are the things that have made the small, intimate Whitehall the choice of so many glittery names when they pass through Chicago—authors like Stephen King and Erica Jong, showbiz biggies such as Liza Minelli, Carol Channing, and Richard Burton, who keep the four lavish tower suites occupied most of the time. Katharine Hepburn reportedly raved about her $400-a-day apartment with its own kitchen and roof terrace where a formal dinner may be served up with a view of the city lights. Sir John Churchill so enjoyed his stay that he sent as a thank-you a signed portrait of his uncle Winston; it now hangs on the wall, causing these quarters to be renamed The Churchill Suite.

You may get a glimpse of some of these celebrities as you take English tea in the lobby in the afternoon or dine in the paneled elegance of the Whitehall Club, a private eating establishment that offers dining privileges to hotel guests. That is, of course, provided you've decided to pass up room service in your own comfortable nest, done up seductively in soft shades of apricot velvet. If you opt for a mini-suite, you'll have a whole dividing wall of mirrors to keep you entertained between meals.

When you're ready to explore Chicago, you're in the heart of the posh Near North Side. There's a personally addressed letter on the dresser telling you what to see and do in town, plus a delightful guide for guests describing Chicago's favorite jogging paths.

The services of a grand hotel with the personal touches of a small inn. That's the Whitehall formula—and it's a winner.

E.B.

Name: The Whitehall
Manager: Michael Littler
Address: 105 East Delaware Place, Chicago, Ill. 60611
Directions: On Chicago's elegant Near North Side, just off North Michigan
    Avenue (the Magnificent Mile), 1 block from the Hancock Building, 3½
    blocks from the lake.
Telephone: (312) 944–6300, toll free (800) 223–5757
Cables/Telex: 25–5157
Credit Cards: American Express, Carte Blanche, Diners, MasterCard, Visa
Rooms: 222, including suites.
Meals: Breakfast 7:00–11:00, lunch 12:00–3:00, dinner 6:00–11:00 (approx.
    $40–$60 for 2); room service around the clock; jacket and tie in the
    dining room.
Diversions: Wallowing.
Sightseeing: Chicago! Chicago!

THE TREMONT HOTEL
Chicago, Ill.

$$$

It's more like a drawing room than a hotel lobby, with fireplace, painted ceiling, printed drapes, candelabra and antique furniture straight out of an English manor house. Upstairs, this eighteenth-century manor house feeling takes the shape of period writing desks, tole lamps, leather wing chairs, engravings on the walls.

The Tremont is chief rival to The Whitehall for the title of Chicago's finest small hostelry, and it has its own host of devotees who dote on its old English charm—as well as its own lavish suites where anyone from the latest rock star to tenor Luciano Pavarotti may be in residence.

Once again there are lavish little touches to make your stay nicer—the morning paper waiting at your door, a concierge in the lobby, Godiva chocolates and a miniature snifter of brandy set next to your turned-down bed at night, even a night butler who'll gladly run out to fetch you a pizza or whatever if you work up an appetite after room service goes off duty at 11:30.

Crickets, the hotel restaurant, is the Chicago outpost of New York's 21 Club. Gothamites will recognize the decor, right down to the corporate symbols and sports gear hanging from the ceiling. It's one of the city's liveliest eating spots and the bar bustles day and night; Cricket's Hearth next door is smaller and more subdued, a peaceful spot for breakfast, lunch, or dinner.

The Tremont staff is multilingual, the clientele is worldly, the pace unhurried. If English manor is just your cup of afternoon tea, here's the place to sip it.

                                                              E.B.

Name: The Tremont Hotel
Manager: Eric Brooks
Address: 100 E. Chestnut, Chicago, Ill. 60611
Directions: Between North Michigan Avenue and Lake Shore Drive on Chicago's Near North Side.
Telephone: (312) 751–1900, toll free (800) 621–8133
Cables/Telex: None
Credit Cards: American Express, Carte Blanche, Diners, MasterCard, Visa
Rooms: 150, 7 suites.
Meals: Breakfast 7:00–10:30, lunch 12:00–2:00, dinner 6:00–10:00, 11:00 on weekends (approx. $50 to $60 for 2); jacket and tie; room service 7:00 A.M. to 10:30 P.M.; piano bar.
Diversions: Guest privileges at McClurg Sports Club (tennis, racquetball).
Sightseeing: Chicago.
P.S. Hotel is currently (into 1981) being refurbished, rooms enlarged, new carpeting and decorating added; special weekend rates.

THE PIONEER INN
Oshkosh, Wisc.

You have to see this to believe it. Behind you is Oshkosh, no doubt a nice enough place, but hardly anyone's idea of romantic. Nor is it even the best side of Oshkosh, but an area of factories and freight cars.

Now, drive about ten feet across a bridge onto "Kini Island," walk through the doors of a fairly ordinary hotel structure—and you might have traveled a thousand miles. On the opposite side of the hotel, across a velvety green lawn, there's absolute serenity, just the crystal waters and picturesque shoreline of Lake Winnebago, and not another thing in sight.

It was an inspired idea creating this twenty-one-acre island in a part of the world where getaways are hard to come by. Pioneer Inn is actually a big complete resort, two-hundred rooms, indoor and outdoor pools, tennis, a marina with boat rentals, waterskiing, fishing, shuffleboard, miniature golf, snowmobiling, and ice fishing in winter—there's never a lack of things to do by day. And by night you can choose from formal and informal dining rooms, and two cocktail lounges, one with live entertainment and dancing.

The outdoor facilities couldn't be nicer, set around that putting green of a lawn, with a gravel path around the edge of the lake just begging for idyllic hand-in-hand strolling. Indoors, the decor is pretty standard motel modern, though the rooms are good size and have big comfortable chairs for lounging plus a private terrace for lake gazing.

Since there aren't many such places in this area, Pioneer Inn is busy, and it attracts plenty of meetings midweek, so be prepared. Nevertheless, back in your room looking out the big glass doors at the view, it's just the two of you and the lake, not another thing in sight.

Don't just request that lake-view room—insist on it. It's what makes Pioneer Inn a very special place.

E.B.

Name: The Pioneer Inn

Manager: John F. Bergstrom

Address: 1000 Pioneer Drive, P.O. Box 2626, Oshkosh, Wisc. 54903

Directions: Route 41 to Oshkosh, follow Ninth Avenue into town to Main
    Street, right turn to 14th Avenue and across bridge to "Kini Island."
    (Plenty of big signs pointing the way as soon as you get into town.)

Telephone: (414) 233–1980, toll free, Wisconsin only (800) 242–0372

Cables/Telex: None

Credit Cards: American Express, Carte Blanche, Diners, MasterCard, Visa

Meals: Breakfast 6:30–11:00, brunch 9:30–2:00 Sundays, lunch 11:00–5:00,
    Sunday lunch from noon on, dinner 5:00–11:00 (until 10:00 Sunday and
    Monday), (approx. $20 for 2); dress optional; coffee shop 11:00 A.M. to
    5:00 P.M.; Caboose Dining Car (snacks, pizza, burgers) 5:30–11:30 P.M.;
    entertainment in Paul L. Cocktail Lounge and Caboose Cabaret, danc-
    ing nightly; room service 7:00 A.M. to 10:30 P.M., to 9:30 Sunday and
    Monday; beverages until 11:00.

Diversions: Indoor and outdoor swimming pools, whirlpool, marina with
    boat rentals; tennis; miniature golf, shuffleboard, fishing, ice skating,
    snowmobiling, ice fishing; golf, riding, racquetball, cross-country
    skiing nearby.

Sightseeing: Oshkosh Public Museum and Paine Art Center.

P.S. 2:00 P.M. checkout makes for delicious lazy Sunday mornings.

THE INN AT PLEASANT HILL
Shakertown, Harrodsburg, Ky.

This is an ironic choice for a lovers' hideaway—the restored village of
a religious sect that banned sex, where boys and girls were never
allowed to be alone together, and where the houses had not only
separate dormitories for each sex but separate doors and stairs. Not
surprisingly, the sect is all but extinct ("celibacy contributed to their
undoing," as one commentator put it) but their village remains as a
placid anachronism, a freeze-frame in the movie of history.

    First, the location. Pleasant Hill is about twenty-five miles
southwest of Lexington, which puts it right on the edge of Bluegrass
Country, along a winding fence-lined lane. This, they say, is the only
historical village in the country where you can spend a night in the

original houses (not inns, but houses). Spooky? Only if total silence punctured by rattling windows and creaky floorboards turn you to Jello; if they do, just make a grab for each other.

The twenty-odd clapboard or birch houses in Shakertown are neatly lined up on either side of an unpaved street which in turn is lined by picket-and-plank fences and mulberry trees.

RAG RUGS, TRUNDLE BEDS. The main lodge, Trustees' House, has been putting up guests since Shaker times, but you can also spend the night in, say, the Ministry's Workshop, or the East Family Sisters Shop (above the spinning and weaving rooms), or the East Family Brethrens' Shop (above the carpenters' tools and broom-making equipment). All the guest rooms feature the ascetic, precise, well-proportioned Shaker decor (it's like living inside a painting by Mondrian); plain walls trimmed with wood in brown or blue, plank floors with handwoven rag rugs, curtains in the Shakers' traditional "dogwood" pattern, stout twin beds (some of them trundles). The Shakers draped everything over wall pegs—sconces, clothes, mirrors, even chairs—and that's the way it is at Shakertown. (Note, by the way, that this creates a resonant acoustic, so take it easy or you may keep the neighbors awake, wondering if they're hearing the spirits of the former inhabitants at one of the "shaking" parties from which they got their name.) Concessions to the twentieth century include tiled bathrooms, air conditioning, fire sprinklers, and television sets (which are as jarring in this setting as a naked body must have been to a Shaker).

MARSHMALLOWS IN YOUR APPLESAUCE. The Trustees' House has four dining rooms, including a summer porch with tall windows overlooking the garden, bare brick walls, and scrubbed wooden tables. The waitresses are dressed in authentic Shaker checked dresses, and Mrs. Kremer's menu is a combination of Shaker and Kaintuck cooking. Village hot breads and the relish tray come automatically. Thereafter you have a choice of four appetizers (including eggs in aspic on anchovy toast), five entrées (say, pork tenderloin, which comes accompanied by piles of fresh vegetables from the village garden, and applesauce with marshmallows). The five choices of dessert include chess pie and Shaker lemon pie—which leave you feeling that at least the Shakers got *some* pleasure out of life.

There are no frivolities here like swimming pools and saunas. Instead you can go for long walks through the fields, or long drives through the Bluegrass Country; but spend at least one morning or afternoon visiting the village exhibits, buying Shaker-inspired gewgaws, and getting to learn something about these remarkable people. In some ways they were ahead of their time. They were pioneers in organic foods and the medicinal use of herbs; they invented several of the labor-saving devices we take for granted—the washing machine, for one; they were pacifists, women's libbers (they believed Christ would appear the second time as a woman), and in a sense they were doing something about the population explosion long before everyone else awakened to its threats. They themselves expected to survive by conversions and adoptions; but since they also had the work ethic with a vengeance, in the end they didn't have much to offer the younger generation. But they left quite a legacy here at Shakertown.

Name: The Inn at Pleasant Hill
Owner/Manager: Ann Voris
Address: Route 4, Harrodsburg, Ky. 40330
Directions: On U.S. 68, about 25 miles southwest of Lexington, about 8 miles from Harrodsburg.

Telephone: (606) 734–5411
Cables/Telex: None
Credit Cards: None
Rooms: 66, 2 suites.
Meals: Breakfast 8:30–9:30, lunch 12:00, 1:00, and 2:00, Sunday 12:30, 1:45,
    3:15, and 6:00, dinner 6:00 and 7:15 (approx. $14 to $18 for 2); no room
    service; informal dress.
Diversions: Walking, wandering around the Shaker exhibits.
Sightseeing: Seasonal calendar of craft events and music and dance presenta-
    tions in the area; Bluegrass Country.
P.S. Special winter weekend packages available. September features 4 Shak-
    er Heritage Weekends, when the village is bustling with additional
    activities. Some small groups.

LODGE OF THE FOUR SEASONS
Lake of the Ozarks, Mo.

$$

There's only one place to stay in these parts and this is it. (The Lake of
the Ozarks, for the record, is a manmade body of water surrounded
by manmade honky-tonk.) Everything you could ask for on a vacation
is a five-minute walk from your bed—a five-story waterfall in the new
atrium, an outdoor pool in a Japanese garden, and an indoor pool; a
spa with saunas, whirlpool baths, massage, exercise rooms, sight-
seeing boat trips on the lake, boats for rent; golf, including an
eighteen-hole Robert Trent Jones course; tennis, fishing, riding,
hiking, waterskiing, archery, games room; a movie theater with
first-run movies. There are ample dining facilities—a restaurant/pub,
French pastry shop, a lakeside coffee shop, and a lavish circular
restaurant called the Toledo Room, hosted by a maître d' who'd be a
credit to most restaurants in New York. After dinner you can whoop it
up in the discotheque or nightclub with live entertainment, or just
relax in the lobby bar.

LANAIS AND CASAS. The lodge's three hundred rooms are spacious,
comfortable, and equipped with telephones, television, and indi-
vidually controlled heating and air conditioning. They're spread out

through the five-story atrium, a four-story lodge, a four-story wing known as the Casadero, lanai rooms facing the pool and Japanese garden, and lakeside casas. The quietest rooms are the casas (except during the boating season, because they're right above the marina), or the Casadero rooms (which also have good views, and balconies for enjoying them).

This is a much better hotel than most people would expect to find out there in the Ozarks among all those hillbillies; in fact, you'd expect a colorful resort like this in Miami or San Juan rather than Missouri, and you may find yourself wishing that there was just a touch more of the hillbilly about the place. Even that the persistent piped music could be coaxed into playing Bluegrass now and again.

Name: Lodge of the Four Seasons
Manager: G. Frederick Davis
Address: P.O. Box 215, Highway HH, Lake Ozark, Mo. 65049
Directions: 170 miles southwest of St. Louis; from Interstate 70, take U.S. 63 or U.S. 65 south, following the signs for Lake of the Ozarks and Bagnell Dam, then drive west 2½ miles from Business 54 to County HH; by air, from Kansas City or St. Louis to Lee C. Fine Airport, Lake of the Ozarks.
Telephone: (314) 365–3001
Cables/Telex: None
Credit Cards: American Express, Carte Blanche, Diners, MasterCard, Visa
Rooms: 300, including 8 suites, 37 mini-suites.
Meals: Breakfast 7:00–11:00, lunch 12:00–3:00, dinner 5:30–10:30; room service, jacket required at dinner in Toledo Room; live music and dancing.
Diversions: Heated indoor pool, spa, movies, bowling; 4 outdoor pools, archery, trap shooting, horseback riding, tennis (6 courts, 2 with lights, pro, ball machines, clinics), golf (18- and 9-hole courses), sailing, waterskiing, bicycles for rent—all on the premises.
Sightseeing: Bagnell Dam, Lake of the Ozarks State Park, Ozark and Stark caverns.

For detailed rate, turn to page 413.

HOTEL MAISON DE VILLE AND
AUDUBON COTTAGES
New Orleans, La.

$$

Even if you've never been there, you probably know from photographs what the typical Vieux Carré townhouse looks like—two-story facade with wrought-iron balconies, and a courtyard with slave quarters at the rear. The slave quarters at 727 Rue du Toulouse date from 1783 and may be among the oldest buildings from the days of the Spanish grandees; the elegant main house was rebuilt in the early eighteenth century, and was at one time the home of M. A. A. Peychaud, the ingenious apothecary who is said to have invented the cocktail. You could almost be persuaded that M. Peychaud still lived behind this grandly carved door and cut-glass window if it weren't for the gleaming brass nameplate announcing Hotel Maison de Ville.

Inside you step back a century or two to the days of the Spanish and French beau monde, into a miniature palace filled with antiques—a Biedermeier love seat, an eighteenth-century commode, a carved trumeau. You may while away your nights of bliss in a Chippendale bed draped with French silk, or a double bed covered with a Belgian sable spread trimmed in black velvet, or twin beds with brass headboards for curling your toes around.

Three of the double rooms are in the slave quarters, connected by a careworn wooden staircase to the courtyard—a leafy, sun-dappled pocket park with a three-tiered cast-iron fountain trickling into a fish pond. This is pure Vieux Carré, and to crown it all you can enjoy several felicities of service: you get your shoes polished when you put them outside your door; you have a concierge to attend to details—like reserving a table for two at Brennan's; ice, mixers, soft drinks, and newspapers are on the *maison;* breakfast arrives in your room on a silver tray—freshly squeezed orange juice, freshly brewed New Orleans coffee, freshly baked croissants. There are only fourteen rooms in the hotel; it's no place to be if you like spacious lobbies and roomy rooms, but if you like gems, here's one.

Recently the gem acquired a new facet: a secret courtyard with half a dozen bungalows dating from the eighteenth century, in "Santo Domingo" style, each with pastel stucco walls, trim gardens, patios, and fountains. John James Audubon lived and painted here in 1821, hence the name—Audubon Cottages. Each cottage has been carefully restored and furnished with antiques, and has acquired a modern kitchen. The cottages are ideal for two or more couples, but you can, if you prefer, reserve just one bedroom. Full room service available at both locations.

Name: Hotel Maison de Ville and Audubon Cottages
Manager: William W. Pretiss
Address: 727 Toulouse Street, New Orleans, La. 70130
Directions: In the heart of the Vieux Carré, a leisurely stroll from everything (but, for all that, quiet and secluded).
Telephone: (504) 561–5858
Cables/Telex: None
Credit Cards: None
Rooms: 12, 2 suites, 7 cottages.
Meals: Breakfast only, 7:30 to noon, room service 7:00 A.M. to 11:00 P.M. for drinks, snacks, and meals from nearby restaurants.
Diversions: Pool; bicycles, tennis, boating nearby.
Sightseeing: New Orleans.
P.S. Open all year, quietest in summer.

THE SAINT LOUIS HOTEL
New Orleans, La.

A count might have lived here a century ago, greeting lovely crino-lined ladies in the courtyard by the fountain. The fact is, there was a bottling plant here until a few years ago when a local entrepreneur who had always wanted a hotel like the Ritz in Paris, pulled the plant down and built this hotel. He spared few expenses—least of all in "aging" the facade to make it look like the sort of place a count might have entertained in a hundred years ago. The predominant color is cantaloupe (or "a melon-smoked-salmon shade" as one of the design-ers calls it), which is the color theme used in bed linen and table linen. The lobby looks like the salon of a Parisian townhouse, domi-

nated by a century-old gilt mirror; beyond it french doors lead
through to the inner courtyard (which, by a directive of the New
Orleans Vieux Carré Commission, must represent 30 percent of any
property).

Begin your stay at the Saint Louis in this delightful spot. Find a
table beneath a slowly turning blade fan, order a cool drink, hold
hands, and admire the banana palms, the golden rain tree, and the
baby weeping willow. Then trot upstairs and ease into the cuddly
terry towel bathrobes hanging in the dressing room. The eighty
bedchambers are luxurious—furnished in the style of Louis XV or
XVI, Empire or Directoire (reproductions, alas, but then people in
cuddly terry towel bathrobes shouldn't expect everything). All the
rooms have air conditioning, color TV, electric shoe polisher, and
bidet.

Name: The Saint Louis Hotel
Owner/Manager: Mark Smith
Address: 730 Bienville Street, New Orleans, La. 70130

Directions: In the Vieux Carré, 2 blocks from Canal Street, and 3½ minutes from Preservation Hall and its Dixieland jazz.

Telephone: (504) 581–7300

Cables/Telex: None

Credit Cards: American Express, Diners, MasterCard, Visa

Rooms: 66, 11 suites.

Meals: Breakfast 7:00–10:30, lunch 11:30–2:30, dinner 6:30–10:30 (approx. $40 to $60 for 2); room service; jacket and tie at dinner.

Diversions: Eating.

Sightseeing: New Orleans.

P.S. June through early September are the quiet months, weekends are quiet most of the year; there may be small groups in residence in winter, and you'd better book at least 1 year in advance for Mardi Gras.

GRAND HOTEL
Point Clear, Ala.

$$

The Point is a giant V formed by two long strips of white sand beach surrounded by turquoise sea. Within the V you have five hundred acres of pines, live oaks, and gardens, and, somewhere among it all, the Grand Hotel. There's an air of quiet elegance about the place, luxury without ostentation. The buildings are muted gray, with brick-and-timber interiors; the fifty bed-sitting rooms have wall-to-wall carpeting, color television, and terraces or balconies facing the gulf or the gardens.

What do you do on a sunny day in Alabama? Just about everything. You can plunge into the freshwater swimming pool (it's enormous—140 feet in diameter); suntan on the white sands; waterski; sail on the bay (there are Rhodes 19, daysailers for rent); play tennis; or tandem through the five hundred acres of pines and live oaks. In the evenings you can stroll over to Julep Point and enjoy the view, or a julep, or a seafood luau. If you have any energy left after the day's activities you can even do a spot of dancing under the stars. Take an after-dinner stroll on the white sands, sniff the salt air, and you could be in the Caribbean.

Name: Grand Hotel

Manager: Jim Pope

Address: Point Clear, Ala. 36564

Directions: Point Clear is 23 miles south of Mobile via Battleship Parkway and U.S. 98, and 49 miles west of Pensacola, Fla.; limousines will meet your plane at Mobile Airport on request; private planes can land at Fairhope Airport, 4 miles away.

Telephone: (205) 928–9201

Cables/Telex: None

Credit Cards: None

Rooms: 170, with 25 suites, 10 villas.

Meals: Breakfast 7:30–9:30, lunch 12:00–2:00, dinner 7:00–8:30; room service during meal hours; jacket and tie at dinner; live music and dancing.

Diversions: Freshwater pool, lawn sports; bikes and waterskis for rent, tennis (10 courts, $3 person per hour, pro, ball machines), golf (three 9-hole courses, $12 per day), fully rigged deep-sea fishing boat for charter.

Sightseeing: Bellingrath Gardens and Mobile's "Azalea Trail." Fort Conde, Fort Morgan, Battleship U.S.S. *Alabama*, the Eastern Shore Art Center.

P.S. Special packages available; 3- to 4-day minimum reservations required on major holidays. Supervised activities for children during summer months.

For more suggestions in this area
turn to Added Attractions, page 375.

In and Around the Rockies

Trip no further, pretty sweeting,
Journeys end in lovers meeting,
Every wise man's son doth know . . .
SHAKESPEARE

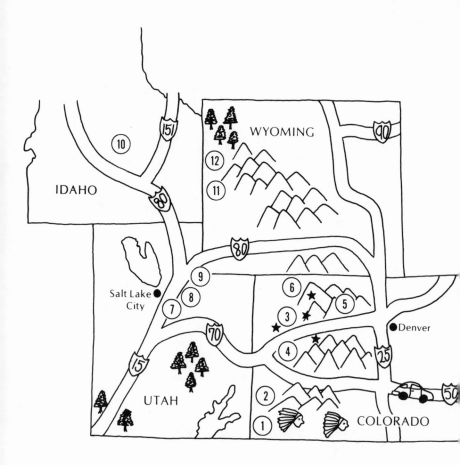

1. Strater Hotel
2. Tall Timber
3. Keystone
4. The Aspen Club
   Condominiums
5. C Lazy U Ranch
6. The Home Ranch
7. Sundance
8. The Lodge at Snowbird
9. Alta Lodge
10. Sun Valley Lodge
11. Jenny Lake Lodge
12. Jackson Lake Lodge
★　Added Attractions

TALL TIMBER

Durango, Colo.

$$$$

If you *really* mean business about getting away from it all, this is the place.

Tall Timber is one of Colorado's best kept secrets: it hides on 180 private acres of the San Juan National Forest. Just getting there is at least one-quarter of the fun. You take the *Silverton*—the last existing narrow-gauge train in the United States. Indeed, this is the *only* way to reach Tall Timber; there are no roads, no trails (and, unbelievably, not one, not a single telephone). The *Silverton* is a real coal-fired, whistle-screaming train, and in its time it has carried some fired-up passengers—Wyatt Earp and Doc Holliday. It follows the canyon of the Rio de las Animas Perdidos, puffing along through ponderosa, piñon, and lodge pole pines, past lakes and waterfalls as clear as a tumbler of Perrier, straight through a double rainbow (sit on the right side of the train for the best heart-turning-over views). At the Tall Timber depot, the train is flagged down, the owners or manager are standing there to welcome you—and you want to pinch yourself because you swear you're dreaming: it's all too good to be real. The train continues on to Silverton, an old mining town. Note the jealous looks on the passengers' faces as they wave good-bye to you.

For here you stand in a perfect Alpine village, sprinkled with daisies and black-eyed Susans and purple asters, hard by the San Juan Mountains and the drifting slant of eagles, and suddenly you're aware of something more remarkable than what you see: the silence. Nothing but a riffle in the aspen leaves, the rush of the Animas (a superb fishing stream that frequently supplies the trout for dinner), and the occasional swack of a tennis ball. This is what the owners of Tall Timber have worked so hard and patiently for: silence, peace, stunning privacy.

Denny and Judy Beggrow hand-designed and hand-built Tall Timber themselves. They began this dream in 1970 and opened for their first guests in 1974. Get them to tell you the story of how the swimming pool was *dropped* three times and why it bears such a striking resemblance to a railroad flatbed car—it speaks to the sublime inaccessibility of Tall Timber.

There is a main lodge and dining room with a soaring fireplace. Denny's father and mother hand-picked and hand-laid thirty tons of rock to build it, and it's magnificent. Tucked away among the cottonwoods and two-hundred-year-old ponderosa are shake-shingled and timbered duplex lodges, so secluded you'll find it hard to see them all. The suites have massive stone fireplaces in the living room, cathedral beamed ceilings, handwoven Navajo rugs, a wet bar, and small refrigerator. A master bedroom with an inside balcony upstairs lets you snuggle off to the snap and glow of embers. There's not even the hum of an air conditioner; at 7,500 feet all you need is something old-fashioned called fresh air.

Tall Timber accommodates only twenty people; it has a staff of twelve in season. This gives you an inkling of how they've made privacy a fine art. Your evening fire is prepared and your bed turned down and fresh fruit or liqueurs set out (or a homemade chocolate mint in the shape of a pine tree laid on your pillow) while you're at dinner. Meals are the only schedule—there are no community sings, no volleyball. If you want to meet the other guests, say so—Tall Timber won't make introductions until you say so. I asked if they have had famous guests. The answer: "If we've had them, we wouldn't tell you." That kind of fierce privacy even Howard Hughes couldn't get with all his money.

Now, if you're beginning to wonder what you're going to do with all this privacy (aside from some obvious attractions), stop worrying. That swimming pool shaped like a flatbed car is heated. There are three warm, bubbly whirlpools, a sauna and cold plunge, an emerald-cut nine-hole putting green, Laykold tennis court (and with only sixteen guests, there's no problem getting court time), five well-marked hiking trails of varying difficulty, a swell waterfall if you like your water brisk, excellent trail horses. And a grand library. Under the eaves above the dining room, it's a perfect spot to sip a silvery-dry martini before dinner and browse. Two thousand very eclectic books from the complete works of Shakespeare, Zane Grey, and Agatha Christie, through *Little Gloria, Grey's Anatomy,* and Henry Kissinger's *The White House Years*. It also contains excellent reference books on flowers and wildlife of the area.

The food? Like everything else about Tall Timber, first-rate. Carefully thought out and conceived. You can have eggs every day for breakfast, but you'd do better to go by the Tall Timber way: alternating days of eggs with perhaps a freshly broiled trout and wonderful concoctions like puff pancakes with fresh strawberries and whipped cream, or fresh pears and rye waffles. One notable lunch that's worth lingering over is a delicious soup made of crisp-cooked fresh, local vegetables, a delicate bacon and fresh asparagus quiche, piping hot, airy zephyr rolls with Judy Beggrow's own homemade chokeberry jelly, and French mint pie—a froth of chocolate and mint. Have the sparkling clear, very delicate iced tea with lunch—it's *sun* steeped for four hours and purists insist it's the best.

Dinners are the likes of prime ribs and Yorkshire pudding, beef Wellington, game hens with Madeira sauce, steak and trout, and a wonderful bourbon-baked ham. The breads, pastry, and desserts are extravagant: pumpkin muffins, apple bread, those sinfully buttery Russian cigarettes, Sally Lunn cake, challah, *sopaipillas*, baked Alaska with *three* kinds of ice cream, *crêpes Sainte Hélène* with homemade coffee ice cream, chocolate sauce, Kahlua and Amaretto flamed over it all. Denny wanted a flaming dessert of his own and got it: flambéed blackberries with applejack brandy and crème de cassis over sour cream pound cake and vanilla ice cream so rich, it's almost yellow. This dessert is divine, and it has no name. I suggest you ask for Denny's V.S.O.F.: Denny's Very Special Own Flambé.

One last note: Tall Timber keeps a personal file record of each guest. If you're allergic to shrimp, you'll never see one again. If you like to nestle in two pillows at night, two pillows you'll get—even when you come back five years later. But you may not stay away that long, if Tall Timber is what you've searched so hard and patiently for: silence, peace, stunning privacy.

S.B.

Name: Tall Timber
Owners/Managers: Dennis and Judy Beggrow
Address: Box 90 G, Silverton Star Route, Durango, Colo. 81301
Directions: Located 25 miles north of Durango, as the eagle flies, and the
         only way to get there is on the *Silverton* narrow-gauge train, which
         leaves Durango every morning at 8:30 A.M. Durango is served by
         Frontier Airlines from Denver and Albuquerque.

Telephone: Mobile radio phone (303) 259–4813, unit 13. (Just like in the
   movies, one person speaks at a time then says "over." As we said, this is
   really getting away from it all.)
Cables/Telex: None
Credit Cards: None (personal checks accepted)
Rooms: 8 suites—4 with 1 bedroom, 4 with 2 bedrooms, all with fireplaces.
Meals: Breakfast 7:30–9:30, lunch 12:30–1:30, dinner 6:30–7:30; informal; no
   room service.
Diversions: Heated outdoor pool, three whirlpools, Finnish sauna, tennis,
   putting green, hiking trails, cross-country skiing, and limited hiking in
   winter; trout fishing; horseback riding (only $12.50 per half day).
Sightseeing: Scenery—waterfalls, cliffs, mountains, streams, plus old lumber
   mills and silver mines along hiking trails.
P.S. Since there are so few rooms (and so many devotees of Tall Timber
   privacy) you must book early—in January, say, for July and August. No
   special facilities for children.

STRATER HOTEL
Durango, Colo.

Here's another pleasant Victorian Revival in a town that looks nowhere near as romantic as its name or history. Still, there's a lot to
explore in the surrounding countryside, where four states (Colorado,
New Mexico, Arizona, Utah) meets, so keep the Strater in mind as a
refuge if you happen to be in this part of the world, any time of the
year except perhaps April and early May.

This red-brick-with-white-trim hotel recently celebrated its
ninetieth birthday but it's a spruce and spry nonagenarian, refurbished to re-create the elegance of its early years when miners and
merchants fought in the saloon, and some fabled poker games took
place in a back room that's now the accountant's office. Through the
years its guest list has included luminaries such as Will Rogers, Louis
L'Amour, Lowell Thomas, JFK, and Gerald Ford.

All the hotel's hundred TV-and-phone-equipped rooms are Vic-
torianized with authentic period furniture. The pinnacles of opulence are Suites 333 (king-size bed, writing desk, modern bathroom,
TV nook with elegant Victorian sofa) and 322 (where you can play

Victoria and Albert in an enormous hand-carved, half-tester bed or in a real old-time, freestanding, four-legged bathtub), and 227.

The Strater's Diamond Belle Saloon is likewise an authentic-looking reconstruction of a Gay Nineties drinking establishment—a tad touristy, perhaps, but there's a hotshot piano player and, according to reliable sources, the bartender makes a mean martini.

MELODRAMA AND OLIO. The Strater has its own Diamond Circle Theater, a three-hundred-seater establishment where $10 will buy you a pair of tickets for a three-act show of melodrama, olio, and vaudeville. *Time* magazine called it one of the three best shows of its kind in the country—and you'll have to take *Time*'s word for it unless you make a reservation for the theater (open from Memorial Day to Labor Day only) when you reserve your room. Likewise if you want a ride on the other attraction that brings five thousand visitors per summer day to Durango—the hair-raising, breathtaking, mountain-clinging ride on the narrow-gauge Denver and Rio Grande Railway. Don't say you weren't warned—five thousand visitors a day. That's a good crowd if you're a Will Rogers looking for an audience or a JFK looking for votes, but if what you have in mind is a quiet, romantic little nook you'd better reschedule your trip.

Name: Strater Hotel
Managers: Earl A. Barker, Jr. (President), Mark Zenpel (General Manager)
Address: 699 Main Avenue, Durango, Colo. 81301
Directions: The town is on U.S. 160, the so-called Navajo Trail, and the hotel is on the main thoroughfare, a couple of blocks from the railroad station; scheduled air services to La Plata Airport.
Telephone: (303) 247–4431
Cables/Telex: None
Credit Cards: American Express, Carte Blanche, Diners, MasterCard, Visa
Rooms: 94, with 2 suites.
Meals: Breakfast 6:00–11:00, lunch 11:00–5:00, dinner 5:00–10:00 (approx. $15 to $25 for 2), with some seasonal variations; room service during dining-room hours; dress optional; honky-tonk piano in the saloon, singing waiters and waitresses in the Opera House Restaurant in summer.
Diversions: No sports facilities in the hotel, but in the neighborhood there are tennis courts, golf courses, bicycles and horses for rent, and skiing at Purgatory, 30 miles north of town.
Sightseeing: Durango, Mesa Verde National Park, Silverton, Purgatory Ski area.

KEYSTONE
Keystone, Colo.

$$

You find the name *Keystone* modifying practically everything you see here on this lovely mountainside a mere seventy-five miles west of Denver. There's a Keystone Village, Keystone Resort, Keystone Ranch, Keystone Lake, Keystone Lodge, Keystone Stables, even a Keystone Gulch.

Right away you get the feeling that the place might be too regimented for you, but hold on. What you have here is the start of a cosmic community. Keystone exists in and of itself, sort of like a Brasilia of the snow country. Its good side is that everything's here, you want for nothing. Its bad side, *everybody's* here as well. But don't despair.

Other guidebooks will steer you to the very core of this busy beehive, the Keystone Lodge. Avoid it, except for meals, for drinks, for socializing. Seek your hideaway in a Keystone condominium. There's an astonishing number of these but you lose all sense of nearness of others once you've retired inside.

Ask for one of the Quicksilver condominiums, just across the high road from all the action. Close your door on the world and make yourselves at home. Kick off your shoes and settle in to a downy sofa. Get a fire crackling in the fireplace, chill a bottle of nice white wine, stock the larder with something to sustain you, and let it snow, let it snow.

You're just a very short walk from the restaurants, bars, and shops in the lodge and in the village. Shuttle buses take you everywhere else.

Take your pick of two mountains for skiing: Arapahoe Basin or Keystone Mountain. There are 810 acres of trails for experts, intermediates, beginners—fifteen lifts whisk you to the top. Hate skiing? Go skating, go swimming in a heated outdoor pool.

There's plenty to do outside of snow season. Golf, fishing, horseback riding, sailing, bicycling, paddleboating, kayaking, swimming, backpacking.

And if you're a tennis nut, Keystone is a terrific place to tighten up your game. John Gardiner's Tennis Club is a mere lob shot away from your condo.

R.E.S.

Name: Keystone Condominiums
Managers: Robert A. Maynard presides over the entire Keystone community; Don Schuster is manager of the condominiums.
Address: Box 38, Keystone, Colo. 80435
Directions: Located 75 miles west of Denver on U.S. 6; take I-70 to the Dillon Exit (205), then take U.S. 6 6 miles east to Keystone. Or check American Limousine Service (303) 393-0653 for daily service between Denver's Stapleton International Airport and Keystone.
Telephone: (303) 468–1234
Cables/Telex: None
Credit Cards: American Express, Diners, MasterCard, Visa
Rooms: 152 doubles in lodge, 700 1, 2, and 3-bedroom condominiums.
Meals: Condominiums have completely equipped kitchens for cooking; there are 11 restaurants in and near the lodge, 6 eating places on the mountainsides; varying hours, prices, and cuisines; dress is casual in all.
Diversions: Downhill skiing (810 acres of trails, 15 lifts), heated outdoor swimming pool, skating, golf, fishing, horseback riding, sailing, bicycling, paddleboats, kayaks, backpacking; tennis nearby.
Sightseeing: Arapahoe Basin, Keystone Mountain, Dillon Reservoir.
P.S. Inquire about various package plans which include the cost of lift tickets.

C LAZY U RANCH
Granby, Colo.

$$$

What this ranch has going for it is its lazy-making setting—a sheltered valley of meadows and pines and streams, eight thousand feet up in the Continental Divide.

It's a real-life working ranch, and in June you can watch the roundups; at other times you can attend nearby rodeos and county fairs. Most people come here, however, for the riding, since it's free. There's a horse for every guest, and once you pick a mount to suit your skills, it's your personal horse all the time you're there. If you can afford to ignore the fact that you're paying for horses but still don't want to ride, you'll find plenty of other pastimes to keep you occupied—a heated pool, Jacuzzi, saunas, racquetball, Ping-Pong, fishing, a skeet range, horseshoe pitching, a jogging track, and a couple of new tennis courts. There are miles of walking trails to lonely groves, and unlimited spectacular sightseeing if you want to go for a drive. If you're here in the snowy months you'll find skiing, ice skating, snowshoeing, sleigh rides, and hot buttered rum before the big fire in the main lodge.

The ranch consists of a big red-roofed lodge facing a lake and flanked by smaller guest cottages. The six rooms in the lodge are the originals, and the most charming. The other rooms are spacious and decked out with "custom-built functional furniture," but they have little personality.

What happens in the evenings? You seem to spend most of the time eating wrangler-sized meals; but the ranch prides itself on its friendly, first-name atmosphere, and if you feel like mixing you'll find conviviality, cocktails, log fires, and a Baldwin grand piano. Forget the conviviality, get to bed early, and get up early to enjoy the mountains and the meadows. Or just B lazy old U.

Name: C Lazy U Ranch

Manager: Peter O. Webster

Address: Box 378, Granby, Colo. 80446

Directions: From Denver, take Interstate 70 and U.S. 40 to Granby, continue a couple of miles to Colo. 125, then go north for 3½ miles; from Rocky Mountain National Park, take U.S. 34 to Granby, then go west on Colo. 125; $110 charge (for 2) if you're picked up in Denver.

Telephone: (303) 887–3344

Cables/Telex: None

Credit Cards: None

Rooms: 12, 24 suites.

Meals: Breakfast 7:30–9:00, lunch 1:00, dinner 7:00; no room service; dress optional; occasional square dancing evenings in summer.

Diversions: Saunas, Jacuzzi, racquetball, table tennis, pool, horseback riding and tennis (2 courts) included in rates; hiking trails, skeet, fishing; golf, skiing, sailing, waterskiing nearby.

Sightseeing: Middle Park, Shadow Mountain, Granby Reservoir, Grand Lake.

THE HOME RANCH
Clark, Colo.

$$$

The Almighty spared absolutely nothing in creating this glorious site in Colorado's high country. It sits at 7,400 feet in the northernmost reaches of the Elk River Valley, totally circled by mountains. And, wonder of wonders, man hasn't mucked up this immaculate vista with any neon improvements.

Step out the door of your private cabin and you're in the midst of the Home Ranch's six hundred acres of quivering aspens, sage, and scrub oak. All yours to explore. Not far beyond are the vast expenses of Routt National Forest and the Mount Zirkel Wilderness Area. Also yours to explore.

This is no ride-'em-cowboy dude ranch. Far from it. First of all, it's very sparsely populated. There are accommodations for only sixteen to twenty guests right now—more to be built soon, but the head count will never exceed thirty to thirty-five. Its second difference from a dude ranch is that you're not surrounded by dust and meadow muffins all day. Everything is green and clear here. And the comforts are exemplary, too.

The community consists of one big log cabin set in a clearing, plus five smaller cabins hidden about in the nearby woods. The big house is where you take your meals and do your socializing. One of the little ones is where you go to get away from it all.

You get your first clue to some of the amenities at your front door. Your simple log cabin has a nice new hot tub on its deck. Inside: a simple, handsome sitting room, complete with wood-burning stove, Navajo rugs and wall ornaments, rugged handmade furniture.

The walls are bare rough-hewn spruce. There's not a gewgaw or gimcrack in sight anywhere. No television or telephone either.

Step beyond to your bedroom. Small and spare, but it has all the essentials: double bed and a puffy down-filled comforter. The bathroom is modern and spotless. There's radiant heat throughout. You may feel like a pioneer, but you needn't shiver like one to enjoy this simple life in the Rockies.

People who yearn for life in the fast lane probably won't like the Home Ranch. Neither will couples who are not on the friendliest of terms. There's much to fill your day here: horseback riding, cross-country skiing, trout fishing in stocked ponds, rock hounding, hiking, sleigh riding. But what you really come down to here is some rare creative solitude and a lovely opportunity for some close sharing—with nature, with one another.

Meals are hearty and wholesome. Everything is homemade, including breads and desserts. Vegetables are from the land. Dinner entrées run to prime rib roasts, chicken, veal, steak. Sharon Jones calls it "family gourmet" cooking. Hmmmmmm. Bring your own wine or settle for what you can rustle up at the general store up the road a piece from the Home Ranch.

R.E.S.

Name: The Home Ranch

Managers: Ken and Sharon Jones

Address: Box 822-K, Clark, Colo. 80428

Directions: U.S 40 to Steamboat Springs, County Road 129 to Clark; or Rocky Mountain Airways commuter plane from Denver to Steamboat Springs, or Frontier Airlines to Hayden; free pickup by arrangement at either airport.

Telephone: (303) 879–1780

Cables/Telex: None

Credit Cards: None; personal checks accepted

Rooms: 5 cabins (three 2-bedroom, two 1-bedroom); 2 more cabins to be built by late 1980.

Meals: 3 meals included in price, single sitting, family style; breakfast 8:00, lunch 12:30, dinner 6:30; no room service; no liquor sold, bring your own; dress casual.

Diversions: Daily horseback riding (except in winter), 10 miles of groomed trails for cross-country skiing, sleigh rides, ice skating, fishing in stocked ponds or at private frontage on Elk River—all included; 18 miles to Steamboat Springs for downhill skiing (provide your own transportation).

Sightseeing: Old goldminers' camp at Hahn's Peak Village, 283-foot waterfall at Fish Creek Falls, gondola rides and shopping at Steamboat Springs.

P.S. Guides available for hunting and fishing trips.

THE ASPEN CLUB CONDOMINIUMS
Aspen, Colo.

$$$$

No wonder the Aspen Club can get away with charging $400 a night for staying here at the height of the season. These are privately owned million-dollar condominiums. There are only twenty in all. No more than eight are ever available for rental to outsiders. So they are scarce, exclusive, loaded with cachet, and very, very desirable among the moneyed movie moguls from Hollywood and New York.

Cats can gaze upon kings. And you can gaze on the ways of today's power people as they let off steam in Aspen. At these prices, you'll surely be looking for a few peak experiences of your own.

Naturally, there's the skiing. The Aspen Club buys you no privileges on the slopes apart from delivering you there and fetching you in a limousine.

Where you really feel cosseted is within the confines of the Aspen Club itself, adjoining the condominiums. Walk over in your tennies or your jogging suit. But be sure to bring your membership card (yours temporarily as a renter). Stargazers and paparazzi are strictly forbidden.

How's this for a simple little health facility? Fourteen racquetball courts, two with galleries to hold a couple of hundred spectators for tournaments. Seven outdoor tennis courts, three indoor tennis courts. Plus squash courts, a full-sized gymnasium, a sixty-foot swimming pool, indoor and outdoor Jacuzzis, steam rooms, saunas, massage rooms.

Everything's done with a lavish, unsparing hand in this select little enclave. Each townhouse bears the personal decorating stamp of its owner. The look varies from home to home, but all are done to the nines.

Nobody really needs three fireplaces in a vacation home, but isn't it nice to know you have them? The master bath is a temple of mirrored self-indulgence with a double Jacuzzi that's big enough for a small Roman orgy. Two or three bedrooms. Full kitchen. Bring your chef and groceries. The only food available anywhere on these swank premises is at the health-food bar in the athletic club.

R.E.S.

Name: The Aspen Club Condominiums
Manager: Annie Conger
Address: 1450 Crystal Lake Road, Aspen, Colo. 81611
Directions: Major airlines to Denver's Stapleton International Airport, connect with Aspen Airways or Rocky Mountain Airways plane to Aspen, limo will pick you up by arrangement. By car, 196 miles from Denver; take I–70 west to Glenwood Springs, then Southeast on U.S. 82 to Aspen.
Telephone: (303) 925–8900
Cables/Telex: None
Credit Cards: American Express, MasterCard, Visa
Rooms: 8 condominiums, 2 or 3 bedrooms.
Meals: None. Fully equipped kitchen in each condo.
Diversions: Gymnasium, swimming pool, steam rooms, saunas, massage rooms, indoor and outdoor Jacuzzis; squash courts, racquetball (14 courts, 2 for tournaments), tennis (7 outdoor, 3 indoor); skiing.
Sightseeing: Mountains and stars; plus shopping, restaurants, and night life in Aspen.
P.S. Spring and fall rates are less than half the rate in skiing season.

SUNDANCE
near Provo, Utah

$$$

Shangri-la is Chinatown at rush hour compared to this: a grove of quaking aspen and pines serenaded by a babbling brook, watched over by the Wasatch National Forest and towering Timpanogos Mountain. You wander along pathways lined with kinnikinnick, drink fresh spring water, and share 4,300 acres of wilderness with inquisitive deer and pot guts (Rocky Mountain ground squirrels). Since there are only nine houses on the estate, you can go from breakfast to dinner without seeing another human.

If you want to know precisely how ravishing Sundance is before you go barreling out to Utah, see *Jeremiah Johnson.* It was filmed there. (And just for the record, the resort was known as Sundance long before Robert Redford made *Butch Cassidy and the Sundance Kid,* and he and his buddies bought up the place.)

The place is a marvel of unspoiled tranquility, partly because of the setting, partly because when Redford and his posse rode in they laid down firm laws: chop one tree, plant two; hide all buildings among the trees; no hunting, ever.

Until ten years ago, there wasn't much here except a short ski tow, thousands of trees, and pot guts; there still isn't much. So what is Sundance? Hard to say. It's sort of a ski resort, but it certainly isn't a hotel—to stay there, you rent one of the nine private vacation homes (cabins, they modestly call them) dotted among the trees. There are no hotel services, except daily maid service.

BOSKY LOVE NESTS. All nine "cabins" are different, and there's no way of knowing which one will be available when you get there. When you arrive, ask Brent Beck to take you on a tour to show you which homes are free. With luck he'll offer you the Magelby Home. This one is named for a local artist who traded his artistic skills for a plot of land, and then built himself a Hansel-and-Gretel cabin of rough-hewn timbers and filled it with stone fireplaces, wood paneling from an old barn, a couple of cuddly bedrooms (one with a fireplace), and antiquey things like old ice skates, a retired bear trap, and an antiquated pedal organ. It's positively the most romantic spot in Utah, and if you hurry you may be able to rent it for $85 a night (in summer).

Although Sundance is basically a ski resort, there's plenty to do here in summer and fall. For a start, those 4,300 acres are great for walking and picnicking. There's a stable with thirty-five horses ($6 an hour), and you can go trotting off on your own without a wrangler along—or with a wrangler, on an overnight pack trip into the back-woods. There's no pool (but you can drive to one of the lakes in the neighborhood for swimming and waterskiing), and no tennis.

Otherwise, Sundance has a main lodge that includes a village store, snack bar, and restaurant. The snack bar's most gobbled lunch is a giant hunk of freshly baked bread smothered with melted butter and honey. It costs fifty cents apiece, and has enough calories for an entire meal, and if you're not careful you may end up looking like a pot gut. Dinner is served in the Tree Room, which has a Douglas fir growing through the roof, Navajo rugs, and stills of *Jeremiah Johnson* on the wall. The steaks and seafood are so good here, people drive over from Salt Lake City for dinner—and the Sundance outdoor theater.

BORDELLO BANDITO. The irrepressible people who run Sundance have built themselves an unusual open-air theater, where they put on plays and musicals which they compose, write, design, and produce themselves. A recent hit was called *Bordello Bandito*, but you might also be there for an afternoon of rock or a moonlight recital of chamber music. Sundance is nothing if not surprising.

They have installed a new ski lift to the top of the mountains, so that Robert Redford can enjoy championship skiing without having to drive over to Snowbird. (It's enough to make you want to be a movie star.) They also plan to hide Sundance. The parking lot, now the first thing to greet you, is being shunted off to a tree-screened location behind the lodge, and the forecourt will be landscaped with more trees. *More* trees? Shangri-la never had it so good.

Name: Sundance
Manager: Brent Beck
Address: P.O. Box 837, Provo, Utah 84601
Directions: Take Interstate 15 to the Provo or Orem Exit, then follow U.S. 189 about 10 miles into the canyon to Utah 80, where you go left (for its seclusion, it's surprisingly accessible); by air to Salt Lake City; and by Amtrak to Ogden.
Telephone: (801) 225–4100
Cables/Telex: None
Credit Cards: American Express, MasterCard, Visa
Rooms: 9 mountain homes.
Meals: Breakfast 9:00–11:00, lunch 10:00–2:00, dinner 5:30–10:00 (approx. $10 to $30 for 2); no room service; dress optional; occasional live music.
Diversions: Outdoor pool, skiing, cross-country skiing (bring your own gear), hiking trails; horseback riding ($6 per hour), golf ($3 per round); sailing and waterskiing nearby.
Sightseeing: Pioneer Museum, Brigham Young University.

THE LODGE AT SNOWBIRD
Snowbird, Utah

$$

Utah has some of the most good-God-will-you-look-at-that scenery on the face of the earth, but until recently the only places to stay were run-of-the-mill motels. New ski resorts are changing all that. The most spectacular of these resorts is Snowbird, six years old and created from scratch eight miles inside Cottonwood Canyon, which is so narrow you can almost throw snowballs from one side to the other. From the skier's point of view the Snowbird statistics are as thrilling as a slalom: 3,100 feet of vertical rise, an average snowfall of 450 inches a year (more than Aspen and Vail *together*), and an aerial tram that hoists 1,000 hopefuls an hour to the top of the runs.

Your first view of the Lodge at Snowbird from the road is a two-story structure of rough-cast concrete and cedar trim, snug with the side of the canyon, and so diffident about its majestic surroundings that you have to peer twice to see the name plate. In the lobby you're confronted with duplex floor-to-ceiling windows framing a stunning view of the slopes, and when you step out onto the terrace you realize you've seen only two of the lodge's seven stories. The other five go *down* the hillside. Seven stories of concrete and a mammoth aerial tram may not sound like the best thing that could happen to a lovely, virgin canyon, but in fact Ted Johnson and Dick Bass, the founder and funder respectively of Snowbird, seem to have been at great pains to preserve and protect the environment. Item: of the total of 860 acres owned by Bass, only twenty acres will actually have buildings (hooray for the high rise); item: no private land is being offered for sale, so they keep control of all the architecture; item: the 150,000 square feet (the equivalent of three and one-half acres) of the Lodge at Snowbird were sited in such a way that only four evergreens had to be removed.

GRANITE FIREPLACES, BENTWOOD ROCKERS. Now for the lodge itself. It has 160 condominium rooms, in three types of accommodations—

bedroom, studio, and suite. The suites are Playboy Seductive, with granite fireplaces, enough logs for a protracted seduction, stylish leather-and-teak Scandinavian sofas and chairs; a kitchen for mixing wicked drinks; and a loft with queen-size beds and bentwood rockers. Each suite's two floors of window open onto that spectacular mountain view, but since the terrace outside the window runs the full length of the lodge and people can pass to and fro, keep the lights low when you're admiring the view if you're admiring each other at the same time. The studios are similar to the suites, but without the loft bedrooms; the bedrooms are spacious, motel-type rooms with two queen-size beds. All the rooms have modern bath/showers, television, room telephones. (Note: the adjoining sixty-eight-room Turramurra Lodge has identical accommodations, same rates.) The only problem at Snowbird is the one you have in most ski resorts: the staff is full of enthusiasm—for skiing rather than housekeeping. Otherwise, a nice place to be, especially in summer when the last skier has gone clomping and stomping off with his zombie boots, and tranquility reigns once more.

All of Snowbird Village's facilities are operating in summer—

nine restaurants, shops, delicatessen, an unusual bar built around the exposed workings of the giant aerial tram. The tram itself is slowed down from its regular six-minute ride for impatient skiers to a twelve-minute ride for leisurely sightseers, from 8,100 feet at the plaza to 11,000 at Hidden Peak. And even if it hauls up a full load of 125 people there are still plenty of out-of-this-world spots among the trees and the peaks.

Name: The Lodge at Snowbird
Manager: Ed Pilkerton
Address: Snowbird, Utah 84070
Directions: Take Interstate 15 to the Sandy Exit, about 20 miles south of Salt
    Lake City, then go east another 12 miles or so on Utah 210; or take
    Interstate 80E to Interstate 125 Belt Route to Wasatch Boulevard,
    follow the boulevard to Little Cottonwood Canyon (Utah 210), then up
    7 miles to Snowbird. By air, to Salt Lake International Airport; by
    Amtrak to Ogden.
Telephone: (801) 742–2222 or, for reservations, (801) 742–2000
Cables/Telex: None
Credit Cards: American Express, Carte Blanche, Diners, MasterCard, Visa
Rooms: 160 (plus an additional 410 at 3 other lodges in Snowbird).
Meals: Breakfast 7:00–11:00, lunch 11:00–4:00, dinner 6:00–10:00 (approx.
    $8 to $40 for 2), plus 9 other restaurants in the resort; no room service;
    informal dress; live music, dancing, disco, wine-and-cheese parties.
Diversions: Heated outdoor pool, therapy pool, sauna, hiking trails; tennis (5
    outdoor, with lights, $8 per court per hour, pro shops, clinics), skiing,
    cross-country skiing, ice skating; horseback riding nearby.
Sightseeing: Wasatch National Forest, symphony concerts, craft fairs, cultur-
    al festivals, Oktoberfest, tram rides.

ALTA LODGE
Alta, Utah

$$

Alta is one of the granddaddies of ski resorts, one of the first in the U.S. to hoist skiers up the mountain with a chair lift; but originally it was discovered by people who were more interested in getting *into* rather than up the mountain—would-be miners with the same gleam in their eyes that you see in skiers' after the first snowfalls of the season. Some people made fortunes in silver up here, and in the last part of the nineteenth century Alta had a population of five thousand. When you go walking in the woods you can still stub your toes on the remains of their homes and mines. Today the population is reduced to a few dozen in summer, nature lovers and the like—hiking, bird-watching, picnicking, savoring the fresh mountain air.

Several of the resort's ski lodges remain open throughout the year, and the most popular is also one of the oldest, the Alta Lodge. Its fifty-six rooms include a few dormitories and some luxurious bed-sitting suites. Most of the latter are in a new chrome-and-glass wing tacked on to the side, with wall-to-wall carpeting, king-size beds, and picture windows, and a few of them also have fireplaces and balconies facing the High Rustler Slope; but some of the most popular rooms are the old-style pine-paneled nooks in the chaletlike main lodge. And there's also a new relaxation building, with two saunas and two hot whirlpools to soothe any overworked muscles. Compared with Sundance, say, or Sun Valley, it's not exceptional, but its off-season rates ($35 to $42) make it a more-than-agreeable spot for a relaxed summer or fall vacation in the heady mountain air, 8,600 feet above sea level, surrounded by the pines and firs of the Wasatch National Forest.

Name: Alta Lodge
Owner/Manager: Bill Levitt
Address: Alta, Utah 84070
Directions: Take Interstate 15 to the Sandy Exit, about 20 miles south of Salt Lake City, then go east another 12 miles or so on Utah 210, and continue for a couple of miles past Snowbird; by air to Salt Lake International Airport, by Amtrak to Ogden.
Telephone: (801) 742-3500
Cables/Telex: None
Credit Cards: MasterCard, Visa (summer only)
Rooms: 56.
Meals: Breakfast 8:00–9:30, lunch 12:00–1:30, dinner 6:30–9:30 (approx. $20 to $30 for 2); coffee in the lobby all day; no room service; dress optional.
Diversions: 2 whirlpools, saunas; tennis, hiking and walking trails, downhill and cross-country skiing (with rentals), helicopter trips nearby.
Sightseeing: See "The Lodge at Snowbird."
P.S. Some special package rates available.

SUN VALLEY LODGE
Sun Valley, Idaho

I think I know why so many celebrities vacation in Sun Valley: no one pays the slightest attention to a passing princess or shah because everyone is so engrossed. There's just so much to do here. The listing below is only part of the story: most winter resorts have cross-country skiing, but few of them have thirty instructors; many resorts rent bicycles but not many give you a choice of standard or three-speed or ten-speed or tandem; and while several resorts have activities for the mind as well as the body, not too many have a Center for Arts and Humanities with workshops in yoga and tai chi chaun, ceramics, and photography.

The way Averell Harriman conceived it, back in the thirties when he was a youthful chairman of the board of Union Pacific Railroad, Sun Valley would be a winter resort in the wilderness—but with an air of sophistication. It soon became the most fashionable, most successful resort in the Rockies; it has been through two new owners and major developments since then, and the original lodge and its sibling inn are now surrounded by acres of condominiums. But the location is probably as invigorating as ever—a natural bowl in the mountains, a vale of aspen and pine and sagebrush, with dazzlingly green fairways and Hemingway's favorite trout stream winding through the foothills.

The lodge itself is set off by trim lawns and duck ponds and masses of flowers. The new owner has decided to replace its distinctive thirties furnishings with contemporary lines and fabrics, and color television has been installed in each room; for anyone who never knew the lodge in the old days the new styling will probably be just fine. Certainly it's comfortable. Several of the suites in the main lodge have fireplaces, a few of them have *two* terraces—one facing the lawns, the other overlooking the ice-skating rink where so many Olympic medalists have been trained. In addition to the lodge, Sun Valley offers you almost as many options in types of accommodations as there are diversions—Lodge Apartments (spacious suites with fireplaces and kitchens, adjoining the lodge), condominiums in all sorts of configurations, beside the pool and tennis courts, in the foothills of the mountains, between the creek and the fairways, right at the base of the ski lifts. How do you choose? For good value, an Atelier Studio (Murphy bed, TV, kitchenette, but no view) rents for just $33 in spring; for a few dollars more you can have a tri-level studio in Villager One; a few more dollars and you get a one-bedroom suite with loft bedroom and full kitchen in Villager Two. If you're a skier, you can ski right to the door of the one-bedroom suites in the Snow Creek condominiums.

Yet with all the activity going on around you, twosomes can still go off on their own and be romantic. The obvious: renting a tandem and cycling the mile into the village of Ketchum for lunch, or renting horses and trotting off through lonesome canyons for a quiet picnic beneath cottonwood trees by the edge of a mountain stream. The unusual, too. In winter, you can hire a horse-drawn cutter and driver, wrap yourselves in blankets, and skim across the snow to wine and dine in a log cabin. And for a grand gesture, how about this: rent the lodge's glass-enclosed swimming pool for the evening, call room service, and have the waiters bring over champagne and dinner. Just the two of you. No one will pay any attention—they'll assume you're just another shah and princess.

Name: Sun Valley Lodge
Manager: Wally Hoffman
Address: Sun Valley, Idaho 83353
Directions: By car, Interstate 84 to Twin Falls, then go north for an hour on U.S. 75 (that's the simplest route, but from Boise you can also take 1–84 to Moutain Home, then U.S. 26 across the windy mesa to U.S. 75, to Blackfoot, then U.S. 26 past Craters of the Moon National Monument to U.S. 75). By air, to Twin Falls (where you can be met by bus or limousine), or by Mountain West Airlines from Boise and Salt Lake City to Hailey, 12 miles south of the lodge.
Telephone: (208) 622–4111 or (800) 635–8261
Cables/Telex: None
Credit Cards: American Express, MasterCard, Visa
Rooms: 140 rooms and suites in the lodge, plus hundreds of condominium apartments.
Meals: Breakfast 8:00–10:00, lunch (indoors or outdoors) 12:00–6:00, din-

ner 6:00–9:30 (maybe later, approx. $22 to $25 for two), plus several restaurants in all price ranges in the valley and nearby Ketchum; room service during dining room hours in lodge, and lodge apartments; dress informal, but usually jackets at dinner in the main dining room; combo in the lounge, lots of entertainment in the neighborhood.

Diversions: Sauna, pool room, bowling alley, 3 heated outdoor pools (glass-enclosed lodge pool open year round), hiking trails, fishing, trap and skeet shooting, ice skating year round, horseback riding (indoors in winter); Arts and Humanities Center with workshops in karate, ceramics, dance, photography, etc.; 58 downhill runs, cross-country trails; tennis (18 courts, no lights, $7 doubles per hour, pro shop, clinics, automated ball machines), golf (18 holes, $12 per round, other courses nearby), sleigh rides, *no* snowmobiles.

Sightseeing: Sun Valley Village; the Opera House, Sun Valley Creative Arts Center (summer concerts).

JENNY LAKE LODGE
Grand Teton National Park, Wyo.

$$$

Think, for one soul-refreshing moment, of the classic Rockies setting—craggy peaks, gouged by glaciers, permanently frosted, soaring above stands of birch and pine. Think of the classic Western homestead—a forest encampment of snug log cabins surrounded by meadows of wildflowers. Think of serenity—no cars, no jets, no jangling telephones, no television, no mobs. Think of mountain streams and elk and trumpeter swans, think of days in the saddle and wide open spaces. Now put all these dreams together and you begin to have an inkling of what Jenny Lake is all about.

This is another of those remarkable Rockresorts that so adroitly blend the wonders of the wilderness with just the right degree of civilized comforts. Here they have some of the most spectacular mountain scenery in the world, a range of rugged peaks leaping right up out of the plain; a mile or two in either direction will bring you to the haunts of elk and moose, and occasionally a deer or young bear will wander into the garden to see what's cooking. One of the cabins dates from the original Jenny Lake settlement (in the twenties), and they're all furnished in the manner of pioneer days—braided rugs, chairs with hide seats, headboards of wood lashed with rawhide; even with the addition of bathrooms, ceiling fans, electric blankets, leather ice buckets, umbrellas, and flashlights, these cabins still give you a real feel of the Old West. It's not until you sit down in the rustic, raftered dining room that you realize the Old West was never like this: maître d', award-winning German chef, seafood Bengali, chateaubriand with sauce bearnaise, *Schwarzwalderkirschtorte*, and a Sunday buffet that stacks the groaning board with more than a hundred different dishes.

Jenny Lake is not for everyone (some people can't figure out why there's no wall-to-wall carpeting, air conditioning, television, and room phones—considering how much it costs to stay there), but for others, this is the ideal combination of wilderness and civilization, like having your *Schwarzwalderkirschtorte* and eating it too. For nonequestrians, it's a shame that horseback riding is included in the rate, because there's contentment enough just sitting on your patio, shaded by birch and pine, surrounded by clumps of chokecherry and Indian paintbrush, admiring the towering Tetons. It's a grand sight.

Name: Jenny Lake Lodge
Manager: Bernard F. Iliff (general manager), Emilio Perez (resident manager)
Address: Grand Teton Lodge Company, P.O. Box 240, Moran, Wyo. 83013
Directions: In Grand Teton National Park. By car, take any of 4 U.S. highways—26, 89, 187, or 287 (if you can, arrive or leave via Yellowstone National Park, next door); by air, daily flights by Frontier to Jackson Hole Airport (14 miles away, each flight is met by the lodge bus); by Amtrak to Rock Springs, Wyo.
Telephone: (307) 733-4647
Cables/Telex: None
Credit Cards: American Express, MasterCard, Visa
Rooms: 30, in individual log cabins.
Meals: Breakfast 7:30–9:00, lunch 12:00–1:30, dinner 6:30–9:00, gargantuan buffet dinner on Sunday, trail-ride breakfasts; room service for continental breakfast; informal dress; liquor service; chamber music once a week, and a harpist plays 4 nights a week.
Diversions: Unlimited horseback riding, bicycles, fishing, hiking (informal or guided, full day or overnight); golf, tennis, and heated pool at Jackson Hole Golf and Tennis Club, 14 miles away; scenic raft trips down Snake River.

Sightseeing: Grand Teton National Park, Snake River, along which the bald
eagle still roosts in all his natural glory, and the National Elk Refuge.
P.S. Reserve early, certainly before the end of April; no groups, few children,
1 baby bear.

JACKSON LAKE LODGE
Grand Teton National Park, Wyo.

$$

This is Rockresort's democratic version of *Jenny* Lake Lodge, an
opportunity for the average traveler to enjoy the splendors of the
Tetons in better-than-average comfort and style. Your anticipation
may falter, though, on arrival: the parking lot may be cluttered with
camper trucks, and the ground-level lobby is almost institutional.
But once you climb the stair to the main lounge, once you get your
first glimpse of its vast windows rising three stories, like vertical
Cinerama, and your first view of Mount Moran reflected in the lake,
your spirits will soar anew. And stay up there. The lodge sits on a bluff
above Willow Flats, and there's a large terrace that becomes a
promenade when guests gather at sunset to scan the Flats for a
glimpse of elk and moose heading for their waterholes; at any time of
the day you have an awesome panoramic view of the entire land-
scape—flats, lake, and the full range of Tetons, constantly changing
form and texture as the sun crosses the sky. You could simply sit here
all day admiring the scenery, without every hopping into your car
and going for tours. The lodge has all the facilities you need: that
impressive lounge, a morning-to-night coffee shop, a rather grand
dining room decorated with murals of the Old West, and the Stock-
ade Bar, decorated with authentic artifacts from the surrounding
settlements. The guest rooms are dispersed among the main lodge,
one-story Patio Suites, and two-story motor-lodge wings at one end.
Since The View is the attraction, that's what you pay for: the least
expensive rooms are just fine if you plan to be out-of-doors most of the
day, but if you insist on a view, ask for a room on the west side of the
main lodge, or a motor-lodge room numbered 580 to 594, where

you'll have a private balcony or patio to watch the elk and moose amble across Willow Flats.

Name: Jackson Lake Lodge
Manager: Bernard F. Iliff (general manager)
Address: Grand Teton Lodge Company, P.O. Box 240, Moran, Wyo. 83013
Directions: A few miles beyond Jenny Lake Lodge.
Telephone: (307) 733-2811
Cables/Telex: None
Credit Cards: American Express, MasterCard, Visa
Rooms: 385, including 42 in the main lodge, the remainder in bungalow and motor-lodge units.
Meals: You can eat in the coffee shop from 6:00 in the morning to 10:30 at night, in the main dining room during regular meal hours (prices from a few dollars to $20 for 2); room service breakfast only (7:30–10:00); dress informal, although you might feel out of place wearing cutoff jeans in the main dining room; cocktail piano nightly, occasional Indian dances, square dancing, movie shows, and lectures.
Diversions: Heated outdoor pool, sundeck, hiking trails; bikes and horses for rent; scenic raft trips, golf, tennis, and boating nearby.
Sightseeing: Yellowstone National Park is 20 miles to the north. Also check under Jenny Lake Lodge.
P.S. Busiest July and August, a few groups other months; lots of children.

For more suggestions in this area
turn to Added Attractions, page 375.

The Desert Resorts of the Great Southwest

It is the hour when from the boughs
The nightingale's high note is heard;
It is the hour when lovers' vows
Seem sweet in every whisper'd word . . .

BYRON

1. The Bishops Lodge
2. Rancho Encantado
3. Sagebrush Inn
4. Arizona Inn
5. Hacienda del Sol
6. Westward Look Resort
7. Tanque Verde Ranch
8. Sundancer Saddle and Surrey
   Ranch Resort
9. Lodge on the Desert

10. Arizona Biltmore Hotel
11. Marriott's Camelback Inn
12. John Gardiner's Tennis Ranch
13. The Wigwam
14. Wickenburg Inn Tennis and
    Guest Ranch
15. Carefree Inn
16. Garlands Oak Creek Lodge
★ *Added Attractions*

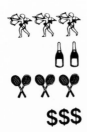

THE BISHOP'S LODGE
Santa Fe, N.M.

Here's a resort that owes its existence to an apricot tree. About a century ago, Archbishop Lamy was wandering through the Little Valley of the Tesuque when he discovered an old apricot tree with particularly succulent fruit. He liked the fruit, and the valley, so he built himself a small hilltop retreat and an adobe chapel with belfry steeple and hand-painted "stained glass" windows. The chapel is still there, and the apricot tree, now a gnarled 350 years old, still welcomes you to the lodge.

At the turn of the century the archbishop's estate was bought by newspaper tycoon Joseph Pulitzer, who built a couple of villas for his daughters; Jim Thorpe's family, in turn, bought it almost sixty years ago and converted it into a resort in 1919—which probably makes it the oldest resort in the Southwest.

IDEAL LOCATION. The location is ideal: a five-minute drive from the bustle of downtown Santa Fe, yet sheltered from the rest of the world, a valley in the foothills of the Sangre de Cristo Mountains, a private estate of eleven hundred acres with five miles of frontage on the Santa Fe National Forest, 7,300 feet above sea level, almost in the desert but shaded by cottonwoods, mountain poplars, crepe myrtle, lilac, Castilian roses—and fruit trees planted by the archbishop. Days are warm and sunny up here most of the year, but even in midsummer the nights are cool and you'll want to snuggle under a blanket.

The resort consists of the main lodge, with lounge, dining room, and cocktail lounge, all with southwest decor, the two Pulitzer villas, and a couple of new wings put up in the past ten years: sixty-five guest rooms and suites in all, and most of them are in authentic Southwest/New Mexico/Mexico decor, or something very close to it. For the record: the dreamiest is room 8, all adobe, with chunky beams, flagstone floor, Navajo rugs, fireplace, and Mexican hand-carved bed; suite 1 is a corner room with patios facing Colorado, plus a small lawn out front, cozy bedroom, fluffy carpets, fireplace, and viga (or rough-hewn beam) ceiling; suites 21 and 22, in the old Pulitzer House, have fireplaces, huge bathrooms with Mexican dressers, parlors (they're both $110 EP or $158 AP but #22 is probably the better buy because it has *two* fireplaces and a small garden). But all the Bishop's rooms are comfortable and/or charming, and eighteen of them have fireplaces.

OLD WOODCUTTERS' TRAILS. Riding is the big thing at the Bishop's. The half-dozen wranglers handle sixty to sixty-five horses in summer (and they're all the lodge's own horses), and if you can prove to the wrangler you know your way about he might let you go off on your own. There are miles of trails in and around the estate, but you can also follow old woodcutters' trails through the forest all the way to Colorado. Better take a picnic lunch along.

But you don't have to be an equestrian to enjoy the lodge. There are five new Laykold tennis courts, a big heated pool with saunas and a Jacuzzi, fishing and trap shooting. You can lie back and do a spot of birdwatching (forty-four species at last count), or you can drive off and visit some of the Indian pueblos around Santa Fe. This is one of the most fascinating corners of America—and the Bishop's Lodge is perfectly located for local excursions.

Evenings at the lodge usually begin with a drink in El Charro, a macho sort of place with saddles, sombreros, and spurs to remind you of *el charro*—the legendary cowboy of Mexico. The food is a mixture of continental and American—mignonettes of beef, Rocky Mountain trout, *boeuf à la Deutsch*, New Zealand spring lamb, Pacific red snapper; the main dining room has a Mexican feel to it, with notched off-white beams, copper chandeliers, murals of Indian ceremonies, "cantina" furniture, and hand-beaten tin doors. On warm evenings you can dine on the terrace and sniff the perfumed air that lured the archbishop here in the first place.

Name: The Bishop's Lodge
Owner/Manager: James R. Thorpe, Jr.
Address: P.O. Box 2367, Santa Fe, N.M. 87501
Directions: 3 miles north of Santa Fe Plaza on Bishop's Lodge Road (via
    Washington Avenue from Plaza, via Camino Encantado from U.S.

285/64/84); by air to Albuquerque (an hour and $65 a couple one way by lodge limousine); by rail via Amtrak to Lamy ($32 per couple by lodge limousine).

Telephone: (505) 983–6377

Cables/Telex: None

Credit Cards: None

Rooms: 65 rooms and suites in 5 lodges.

Meals: Breakfast 8:00–9:30, lunch 12:00–1:30 (Sundays 11:30–2:00), dinner 7:00–8:30 (6:30–9:00 in summer), approx. $20 to $40 for 2; room service during meal hours; jacket and tie for dinner.

Diversions: Sauna, therapy pool, table tennis, solar-heated outdoor pool, badminton, croquet, stocked-pond fishing, all free; tennis (5 courts, $5 per court per hour, pro shop, ball machine, clinics), horseback riding ($12 per ride, 1½ to 2 hours), skeet-trap shooting; bicycles for rent nearby.

Sightseeing: Sangre de Cristo Mountains, Santa Fe National Forest, Mission of San Miguel, St. Francis Cathedral, Palace of the Governors, Santa Fe Opera, Fine Arts Museum, Museum of International Folk Art, Wheelwright Museum (Navajo artifacts).

P.S. Special programs for children during summer; small conventions in spring and fall.

RANCHO ENCANTADO
near Santa Fe, N.M.

$$$

Beautiful. No, enchanting, like it says. By day there's desert as far as the eye can see; by night, there are stars as high as the eye can see; and there are interiors filled with art, artifacts, and antiques.

The ranch's 168 acres are surrounded on three sides by the Tesuque Indian Reservation and on the fourth by the Santa Fe National Forest; to the east are the Sangre de Cristo Mountains, to the west (away to the west) the Jemez Mountains. The grandeur of the setting and the charm of the ranch have corraled the likes of Henry Fonda, Kirk Douglas, Gregory Peck, the Duchess of Argyll, and Prince Rainier and Princess Grace of Monaco. Some posse.

The ranch got its start back in the early thirties when a young

lady who learned her innkeeping at The Bishop's Lodge decided to branch out on her own; she chose this spot and had her brother-in-law put up the buildings (he also made a lot of the furniture, some of it still here in the lobby). But the ranch's present name and personality are the creation of its present owner, Betty Egan, a widow from Cleveland, who started a new life here fourteen years ago with her four teen-agers. Among them, and with the imagination and taste of their interior designer, Donald Murphy, they've created the sort of guest ranch you always hope a desert ranch will look like.

The lobby's quarry tile floors and raftered ceiling set the tone; the lounge is a casually elegant room with a huge adobe fireplace, cowbells, a skylight above the fire, rawhide tables and lamps, and handwoven cushions. The dining room is three tiers of white adobe, decorative tiles, and quarry tile floors, with most of the tables commanding a view through tall windows and across the terrace to unending, unspoiled desert. There are lots of neat little touches about the place—like a wall plaque with nineteen (19) types of barbed wire, and a hand-carved armoire concealing a cigarette machine.

The twenty-eight guest rooms are equally enchanting—all in southwestern style, with Franklin stoves or adobe fireplaces, antique lamps, raftered ceilings, tiled floors, Indian rugs and wall hangings, *retablos*, and so forth. The quietest rooms are in the cottages (they also have fireplaces), but the prettiest is probably #8, up a beautiful tiled stairway to the second floor of the main lodge. All the rooms have private bathrooms with tub/showers, but no television (you can have one installed if you're gauche enough to ask for it).

Despite all this luxury, Rancho Encantado is an outdoorsy sort of place. One of its earliest horse-riding guests, a Mrs. Sage Underwood, used to turn up with her own cowboy; today she'd probably be happy to rely on the wrangler. His stable has ten frisky horses (horses rent for $8.75 an hour, and you'll probably have to be accompanied by a wrangler). There's also an elevated swimming pool with sun terraces and a stunning view across the desert. (Sharpshooters will find the trap range across the road; tennis buffs can while away the time between sets playing pool or having a beer in the Cantina Lounge, next to the courts.)

It would be a shame if the ranch's meals were a letdown for its lovely dining room. They're not. Wines? Everything from Paul Masson's Cabernet Sauvignon to a Rockerfellerish Château d'Yquem. If it means the difference between staying here and not staying here, settle for the Paul Masson. Or a glass of beer. Or even a glass of water.

Name: Rancho Encantado
Manager: John T. Egan
Address: Route 4, Box 57C, Santa Fe, N.M. 87501
Directions: In Tesuque, 8 miles north of Santa Fe, on State Highway 22, off Route 285.
Telephone: (505) 982–3537
Cables/Telex: None
Credit Cards: American Express, Carte Blanche, Diners, MasterCard, Visa
Rooms: 28 rooms, 9 suites
Meals: Breakfast 8:00–10:00, lunch 11:00–1:30, dinner 6:00–9:00 or 6:00–10:00 during the opera season (approx. $12 to $20 for 2); informal dress; recorded and live music.
Diversions: Game room, parlor games; heated outdoor pool, archery, hiking

trails, tennis (3 courts, no charge); horseback riding ($8.75 per hour); skiing, sailing nearby.

Sightseeing: See "The Bishop's Lodge."

P.S. Make your reservations far in advance, especially during the opera season.

SAGEBRUSH INN
Taos, N.M.

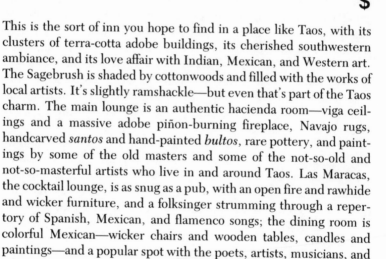

This is the sort of inn you hope to find in a place like Taos, with its clusters of terra-cotta adobe buildings, its cherished southwestern ambiance, and its love affair with Indian, Mexican, and Western art. The Sagebrush is shaded by cottonwoods and filled with the works of local artists. It's slightly ramshackle—but even that's part of the Taos charm. The main lounge is an authentic hacienda room—viga ceilings and a massive adobe piñon-burning fireplace, Navajo rugs, handcarved *santos* and hand-painted *bultos*, rare pottery, and paintings by some of the old masters and some of the not-so-old and not-so-masterful artists who live in and around Taos. Las Maracas, the cocktail lounge, is as snug as a pub, with an open fire and rawhide and wicker furniture, and a folksinger strumming through a repertory of Spanish, Mexican, and flamenco songs; the dining room is colorful Mexican—wicker chairs and wooden tables, candles and paintings—and a popular spot with the poets, artists, musicians, and assorted dilettantes and characters who've been here long enough to call themselves *taosenas*.

The guest rooms are grouped around a courtyard at the rear and linked by a shady ramada—except for a few rooms in the second story of the main building, and one rather drafty room in the penthouse of the mission-style tower. They're also in southwestern style, and some of them have adobe fireplaces in the corner (they're the most popular buys, because although you may think you're out in a blazing desert in Taos, in fact you're seven thousand feet up and it can get chilly there, even in midsummer). Twenty-two new rooms have been added in recent years, each with two oversize single beds, with

rust-brown-black bedspreads, ample closets, and color TV. Rooms
on the second floor are quieter. A second new wing, twelve two-room
suites, overlooks the pool, has superb views of the Sangre de Cristo
Mountains, but picks up traffic noise.

Unfortunately, there's nothing very Taosy or romantic in the
inn's setting—plunk by the side of the highway like any common or
garden motel; and the South Santa Fe Road only proves that the main
drag into a cultured, historic spot like Taos can be as dreary as any
other main drag. So use the Sagebrush Inn as a base for exploring the
art galleries, boutiques, restaurants, old churches, that marvelous
multistory Indian pueblo just north of town, and the other sights of
this extraordinary corner of the United States. Otherwise don't leave
your cozy little Sagebrush room except to lounge in the lounge, drink
in Las Maracas, or replenish your energy in the solar-heated dining
patio.

Name: Sagebrush Inn
Owner/Manager: Ken Blair
Address: P.O. Box 1566, Taos, N.M. 87571
Directions: 2 miles south of Taos and just north of Rancho de Taos, on the
    south Santa Fe Road (U.S. 68).
Telephone: (505) 758–2254
Cables/Telex: None
Credit Cards: American Express, Carte Blanche, Diners, MasterCard, Visa
Rooms: 60.
Meals: Breakfast 7:30–10:30, lunch 11:30–2:30 (June through September
    only), dinner 5:30–10:00 (approx. $15 to $24 for 2); no room service;
    informal dress.
Diversions: Heated outdoor pool; tennis (2 courts, $3.50 per court per hour).
Sightseeing: Taos, The D. H. Lawrence Ranch and Shrine, The Harwood
    Foundation, The Millicent A. Rogers Memorial Museum, Rodeo de
    Taos, Kit Carson's house.
P.S. Busiest July and August, and weekends during the skiing season.

For detailed rate, turn to page 413.

ARIZONA INN
Tucson, Ariz.

$$

Lawns everywhere. Beds of violets and poppies. Anchor doves flitting among the palo verde, poplars, bottlebrush, and longneedle pine. Eight gardeners silently trimming, weeding, watering. You could easily fool yourself into thinking you're out in the country. In fact, you're smack in the middle of suburbia, and the Arizona Inn is merely a cocoon coddling you from the real world.

It wasn't always that way.

When it first opened forty-odd years ago, the Arizona was indeed away out in the middle of the desert, but then the almost perfect climate of Tucson lured more and more vacationers to the area, and then more and more residents, and slowly the city besieged the inn. You'd never guess that from inside the inn, and there's no reason to leave. You have everything you need for unwinding right there within the pink stucco walls of this fourteen-acre oasis.

You have a private patio for sunbathing; an uncrowded swimming pool with a sun terrace on one side and a leafy arbor on the other; a couple of Har-Tru tennis courts (floodlit for evening play) and a pro shop; a croquet lawn and a putting green; and a pampering staff.

STRAWBERRIES, FIGS, AND BAKED WINESAP APPLES. Goodness, how you'll be pampered. Morning paper waiting at your door. Breakfast on your patio (anything from muffins, strawberries, apricots, and figs to hot clear bouillon, kippered herring, and baked winesap apple). Lunch by the pool. Dinner by the fire in your room. Fresh flowers and finger bowls in the dining room.

This is the sort of place where personal service still means *personal* service. The poolside waiter gets quite upset if he can't remember your name when you order your second round—and the fact that he's been remembering names correctly for over thirty-seven years doesn't console him. Almost half the staff have been at the Arizona Inn for twenty years or more (not too many hotels can make a claim like that), which is probably one reason why so many of the guests have been coming back year after year since the inn was surrounded by desert. They're not only loyal, they're a pretty distinguished group, too—from Winston Churchill and assorted English lords to Salvador Dali and Cary Grant. John D. Rockefeller liked it so much here he kept a cottage for his permanent use. And apparently the inn still gets the patricians, because the registration card includes space at the bottom for the names of your chauffeur and maid.

This special place came into being in a rather unusual way. Shortly after World War I, a local lady by the name of Miss Greenway (the first congresswoman from Arizona) started a plan to help veterans adapt to postwar conditions: they made furniture by hand, their wives decorated it, Miss Greenway bought it. They must have been eager beavers because after a short time Miss Greenway had more furniture than she could use. So she built an inn out in the desert.

But don't get the idea that the Arizona Inn is a rickety place filled with old handmade furniture. It isn't. Miss Greenway added some of her own family heirlooms, and regional decorations made from copper and cactus. It's a luxurious place, with a full-time decorator on the staff to make sure everything stays immaculate. The lounge is fit for a Spanish grandee—dark wooden ceiling and rafters, stately furniture grouped around a huge fireplace, and custom-designed carpets handwoven in Morocco. The rooms are equally comfortable, with armchairs, desks, coffee tables, card tables, walk-in closets, handblocked linen spreads, original paintings, air conditioning for the summer months, television (they finally gave in), private patios—or, in some cases, private gardens, patios within patios.

Name: Arizona Inn
Owner/Manager: John S. Greenway/Robert Minerich
Address: 2200 East Elm Street, Tucson, Ariz. 85719
Directions: Leave Interstate 10 at the Speedway Boulevard Exit, go east on Speedway to the University of Arizona, turn left on Campbell, drive 5 blocks, turn right, and you're on East Elm, almost at the entrance; also scheduled air and Amtrak service.
Telephone: (602) 325–1541
Cables/Telex: 165523
Credit Cards: American Express, Carte Blanche, MasterCard, Visa

Rooms: 85, 8 suites, 3 private homes.

Meals: Breakfast 7:00–9:30, lunch 12:00–1:45, dinner 6:30–8:30 (approx. $18 to $22 for 2); room service during dining-room hours; jacket and tie for dinner in winter.

Diversions: Heated pool, croquet, table tennis, putting green, tennis courts (2 courts, no lights); golf course, horseback riding, hiking, skiing nearby.

Sightseeing: Old Tucson, Arizona State and Historical museums, Arizona—Sonora Desert Museum, Mission San Xavier del Bac, Sabino Canyon, Coronado Forest Preserve, Saguaro National Monument. Mexico is just 65 miles south.

P.S. Open all year, peak months (mostly elderly clientele) January through April; small groups during summer.

HACIENDA DEL SOL
Tucson, Ariz.

$$

The well-to-do of Tucson are taking to the hills these days, to the foothills of the Catalinas, but the Home of the Sun beat them to it. Its knolltop perch will probably stay unspoiled for years to come, too, because the owner of this swatch of desert lives on the neighboring knoll and he likes the view just as it is. You're welcomed to the hacienda by a mission gateway, and a gently splashing blue-tiled fountain and a pathway shaded by orange and grapefruit trees lead you inside to a cloisterlike cluster of adobe casitas, all arches and red-tiled roofs. Very Mexican, very Spanish.

The hacienda was built originally as a girls' school, back in 1929, and transformed into a guest ranch in 1946; when the Hartmans took over about ten years ago, they moved in their personal collection of Mexican and Indian art—Aztec suns, gods' eyes, hand-painted chairs, hand-beaten tin screens and chandeliers. The dining room is roofed by heavy carved beams, highlighted by silver lamps and sconces; the lounge has a blue adobe fireplace and a collection of Navajo rugs and Kachina dolls. It's the Southwest with style and taste.

It's a wonderfully detached, soothing place, up there above the city. You can lounge in the courtyard beneath the orange and

grapefruit trees or in the glass-enclosed therapy pool with a view of the Catalinas. At tequila time you can pull up a chair by the windows of the Casa Feliz, look down on Tucson's sprawling lights, and pretend they're moonlight shimmering on a lake; then a leisurely dinner in that beautiful dining room (the hacienda's chef was recently invited to spend a summer cooking aboard the Norwegian royal yacht); afterward, a stroll around the garden before turning in for the night. If you want something to read, the hacienda's library fills two walls (one of the country's leading publishers spends a few weeks here ever year).

Despite all this charm and style, the hacienda is really a ranch; it has its own stable and its own string of fifteen horses, and its friendly wranglers will take you riding up beyond the foothills of the Catalinas to Piñon Canyon and Finger Rock.

Name: Hacienda del Sol
Owner/Manager: Robert E. Hartman
Address: Hacienda del Sol Road, Tucson, Ariz. 85718

Directions: Follow Campbell Drive from the University of Arizona to River
  Road; turn right, drive until you come to Hacienda del Sol Road, and
  stay with it all the way (about 8 miles from downtown Tucson).
Telephone: (602) 299–1501
Cables/Telex: None
Credit Cards: None
Rooms: 31 rooms, 7 suites, 5 villas.
Meals: Breakfast 8:00–10:00, lunch 12:30–1:30, dinner 6:30–7:30; room ser-
  vice during meals; jacket at dinner.
Diversions: Heated outdoor and indoor pools, therapy pool, exercise room,
  hiking trails, putting green, shuffleboard, horseshoes, occasional
  movies and games in the evening, tennis court (free), horseback riding
  ($5 per hour), golf (championship courses nearby).
Sightseeing: See "Arizona Inn."
P.S. Quietest times are first 2 weeks in November, first 3 weeks in January,
  but relaxing anytime. Rates listed are for November 1 to May 1 *only*;
  closed during summer.

WESTWARD LOOK RESORT
Tucson, Ariz.

From the distance, it looks like a Greek village, a terraced hilltop of
dining room and tennis courts, swimming pool and therapy pool, and
a cluster of townhouse suites on the lower tier, the whole held
together by well-tended gardens and winding pathways. The surrounding acres of desert may look scraggly and bleak, but if you were
to spend an afternoon walking around and counting the different
types of plant and flower you'd have enough names to fill a foolscap
page—everything from periwinkle to cow's-tongue cactus. These
acres of desert also serve to isolate the Westward Look from its
neighbors, which gives it its quiet, unhurried air. It's probably the
best of these Tucson hideaways for tennis buffs, even though its
altitude (3,200 feet) exposes the courts to occasional gusts of wind that
play havoc with lobs.

The so-called Posada rooms are standard-sized, standard-equipped units, grouped around the swimming pool and therapy pool; the townhouse, or Fiesta, rooms have an extra dining area, kitchen, and refrigerator. Some have better views than others, but don't lose any sleep on that point because Tucson is not the most exciting cityscape in the land. In any case, if you want to admire the twinkling city lights you can do that from the dining room, the Gold Room no less, which has floor-to-ceiling windows and soft lights. You may be grateful here for something to look at, other than the parchment menu, because the service confirms that old rule of thumb about waiters: the fancier the shirt, the chancier the service. A shame, because it's not every resort where you can play a few sets of tennis, soothe your muscles in a therapy pool, then settle down to *boula-boula* (that's clear turtle soup topped with pea soup), *escalope de veau Oscar,* or *scampi Bretonne,* followed by slices of mango flamed with Martinique rum. If you want to enjoy your *boula-boula* without suffering the ineptness of frilly-fronted waiters, stay in your room and have your dinner carted down (or up) the hill. It's *faster* that way.

Name: Westward Look Resort

Manager: Joe Darling

Address: 245 East Ina Road, Tucson, Ariz. 85704

Directions: Take Interstate 10 to Ina Road Exit, go east on Ina Road; the resort is ½ mile beyond Oracle Road (U.S. 80/89).

Telephone: (602) 297–1157

Cables/Telex: None

Credit Cards: American Express, Carte Blanche, MasterCard, Visa

Rooms: 93, half of them poolside, half of them townhouse-style semisuites (and 9 rustic casitas adjoining the tennis courts).

Meals: Breakfast 7:00–10:00, lunch 11:30–2:30, dinner 7:00–10:00 (approx. $20 to $40 for 2); room service during meal hours; jacket for dinner in winter; combo every evening except Monday in the stygian Lookout Lounge.

Diversions: Heated outdoor pool and therapy pool; tennis (8 courts, 3 lighted, pro shop, ball machines, clinics), horseback riding ($3.50 an hour); a selection of golf courses nearby.

Sightseeing: See "Arizona Inn."

P.S. May be difficult to reserve a room during the Tucson Open Golf Tournament.

TANQUE VERDE RANCH
Tucson, Ariz.

$$

Many desert moons ago, the Tanque Verde's owner was strung up by the neck over the rafters of what is now the Reading and Card Room. Not by irate guests, but by outlaws out for his petty cash. That was back in the days when the ranch was a stagecoach stop on the San Pedro run, and it had its fair share of Injun raids and cattle rustling. Nowadays, the posses heading out of the corral are harmless and wobbly tourists, and the ranch is one of the most peaceful spots in Arizona.

It could hardly be anything else, given its location. It's 2,800 feet up in the foothills of the Tanque Verde Mountains; its eastern border is 1,385,307 rugged acres of the Federal Coronado Forest Preserve, and its southern border is the 63,000-acre Saguaro National Monument. Tucson is twelve miles and twenty-nine dips away along the

Speedway Boulevard. All that wilderness shuts out the rumbles of civilization and you're left with the cry of the coyote and the assorted chirps, warbles, cries, and whistles of the red-shafted flicker, LeConte's thrasher, the bridled titmouse, Williamson's sapsucker, and the lesser scaup. There's a birdbath in sight of every room, so you can sit on your porch and watch the cavortings of the common bushtit, black phoebe, boat-tailed grackle, and Inca dove. Look farther and you may spot a bald eagle. More than 196 species have been spotted here. (There's a bird-banding every Thursday, and guests are invited to join in.)

Most people don't come here, though, to watch the birds. They come to ride over desert trails, past giant saguaro, and up into the mountains to *Campos Americanos* and the *Puerto de Cabeza de la Vaca* (the Cow-headed Saddle). This is very much a horse-and-wrangler type of ranch—and you can take your pick from a string of eighty palominos, appaloosas, sorrels, and buckskins. Unlimited riding (but only with escort) is included in the rate, so most people ride. But if you get saddle sore, don't despair. There's plenty to do down on the ranch (see listing).

The oldest part of the ranch, dating from 1862, is now the office/lounge, alongside a low-ceilinged wing of adobe rooms sheltered by an authentic ramada of rough-hewn timbers topped by a roof of ghost saguaro. Hammocks dangle between the timber pillars. Antique Mexican pottery dots the garden, among the eucalyptus, pepper, and wild orange tree (if you're lucky you may even sample a wild orange pie some evening at dinner).

Across the garden is the old adobe bunkhouse, which has gone through a few transformations and become the Dog House Bar—a bottle club with flagstone floor, adobe fireplace, rawhide chairs, and pictures of Wild Bill Hickok, Wyatt Earp, Luther Patton, and that notorious Wild West dog-kicker, W. C. Fields. This is the gathering place after a day riding the range. Here, or up on the sundeck above the Sonora Health Spa and Recreation Center. The spa is where you'll find Tanque Verde's indoor pool, sauna, and exercise rooms. Unlikely items on a dude ranch? But this is no ordinary dude ranch.

THE PH.D. AND THE STEWARDESS. How could it be with a manager who speaks fluent French, Chinese, and Japanese, and earned his Ph.D. with a thesis entitled "A Russian Agronomist's Influence on

Japanese Agriculture"? DeeDee Cote was a stewardess who used to come here between flights to ride her favorite horse, Champ, before she realized she was really coming because she was in love with the manager. So they got married.

And where else will you find a dude ranch with one German and one French chef, and a pastry chef from Berlin? So you won't have to settle for chuckwagon food. Some evenings you'll find German dishes, other evenings Polynesian or Mexican.

Tanque Verde's sixty patio lodges and cottages all have private baths, individual thermostat controls for heating and air conditioning, and room phones, but no TV. Many of the rooms have log-burning fireplaces, many have private patios. No two rooms are alike, so take a peek and pick the one that suits you before you move in. Room 7, for example, is a suite with adobe fireplace, fitted carpet, wood walls; suite 22 has corner windows facing the sunset, a garden patio and fireplace; and if you're more interested in riding than in comfort, you can have a small "ramada" room (only $79—but remember that includes all meals *and* riding).

Name: Tanque Verde Ranch
Owner/Manager: Bob Cote
Address: Route 8, Box 66, Tucson, Ariz. 85710
Directions: Follow East Speedway east until it goes no farther—15 miles from the center of Tucson.
Telephone: (602) 296–6275
Cables/Telex: None
Credit Cards: None
Rooms: 47, 13 suites.
Meals: Breakfast 8:00–9:00, lunch 12:30–1:30, dinner 6:30–8:00; no room service; informal dress.
Diversions: Heated outdoor and indoor pools, therapy pool, sauna, exercise rooms, shuffleboard, table tennis, occasional movies and square dancing in the Bottle Club; tennis (4 courts, 1 lighted), horseback riding, hiking trails, bird-banding.
Sightseeing: See "Arizona Inn."
P.S. Busiest season December through April. Special packages available.

THE LODGE ON THE DESERT
Tucson, Ariz.

$$

The name made sense back in the thirties when the Lininger family first opened the doors of their hacienda to paying guests. The Lodge on the Desert truly was a lodge on the desert. The city of Tucson has long since corraled the Liningers, however, and, as happened with the Arizona Inn, their pleasant little "club resort" is now surrounded by tidy homes, a city park, and multilane gridwork of avenues. But once inside the garden walls, you quickly forget the Sun Belt boomtown outside. This peaceful, homey hacienda is still lovingly and graciously run by the Lininger clan; a son and a daughter-in-law now man the front desk, supervise waitresses, give guided tours, and along the way pick up fallen coat hangers on closet floors. It is the kind of place where last year's magazines and a forty-year accumulation of left-behind best-sellers fill every shelf and tabletop in the lounge, where the loudest sounds in the shady gardens are the whacking of a croquet mallet or the whooshing of a shuffleboard puck.

Lazy, lazy days, then, are the only order of business. A lap or two in the little, no-nonsense swimming pool. A game of chess or checkers. Siesta in a lawn chair. Tucson beckons—or perhaps not.

Lodge on the Desert was built in typical adobe hacienda style as a series of one-and-two-story casas set somewhat higgledy-piggledy and connected by belltower archways and meandering paths. Desert gardens, barely pruned from the existing wild landscape, fill the spaces between buildings; palms and flowering bushes shelter guest-room windows with leafy privacy; and hacienda walls shut out the city as they once shut out rattlers and other desert critters when the lodge was young. Rooms are big and apartmentlike with beamed ceilings, tiled baths, and large, walk-in closets (no wonder a few repeat guests now make the Lininger's hacienda their year-round residence). The look of the accommodations is basically easy-care adobe and quarry tile and the overall impression is of comfort and good taste. Much of the furniture is more functional than fashionable, but here and there are scattered Mexican antiques or original 1930s Monterey chairs and chests of drawers. All but a dozen rooms have fireplaces, several have adjacent kitchens or kitchenettes, and one of the suites, on the second floor above the lounge, even has its own private sundeck, private 30-foot swimming pool *and* private panoramic view over the city to the Catalina Mountains in the east or those glorious Arizona sunsets in the west. And from there you can even still see the desert.

L.E.B.

Name: The Lodge on the Desert
Owner/Manager: Schuyler W. Lininger
Address: 306 North Alvernon Way, Tucson, Ariz. 85733
Directions: Leave Interstate 10 at either the Speedway or Congress Street
     Exit; travel east to Alvernon Way; the lodge is between East Broadway
     and East Fifth streets.
Telephone; (602) 325–3366, toll free AMRES (800) 317–9157
Cables/Telex: None
Credit Cards: MasterCard, Visa
Rooms: 35, 2 suites.
Meals: Breakfast 7:00–9:30, 7:30–9:00 on weekends, lunch 12:00–1:30, Sun-
     day brunch 11:30–2:00, dinner 6:00–8:30 (approx. $15 to $20 for 2);
     room service during dining hours only; jackets for dinner during the
     winter season; no shorts.
Diversions: Outdoor pool (or private 30-foot pool in suite 64), shuffleboard,
     croquet, darts, Ping-Ping; two 18-hole golf courses, 21 lighted tennis
     courts, 6 racquetball courts nearby.
Sightseeing: See "Arizona Inn."

SUNDANCER SADDLE AND
SURREY RANCH RESORT
Tucson, Ariz.

$$

Only thirty guests can bunk down here at one time, and since horseback riding is included in the room rates and the ranch is surrounded by six mountain ranges, most of those thirty people spend as much time in the saddle as their flesh will allow. Their enthusiasm makes for a clubby atmosphere, helped along by the rawhide-and-blue-tiled cantina, a bottle club where wranglers and riders get together after their days in the sagebrush and saguaro. Helped along, too, by the *Pátron Grande* and his wife Colette, now in their twenty-ninth season at the ranch.

Jack Jackson's etc. etc. Resort is an informal, easygoing sort of place, casual as a cowpoke; no jacket or tie for dinner here (but you are expected to be in their Mexican-style dining room ready to sit down to a family-style meal at seven o'clock pronto). After dinner, you can pull up a chair before one of the fireplaces; or dodge the color TV in the lounge and play a few games of billiards in the raftered game room; or join a square dance on the terrace. More likely, you'll want to slip off to bed and get a good night's sleep to prepare you for tomorrow's breakfast ride up into the Tucson Mountains.

Name: Sundancer Saddle and Surrey Ranch Resort
Owner/Manager (or "Pátron Grande"): Jack J. Jackson
Address: 4110 Sweetwater Drive, Tucson, Ariz. 85705
Directions: Leave Interstate 10 at Grant Road Exit; drive west 1 mile to Silverbell Road, north 2½ miles to Sweetwater Drive, west 1¼ miles on Sweetwater. If you're coming by air, they'll pick you up at the airport.
Telephone: (602) 743-0411
Cables/Telex: None
Credit Cards: None
Rooms: 14 casitas.
Meals: Breakfast 7:30–9:00, buffet lunch 12:30 by the pool or on the terrace, dinner 7:00 (served family style, bring your own wine); room service available; informal dress; live music and dancing on the terrace, Sunday evening barbecues, cookout rides.
Diversions: Billiards, backgammon, Aqua'ssage hydrotherapy pool; heated outdoor pool, hiking trails, horseback riding, sunbathing tower, shuffleboard, putting green, tennis (1 court)—no charge; and "any mixed doubles team that can beat Jack and Colette Jackson in two out of three sets will be offered a free day's stay on their next visit"; 5 golf courses nearby.
Sightseeing: See "Arizona Inn."
P.S. Special air-tour packages available. Minimum stay of 3 nights. Closed April 30 to October 31.

ARIZONA BILTMORE HOTEL

Phoenix, Ariz.

$$$

The lobby, lounge, and dining room have ceilings of pure gold leaf; Frank Lloyd Wright had a hand in the design, and the master's touch can be seen in murals and chandeliers, and in the texture and motifs of the unique facade. No ordinary resort this. But it may be heading that way.

Phoenix developers now have the Biltmore in a full nelson and some of the sense of spaciousness has gone. That splendid driveway sweeping from 24th Street to this Cloud Nine is no longer lined only with groves of orange trees but more and more with homes (classy homes, true, but hardly as pleasing to the soul as orange trees) and out back, beyond the pool and cottages are casitas, condominiums, and a new conference center that are circling the Biltmore like a posse around the James Gang. To top it all off, the fourth owner in less than a decade has taken over (the Westin, formerly Western International, Hotel group), and presumably they'll continue to put more emphasis on group business.

Still, the Arizona Biltmore *is* one of a kind, and it does offer at least some of the style of a resort in the grand manner: room service comes with all the trimmings, including white gloves on the waiters, and guests still dress to nines for sumptuous dining beneath the gold leaf.

The Biltmore's 410 guest rooms and 46 suites are classics in the Frank Lloyd Wright manner, revivified with pastel colors and geometric wall hangings. The most romantic rooms are in the fifteen cottages behind the main building, facing acres of lawns and beds of snapdragons and calendula. The new Paradise and Valley wings (constructed at great expense to match the texture and color of the original buildings) have biggish boudoirs with deep-pile carpeting, armchairs, and color TV; rooms on the first and fourth floors have patios (the rooms on the top are smaller, but you have more privacy on your patio), and you'll have a view either of the famed blue-tiled pool or the gardens and Squaw Peak.

Other recent features include more tennis courts, more fairways, and the spectacular Orangerie, dripping with long Art Deco chandeliers, and a new terrace café with blue-and-white patio furniture. The gardens are still one of the delights of the Biltmore: thirty-nine acres of flowers, fan palms, and weeping bottlebrush trees, cholla, and saguaro cactus. You can step from your room, reach up, and help yourself to an orange or grapefruit. No apples, but Eden enough. Especially if you didn't know the Biltmore in the old days.

Name: Arizona Biltmore Hotel
Manager: Cecil Ravenswood
Address: 24th Street and Missouri, Phoenix, Ariz. 85016
Directions: Just off 24th Street, between Camelback Road and Lincoln Drive, 20 minutes from the airport, interstates, and Amtrak depot.
Telephone: (602) 955–6600, toll free (800) 228–3000 (or any Westin hotel)
Cables/Telex: 165–709
Credit Cards: American Express, Carte Blanche, Diners, MasterCard, Visa
Rooms: 410, 43 suites.
Meals: Breakfast 6:30–10:30, lunch 11:30–2:30 (indoors, on the patio, by the pool), dinner 6:30–10:30 (approx. $40 to $45 for 2); room service 6:00 A.M. to 11:00 P.M.; jacket and tie for dinner (informal dining in the Mexican-style Adobe Steak House); live music and dancing nightly in the Aztec Lounge.
Diversions: Therapy pool, sauna, exercise rooms, heated outdoor pool, jogging trails; tennis (18 courts, 17 lighted, $2.50 per person per hour, pro shop, ball machines, videotape, clinics), golf (36 holes, green and cart fees $21–$27), bicycles for rent; horseback riding nearby.
Sightseeing: The Desert Botanical Garden, Heard Museum, Pueblo Grande Museum, Phoenix Art Museum, Pioneer Arizona, Arizona Museum, Phoenix Little Theater, Civic Plaza Symphony Hall, Celebrity Theater, the Rodeo of Rodeos (March).
P.S. Special rates available during summer months.

For detailed rate, turn to page 413.

MARRIOTT'S CAMELBACK INN
Scottsdale, Ariz.

$$$

This sand-colored enclave blends into sixty-five acres of desert (and concrete) in the foothills of Mummy Mountain across the way from Camelback Mountain. Its most distinctive buildings, the circular Chaparral Restaurant and Cantina Lounge, look like grounded UFO's and behind them, adobe-style casitas encircle a giant pool and a dazzlingly colorful garden, planted, in springtime, with a thousand daffodils and ranunculus and anemone bulbs. The Camelback guest rooms, too, are larger than usual (they're over five hundred square feet, for the record), and color TV, wet bars, and separate dressing areas come as standard equipment. The most unusual Camelback lodgings are the five-sided rooms inspired by the Indians' ceremonial *kivas* (beamed ceilings, oversize beds, rainbow headboards), but many of them are in a heavy-traffic location between the driveway and the tennis court; for privacy, the quietest rooms are closest to the mountain, but a good hike from the hub of the complex. To compensate for that, several of the suites up here have fireplaces, complete kitchens, and their own pools. If you can, check into one of the twenty-five Arizona Patio Rooms, on the second floor of the casitas, with secluded decks for intimate sunbathing.

But your problem in Phoenix may not be so much deciding which *room* but which *hotel*—Camelback or Biltmore. Each has its loyal following, but for those who have yet to sample the luxuries of either, here are a few comparisons. Many people find the informality of the Camelback more relaxing, whereas the Biltmore's grandeur tends to put some people on their Sunday-best behavior; at the Camelback, you can park your car almost at your doorstep, which gives you an added degree of privacy, if that's a consideration (but in turn that accounts for the extra concrete—you can't have it both ways); at certain times of the year the Camelback is cheaper (but since each hotel has its own pattern of seasons you'll have to study dates closely); at dinnertime you can choose between the Biltmore's European-style elegance and the Camelback's pseudo-sophisticated, outrageously red plush Chaparral Restaurant that now prides itself on the incongruous combination of *nouvelle cuisine* and flambéed specialties.

It's a tough choice, unless you happen to be a thrifty tennis player who fancies red plush.

Name: Marriott's Camelback Inn

Manager: Dave Rolston

Address: P.O. Box 70, Scottsdale, Ariz. 85252

Directions: On 5402 East Lincoln Drive, the main east-west road on the north side of Camelback Mountain; about 10 minutes from Scottsdale, 20 minutes from downtown Phoenix, Sky Harbor Airport, and the Amtrak depot.

Telephone: (602) 948–1700; toll free (800) 228–9290

Cables/Telex: 910 950 1198

Credit Cards: American Express, Carte Blanche, Diners, MasterCard, Visa

Rooms: 413 rooms and suites.

Meals: Breakfast 6:30–11:30, lunch 11:45–2:00, dinner 6:00–10:30 (approx. $20 to $30 for 2, although you can eat much more cheaply in the inn's attractive coffee shop); room service 7:00 A.M. to 10:00 P.M.; jackets requested in the Chaparral Room.

Diversions: 2 heated outdoor pools, 2 therapy pools, hiking, shuffleboard, table tennis; tennis (10 courts, 5 lighted, $6–$8 per court per hour), golf (36 holes, $17 per round in winter, $8 in summer), pitch-and-putt golf ($2.50), bicycles ($5 per day); horseback riding nearby.

Sightseeing: See "Arizona Biltmore."

P.S. A variety of off-season value packages available in June, July, and August.

JOHN GARDINER'S TENNIS RANCH
Scottsdale, Ariz.

From the main road you can barely pick out the ranch, so neatly does it blend in with the foothills of Camelback Mountain, but once you get there the statistics are impressive. Tennis courts? Two dozen of them, and if you rent the Casa Ken Rosewall you'll have a private court on your roof. Pros? Thirty-six. Swimming pools? A total of nine, including six private casa pools. If you join one of the famed clinics, you'll be on the courts for three and a half hours a day, battling it out with a computerized ball machine that pops out three thousand balls an hour. Everyone takes his or her tennis seriously here, but there are enough duffers and fluffers to keep the great Rosewall and his pros wincing; and whatever the state of your game you can enjoy the luxury of John Gardiner's Ranch.

Most of the accommodations are in forty-odd casitas—each with beamed ceilings, open fireplace, spacious patio, air conditioning, but, oddly enough, a square tub/shower rather than the stretch-out-in kind of bathtub you'd probably welcome after all that dashing around on the courts. The casas offer really deluxe accommodations, with fieldstone fireplaces, color TV, private therapy pools; six of them have private pools and private tennis courts. Most spectacular of the bunch is Casa Rosewall, which has beds (and bathrobes) for eight guests ($500 a day, but divide that by eight and it's not prohibitive).

What sets the Gardiner Ranch apart is not only the thoroughness of its clinics and the luxury of its rooms, but the thoughtful touches. Orange juice, coffee, and a newspaper appear on your doorstep every morning before you join the clinic; your room comes stocked with setups, coffee, and tea; your MAP rate includes buffet lunch rather than dinner, on the theory that tennis players are more likely to want to have lunch at the ranch, then dress up in the evening and sample the scores of good restaurants in the neighborhood. Finally, on the rare occasions when rain stops play and eveyone is fidgeting to get back on the courts, John Gardiner pops open the champagne and fills everyone's glass. On the house. That's the sort of hospitality that has attracted such budding Rosewalls as Elton John, David Frost, and Art Buchwald.

Name: John Gardiner's Tennis Ranch
Manager: Vik Jackson
Address: 5700 East McDonald Drive, Scottsdale, Ariz. 85253
Directions: Between Scottsdale Road and 44th Street, 1 block south of Lincoln Drive.
Telephone: (602) 948–2100
Cables/Telex: None

Credit Cards: American Express
Rooms: 105, in various casitas and casas.
Meals: Breakfast 7:30–10:30, lunch 12:30–3:30 (buffet), dinner 7:30–10:30;
    room service (limited) 11:00 A.M. to 7:00 P.M.; jacket and tie at dinner;
    occasional live music and dancing.
Diversions: 3 heated pools, 2 therapy pools, sauna, massage therapists,
    Jacuzzi, tennis (24 courts, no charge, 36 pros, no lights, ball machines,
    clinics); golf, horseback riding nearby.
Sightseeing: See "Arizona Biltmore."
P.S. Special packages available.

THE WIGWAM
Litchfield Park, Ariz.

Back in World War I the United States needed Sea Island cotton fast
for revolutionary new tires. So the Goodyear Tire and Rubber Company rolled to the rescue and went into the cotton plantation business
on a stretch of desert seventeen miles west of Phoenix. To keep its
uprooted executives happy, the company built a guesthouse, known
as the Organization House, which became so popular that it was
converted into a resort in 1929. That may seem an unpromising
beginning for a resort inn, but you just try to get a reservation here in
February or March. The only signs of the ownership are occasional
fly-overs by the Goodyear blimp, and the name of the resort's golf
course—the Goodyear Gold and Country Club. Even a B. F. Good-
rich stockholder couldn't be offended.

The Wigwam is surrounded by a garden suburb, Litchfield
Park, which in turn is surrounded by a fourteen-thousand-acre operating ranch that branched out from the original cotton to alfalfa,
grains, and melons; but several of these fourteen-thousand acres are
still native desert where the inn's wranglers will lead you along
cactus-lined riding trails.

CASITAS AND EUCALYPTUS. The inn itself is a series of one- and two-
story sand-colored stucco casitas sheltered by palms, eucalyptus,

bougainvillaea, and citrus trees (lemon, lime, grapefruit, and orange) or flanked by the velvet fairways of Robert Trent Jones's masterful golf course.

The 220 rooms are divided into five types of accommodations— something for everyone. Even the simplest rooms give you space to stretch out, and they all have TV, refrigerators, and individually controlled air conditioning.

The Wigwam probably has more lounges than any other hotel anywhere, with all sorts of quiet nooks and crannies, fireplaces, potted plants, magazines, and an ongoing jigsaw puzzle or two. But with winter weather like Arizona's, you'll probably prefer to do your lounging around the pool, or on the rooftop solarium. The Goodyear Golf and Country Club, besides forming a lovely background for the inn, is also one of the most famous golf clubs in the Southwest, with three superb golf courses. Until recently it was golf that lured visitors to the Wigwam, but in 1973 the resort opened a new tennis club, with eight Plexipave courts, a pro shop, and four practice alleys with automatic ball pitching machines to give your strokes a workout. The Organization House has come a long way.

Name: The Wigwam
Manager: Reade Whitwell
Address: Litchfield Park, Ariz. 85340
Directions: 17 miles west of Phoenix on West Indian School Road.
Telephone: (602) 935–3811
Cables/Telex: None
Credit Cards: None
Rooms: 220, 16 suites, in groups of casitas and villas.
Meals: Breakfast 7:30–9:30, continental breakfast 9:30–11:00, lunch 12:00– 2:00, dinner 6:30–9:30; room service 7:00 A.M. to 11:00 P.M.; jacket and tie at dinner; dinner-dancing nightly, live music in lounge nightly, occasional fashion shows and square dancing; weekly Sunday buffet lunch.
Diversions: Heated outdoor pool, therapy pool, sauna, walking trails, bad- minton, shuffleboard, volleyball—all free. Tennis (8 courts, 6 lighted, $6 per hour, pro shop, ball machine, clinics), golf (three 18-hole courses, $13.50 per day, carts $13 per round), horseback riding ($11 for 2½-hour ride); bicycles for rent, trap and skeet shooting.
Sightseeing: See "Arizona Biltmore."
P.S. The big push is during February, March, and the first week of April,

when the regulars move in for weeks at a time and you'll be lucky to get a reservation for less than a week; small groups at other times. Very special programs during traditional holidays. Golf, tennis, and riding packages available.

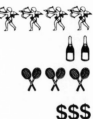

WICKENBURG INN TENNIS AND GUEST RANCH
Wickenburg, Ariz.

$$$

The ranch hand who drove us to our casita in a golf cart pointed to the pile of mesquite on the porch: "Let me know if you want a fire set, either in the parlor or up on the roof." The roof, up a spiral stair, is a private deck for sunbathing by day or star-gazing by night, with a small adobe-style fireplace in one corner. The Wickenburg Inn, I decided, is what a desert resort is all about.

The owners, Chicago businessmen Jean Kempner and Warren Jackman, set out to create "the most beautiful desert resort in the country," and for my money they come very close. Everything possible has been done to preserve the character of the desert. A dirt road bounces you through the scrub to the parking lot, but from there on you get around on foot, horseback, or golf cart. A naturalist-in-residence keeps the staff on its toes to make sure the ecology is not disturbed, but he's also eager to tell guests about the one night of the year when the spade toad comes out after rain; bird feeders encourage the hummingbird and mountain bluebird to pay a call and sing a song. The riding and walking trails go on for mile after desert mile, but the owners have spared a thought for the saddle-sore and built an arts and crafts center where guests can indulge in macramé, stone-grinding, and other old-style crafts.

BOOKS, FRUIT, WINE. Apart from ten rooms in the main lodge (perfectly adequate, if you don't take a peep at the casitas), accommodations are in dust-colored casitas that hug the dust-colored hillsides. They're built in the adobe brick-and-beam manner, furnished with comfortable seats and sofas (with at least one antique per room), bathrooms with modern fixtures and rustic decor; each room has a

shelf or two of books, and the casitas have small refrigerators and the makings for tea and coffee (regular *and* decaffeinated). Arriving guests are welcomed with a tray of fruit and a half-bottle of wine; beds are turned down every evening when you're at dinner. The inn's cooking is ranch-style hearty without frills, but the culinary highlight of the week is the cookout on Eagle Flats, a mesa setting of sagebrush and yuccas and chollas. You don't have to be a John Wayne to get to Eagle Flats; half the guests get there on horses, others by haywagon, and the unrepentant dudes by golf cart. Steaks are cooked over mesquite, accompanied by cowboy beans and beer biscuits; when the last deep-dish apple pie has been gobbled up, everyone gathers around the campfire and Ed Cheek and his wranglers get out their guitars and strum through a few western ditties. With some style, too. The party usually continues back at the lodge, but there, alas, with amplification. Time to duck out, follow the lanterns up the hillside to your casita, uncork that half-bottle of wine and, if you're smart enough to have a deluxe casita, climb to your rooftop deck, light the fire, and toast the stars.

Name: Wickenburg Inn Tennis and Guest Ranch
Manager: Ed Cheek
Address: P.O. Box P, Wickenburg, Ariz. 85358

Directions: By car, 1½ hours north of Phoenix; from the town of Wickenburg, take Highway 93 a mile or so north of town, then go northeast on U.S. 89, and the entrance to the inn is a couple of miles away on the right (but you have to watch carefully to spot the sign); the inn's limousine can be alerted to pick you up at the airport or Amtrak station in Phoenix, and there's an airfield for private planes at Wickenburg.

Telephone: (602) 684–7811

Cables/Telex: None

Credit Cards: American Express, Diners, MasterCard, Visa

Rooms: 51 (10 in main lodge, the remainder in hillside casitas, including deluxe suites).

Meals: Coffee and rolls 7:00–11:00, breakfast 8:00–9:30, lunch 12:30–1:30, dinner 7:00–9:00; cookouts twice a week, with country and western music.

Diversions: Heated outdoor pool, tennis (11 courts, pro shop, ball machines, clinics, no lights), horseback riding, arts and crafts center, wildlife study—all free; 9-hole golf course nearby.

Sightseeing: See "Arizona Biltmore."

P.S. "During major holidays, children are expected to join their peers . . . under the supervision of trained counselors." Some group tours in summer. October and November are ideal months.

CAREFREE INN
Carefree, Ariz.

Take a bike ride in the desert. Chase a roadrunner through the cactus. Hunt for white-speckled quartz. Walk down to Cave Creek, push through the swing doors of a saloon, and have a drink with real cowboys. Explore the neighborhood for ghost towns, old gold mines, Hohokan ruins and Indian petroglyphs. Up there in Carefree you're closer to the desert than in Phoenix or Scottsdale. But hurry. Carefree isn't exactly car-free, and it's getting more built up every day.

Carefree is a new town, a planned community that has some respect for the desert. It's 1,400 feet higher and thirty-five miles northeast of Phoenix. Up here the sun shines smoglessly nine days out of ten; and some people will swear it's the most beautiful spot on earth when the palo verde blooms yellow in the spring, or when summer showers turn the ocotilla crimson.

The inn itself looks like a motel—a pair of two-story wings embracing a pool surrounded by rocks and cacti. There are also a few casitas with kitchens, wet bars, and sunken tubs, and some new townhouse-style units across the parking lot that surround their own small pool and face the golf course, the desert, and the hills beyond. The rooms are oversize, the beds are oversize, the closets are over-size, and they all have balconies, refrigerators, electric blankets, electric alarms, color TV, and room phones. Nothing exceptional—just very roomy and very comfy, and recently refurbished to the tune of $1,000 a room.

But you're not going to be indoors much, especially with the lights on. Most of the time you'll be playing tennis (six Laykold courts, five floodlit, all free), riding horses over old territorial trails to Bronco Butte or Apache Peak, or playing golf on two of the most spectacular courses in the Southwest.

In the evenings you can dine formally or informally (some folks drive all the way up from Phoenix for dinner here); and if you want a change of cuisine, you can drive over to Carefree town and dine beneath the stars in the patio of a Spanish restaurant.

Summer rates here are a steal. And don't let the thought of Arizona's summer temperatures put you off. Carefree is situated in the hills, where temperatures average 84.5 degrees in July, 87.8 in August, but the average relative humidity is 10 percent to 20 per-cent. That shouldn't stop you taking a bike ride in the desert—especially if you go by tandem.

Name: Carefree Inn
Manager: Dick Osgood
Address: Box 708, Carefree, Ariz. 85331
Directions: About 20 minutes north of Scottsdale; keep driving on Scottsdale Road until it becomes Tom Darlington Road, turn right on Cave Creek Road at Spanish Village and continue until you see the signs for Care-free Inn; air-conditioned limousine service to and from Phoenix Sky Harbor Airport, about 40 to 50 minutes.
Telephone: (602) 488–3551
Cables/Telex: None
Credit Cards: American Express, MasterCard, Visa
Rooms: 200, including 86 suites, plus villas.
Meals: Breakfast 7:00–11:30, lunch 11:30–5:00, dinner 5:00–10:00 (approx. $20 to $25 for 2); no room service; informal dress; live music and dancing.

Diversions: Heated outdoor pool; tennis (6 courts, lighted, free in summer, $1.50 per person per hour at other times, pro shop, clinics), horseback riding (165 to 200 horses, $4 an hour, $8 on cookout rides, also overnight pack trips), bicycles (standard, 3-speed, 10-speed for both men and women, by the hour or day), golf (two 18-hole courses nearby, $10 a round in winter, $5 in summer), trap and skeet shooting, hiking trails, trail rides by 4-wheel "Jackrabbits," charter flights to Grand Canyon, etc.

Sightseeing: See "Arizona Biltmore Hotel."

P.S. Open all year, busiest in winter, great bargain in summer (remember, it's cooler here than in Phoenix), but check for conventions.

GARLAND'S OAK CREEK LODGE
Sedona, Ariz.

Childhood fantasies of mountain hideaways and woodland romance flood your imagination shortly after you turn off the highway. The driveway to Garland's Oak Creek Lodge, in the heart of Arizona's cool and leafy Oak Creek Canyon, dips beneath the branches of tall oak and fir trees, and water laps against the car wheels as you cross the creek bed. Just to be in a car seems suddenly strange and precarious on the narrow climbing roadway. Then you enter a sunlit clearing in the Ponderosa pines and know at once it's time to leave behind your car and any cares you brought as excess baggage. Garland's is a place that invites you to climb a tree and munch a just-picked apple, to throw out a line and catch a rainbow trout or German brown, to cuddle in front of the fire in your own log cabin and let nature take its course.

Arizona city folks (and magazine writers) rave about the food at Garland's, a worthy combination of American and French dishes and techniques, thanks to the Arizona upbringing and Parisian training of Susan Garland, the innkeeper's sister and the resort's former chef. "Like Mother used to make" and "fresh from the garden" are Susan's guiding principles (she still keeps an eye on the kitchen), so you can expect peaches from the orchard in fluffy sour cream muffins, and trout from the creek as a simple pan-fried *entrée meunière*. Eggs, too, are fresh from the yard and owner Gary Garland is known for his hearty breakfast specialties named for colorful local Sedona residents (Eggs Anderson is a lonely hard-boiled egg on a plain white plate; Eggs Pendley, a creamy vegetable version of Eggs Benedict). But to fuss endlessly over the food at Garland's Oak Creek Lodge seems, sadly, to miss the point of this mountainside retreat (elevation: 5,000 feet), which has more to do with hand-crafted pine furniture, home-sewn eyelet curtains, and log cabins built from scratch by a gentleman who has summered in this idyllic setting since he was a boy. As Gary expresses it, "We do the best we can, without pretense . . .what we offer is a wholesome, peaceful place to stay . . . a kind of life that has almost been lost."

When Gary, his sister, brother, and parents first spent summers in Oak Creek Canyon, the lodge and orchard they now own was a local mecca named Todd's Lodge. Built in the 1920s on the site of a territorial homestead, it was a down-home establishment with a fruit ranch out back (peaches, plums, apricots, cherries, and twelve varieties of apples) that had a row of fishermen's cabins overlooking the creek and a powerful reputation in the area for good fried chicken and apple pie (the fishing and the food regularly attracted miners from nearby Jerome in the days before the copper played out). When the Todds were ready to sell their 10-acre spread in the late 1960s, it was the Garland family (Dad was president of Garland Steel Co.) that decided to buy, and thereby preserve, their favorite vacation spot. From the beginning it was a family project with each of the younger Garlands playing a role. Gary, by then an engineer, built three more cabins; Dan, a horticulturist, planted, pruned, and irrigated the orchard and gardens (vegetables, herbs); Susan developed the menus and recipes for the restaurant; and Gary's wife, Mary, filled in as interior decorator, assistant chef, and front-office manager. Although the Garlands couldn't resist adding a few of their own touches of style and sophistication (classical music tapes mixed with Gene Autry and Joan Baez, *filet mignon Bordelaise* and a skylight in one of the larger cabins), they never compromised the simplicity and peaceful life-style they treasured in Oak Creek Lodge. The accommodations are still simple shelters with a minimum of furniture and stall showers in the bathrooms (there's not a television set or room phone in sight) and the activities are still limited to wading in the creek, walking in the woods, or, as the information sheet suggests, letting the world go by until it's time for dinner. If you have a yen for golf, tennis, or a chlorinated swimming pool, you'll simply have to get in your car and go elsewhere. This mountain hideaway is strictly for playing out childhood fantasies of woodland romance.

L.E.B

Name: Garland's Oak Creek Lodge

Owners/Managers: Gary and Mary Garland

Address: P.O. Box 152, Sedona, Ariz. 86336

Directions: Follow U.S. Highway 89A 8 miles north of Sedona or 20 miles south of Flagstaff and turn off near Banjo Bill Campground (note: the Garland's sign is small and easily missed; also, when Oak Creek is high, you may have to park near the highway and proceed to the lodge via the footbridge).

Telephone: (602) 282–3343

Cables/Telex: None

Credit Cards: MasterCard, Visa

Rooms: 11 cabins.

Meals: Breakfast 8:00–10:00, no lunch served, dinner (1 sitting only) 7:00, with cocktails from 5:00 (approx. $25 for 2); no room service; dress code is "casual but sharp"; player piano, taped music in the lounge only.

Diversions: Walking in the woods, fishing in the creek, tree-climbing in the orchard; golf, horseback riding, tennis in the area.

Sightseeing: Sedona is an artist's colony located in the heart of the famous Red Rock Country; it is the gateway to both the Verde Valley and Oak Creek Canyon; Arizona Snow Bowl (winter sports area), Flagstaff, Montezuma's Castle, Meteor Crater, Tuzigoot National Monument (pueblo ruins), Jerome (a mining ghost town), and in Prescott, the Sharlot Hall Arizona Historical Museum and the Smoki Museum.

P.S. Garland's is open only between April and November (exact dates vary annually) and, even then, it is closed to overnight guests and diners from Sunday noon to Monday noon. Also, be sure to book well in advance; previous guests get first refusal on favorite cabins and preferred dates (many anniversaries are celebrated at Garland's) and even regulars book weekends a year in advance (mid-week dates can possibly be reserved on shorter notice).

For more suggestions in this area
turn to Added Attractions, page 375.

Sunny Southern California

The sweetest hours that e'er I spent,
Are spent amang the lasses, O!

BURNS

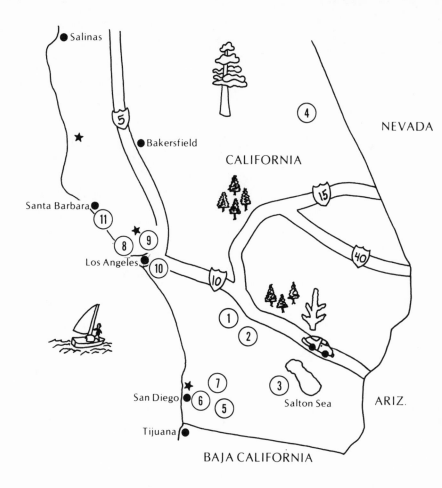

1. Ingleside Inn
2. La Quinta Hotel
3. La Casa del Zorro
4. Furnace Creek Inn and Ranch Resort
5. Rancho Bernardo Inn
6. La Valencia Hotel
7. The Inn at Rancho Santa Fe
8. Beverly Hills Hotel
9. Bel-Air Hotel
10. Westwood Marquis Hotel
11. Marriott's Santa Barbara Biltmore
★ *Added Attractions*

INGLESIDE INN
Palm Springs, Calif.

$$$

I imagine this is how movie stars live: a lovely old hacienda with red-tiled roof, a cool veranda facing a lawn and pool, a pillared patio at the rear with a cherubic fountain among the flowers; the San Jacinto Mountains provide a backdrop just beyond the garden gate, Saks Fifth Avenue is one convenient block away in the other direction. Coming from Saks with your bundles of Puccis, you enter Ingleside through elegant gateposts, along a curving driveway strewn with Rolls-Royces, Aston Martins, and Cadillacs. (But no Pierce-Arrows, although the hacienda began life as the estate of the heirs to the Pierce-Arrow millions.) In the thirties through fifties it became a very chic, very exclusive hideaway for Samuel Goldwyn, Howard Hughes, Liz Taylor, Cyd Charisse, and a galaxy of other celebrities. Now the inn has come full cycle, having been bought up three years ago by Mel Haber, who also made his millions or whatever from automobiles, marketing what is politely referred to as "automotive novelties." In other words, those tacky little dolls and animals that wink at you from rear windows. Treat them with new respect from now on, because they enabled this Brooklyn entrepreneur to pour something like half a million dollars into rehabilitating Ingleside, in the process creating one of the most delightful, most unusual inns in the country. Unusual because on one hand it's unabashedly indolent, on the other it's congenial and "with it." Mel Haber himself is a walking birthday party, and this has become *the* place for the stars, starlets, and statesmen of Palm Springs. They flock to the Casablanca Lounge to imbibe, in an environment of wicker and rattan, ceiling fans with brass filigree, a grand piano with a copper lid; then to the glass-enclosed terrace of Melvyn's Restaurant to dine. Frank Sinatra held his prewedding dinner here, movie stars are married on the front lawn. Into the bargain, the food is first rate, the dapper waiters are not at all starstruck, and so far as I could tell, everyone seemed to be getting proper attention.

If you want to observe the people parade, spread out on one of the luxuriously padded leather loungers beside the pool. But if you want to escape, simply retire to the leather-and-marble library and have a game of backgammon, or head for the tranquil patio and read a good book beside the fountain. It's another world. Most of the guest rooms and suites are grouped around this patio, each one a boudoir fit for a star, furnished with antiques and objects carted over from Europe by the Pierce-Arrow clan. My suite had a Limoges cigarette lighter and ashtray on a Louis XVI night table and jade doodads on a Chippendale chest of drawers; every suite comes equipped with steam bath, stocked refrigerator, and matches with your initials emblazoned in gilt. I'm told that Lily Pons came here for a few nights and stayed for thirteen years; you may want to do the same.

Name: Ingleside Inn
Owner/Manager: Melvyn (Mel) Haber
Address: 200 West Ramon Road, Palm Springs, Calif. 92262
Directions: Corner of West Ramon Road and Belardo Street, between Palm Canyon Drive and the San Jacinto Mountains; ask for directions to either the Ingleside Inn or Melvyn's Restaurant.
Telephone: (714) 325–1366
Cables/Telex: None
Credit Cards: American Express, MasterCard, Visa
Rooms: 28.
Meals: Complimentary continental breakfast in your room, on the veranda, or beside the pool; luncheon 12:00–3:00; dinner 6:00–11:00; champagne brunch Saturdays and Sundays 9:00–3:00; room service from 7:00 A.M. to midnight; refrigerators in every room stocked with beverages and light snacks (complimentary); dress—informal, but "stylish" informal; piano bar in the Casablanca Room, strolling violinist on weekends.
Diversions: Pool, luxurious loungers, therapy pool, private steam baths in every room, croquet and shuffleboard; tennis, golf, and horseback riding nearby.
Sightseeing: San Jacinto Mountains, the Palm Springs Desert Museum, the Agua Caliente Indian Reservation, the Moorten Botanical Gardens, or if you're starstruck by more than your companion, the homes of the rich and famous.

LA QUINTA HOTEL
La Quinta (near Palm Desert), Calif.

$$$

It gets its name from stagecoach days when journeys took a breather on the fifth day, *la quinta*, for refreshment and, when the passengers were compatible, revelry. This La Quinta came along in the twenties, an oasis at the base of the Santa Rosa Mountains—forty-nine Spanish-style bungalows spread over twenty-eight acres of trim gardens. All the accommodations are bungalows with two or three bedrooms, furnished in tasteful southwestern style, each with a private entrance somewhere among the tangerine and grapefruit trees, or the palms growing dates for the chef's homemade date ice cream and date cake. Dinner here runs to six courses, and might include poached salmon court bouillon, veal sauté Marengo, and roast rack of lamb.

WESTERN WHITE HOUSE. La Quinta is part of a larger, eight-hundred-acre estate, and both the landowners and the hotel's "distinguished clientele" are top drawer. During Eisenhower's presidency, La Quinta frequently served as his Western White House. The lure was obviously the estate's exclusive golf course, where a round will set two players back almost $80, including carts, which are obligatory. Forget it. There's plenty to enjoy here besides golf, and a staff of 110 to pamper just 320 guests. They're a friendly group too, despite the top-drawer clientele—just the sort of people you'd be happy to see on *la quinta*.

Name: La Quinta Hotel Golf & Tennis Resort
Manager: Robert T. Silva
Address: P.O. Box 69, La Quinta, Calif. 92253
Directions: On Highway 111, about 20 miles south of Palm Springs, 7 each from Palm Desert and Indio; by air to Palm Springs, by Amtrak to San Bernardino (about 69 miles away), and you can arrange to have the hotel pick you up at the airport or station.

Telephone: (714) 564–4111
Cables/Telex: None
Credit Cards: MasterCard, Visa
Rooms: 160 in cottages with 2 to 6 bedrooms.
Meals: Breakfast 7:30–10:00, lunch 12:00–2:30 (indoor or outdoor), dinner
     6:30–9:00; room service during dining-room hours; jacket and tie at
     dinner; trio 6 nights a week.
Diversions: Heated outdoor pool; masseur, tennis (6 courts, 4 lighted, $8 per
     person per day, pro shop, ball machine, backboard), golf (championship
     Pete Dye 18-hole course, $40 green fee includes cart, unlimited range
     balls).
Sightseeing: See "Ingleside Inn."

LA CASA DEL ZORRO
Borrego Springs, Calif.

$

Back in the thirties, Zorro was known as the Desert Lodge, an
adobe-style hideaway for Hollywood adventurers who wanted a taste
of the desert. That's certainly what they found in the Anza-Borrego
wilderness, the largest state park in the nation, mile after moonscape
mile of seemingly lifeless, bewitching desert. Yet Borrego Springs is
only an hour and a half by car from Palm Springs, a little over two
hours from San Diego. It huddles beneath the eight-thousand-foot
peaks of the Santa Rosa Mountains, a mere hamlet with a few shops, a
restaurant, a bar or two, golf course, landing strip, and the Casa del
Zorro.
     The Casa is half-hidden in an oasis of tamarisk trees and roof-
high oleanders—the original, refurbished lodge, a motel-style wing
of rooms, and eighteen individual cottages in the garden at the rear.
The lodge's dining room recalls its pioneer heritage with original
paintings of old California and the Butterfield Stagecoach, which
used to pass nearby; the bar is hung with antique copper and brass,
but the guest rooms lack any special charm, spacious and comfortable
though they are (each has air conditioning, a phone, and color TV).
The chief attractions here are the rates (a one-bedroom cottage with
kitchenette for as little as $40 a night) and, of course, the solitude.
You can drive from the Casa across the desert to the Salton Sea and

pass maybe a couple of other people along the way. The Salton Sea (234 feet below sea level) merits only a short visit (maybe time for a below-sea-level swim), and Salton City is a noncity of subdivisions and utility poles; so you probably won't hang around long before driving back across the moonscape to your comfortable Casa for a taste of Polynesia—steak teriyaki or *mahi mahi*.

Name: La Casa del Zorro
Manager: Donald P. Gillette
Address: Borrego Springs, Calif. 92004
Directions: From Los Angeles, take the new Montezuma Road via Warner Springs; from San Diego, State Highway 78 via Santa Ysabel; from Palm Springs and points east, State Highways 86 (south) and 78 (west).
Telephone: (714) 767–5323
Cables/Telex: None
Credit Cards: American Express, Carte Blanche, Diners, MasterCard, Visa
Rooms: 16, 18 cottages.
Meals: Breakfast 7:30–11:00, lunch 11:30–2:00, dinner 6:30–9:00 (approx. $12 to $15 for 2); jackets for dinner (October 1 through May 31).
Diversions: Large heated outdoor pool, tennis (2 lighted courts), putting green, badminton, paddle tennis, shuffleboard; golf 8 miles away.
Sightseeing: Borrego Valley in Santa Rosa Mountains, scenic drives through Santa Ysabel in the back country to nearby San Diego.

FURNACE CREEK INN AND RANCH RESORT
Death Valley, Calif.

Natural waterfalls tumble over rocks into a tropical garden of ferns and palms (and one intrepid rose bush); the big swimming pool is filled with spring water, naturally heated to 87 degrees; in the evening, you can dine off fig glacée and chicken breast with artichoke hearts, prepared by a Swiss chef and served in the dining salon of a Spanish *palacio*. That may not be the way you picture Death Valley, but that's the way it is in the oasis known as Furnace Creek Inn. Don't let the word *furnace* fool you: it has nothing to do with the temperature outside, but refers rather to the old ore smelting furnaces built here in the 1800s. In fact, don't let the valley's ominous name fool you

either; death it may have inflicted on early settlers trying to walk across the borax-covered floor of the valley, but during the season when the inn is open—fall through spring—the temperature *at midday* averages only 80 degrees, and guests sunning themselves by the pool can look across the valley to snow gleaming on the peaks of the Panamints.

The inn itself is right on sea level, a granitelike palacio with red-tile roofs; its solidly furnished rooms are cooled by air conditioning (at night you may need a blanket, though), and many of them have patios or balconies with views across the valley. The ranch is lower (two hundred feet *below* sea level, in a grove of date palms), with 164 of its rooms in new two-story, motel-type wings adjoining "the only eighteen-hole grass fairway course below sea level"; it's good value, and it remains open throughout the summer. Both are operated by the Fred Harvey Organization.

Plan to spend at least three days here because there are so many things to see in Death Valley—Scotty's Castle, Twenty-Mule Team Canyon, ghost towns, fourteen square miles of sand dunes (magical at sunset), Badwater (at 272 feet below sea level the lowest point in America), to say nothing of secluded picnic spots among the juniper and piñon; and you will also want to leave some time for enjoying the tropical garden and the spring-fed swimming pool.

Name: Furnace Creek Inn and Ranch Resort

Manager: Alpheus C. Bruton

Address: Death Valley, Calif. 92328

Directions: Just over 2 hours by car from Las Vegas (via U.S. 95 and State Highways 29, 127, and 190); from Los Angeles via Mojave and Olancha (290 miles via State Highways 14 and 190); by private plane, or charters from Las Vegas, to the landing strip at the ranch.

Telephone: (714) 786–2345; out-of-state toll free (800) 227–4700; in California, (800) 622–0838

Cables/Telex: None

Credit Cards: American Express, Carte Blanche, Diners, MasterCard, Visa

Rooms: 69 rooms in the inn (plus 225 in the ranch, of which 164 are new and appropriate for readers of this guide).

Meals: Breakfast 8:00–9:00, lunch 12:00–1:30, dinner 6:00–8:00; some cookouts, separate hours (and modest prices) at the ranch restaurants; room service during dining-room hours (inn only); jackets at dinner (inn only); trio seven nights a week in inn supper club.

Diversions: Table tennis, badminton, movies, bingo; outdoor pool, tennis (4 courts with lights); additional pool, tennis courts, golf (18 holes, $8 per round), horseback riding ($8 for 2 hours) at the ranch.

Sightseeing: Scotty's Castle, Twenty-Mule Team Canyon, Badwater, and the entire Death Valley Monument National Park, including mountains, canyons, and dunes.

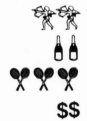

RANCHO BERNARDO INN
Rancho Bernardo (San Diego), Calif.

The first owner of this Spanish land grant was an English sea captain, Joseph Seven Oaks, who retired from the sea to the life of a Spanish grandee—with the name Don José Francisco Snook. Snook's nook was all hills and vales with a smattering of trees; now it has forty thousand trees, twenty thousand inhabitants, shopping centers, riding stables, and a golf course. And right in the middle of it all—the inn.

Hardly the most *idyllic* spot for a hideaway, but if you plan to play golf or tennis together, you'll find the Rancho Bernardo Inn one of the most convenient places in the Southwest.

The inn is girdled by forty-three holes of championship golf (including an Executive Course with no par fives), driving range, practice trap, and putting green. (The green fee is only $14 a day for inn guests, and they get priority on starting times.)

The inn also has a Jacuzzi, two heated swimming pools, and you can rent bikes, but its most famous sporting facility is probably its tennis college. The college consist of six courts (four lighted), videotape instruction, and practice machines; its two-day crash course keeps you thinking tennis, playing tennis, and watching tennis from nine in the morning to nine at night. Exhausting. Better plan on following through with a two-day crash course in love.

OVERSIZE ROOMS, OVERSIZE BEDS. The 150 rooms are said to have Spanish decor. They're as Spanish as Don José Francisco Snook. However, they *are* spacious, and they do have two oversize beds (plenty of space for post-tennis back-rubbing), private decks or patios, double washbasins, and a few nice little touches, like color TV sets concealed in handsome armoires, and heat lamps in the bathroom. The rooms overlook the golf course, swimming pool, tennis courts, or parking lot: ask for second-floor rooms in the 400 and 500 wings, with a view of the fairways.

Name: Rancho Bernardo Inn
Owner/Manager: James W. Colachis
Address: 17550 Bernardo Oaks Drive, San Diego, Calif. 92128
Directions: Take U.S. 395 from San Diego to the Rancho Bernardo Exit (about 25 minutes from downtown San Diego, 30 minutes from San Diego airport); from Los Angeles (2 hours), by Interstate 5 south to Oceanside, then Calif. 78 east to Escondido, and from there south on U.S. 395.
Telephone: (714) 487–1611
Cables/Telex: None
Credit Cards: American Express, Carte Blanche, Diners, MasterCard, Visa
Rooms: 150, 7 suites.
Meals: Breakfast 7:00–11:00, lunch 11:30–2:30, dinner 6:00–10:00 (approx. $30 to $50 for 2); room service 6:30 A.M. to 10:00 P.M.; jackets required in main dining room; live music and dancing.
Diversions: Table tennis, shuffleboard, 2 outdoor pools, hiking trails, badminton; tennis (16 courts, $6.50 per hour per court, 2 with lights, pro, ball machines, clinics), golf (18 holes, $14 per round), bicycles for rent; skiing, sailing, waterskiing nearby.

Sightseeing: Presidio Park museums, Balboa Park, The Museum of Man, San
      Diego Zoo, Natural History Museum, Maritime Museum, "Old Town,"
      Sea World, San Diego Opera, Symphony, Mission San Diego de Alcala,
      Tijuana.

P.S. Busiest January through April, but the weather's perfect for tennis, golf
      all year.

LA VALENCIA HOTEL
La Jolla, Calif.

Groucho Marx used to skulk behind the pillars in the lobby and leer
at startled ladies. Charles Laughton visited the bar every afternoon in
summer to order "a pot of real hot tea, please." Evangelist Aimee
Semple McPherson used to slip off here for weeks at a time with her
current boyfriend ("She was a grand woman," says a longtime member of the staff, "but oversexed"). Those were the days when everyone who was anyone in Hollywood went to La Valencia to get away
from it all—Greta Garbo, John Gilbert, Ramon Navarro, Joan Craw-
ford, David Niven, Gregory Peck, Audrey Hepburn—the whole
gang.

      La Jolla is no longer the unspoiled little seaside village it was in
Hollywood's heyday, and the Valencia Hotel now competes with
bulky condominiums, but they're by no means has-beens.

      La Valencia is still, as it has been since it opened its doors in
1926, *the* place to go in La Jolla. Its Mediterranean entrance is still
shaded by jungly podacarpus; little old ladies still have luncheon in
the mosaic courtyard; and a jigsaw puzzle still waits on the table for
someone to drop in the magic piece.

TERRACES, TILES, AND POTTED PLANTS. The hotel sits on a bluff above
a bluff above La Jolla's famous rocky cove. Its gardens terrace down
the hillside, then sweep around the swimming pool to the street and
the park by the edge of the ocean. Pictorial tiles jostle with clumps of
flowers for the chance to beguile your eye, and create petaled nooks if
you want to be alone. The hotel itself is eleven stories of pink stucco,
Spanish style, with a pink tower. Beyond its leafy patio you enter a

cool lobby leading to the big-windowed lounge overlooking the ocean—an impressive room with Spanish tiles, potted plants, a golden piano, tiled fountain, and a hand-painted ceiling. This, you feel, is how a hotel in California should look.

The decor in the guest rooms is understated and graceful, with richly striped wallpapers, handwoven Portuguese bedspreads, beamed ceilings, and elegant sofas and armchairs from England, Italy, Spain, and France. The corner rooms on the eleventh floor ($55 at the height of the season) also have small sundecks. There are also a couple of unusual rooms in a bungalow in the garden, if you want extra privacy, but they're not quite "La Valencia": Room 3 has an attic ceiling, white walls and furnishings, and a king-size bed, and #2 downstairs is a suite with a fireplace. The hitherto conventional new West Wing has been redone in Ficks Reed and McGuirre South California seaside style.

OUTDOOR AND TOWER-TOP DINING. For a hotel its size, La Valencia presents you with plenty of options when it comes to dining. You may be tempted to stay a few days longer so that you can sample a different eating spot at each meal. Say, lunch on the patio and dinner in the elegant ocean-view Surf Room (steak au poivre, rack of lamb persillade for two, veal Oscar). Second day, lunch in the Skyroom on the tenth floor, with windows on three sides (and a grandstand view of migrating whales if your timing is right); then dinner on the patio beneath the moon. Third day, lunch on the patio and dinner in the Café la Rue, next to the Whaling Bar. The Whaling Bar itself is one of La Jolla's favorite watering spots—a shuttered, leather-boothed room with authentic harpoons, New Bedford lanterns, pewter candles, and paintings of whaling scenes. And, all the posh notwithstanding, you never have to wear a jacket and tie at La Jolla.

SUN, SURF, AND SNORKELING. The hotel's freeform swimming pool is one of the more placid spots in La Jolla for working up a tan. A few steps from the garden entrance, though, and you can be taking a dip in the surf, or floating off with a snorkel to discover some of the region's unusually prolific underwater life. You never know what's going to pop out from behind a rock and leer at you.

Name: La Valencia Hotel
Manager: Richard P. Irwin
Address: 1132 Prospect Road, La Jolla, Calif. 92038
Directions: 14 miles north of San Diego; get off Interstate 5 at the San Clemente Canyon Road cloverleaf and follow Ardath Road to and around the waterfront.
Telephone: (714) 454–0771
Cables/Telex: None
Credit Cards: American Express, MasterCard, Visa
Rooms: 95, 10 suites.
Meals: Breakfast 7:30–10:30, lunch 12:00–2:30, dinner 5:00–10:30 (approx. $12 to $20 for 2); room service during meal hours; dress optional; piano in bar.
Diversions: Heated outdoor pool, therapy pool, sauna, exercise room; ocean beach across the street; tennis, golf, bicycles, sailing, waterskiing nearby.
Sightseeing: La Jolla art colony, cliffs, sea caves.
P.S. Busiest in summer, but beautiful anytime of the year (average temperatures vary only about 10 degrees between winter and summer).

THE INN AT RANCHO SANTA FE
Rancho Santa Fe, Calif.

It was raining outside and mystery-writer Helen MacInnes was standing in the lobby armed with a golf umbrella. We discussed the weather, traded accents, and discovered we came from the same rain-haunted part of Scotland. Then, this being California rather than Scotland, the rain stopped, and she went striding off through the garden, no doubt concocting some intricate new plot for her next best-seller.

When you think of it, the Inn at Rancho Santa Fe is the perfect setting for a thriller—secluded, unhurried, slightly mysterious. This Santa Fe is only twenty-seven miles north of San Diego, but it's a cousin of its New Mexico namesake through the Atcheson, Topeka and Santa Fe Railroad. Apparently, at the turn of the century, an ATSFRR bigwig went off to the antipodes, brought back eucalyptus trees from Australia and New Zealand, and planted them on this old Mexican land grant. His intention was to create an endless supply of railroad ties for his company, but the plan didn't take root. The trees, however, did. They grew and grew and grew into a languid grove. In the twenties the ranch was transformed into one of the country's first planned communities (although it doesn't *look* regimented) and the inn was built in 1924.

It's an enclave of adobe cottages adding up to seventy-five rooms, but if you didn't know it was there you'd drive past it. The inn's six gardeners (six gardeners to only seventy-five rooms—remarkable) seem to feel it's their duty to disguise the inn, to hide it behind a proliferation of eucalyptus, Brazilian peppers, acacia, strawberry trees, avocado trees, and bougainvillaea. They've certainly created one of the most fragrant hideaways in the West.

MULTILEVEL GARDEN. The gardens and cottages are on several levels, and as you weave among the foliage to your room it's easy to forget that you're in an inn. All the rooms have views of the gardens, the trees, or the mountains beyond. All have showers, all but five have baths; and a third of them have fireplaces and kitchens. The decor is as varied as the flora and fauna. My own favorite is #221, with period decor and wallpaper and a large sundeck overlooking the dell at the rear; room 38 has a window alcove, armchairs, french doors on to a terrace, a concealed wet bar; and #35 has hideaway beds and huge windows overlooking the terrace and lawn, a pullman kitchen, and a eucalyptus-burning fireplace.

Even the menu is remarkably varied for an inn this size, serving everything from snacks to continental dishes. It's surprisingly inexpensive, too—say, Bayshore combination seafood plate (tutuava, shrimp, scallops, bluepoint oysters) for $4.50, stuffed crepes with bay shrimp for $4, steaks and roast beef from $8, with a wine list to match. You can enjoy your meal in the sunny Garden Room overlooking the pool, the leather-and-wood-paneled Vintage Room, the Patio Courtyard and, in summertime, by the pool.

BARONIAL LOUNGE, FOUR-THOUSAND-VOLUME LIBRARY. The Inn at Rancho Santa Fe is essentially a place for relaxing, for lounging by the pool, with maybe an occasional game of tennis on the inn's three courts (free), or a round of golf over one of the three courses nearby (green fees from $9). In summer you can drive four miles to Del Mar, where the inn has a beach bungalow (they'll also make up picnic lunches for you). Between swims and games, you can retire to the peace and quiet of the inn's baronial lounge, with its raftered ceiling, big open fire, voluminous sofas, Chinese screens, and models of sailing boats. A comfy, clubby place for a predinner sherry or after-dinner brandy. You can also browse for an hour or two in the inn's four-thousand-book library. Maybe you'll pick up a thriller you won't be able to put down—which is as good a way as any of spending a rainy afternoon, next to writing one.

Name: The Inn at Rancho Santa Fe
Owner/Manager: Dan Royce
Address: Box 869, Rancho Santa Fe, Calif. 92067
Directions: From Interstate 5 take the Encinitas Boulevard or Lomas Santa Fe exits (from the north), the Via De La Valle Exit (from the south); the inn's limousine will pick you up at the airport in San Diego ($20 per trip for two); by Amtrak to Del Mar.

Telephone: (714) 756–1131

Cables/Telex: None

Credit Cards: American Express, Diners, MasterCard, Visa

Rooms: 70, 5 two- or three-bedroom villas.

Meals: Breakfast 7:30–10:00, lunch 12:00–2:30 (also served on outdoor terrace), dinner 6:30–9:00 (approx. $15 to $20 for 2); room service during dining-room hours; jackets at dinner in Vintage Room, optional but preferred in Garden Room; live music and dancing on patio during summer ($2.50 per person cover charge).

Diversions: Pool, croquet, bowling on the green, badminton, Ping-Pong, horseshoes, shuffleboard, tennis (3 courts, no charge); beach cottage at Del Mar; golf nearby.

Sightseeing: Santa Fe, Mexico, Palomar Observatory, Scripp's Institute of Oceanography, Sea World, The Wild Animal Park, the San Diego Zoo.

BEVERLY HILLS HOTEL
Beverly Hills, Calif.

$$$

"Daddy, this is such a beautiful hotel, and we love it so, I wish you'd buy it for us." So Daddy did, Daddy being Detroit lawyer and financier Ben Silberstein. Daughter Muriel was eighteen at the time she dropped the hint, and the Beverly Hills Hotel was a trifling $5¼ million. Today, it's worth $30 million. Maybe more.

Long before there was a Beverly Hills there was a Beverly Hills Hotel. When it opened in 1912, Sunset Boulevard was a bridle path, and the new pink-and-green stucco structure was surrounded by bean fields. Its original function was to attract people to the area so that they'd buy land and build homes. And buy and build they did—the Pickfords, Tom Mix, Harold Lloyd, W. C. Fields.

Today the Beverly Hills Hotel sits among broad avenues lined by royal palms and million-dollar homes, screened from the world by twelve acres of lawns and jungly gardens of banana trees, ginger plants, oleander, and jacarandas, a haven for celebrities and nonentities alike.

The haven consists of 325 rooms, all individually designed, most of them in the main building. The remainder are in bungalows tucked

away among the jacarandas and date palms and bougainvillaea—
perfect spots for trysting lovers and bashful movie stars because you
can get to them through the foliage, without ever showing your face
in the lobby. Renting a bungalow is like having your own home in
posh Beverly Hills; each one has one to four bedrooms (you can rent
them separately), plus parlors, natural fireplaces, dining alcoves,
kitchens, wet bars, and garden patios. They're all luxuriously decorated—even the single rooms come with a small refrigerator.

The bungalows are expensive ($90 a bedroom, $600 or more for
the lot), but they're still the most popular accommodations in the
hotel. Except, perhaps, for suite 486 on the top floor of the main
building—a sumptuous peach-colored $215-a-night suite with gold
faucets, marble tubs, and a wet bar with a hundred glasses in case
you're planning a little get-together. In recent years, this suite has
hosted Prince Philip, Johnny Carson, Princess Grace and her prince.
Big names, but then the history of the Beverly Hills Hotel is an
anthology of anecdotes about the great and famous. Like the time
Katharine Hepburn walked from the tennis courts to the pool,
climbed the diving board, and performed a perfect backflip—still in
her tennis togs and shoes. Or the day cartoonist George McManus
unscrewed a button marked "Press" from a urinal in the men's room,
stuck it in his lapel, and gate-crashed a party as a newspaperman.

BEAR STEAK FOR DINNER, CHAMPAGNE FOR BREAKFAST. To keep its
guests happy, the Beverly Hills has an army of four hundred reception clerks, bellhops, waiters, chambermaids, and chefs waiting to
show you a thing or two about personal service. If you've been here
before and made it known that you prefer a room at the rear, you'll
get a room at the rear without asking; if you're the oil tycoon who has a
penchant for bear steaks, a special order has already gone through to
Alaska and your bear steak is waiting for you in the freezer; and if
you're Brigitte Bardot you'll find the customary bottle of champagne
on your breakfast tray. The hotel keeps track of these facts with a
huge revolving card index system that records the basic facts plus the
whims, foibles, and preferences of every guest who has signed in
during the past five years; and special briefing cards are issued to key
personnel, who are also expected to add to the list of foibles. The first
test of Beverly Hills service is to pick up your telephone the minute
you enter your room, and one of the hotel's forty operators will

address you by name. (Or should. Last time I stayed there, she didn't, but maybe she didn't know how to pronounce it, and was too polite to guess.)

HAMBURGERS WITH ROSES. If you want an excuse to telephone, call room service. This is another of the hotel's fortes. Obviously, if a big oil tycoon wants bear steak, he gets it. How about ordinary mortals? Try ordering a hamburger. It will arrive within twenty minutes on a silver tray, with your beer in an ice bucket and one perfect red rose in a bud vase. (There are roses everywhere; the hotel goes through a hundred dozen roses a week.)

You can also look forward to a rose with breakfast in bed, but here's another suggestion. Enjoy a whole gardenful of flowers with your muffins and coffee—in the Loggia, just beyond the fabled Polo Lounge, a patio built around an aging Brazilian pepper tree with pink azaleas dripping from its branches. The edge of the patio is scalloped with little alcoves of white brick, surrounded by hibiscus, camellias, birds of paradise, pituporum, and night-blooming jasmine, where you can linger over your fresh strawberries and cream and listen to the birdsongs. It's a lyrical way to begin a day. There are, to be sure, some people who find the Beverly Hills Hotel less than lyrical. Some people think it's overpriced (and cubic foot for cubic foot it probably is, if you're interested in cubic feet). Some find the plumbing intrusive. Some people get fidgety waiting for the valet to bring their car round from the parking lot (a rather noisy production number in the evening, so demand a room at the rear), and others think that a $6 cab ride from downtown Hollywood is $6 too far. But for its loyal fan club, it's a matter of "Daddy, this is such a beautiful hotel, and we love it so, we hope you won't sell it." Even for $30 million.

Name: Beverly Hills Hotel
Manager: Robert J. Marsili
Address: 9641 Sunset Boulevard, Beverly Hills, Calif. 90210
Directions: The simplest way, probably, is to get onto the San Diego Freeway (Interstate 405), get off at the Sunset Boulevard ramp, and drive east until you come to a big pink-and-green building sticking up above the palm trees.
Telephone: (213) 276–2251
Cables/Telex: BEVHILL/691459

Credit Cards: American Express, Carte Blanche, Diners, MasterCard, Visa
Rooms: 325, 50 suites, 20 bungalows.
Meals: Breakfast 7:00–11:00, lunch 12:00–3:00, dinner 6:30–10:00 (anything
    from a few dollars to a hundred); room service 6:30 A.M. to 1:00 A.M.;
    jackets at dinner.
Diversions: Heated outdoor pool; 2 tennis courts ($2.50 per person per hour);
    Pacific Ocean 20 minutes away.
Sightseeing: Beverly Hills.
P.S. Busy all year round—but one of the few hotels in this guide that's *less*
    crowded on weekends; no need to worry about conventioneers ever
    (the hotel won't even allow name tags), but forget about staying here on
    Emmy Awards night and so on, unless you want to book now for 1984.

BEL-AIR HOTEL
Westwood Village, Los Angeles, Calif.

Truman Capote calls it "the greatest hotel in the world." Hotel? It's a
magic bird cage in an enchanted garden. The first sights you see are
an arched stone bridge, a white wrought-iron chair at one end, and
masses of flowers everywhere. Walk across the bridge and you look
down through the foliage to a lake with swans, and pathways winding
to nowhere. Al Peiler and his team of gardeners have created a
wonderland with pampas grass, jade plants, candytuft, tree ferns,
tulip trees, red azaleas, ginger plants, coral trees, rose vines climbing
stucco walls to tiled roofs, two sturdy oaks, and a rare silk floss tree, or
chorisia speciosa, which is famous in horticultural circles. Opossum
and deer often come down from the canyon to feed on the lawn.

EXERCISE RING, HORSE HOSPITAL. Actually the hotel's beginnings
were earthy—it was once a stable. The estate known as Bel-Air,
hideaway of the upper echelon of show business, was founded by
Alphonso E. Bell, a man of the cloth who happened to strike oil on his
dairy farm and put his blessing into real estate. To attract the right
type of resident he built a stable, with exercise ring, milk shed, and
horse hospital. A stable it remained from the 1920s to 1944, when it
was converted into a hotel. Very skillfully, too—you'd never suspect

that room 109 was once a horse hospital. The hotel is now owned by
financier Joseph Drown, who wanted a hotel that is "relatively small,
typically Californian in looks, built among gardens, around patios."
He wanted, he got.

Bel-Air's Shangri-la has a cloisterlike look, with Spanish arches,
courtyards, patios, fountains, white and pink corridors linking white
stucco bungalows with clay-tiled roofs—sandwiched between the
garden and the sheer green wall of the canyon.

WOOD-BURNING FIREPLACES, GARDEN PATIOS. All the guest rooms are
different (except for an unexpected paper wrapper round the toilet
seat announcing "Sanitized for your protection"). Each room in its
individual way is a classic of refined elegance. Or elegant refinement.
Most of them have wood-burning fireplaces and garden patios.
Some, like suite 160, have a marble fireplace, a small refrigerator,
and a patio the size of most people's homes; suite 122 has a carved
wooden fireplace, and harmonized wallpapers, drapes, upholstery,
and bedspreads that change hue discreetly from parlor to bedroom.
The most fairytale of the rooms is #240, halfway up a moss-topped
tower, with a bay window and love seat overlooking Swan Lake. It's a
tiny world all its own. It even has a small patio where you can have
breakfast or sunbathe.

The Bel-Air is the ideal little hideaway. You don't even have to go through the lobby, which doesn't look like a lobby anyway, more like a mansion lounge, with a large log-burning fireplace; in one corner is a tiny office, where reservations manager Phil Landon sits with a jar of jelly beans on his desk, and quietly caters to the erratic tastes of the rich and the distinguished—princesses, movie stars, society (like the multimillionaires who used to arrive with their own bed linen and toilet tissue), performers, and people so famous they need only one name. Some stable.

Ironically, you have to leave the stable if you want to go horseback riding. The only sports facilities are an egg-shaped pool and sun terrace. That's it. The Bel-Air is definitely a place for dalliance. Enjoy the garden. Enjoy the pool. Enjoy each other. Linger over dinner. The romantic atmosphere in the dining room is kindled by soft candlelight, cozy booths, and a fireplace carved into the canyon rock and surrounded by Hawaiian-style greenery; here Chef Roger Smith serves up the sort of meal you want to spend an entire evening with—local fare with a continental flavor, like Catalina sanddabs *sauté belle meunière*, broiled salmon Mirabeau, roast rack of lamb *boulangerie* or *medaillons de veau Veronese*. Even when you've added vegetables and wine and all the trimmings you can still come out for under $50 for two.

The problem is—even if it means going over $70—in an atmosphere like this it's almost blasphemy not to order champagne.

Name: Bel-Air Hotel
Manager: James H. Checkman
Address: 701 Stone Canyon Road, Los Angeles, Calif. 90024
Directions: Drive east on Sunset Boulevard from San Diego Freeway to Stone Canyon Road, then turn left to Calif. 701; if coming from Hollywood, drive west on Sunset to Stone Canyon Road (which dead-ends into Sunset Boulevard) and turn right. Stone Canyon is located almost at the center of UCLA facing Sunset Boulevard on the south.
Telephone: (213) 472–1211
Cables/Telex: None
Credit Cards: American Express, Carte Blanche, Diners
Rooms: 46, plus 22 suites.
Meals: Breakfast 7:30–noon, lunch 12:00–3:00, dinner 6:00–11:00 (approx. $50–$70 for 2); room service from 7:30 A.M. to 9:30 P.M.; jacket and tie at dinner; pianist and vocalist in lounge, after dinner.
Diversions: Heated outdoor pool, walks to the reservoir.

Sightseeing: Los Angeles, Beverly Hills, UCLA.

P.S. Busy at any time of the year, but you never have to worry about conventions—they're not allowed over the bridge.

WESTWOOD MARQUIS HOTEL
Westwood Village, Los Angeles, Calif.

$$$

Nothing at the Westwood Marquis is less than a suite, the smallest going under the euphemism of studios; and the largest and grandest being on the penthouse floor with their own personal concierge and butler.

But aside from space, what most endears this hotel to those who spend weeks and months at a stretch in L.A. (you'd be surprised how long it can take to shoot a Miller Lite commercial) is how un-hotelish it is here. And you begin to notice before you're even out of your limo.

Out on the sidewalk waits a small, elegant glass elevator. Not for you—for your luggage. This way, you never have to watch battalions of sweating bellmen lurching under the weight of your matched Vuitton. Magically, it disappears ahead of you without inflicting a stab of guilt for the lifting-carrying classes. The lobby's welcome mat is Aubusson, the walls marble and tapestries, the furnishings live orchids and Louis XIV. And the first face you see is a very pleasant one belonging to a statuesque concierge in floor-length velvet, who proves never too busy or bored to remember your name and figure out how to solve your every problem, including some even your mother couldn't handle.

The guest suites may not be exactly like home, but what fun would that be? No two (out of 250) are exactly alike, and although California tastes tend to be a little . . . er . . . *livelier,* shall we say? than the rest of the world's, surely even Billy Baldwin would shed no tears here. Tables are heavy glass and solid brass. Television sets are hidden away in walnut cabinets. Bathrooms (sometimes two to a suite) are big and full of multi-sinks, vanity tables, a telephone, and enough thick yellow bath towels to dry off the L.A. Rams.

One distraction, which has been known to drive an occasional guest to sleeping in the hall, is the hotel's ubiquitous heating-cooling system. It isn't that it makes noise—it just sort of *breathes* on you. All the time in every room. There's no shutting it off no matter what you do with the thermostat. Most people find it like scuba-diving: once you get used to it, you forget what life was like before. Then again, there are those who don't.

As for the food, *every*body in West L.A. (which is the only part to be in anyway) lunches and brunches at the WM's gazebo as religiously as they drink at the Polo Lounge. And apparently for the same reason. Because *every*body is there, including stars of stage, screen, and "Dallas." It is an extremely pretty room, all trellises and garden furniture. But while the goodies at the buffet table look very good indeed, they actually turn out to be less than meets the eye. As for dinner, forget it here. Both food and service fail to live up to their pretensions.

But just a couple of magnolia-scented blocks away is the center of Westwood Village with dozens of restaurants, shops, and above all else—movie theaters. All the films you couldn't see at home because of the lines or because they just never opened there are playing here with plenty of popcorn and no lines. And this may be the only place in southern California that you can get to by *walking*.

In fact, one of the nicest things about the WM is where it is. Right on the edge of the UCLA campus, but with Beverly Hills shopping just ten minutes away and Malibu about thirty.

Although the hotel has sauna, steam room, and pool, don't count on it to give you a George Hamilton tan. For the sun sets below its horizon promptly every day at two.

Anyone who's ever left home knows no hotel is perfect, but the style and comfort and service of the Westwood Marquis come as close to it as any hotel I've encountered on the West Coast. Ask for a suite with a view (either of the sun setting over Beverly Hills or a hundred miles of downtown L.A.), uncork the Burgundy the manager sends up to say welcome, and relax. If you're not in God's country at least you're in the best hotel in L.A.

                                                                      C.P.

Name: Westwood Marquis Hotel
Manager: Jacques P. Camus
Address: 930 Hilgard Avenue, Los Angeles, Calif. 90024
Directions: Approximately 20 minutes north of Los Angeles International
     Airport in Westwood Village; 2 blocks from the UCLA campus.

Telephone: (213) 475–8765
Cables/Telex: 181835 (incoming telex)
Credit Cards: American Express, Carte Blanche, Diners, MasterCard, Visa
Meals: Breakfast 7:00–10:00, lunch 11:00–2:30, dinner 5:30–10:30 (approx.
   $40 to $45 for 2); informal; full room service, 24 hours a day; entertain-
   ment in lounge, taped music in lobby, dining room.
Diversions: Swimming pool, sauna, massage, gymnasium, exercise room;
   tennis, golf, horseback riding, beach, water sports nearby.
Sightseeing: Los Angeles.
P.S. Occasional groups, limited in size.

MARRIOTT'S SANTA BARBARA BILTMORE
Santa Barbara, Calif.

The beamed ceilings and waxed flagstone floors, the panels of antique
Mexican tiles, and the immense bowl of fresh chrysanthemums give
you your first clue about what to expect at the Biltmore. Just step
through the arched door and you can tell you're going to find a lot of
low-key luxury. And you do.

Each of the 176 rooms is different. Each has a distinctly well-
bred look—the kind you see only in fine houses or good country
clubs. The bedspreads and draperies, for instance, aren't shiny. They
look like Fortuny fabrics (perhaps they're copies), but the bed linens
are indeed Wamsutta supercales. *Three* sheets per bed. The bath is
well appointed, too: after your bath, you can wrap yourselves up in a
Fieldcrest Royal Velvet towel—all twenty-seven-by-fifty inches of it.
The beds, too, are outsized (perhaps because the fifty-year-old Biltmore was the dream child of a lanky cowboy, the late Robert Odell).
Ask for an extra-wide or an extra-long one—or both. In either case,
the mattress will be a bouncy Beautyrest of a Serta Perfect Sleeper.

And where do you find ice? In your armoire, of course. In a
concealed refrigerator. (The inevitable TV set here, hooked up for
Home Box Office, however, is in full unsightly view.) Most of the
rooms also have window seats, upholstered settees, or sofas, and
many of them have fireplaces (burning, alas, gas and not wood, but

the effect is still quite beguiling, especially when you're shrouded in your twenty-seven-by-fifty towels).

CHILLED OYSTERS, BIRDS OF PARADISE. At teatime, guests with unflagging spirits can stoke up on shrimp or chilled oysters. (What true lover would ever pass the chance of lunging into some nice oysters, particularly just after a siesta?) At night, outdoor torches are ablaze for dining al fresco, so you can still admire the Biltmore's hibiscus, bougainvillaea, and birds of paradise—and the fresh flowers on your table, grown not in some distant hothouse but right here on the grounds. Which are considerable—some twenty-one acres of prime land by the very edge of the Pacific (there's a small, but sandy nonetheless, beach right across the street). There, by the grace of you know who, you'll be seeing some startling scarlet sunsets. They're just about the most ostentatious touches tolerated around this lovely low-key place.

                                                                    R.E.S.

Name: Marriott's Santa Barbara Biltmore
Manager: Thomas H. Gowman
Address: 1260 Channel Drive, Santa Barbara, Calif. 93108
Directions: Take Calif. 101 to the Olive Mill Road Exit, a few miles south of
    Santa Barbara, then follow the road to the shore and Channel Drive; 1½
    hours from Los Angeles, 6½ from San Francisco; by air, to Santa
    Barbara Airport (limousine service); by Amtrak, the *Coast Starlight*.
Telephone: (805) 969–2261
Cables/Telex: None
Credit Cards: "All major credit cards"
Meals: Breakfast 7:30–10:30, lunch 12:00–2:30, dinner 6:00–10:00 (approx.
    $30 for 2); jacket and tie; full room service 7:00 A.M. to 11:00 P.M.; music
    and dancing in dining room; combo in lounge.
Diversions: 2 heated swimming pools, golf (18 holes), badminton, bicycles,
    croquet, pickleball; tennis, horseback riding, beach, water sports,
    whale watching nearby.
Sightseeing: In Santa Barbara: Mission Santa Barbara, Lobero theater.
P.S. Basically a summer resort, but with this climate you can come at any
    time; some groups.

San Francisco and Its Neighbors

And when the west is red
With the sunset embers,
The lover lingers and sings
And the maid remembers . . .

ROBERT LOUIS STEVENSON

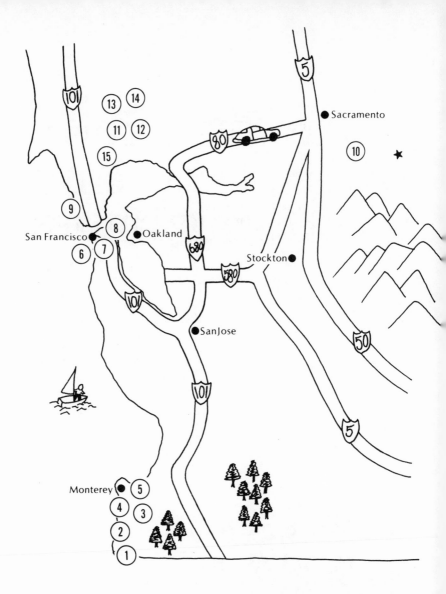

1. Ventana
2. Highlands Inn
3. Quail Lodge
4. The Sandpiper Inn
5. The Lodge at Pebble Beach
6. Miyako Hotel
7. The Stanford Court
8. The Mansion
9. The Pelican Inn
10. Sutter Creek Inn
11. The Magnolia Hotel
12. Burgundy House
13. Bordeaux House
14. The Wine Country Inn
15. Sonoma Mission Inn
★ *Added Attractions*

VENTANA
Big Sur, Calif.

$$$

If you'd like a preview of your entry into Valhalla, walk out along the enormous concrete deck of Ventana, and watch a big cloud bank come drifting in over the Pacific (look *down*, the ocean's way below you). Now you know what it's like to be sitting on top of the world. The Ventana is not short on mortal pleasures either. Management pretends to know nothing of the group therapy sessions that go on in the Japanese therapy pools and saunas during the wee hours. But love, and lust, always find a way, don't they? There has already been one wedding amidst the poppies here, and more are inevitable—the place is that romantic. Ask any couple sitting around the pool sipping Chablis. They hoot if you happen to wonder where you go for tennis. "Nobody comes to Ventana to be competitive, you come to share with one another."

Only forty-eight people get to share at one time. Most of the twenty-four guest rooms have ocean views (cloud banks and morning mist permitting), others face the Santa Lucia Mountains and the redwoods. All are simply and beautifully decorated. Wicker, rush, caning, natural wood—these are the substances that give Ventana such a terrific look. The homemade quilts from Nova Scotia, Franklin stoves, and handpainted and hard-carved headboards don't hurt either.

Continental breakfast is served in your room or by the open hearth in the guest den. (You also have a wet bar in your room, in case you want to hoard juices or wines.) For your other meals you walk or drive to the real showplace of this superb establishment, the ocean-view restaurant. Have lunch outdoors, on the deck, and drink in the forty-mile panorama of Big Sur coastline and Pacific Ocean. In the evening, enjoy dinner by candlelight in the beamed and timbered dining room. The napery is soft lilac, the music is Mozart, and wonder of wonders, the food is excellent. If the chef has his poached salmon on the menu, leap at it. Next night, try the tender-pink roast leg of lamb. And for dessert, *demand* the pear tart with almonds. You can swim it all off tomorrow. Or steam it all off tonight. In the sauna, that is.

R.E.S.

Name: Ventana
Manager: Robert E. Bussinger
Address: Ventana Village, Big Sur, Calif. 93920
Directions: 28 miles south of Carmel, on the coastal highway; Shell Station at entrance.
Telephone: (408) 667–2331, (408) 624–4812
Cables/Telex: None
Credit Cards: American Express, Carte Blanche, Diners, MasterCard, Visa
Rooms: 40, 2 suites; some with fireplace and/or terrace.
Meals: Continental breakfast 8:00–10:00, lunch 11:00–3:45, dinner 6:00–9:30 (approx. $35 to $45 for 2); lunch and dinner also served on outdoor terrace; room service for breakfast only; informal dress.
Diversions: Heated outdoor pool, therapy pool, sauna, hiking trails.
Sightseeing: Big Sur coastal scenery, the Pacific; in Carmel: Carmel Mission historical museum, Del Monte Forest (complete with giant redwoods), Mission San Carlos Borromeo.
P.S. 2-night minimum stay on weekend, 3 nights on holiday weekend.

HIGHLANDS INN
Carmel Highlands, Calif.

$$$

The cocktail lounges are called the Sunset Room, the Lauder Room, and the Owlery Bar, and look toward the Bird Rocks of Point Lobos (one of the most unspoiled, unusual peninsulas along the entire California coast); the dining rooms overlook Yankee Point and its dramatic cedar-sided homes and crashing surf. Highlands Inn is a nest high on the granite cliffs above a cove, and as if the natural setting weren't enough, the Ramsey family has transformed this fourteen-acre hillside into a botanical garden with rare plants from New Zealand, Japan, Australia, Peru, South Africa, Japan, and Ethiopia—two thousand varieties of flowers from California lilac and Ponderosa lemons to heather and cypress.

CREDENZAS AND CHICKERINGS. The inn's lobby is a depository of antiques, including a cherry-wood credenza said to have been carpentered by Mormon Brigham Young for his sixteen-year-old fourth wife, a huge court cupboard belonging to the Emperor Franz Josef, and the first Chickering grand piano in California. The original guest rooms are Hansel-and-Gretel cottages secluded among the foliage and flowers; quiet, secluded, comfy, they strike the right note between rustic and modern. Not all of them have the views of the ocean and that's why the more functional lanai rooms are most popular.

Some of the lanais are quite luxurious. Room F4, for example, has a superb view, with a large balcony overlooking Yankee Point, a tiled lanai with wrought-iron furniture, white rough-hewn pine walls, and king-size bed; and there are several rooms with balconies or patios to make the most of the sun—breakfast on the patio by the pool, dinner on the balcony overlooking the ocean. Lanai 24 is a suite with an enormous patio for sunning and dining, acres of window, a pink scatter rug in front of a fire, a red/white/blue bedroom with his and hers closets. In other words, among the inn's 105 rooms is something to suit every taste.

Your room rates include an eight-course dinner, and there's an extraordinary wine list that ranges from humble Californians at $8 a bottle to an aristocratic Château Lafite Rothschild at $120. How's that for an elegant way to celebrate the sunset?

Name: Highlands Inn
Manager: Paul C. Reed
Address: P.O. Box 1700, Carmel-by-the-Sea, Calif. 93921
Directions: In Carmel Highlands, 4 miles south of Carmel, on scenic Highway 1, up a steep hill.
Telephone: (408) 624–3801
Cables/Telex: None
Credit Cards: American Express, Barclaycard, Carte Blanche, Diners, Eurocard, MasterCard, Visa
Rooms: 105, 2 suites.
Meals: Breakfast 8:00–10:00, lunch 12:00–2:00, dinner 6:30–9:00, (6:00–10:00 Fridays and Saturdays); room service; jacket and tie at dinner; live music in the lounge.
Diversions: Heated outdoor pool, shuffleboard; golf, tennis, horseback riding, bicycles, boating nearby.
Sightseeing: See "Ventana."
P.S. Busiest in summer, but the view is spectacular at any time of the year, some groups in off-season.

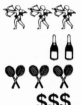

QUAIL LODGE
Carmel Valley, Calif.

Someone went to a lot of trouble and expense here to create a perfect nest for lovers. A split of private-label champagne welcomes you to a room of muted colors, Ficks Reed furniture, Swedish string lamps, Fieldcrest towels, custom-made soap, rockstone tiles in the bathroom, electric percolator, *ground* coffee and ceramic mugs.

There are ninety-six of these rooms in beautifully designed board-on-board redwood cottages, some overlooking a lagoon with a Japanese bridge, others overlooking the golf course. They all have patios (but if you plan to spend much time on your patio, choose the rooms overlooking the golf course—they're farther from the highway).

DUCKS ON THE FAIRWAYS, DOVES IN THE LOBBY. Quail Lodge is part of
the Carmel Valley Golf and Country Club, where the valley pushes
aside the hills and spreads down to the sea. Most of the floor of the
valley is the golf course, which golfers share with ducks, deer,
opossums, and raccoons. The clubhouse is a handsome white building surrounded by flowers and flowering plum trees, and with a big
white wrought-iron cage of temple doves in the foyer. The club
facilities are available to the lodge's guests.

But isn't it only fair that since someone took all that trouble with
color schemes and fabrics, you should spend a lot of time in your
room?

Name: Quail Lodge
Manager: Hoby J. Hooker
Address: 8205 Valley Green Drive, Carmel, Calif. 93923
Directions: 4 miles along Carmel Valley Road, east of Calif. 1—that is, 5
  minutes from Carmel-by-the-Sea; by air to Monterey Airport, and from
  there by airport limousine.
Telephone: (408) 624–1581
Cables/Telex: None
Credit Cards: American Express, Carte Blanche, Diners, MasterCard, Visa
Rooms: 96, including 12 suites.
Meals: Breakfast 7:30–11:30, lunch 11:30–2:30, dinner 6:30–10:00 (approx.
  $18 to $30 for 2); room service 7:30 A.M. to 11:30 A.M. for breakfast, 8:00
  A.M. to midnight for liquor; jackets in Covey dining room; live music
  weekends.
Diversions: Outdoor heated pool, sauna (for men), hot tub, hiking trail;
  tennis (4 courts, pro, $8 per hour), golf (18 holes, $15 per round),
  bicycles for rent; sailing and boating nearby.
Sightseeing: See "Ventana."
P.S. Busiest in summer, but you can play golf or tennis any time of the year.

THE SANDPIPER INN-AT-THE-BEACH
Carmel-by-the-Sea, Calif.

Innkeeper Graeme Mackenzie was watering his roses as new guests
arrived at The Sandpiper, and his warm greeting tipped them off to

the general cordiality to be found during a stay at this small country inn.

Irene Mackenzie is continually redecorating all fifteen rooms country English style. Every room has a brand-new Serta Perfect Sleeper (king or queen size), Mackenzie antiques from Scotland and the Orient, and fresh flowers in all the bedrooms. Some rooms have glorious views of Carmel Beach; others wood-burning fireplaces. Homey as the inn looks, it has recently been brought totally up to date in one convenience: private baths in every room.

Feel free to make tea, or chill your Riesling, in the Sandpiper kitchen; soft drinks are stored in the big refrigerator, and you pay for them on the honor system. Continental breakfast is served by the big open fireplace in the living room. Guests socialize here, and plan their days. What is there to do? The beach is a mere half-block away. (There was a sand-castle contest going on during our visit on a coolish October weekend.) Or you can hire a bike—the Mackenzies have ten-speeders to tour the Seventeen-Mile Drive, for wheeling into town, or visiting the two-hundred-year-old Mission San Carlos Borromeo. The Mackenzies can also advise you of the specialities at all the restaurants in the area. (Graeme Mackenzie is president of the Carmel Innkeepers Association, so he has connections, if you want to make a reservation.) Likewise, if you want to make arrangements for golf or tennis clubs, he's the man to ask.

But maybe the thing to do is just sit around the fire and mingle with the other guests. The Mackenzies are well known in international circles, and their guest list shows names from sixty-four countries.

It's quiet here, too. The only buildings in the neighborhood are private houses. Strict zoning laws prevent any commercial encroachments. Your luck. It's like living in a pleasant private home in a jealously guarded enclave of privacy—and rose gardens.

R.E.S.

Name: The Sandpiper Inn-at-the-Beach
Owners/Managers: Graeme and Irene Mackenzie
Address: 2408 Bayview Avenue at Martin Street, Carmel-by-the-Sea, Calif. 93923
Directions: From Highway 1, go down Ocean Avenue to the stop sign at the beginning of the village; turn left then second right into 8th Avenue, go

all the way to the beach, turn left, drive along Scenic Avenue to the large stop sign in the middle of the road; next left is Martin Street, and the inn is 50 yards up on the right.

Telephone: (408) 624–6433

Cables/Telex: None

Credit Cards: MasterCard, Visa

Rooms: 15, including 2 Carmel Cottage rooms.

Meals: Continental breakfast 8:00–10:00; no other meals, but guests have use of the kitchen for storing wines and cheese, or making a pot of tea or coffee; room service for breakfast after 9:00; dress casual at all times.

Diversions: Backgammon, bridge, chess; 10-speed bicycles for hire; golf, tennis, horseback riding, hill walking, mountaineering, surfing, scuba-diving, polo, etc., nearby.

Sightseeing: See "Ventana."

P.S. Minimum stays in effect for all holidays and during some special events, such as the Crosby Pro Am Golf Tournament (check in advance for dates). No children under 12, and no pets.

THE LODGE AT PEBBLE BEACH

Pebble Beach, Calif.

$$$

You wake up in the morning and step out onto the balcony and there spread out before you is a sight that will open wide the bleariest love-hooded eye: the eighteenth fairway of the Pebble Beach course running alongside the surfy Pacific, a flock of mudhens picking the grass, the whole scene set in a curve of bay with rocks and pounding waves and pine and cypress trees. "A monument to the blessing nature can bestow on a golf course," as golf writer Pat Ward-Thomas called it. Even if you're not a golfer you'll probably still concede that a golf course is prettier to wake up to than a baseball diamond.

Golf made Pebble Beach famous, but you don't have to play the game to wallow in the good life.

PRIVATE FOREST, SEVENTEEN-MILE DRIVE. The present-day Pebble Beach Lodge is a white, gleaming structure of slightly classical pro-portions, surrounded by two-story villas housing 159 rooms with views of the golf course or the ocean or both. It's on the famous Seventeen-Mile Drive around the Monterey Peninsula, which means it's part of the Del Monte Forest, a private reserve decked out with some of the loveliest mansions you've ever squinted at behind fences and hedgerows—a setting of almost unalloyed peace, even in August, when Carmel itself is awash in Bermuda shorts. The guest rooms have big windows, big closets, big balconies, big beds; color TV, refrigerators, and log-burning fireplaces; and they've all been gingered up from ceiling to underfelt in the past few years. Since the rooms are all alike, more or less, the main difference is the view, and for my money the best views are from the rooms in the villas known as Colton, Alvarado, and Portola.

The main dining room, one floor above the fairway level, overlooks the ocean, and (nice touch) the tables that are not next to the window are turned to face the view. Up here, the table d'hôte menu offers you a choice of Monterey Bay sea bass, crisped duckling with orange sauce, roast rack of lamb; downstairs in the Club XIX, you have a slightly fancier menu—poulet grillé, beef bourguignon, or fresh salmon (in season).

One problem with a dining room that serves good food is that it becomes popular with the locals, and on weekends you have to reserve a table—and sometimes you can't get a reservation. In this case, who needs it? Just call room service and have them set up your meal in front of the log fire, or out on the balcony where you can listen to the surf as you sip your Pommard.

Name: The Lodge at Pebble Beach
Manager: Leif Jensen
Address: Pebble Beach, Calif. 93953
Directions: Take Calif. 101 to Carmel or Monterey, then follow the signs to Seventeen-Mile Drive; by air, scheduled services to Monterey Peninsula Airport (lodge limousine, $6 per couple each way).
Telephone: (408) 624–3811
Cables/Telex: None
Credit Cards: American Express, Diners, MasterCard, Visa
Rooms: 159 rooms and suites.
Meals: Breakfast 7:00–11:00, lunch 12:00–2:00, dinner 7:00–10:00 (approx. $30 and up for 2); room service 7:00 A.M. to 10:00 P.M.; jacket and tie in the dining room; trio and dancing on weekends.
Diversions: Heated freshwater pool, saunas, walking, jogging; horseback

riding (34 miles of trails); tennis (14 courts, $3 per person per 1½ hours, pro shop), golf (three 18-hole championship courses, $12 to $32 per round).

Sightseeing: Monterey Peninsula; also see "Ventana."

P.S. May, September, and October are the big months, but the climate is springlike year round; avoid the weeks of the Bing Crosby Pro-Am and other tournaments; some seminars and groups throughout the year.

MIYAKO HOTEL
San Francisco, Calif.

$$

What do you say to a sauna for two without leaving the privacy of your own room? Voluptuous? Then reserve one of the fourteen suites with sauna baths.

Or sample an oriental evening in one of the four Japanese rooms, with *tatami* mats and those voluminous quilts known as *futons*, which are spread on the floor to become beds. Have your dinner brought up, eat it cross-legged on the floor, and then when you're finished simply roll over onto bed. Soft lights glow in an indoor bamboo garden to add a moonlight-over-Fujiyama touch to your frolics on the *futon*.

Even the ordinary rooms at the Miyako let you indulge in a delicious Japanese tradition—the sunken tub made for two, complete with low stool and bucket for sloshing each other with cold water between bouts in the hot tub. The hotel thoughtfully supplies a specially imported perfumed powder that brings California's public utility water to the proper color and fragrance. In your subsequent state of euphoria, you may not notice the other features of the room—the delicate gold-brown-yellow decor of Japan, a *tokonoma* (the niche for flowers or Buddhas), *shoji* screens, brocade quilts, and chairs covered with Japan's traditional chrysanthemum motif. There's also color TV—a Japanese make, of course.

Now why on earth would you want to stay in a Japanese hotel in San Francisco? Apart from saturnalian plumbing, none—except that Nihonmachi, the Japanese equivalent of Chinatown, is one of the oldest parts of the city the Japanese call Soho. Plus the fact that you have less chance in this 208-room hotel of being swamped by a convention, which is a possibility in other top hotels.

MISO-SHIRU, SASHIMI, AND TEMPURA. You can also enjoy Japanese food here—in the hotel or in the restaurants of Nihonmachi. The room service has a few Japanese dishes among the regular occidental delicacies like club sandwiches and teriyakiburgers, but if you speak nicely to the maître d' in the dining room, you can order up a meal from the regular menu—miso-shiru (soy bean soup), sashimi (raw fresh tuna or sea bass from Fisherman's Wharf, thinly sliced), and tempura (butterly shrimps and vegetables deep fried in a special batter).

And if you really want to pamper yourselves, pick up the telephone and order room-service massage.

Name: Miyako Hotel
Manager: Larry Alexander
Address: 1625 Post Street, San Francisco, Calif. 94115
Directions: Ask for the Japanese Trade Center, or look for its peaked Peace Pagoda; a 5-minute cab ride from Nob Hill, about 10 minutes from Fisherman's Wharf.
Telephone: (415) 922–3200 (or any Westin, formerly Western International, hotel)
Cables/Telex: 278063
Credit Cards: American Express, Barclaycard, Carte Blanche, Diners, Eurocard, MasterCard, Visa
Rooms: 208, 14 suites.
Meals: Breakfast 6:30–11:30, lunch 11:30–5:00, Sunday brunch 11:30–2:30, dinner 5:00–11:00 (approx. $14 to $30 for 2); room service 6:30 A.M. to 11:00 P.M.; dress optional; live music and dancing.
Diversions: Japanese tubs—what more do you want?
Sightseeing: San Francisco, particularly Nihonmachi.
P.S. Special packages available; meeting facilities for up to 1,000.

For detailed rate, turn to page 413.

THE STANFORD COURT
San Francisco, Calif.

You don't really need the two chocolate bonbons left on your pillow every night. You don't really need the little marvel that warms your bath towels. And heaven knows you don't need a second TV in the dressing room. But you're going to feel so cosseted once you've had them that you won't give a damn that your room rate sounds more like a donation to a fund-raising dinner. But then these are not everyday hotel rooms—they were decorated and furnished for a cool $43,000 per room.

Walk through the carriage courtyard, beneath the vaulted glass dome, past the Beaux Arts fountain, into the subdued, antique-filled lobby and you'll find it hard to believe that you're in a hotel opened as recently as 1972. The whole place has such a look of noble dignity about it you'd swear its feeling for the grand hotel tradition began in an earlier era; but it looks and feels that way partly because it does indeed have an architectural heritage. No jerry-built glass-and-steel box this. It dates back to 1912, when it was opened as an eight-story luxury apartment complex, high on Nob Hill, on the site of an enormous mansion owned by Leland Stanford. When the house was converted to a hotel each room was designed individually by one of the city's top decorators; rooms, lobby, and hallways were enriched with tapestries and marble, here an antique clock from the Roth-schild estate, there a Baccarat chandelier from the *château* of Chambord. A French chef, groomed in Monte Carlo's Hotel de Paris and Paris's Hotel Crillon, was called in to take charge of the stylish restaurant, Fournou's Ovens. It's highly acclaimed and appropriately expensive; but The Stanford Court is an easy walk to a number of less costly three- and four-star restaurants. Daytime sightseeing is a cinch too: *two* cable-car lines go past the front door. If you're early-to-bedders, ask for a room facing the spacious court (no view, but very quiet) or Pine Street (good view, yet still no sound of the cable cars). For the best view, check into a room on the California Street side, if the clang, clang won't bother you (in any case, the cable cars return to their barn somewhere between eleven and midnight). Incidentally, we have no idea how they keep the interior so quiet. You won't hear a peep from the hallways. Not the maids. Not the breakfast carts. Not even the television in the bathroom next door.

R.E.S.

Name: The Stanford Court

Managers: James A. Nassikas (president), William F. Wilkinson (vice-president and general manager)

Address: Nob Hill, San Francisco, Calif. 94108

Directions: At the corner of California and Powell streets, 5 minutes from Union Square, 10 minutes from Fisherman's Wharf.

Telephone: (415) 989–3500

Cables/Telex: 34-0899; STANCOURT

Credit Cards: American Express, Barclaycard, Diners, Eurocard, Master-Card, Visa

Rooms: 402 rooms and suites.

Meals: Breakfast from 7:00 A.M., lunch to 6:00, high tea 4:00, dinner 5:30–11:00 in Fournou's Ovens ($35 and up for 2); room service 7:00 A.M. to midnight; jacket and tie in Fournou's Ovens.

Diversions: The lobby, the people.

Sightseeing: San Francisco.

P.S. Primarily a business executives' hotel, but romantic nevertheless; no conventions, only a few small seminar-type groups, and name tags and that sort of thing are not encouraged.

P.P.S. from I.K. I stayed here recently and found it even more attractive than I had anticipated. Fournou's Ovens has been skillfully expanded with an indoor/outdoor glass and wrought-iron conservatory, in three-stepped levels along Powell Street. I was equally impressed with Café Potpourri, with its Victorian leather-and-aspidistra atmosphere, ostensibly the hotel's coffee shop, but most hoteliers would give an arm and a leg to have such a room as their main restaurant. Throughout the hotel, the quality of the service, the personal attention, and the perfectionist attention to detail restore one's hope for the tradition of innkeeping in the grand old manner.

THE MANSION
San Francisco, Calif.

$$

Nothing in the staid surroundings of Pacific Heights quite prepares
you for the drollery of The Mansion. Its Queen Anne Revival facade,
all buff and rust and white, signals from its perch above a terraced
flower garden. You walk up two flights of masonry steps, past four
monumental sculptures by Erskine Bufano, through a big oak door
and into the grand foyer. Bach drifts through from one of the parlors;
a wraparound mural dramatizes some highlights in the social history
of the city, but before you have a chance to figure it all out, a young
manservant in white alpaca jacket takes your luggage and leads you
up an elegant stairway, past mannequins in turn-of-the-century garb,
to your room. He will reappear a few minutes later proffering a tray
with glasses of wine to ease the chore of unpacking. The bedcham-
bers are all different sizes, but even the former maids' quarters are
larger than the average motel room. Each is outfitted with fur-
nishings of the period circa 1890 to circa 1940—marble-topped night
stands, white ironstone ewers and basins, chairs upholstered in
tufted purple velveteen. Beds have brass or carved-wood head-
boards, with sachets of fragrant potpourri on the pillows; bedside
reading might be anything from *How to Win Friends and Influence
People* to *Learning to Sail* to *Everything You Never Wanted to Know
About Sex*. The bathrooms (all but one are semiprivate) are floored
with the original octagonal white tiles, augmented by tiny oriental
rugs to keep your toes warm. The conversation piece of each room is a
full-length mural depicting the San Francisco worthy for whom each
room is named—Emperor Norton, Sunny Jim Rolk, et al.

More murals: in the parlor, wild flowers and butterflies, a stag
and unicorn frolicking by a stream, a winged pig with a beatific smile
flying above a meadow. More pigs: in the kitchen-cum-pantry, mu-
rals extol the pig—pigs eating grapes, pigs playing musical instru-
ments, pigs serenading pigs, all confirming owner Bob Pritikin's view
that life should be one big "picnic." In addition to being boss of a local

ad agency, Bob Pritikin is a music lover and organizes evening concerts around a baby grand adorned, need it be noted, with more pigs; and should the evening become too solemn, he is likely, as the resident virtuoso on carpenter's saw, to turn the *soirée musicale* into a *sawrée musicale* by rasping out his rendition of "I left my heart in Sawn Francisco." As another of the city's leading admen remarked: "The Mansion is a grand place for lovers who want to giggle as well as sigh."

A.M.

Name: The Mansion
Manager: Charles Brown
Address: 2220 Sacramento Street, San Francisco, Calif. 94109
Directions: In Pacific Heights, one of the city's prestigious residential neighborhoods; between Laguna and Buchanan streets. About 2 miles from the financial district, 10 blocks from Union Street.
Telephone: (415) 929-9444
Cables/Telex: None
Credit Cards: American Express, MasterCard, Visa
Rooms: 16
Meals: Breakfast (continental) served in bed from 7:00–10:00 weekdays, 7:00–11:00 weekends, dinner 7:30–11:00, 8:30–11:00 Thursdays, Fridays, Saturdays (approx. $46 for 2, including wine); room service 7:00 A.M. to 11:00 P.M. for beverages and snacks; taped Bach, occasional live recitals or chamber music.
Diversions: Backgammon and chess in the library, billiards room; tennis in Lafayette Park, 2 blocks away.
Sightseeing: San Francisco.

THE PELICAN INN
Muir Beach, Calif.

You're winding up and up through the eucalyptus groves above the Golden Gate, with Muir Beach just ahead and San Francisco just behind, and what's this? Too much champagne in your morning Mimosa? A remake of *Tom Jones* complete with a swatch of English countryside?

None of the above. It's the Pelican, an honest-to-Shakespeare Elizabethan farmhouse—whitewashed and timbered to its slatey roof outside and chugging out pints of Guinness and Stingo within. The fact is, it was created lock, stock, and priest hole* no more than three years ago by a nostalgic Englishman, who had long ago come to San Francisco with but one regret. That he'd had to leave behind the famous old country pub that had been in his family for four generations.

But if he couldn't take it with him, he could at least re-create it within easy commuting distance of his San Francisco office. So when you tire of the rococo reaches of the big-city hotels, you can escape to Charles Felix's vest-pocket pub, a twenty-minute ride from the city and a stone's throw from the beach.

There are six tiny guest rooms overlooking the garden and a stable full of horses. Along with fresh and flowery curtains blowing in the window and big, soft beds even Falstaff might have envied, there hangs in each room a small stone whose sole purpose, as it has been for four hundred years, is to prevent rickets in case of pregnancy. And the rest of the house is just as authentic, much of it a direct steal from the English original, including the leaded glass windows and the beautifully burnished antiques. Even the fireplace is an exact replica, made with ancient bricks, of one invented by a British royalist who barely escaped George Washington with his life.

But there's much more to the Pelican than soft beds and old beams. There's the rare pleasure of sitting down with a warm and witty innkeeper and sharing his love of doing what he's doing. The fire is lit. Tales are told. A hint of hot shepherd's pie works its way in from the kitchen.

"We want people to come here and utterly relax," he says. "Everything is hand-prepared and it takes time." And caring. Which shows up in a dozen welcome details. Every day at sundown, a tiny carafe of sherry and a pair of glasses are brought to your room. There are no fewer than nine different British stouts and beers at the bar—and the innkeeper's wife will warm them up for you if you don't like them chilled American style. The fare is very British and very good. Cheshire and Stilton cheeses, bangers and mash, fresh salads, homemade bread, wine and mead. And, of course, afternoon tea by

*A hidden compartment in every good sixteenth-century Catholic's fireplace, where the local pastor could be sheltered from the king's displeasure.

the fire or on the flower-hedged terrace. Fresh flowers show up by your bedside, and the morning paper comes with your breakfast.

What else happens at the Pelican depends on you—and the innkeeper's whim. There's swimming on the protected beach and tours through the redwood forests of nearby Muir Woods. Shakespearean love scenes are sometimes read in front of the fire. And you can even order up an Elizabethan banquet for yourselves, replete with minstrels and serving wenches.

This is an exceptional find created by an exceptional man. But even in three short years word travels. So to get a room at the Pelican in anything but the darkest, drizzliest season, book ahead several months.

C.P.

Name: The Pelican Inn
Manager: David Jones
Address: Muir Beach, Calif. 94065
Directions: On Highway 1, just 25 minutes north of San Francisco.
Telephone: (415) 383–6000
Cables/Telex: None
Credit Cards: MasterCard, Visa
Rooms: 6.
Meals: English breakfast 8:15–10:00, lunch 11:00–4:00, dinner 5:00–9:00 (approx. $10 to $15 for 2); informal; room service 8:00 A.M. to 11:00 P.M.; taped music (classical) in dining room and lounge.
Diversions: Beach swimming, walking trails; horseback riding, water sports, darts nearby.
Sightseeing: Muir Beach, Golden Gate National Recreation Area, Muir Woods (redwoods); nearby: Sausalito, Mill Valley, Tiburon.
P.S. Some small, *very* small, seminar groups.

SUTTER CREEK INN
Sutter Creek, Calif.

$

Swinging couples you've heard of, but swinging *beds?* This pendulous experience is something you can look forward to in "The Hideaway, "The Storage Shed," "The Tool Shed," or "The Patio." The beds are suspended (securely, unless you have in mind something very peculiar) from the ceiling by sturdy old chains from ghost mines, which is only natural since this is the heart of the Mother Lode Country.

The inn itself is a 115-year-old house, the former home of a California senator, and became an inn only a few years ago when Jane Way happened to be passing by and fell in love with it. It wasn't for sale, so she waited until it was (or maybe she willed it—she's that kind of lady). Having acquired the house, and with no more experience of running an inn than any other housewife who has reared a family, she then set about transforming it into one of the most delightful country inns on either side of the Great Divide.

And ingeniously, too. She scoured the antique shops and auctions for cranberry scoops that became toilet paper holders, old washtubs for shower stalls, a sled for a magazine rack, a portable bidet for a coffee table. The rooms are stuffed with canopy beds, hand-painted chairs, rockers, and other antiques and curios.

There are now seventeen rooms in the main cottage and in a cluster of smaller cottages in the garden. Take your pick. Some suggestions: The Hideaway, The Patio, The Cellar (which has a fireplace, patio, and pencil post bed), the Lower Washhouse, The Canopy Room (canopied twin beds, but slightly cramped), and The Library (a comfy room, but unfortunately on the ground floor between the kitchen and the parlor, where you can while away odd minutes with something from the shelves—say, *Design for Steam Boilers and Pressure Vessels, New Patterns in Sex Teaching* or *What the Bible Is All About*).

SHERRY ON THE HOUSE, BRANDY IN THE COFFEE. Jane Way has also filled her inn with friendly little touches, like strategically located decanters of sherry; when you feel like a snort you simply help yourself. And if you're astir before breakfast, you can help yourself to coffee with a dash of brandy "to get you ready for an afternoon nap." Breakfast is taken family style in the brass-and-copper Colonial kitchen. After breakfast, you're on your own. There's nothing to do here—no pool, no television—but just enjoy yourself. You can lounge in the hammock or laze in the garden in the shade of the flowering quince, willows, and daphne. You can play chess or Parcheesi in the pale-green parlor. Or settle into one of the deeply upholstered sofas by the fire and read *Punch*.

Otherwise, take a stroll down the arcaded main street of Sutter Creek, and check out the antique stores. Or go for a drive through the foothills of the Sierras and discover the relics of Mother Lode and all her little nuggets—abandoned mine shafts, the tumbledown shacks of Forty-niners, cemeteries where simple headstones mark the graves of young men who died old deaths. You can even try your hand panning for gold (the best time is spring, when the snows melt).

Name: Sutter Creek Inn
Owner/Manager: Jane Way
Address: 75 Main Street, Sutter Creek, Calif. 95685
Directions: About 50 miles southeast of Sacramento via Calif. 16, heading for Jackson; or via Calif. 88 out of Stockton, again heading in the direction of Jackson, which is 4 miles south of Sutter Creek on Calif. 49.
Telephone: (209) 267–5606
Cables/Telex: None
Credit Cards: None
Rooms: 17.
Meals: Hot breakfast only; for dinner, Jane Way recommends The Palace across the street; no room service.
Diversions: Pool; tennis, golf nearby.
Sightseeing: Antique stores, the foothills of the Sierras, the relics of bygone mining days.
P.S. "No children under 15, no pets, no cigars." Jane Way is something of an expert on reading palms and analyzing handwriting.

THE WINE COUNTRY INN
St. Helena, Calif.

$$

In the Napa Valley countryside around St. Helena you'll chance upon many farms and wineries sturdily built of fieldstone and Douglas fir. A few steps from one of these wineries, Freemark, you'll find another of these sturdy barnlike structures, looking like it's been there for decades. It's the Wine Country Inn, and it's been there only a few years, and every brick and every timber was put there by the owners and their family. Ned and Marge Smith began planning their dream back in the Sixties, while he was looking to his retirement from the frenetic world of broadcasting. In 1973, they toured New England, visiting a score of inns, filling notebooks with ideas to adopt, mistakes to avoid. One conclusion: to get what they wanted, they should build a new inn from the ground up.

So they did, with the help of their five youngsters and Ned's eighty-two-year-old mother. One son learned masonry and supervised the construction of the stone footings and four-story chimney; another son supervised the framing, a third plastered and painted; a fourth did all the fine carpentry. Marge and daughter Kathy made quilts, Grandma did the crewel work. And so the Smith's inn came to fruition in the finest wine-country tradition.

No two rooms are alike in shape or decor ("We figured that our friends would have to come back twenty-five times before they repeated themselves"), but each has a view of vineyards and oak-covered hills. Most upstairs rooms have private balconies, ground-floor rooms have patios or private gardens, and many have working fireplaces. Several rooms have fourposter beds with testers designed and sewn by Marge, and all but two rooms have small refrigerators where guests can chill the Chardonnays they bought at the nearby wineries. A recent addition, the Brady Barn, includes two suites with sitting rooms and offers the most privacy. Piles of magazines and books take the place of TV sets, but rooms in the main building have classical music piped in from a local FM station.

Breakfast—a spread of fruit of the season, fruit juices, and several kinds of pastry—is served buffet style on the fine old pine table in the sunny common room, but many guests enjoy the first meal of the day on the garden terrace, in the fresh morning Wine Country air with its hint of wild mustard and poppies.

A.M.

Name: The Wine Country Inn
Manager: Kathleen Hunter
Address: 1152 Lodi Lane, St. Helena, Calif. 94574
Directions: St. Helena is on Route 29, between Napa and Calistoga; Lodi Lane is 2 miles north of St. Helena, next to the Freemark Winery, and the inn is just on the left, a few yards down the lane.
Telephone: (707) 963–7077
Cables/Telex: None

Credit Cards: MasterCard, Visa

Rooms: 25, including 2 suites, in 3 lodges.

Meals: Breakfast only 7:30–9:30; no room service, no bar. For other meals, the inn will give you advice on nearby restaurants and menus, and make reservations for you.

Diversions: None; golf (including Johnny Miller's home course at Silverado), tennis, horseback riding, hot-air ballooning, sail plane soaring and quarterhorse races nearby.

Sightseeing: The wineries; the Silverado Museum (memorabilia of Robert Louis Stevenson).

P.S. Some small groups (up to 20 people).

THE MAGNOLIA HOTEL
Yountville, Calif.

$$

There's double enticement awaiting you at this very small hotel in the Napa Valley. First, the wine cellar—some fifteen thousand bottles being laid down by new owners Bruce and Bonnie Locken. The second lure is the stockpot forever simmering at the back of the stove, and the cooking smells are irresistible. Dinner at the Magnolia offers a choice of two entrées. But what entrées! During our visit, it was poached salmon with hollandaise sauce or roast pork Normande. Prices are higher than you might expect in a place called Yountville, but then the food is better than you'd expect in a place called San Francisco.

In the Magnolia's brick-and-fieldstone dining room the atmosphere is joyous and convivial, becoming more joyous and convivial as the dinner wine flows and the logs crackle in the fireplace. The luckiest diners are those who had the foresight to reserve the few rooms in this quaint hostelry, who can stumble directly to nearby brass beds with crocheted bedspreads. Staying here is like a visit to Grandmother's—if Grandma was considerate enough to leave a cut-glass decanter of port in every room. Will all this gustatory indulgence catch up with loving couples? It needn't. You can work some off with long swims in the Magnolia's pool, or steam it off in the hot-water spa. You can drive up to Calistoga for a taste of the local mineral water or, yet another enticement, a Calistoga mud bath.

R.E.S.

Name: The Magnolia Hotel
Owners/Managers: Bruce and Bonnie Locken
Address: 6529 Yount Street, Yountville, Calif. 94599
Directions: In the Napa Valley, on Route 29, about 60 miles north of San Francisco.
Telephone: (707) 944–2056
Cables/Telex: None
Credit Cards: None
Rooms: 11, in the main building or Garden Court, some with fireplaces.
Meals: Breakfast 9:00 prompt in the family dining room, no lunch, dinner (Friday and Saturday *only*) 5:30–9:30 (5 courses, approx. $40 to $42 for 2); no room service; informal dress.
Diversions: Pool, hot-water spa; bicycles, mud baths, and wineries nearby.
Sightseeing: See "The Wine Country Inn."

BURGUNDY HOUSE
Yountville, Calif.

$ $

All five guest rooms in this *petite auberge* were solidly booked for eight weekends in advance when we checked the reservation list. So were the three cottages the Burgundy maintains across the street. Week*days*, of course, would be an easier matter. But you'll see why the place is so popular after browsing around for a bit. That baker's rack, those tea-caddy lamps, the game table are not the common-place bric-a-brac you might see in any old inn. They're really old, really French—and for sale. Hosts Mary and Bob Keenan were and are antique dealers. They opened Burgundy House as an antique shop, and it "just sort of became an inn" because of all the people who begged to stay over. The Keenans have lavished a lot of love and good taste in making the guest rooms beautiful too. Put in a bid for the sole room downstairs (the only one with a private bathroom) and you also get your own garden patio. Just waltz through your french doors and have morning coffee under the old chestnut tree. Rooms upstairs give you a better view of what you've come to see—unending vineyards of grapes, grapes, grapes. Bring binoculars and see if you can tell the Chardonnays from the Cabernets. Upstairs guests share the two baths, but the bathrooms are so old-timey, so leafy with ivy and ferns, you're not likely to mind. Sharing can't be all that bad, because people keep coming back to Burgundy House time and again.

Sing in the shower, if you like (make it something from *The Most Happy Fella*, which was set in this very region)—noise is no problem here, because the fieldstone walls are twenty-two inches thick. Burgundy House was built in 1879 by a Frenchman, and it still looks— well, Burgundian. Continental breakfast is served on the huge harvest table downstairs. The inn is too small to provide anything more ambitious, but you can walk down to the old pony-express station for your other meals, or across the courtyard and to Mama Nina's for northern Italian cuisine. For aperitifs you go no farther than your dresser, where the Keenans have a decanter and glasses at the ready.

R.E.S.

Name: Burgundy House
Owners/Managers: Bob and Mary Keenan
Address: 6711 Washington Street, Yountville, Calif. 94599
Directions: In the Napa Valley, on Route 29, about 40 miles north of Oakland.
Telephone: (707) 944–2855
Cables/Telex: None
Credit Cards: American Express, Diners, MasterCard, Visa
Rooms: 5 in the inn, and 3 cottages across the street.
Meals: Continental breakfast only, but rates include all wine drinking.
Diversions: The countryside, the wineries; tennis, golf nearby.
Sightseeing: See "The Wine Country Inn."

BORDEAUX HOUSE

Yountville, Calif.

$$

Beds dominate the rooms here, queen-size beds mounted on hip-high platforms so that lovers can gaze into the fireplace. Each room has a fire and a bathroom, each is furnished with antiques and decorated in soft tans and rich burgundies that echo the colors of the region's wine. Even the warm color of the thick carpet makes it feel cozier between the toes.

The Keenans opened this six-room gem in 1980, a slightly more luxurious version of their Burgundy House. As in Burgundy House, decanters of wine come with every room in case you want to sip a Zinfandel as you lie on your platform gazing at the fire.

A.M.

Name: Bordeaux House
Owners/Managers: Bob and Mary Keenan
Address: 6600 Washington Street, Yountville, Calif. 94599
Directions: Same as Burgundy House, give or take a block or 2.
Telephone: (707) 944–2855
Cables/Telex: None
Credit Cards: American Express, Diners, MasterCard, Visa
Rooms: 6.
Meals: Continental breakfast only, 7:30–11:30.
Diversions: None at the inn; tennis, golf nearby.
Sightseeing: See "The Wine Country Inn."

SONOMA MISSION INN

Boyes Hot Springs, Calif.

$$

The name probably leads you to expect some kind of pink stucco building, with arched doorways, a tower, peaceful gardens, and fountains in the forecourt. And that's exactly what you'll find here, all freshly spruced and titivated. But the name hardly prepares you for the chic San Francisco decor of the interior. A few years back a wealthy real estate tycoon, Edward Safdie, decided he'd like to have his own inn, found this twenties mission-revival hotel in decrepit condition, and commissioned a leading Bay Area decorator, John Dickinson, to restyle the entire thing. At a cost of $100,000 per room. And what an exquisite job he has done. Some people might find it precious, but what he has contrived is a masterful blend of mission and modern, boudoir and bivouac.

You step from the fountained forecourt into an airy lobby with bleached-beam ceiling, tiled floor, and massive fireplace—as you'd expect in a mission. But two large screens of clay-colored canvas and upholstered chairs focus attention on the fire and make an intimate corner in an expansive lobby. In the guest rooms, beds have been fitted with baldachins of canvas that match bedspreads and drapes, also of canvas, in one of three stylish color schemes—clay, taupe, or camel. Ceiling fans add a touch of Raffles nostalgia. Each room also comes with revolving bedside tables, AM/FM radio, wake-up alarm, small TV, Parsons-style desk, and a pair of boudoir chairs.

Of the hundred rooms, the most popular are in the two-story Pool Wing, where the four end rooms, known as Country Inn Suites, have the same basic decor and refinements, but with the addition of small sitting rooms overlooking the garden. The rooms in the other wing, leading off from the lobby in the opposite direction, are identical in size and style, and the only disadvantage, probably a minor one, is that they get some traffic going to and from the restaurant; on the other hand, if you plan to use the tennis courts more than the pool, this wing is more convenient. But if you insist on having breakfast in bed, beneath your canvas baldachin, canvas bedspread tucked under your chin, none of the above will do, since room service is available only in the dozen rooms directly above the lobby.

Designer Dickinson's *pièce-de-resistance* may be the restaurant, the Provençale: big open fire for winter, ceiling fans for summer, tables arranged for *intime* dining, everything from walls to napkins awash in a sea of pink—coral, cameo, rose. With a new chef from London's tony Connaught Hotel, dinner here can be a very romantic occasion. More romantic than the name might lead you to expect.

Name: Sonoma Mission Inn

Manager: Mrs. Leslie Moore

Address: 18140 Sonoma Highway, Box 1, Boyes Hot Springs, Calif. 95416

Directions: On Route 12, 2 miles north of the town of Sonoma, less than an hour from the Golden Gate Bridge.

Telephone: (707) 996-1041, toll free (800) 862-4945

Cables/Telex: None

Credit Cards: American Express, Diners, MasterCard, Visa

Rooms: 100, including 5 suites.

Meals: Breakfast 7:30–9:30, lunch 11:30–3:00 (outdoors in summer), dinner 6:00–10:00 (approx. $40 to $45 for 2); informal; room service for drinks only; live music in lounge on Friday.

Diversions: Heated swimming pool (with "Arabian Nights" cabanas), massage (full-service spa to come), tennis (3 courts, lighted, free except during weekends in summer); golf, horseback riding, ballooning nearby.

Sightseeing: Sonoma Town Square and other historic sights, the home of author Jack London, the wineries.

P.S. Some small groups, children "not encouraged."

For more suggestions in this area
turn to Added Attractions, page 375.

The Pacific Northwest

... for love is heaven, and heaven is love ...

BYRON

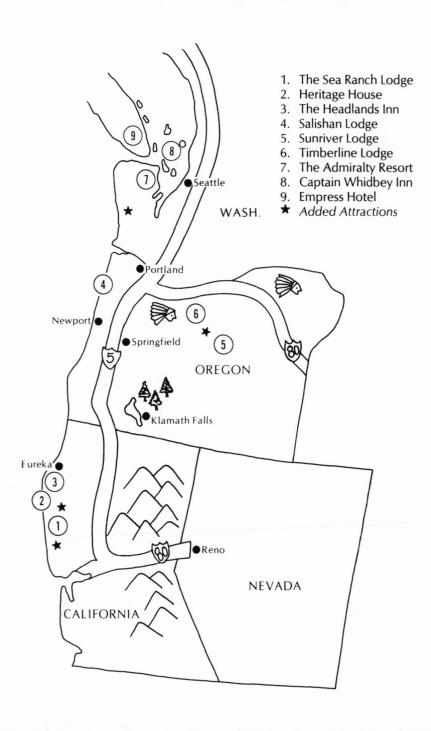

1. The Sea Ranch Lodge
2. Heritage House
3. The Headlands Inn
4. Salishan Lodge
5. Sunriver Lodge
6. Timberline Lodge
7. The Admiralty Resort
8. Captain Whidbey Inn
9. Empress Hotel
★ *Added Attractions*

WASH.

Seattle

Portland

Newport

Springfield

OREGON

Klamath Falls

Eureka

Reno

NEVADA

CALIFORNIA

THE SEA RANCH LODGE

Sea Ranch, Calif.

Sheep graze in meadows. The ocean lunges at headlands and scours coves. Fog rolls in, gulls scurry, wrens and finches skitter among huckleberry and beach grass. So starkly beautiful is this isolated windswept coast you could almost be in the Highlands of Scotland, half expecting, as you round the next bend, to come upon a ghostly castle.

What you come upon instead is a large redwood sign adorned with a stylized ram's horn. This is the entrance to Sea Ranch, once a working ranch, now an estate with some three hundred architect-designed homes spread over fourteen miles of meadowland between the ocean and the redwoods. The owners have gone to such great length to preserve the unspoiled beauty of the setting (all the homes of native redwood) they've banned garden fences and hedges so as not to interrupt the sweep of the meadow.

The lodge itself is a combination of traditional ranch house and contemporary California styling, with picture windows that gobble up splendid seascapes of headland and ocean, fields brightened by monkey flower and paintbrush, a tumbledown barn and weathered grapestake fences. Guest rooms manage to proffer most of the amenities (private bathrooms, electric blankets, bentwood rockers) while retaining an appropriately rustic feel with rough pine plank walls, canvas windowshades, and, in some, wood-burning stoves. Of the twenty rooms, #10 and #11 have corner windows with views along the coast as well as out to sea (but no fire). Since there is neither TV nor radio in your room, you'd better put in a bid for #19 and #20, both of which have very private patios with hot tubs from which you can contemplate the stars, the moon, and the mysteries.

Bubbling in your hot tub, or snuggled before your fire, you'll probably forgive the lodge a few shortcomings: no room service, no porter service, and those times when one suspects that the owners have put more emphasis on primary colors, bold graphics, and award-winning design than on the refinements of innkeeping. If you're a stickler for service, continue up the coast to Heritage House, but if you love the great outdoors—feeling the hint of spume on your cheeks, watching a family of starfish losing an epic battle to a horde of hermit crabs, or listening to the crashing of waves among the sea-stacks—then you won't mind trotting over to the dining room in the morning for breakfast—with a view.

Name: The Sea Ranch Lodge
Manager: Ron Fitzgerald
Address: P.O. Box 44, Sea Ranch, Calif. 95497
Directions: On the Shoreline Highway (Calif. 1) 29 miles north of Jenner, about 110 miles north of San Francisco (3 hours by the inland route, 4–4½ via lovely Calif. 1).
Telephone: (707) 785–2371
Cables/Telex: None
Credit Cards: MasterCard, Visa
Rooms: 20, 8 with wood stoves, 2 with hot tub.
Meals: Breakfast 8:00–11:00, lunch 12:00–3:00, dinner 6:00–9:00 (approx. $15 to $20 for 2); casual dress; no room service; TV in bar.
Diversions: Cliff walks at the lodge itself; heated pool and sauna at the tennis club, 5 minutes away (4 courts, no lights, free); golf at the north end of the ranch (9 holes, $10 per day, bring your own equipment); some 50 miles of hiking trails through open meadows and forests of fir and redwood.
Sightseeing: Fort Ross (restoration of Russian fur-trading settlement) to the south; Fort Bragg, Mendocino, etc.; to the north (see "Heritage House"), redwood forests inland.
P.S. September and October have the best weather. Many of the splendid homes at Sea Ranch are available for rent by the week or month, from as little as $110 a weekend for 4 people—for details, write P.O. Box 123, The Sea Ranch, Calif. 95497, or call (707) 285–2427.

HERITAGE HOUSE
Little River, Calif.

Take a walk around the cove. Sing love songs into the wind. Put your arms around each other's necks to keep the chill out. Listen to the ocean raging at the land.

A hundred years ago this site was a cove for shipping redwood ties, and for smuggling in liquor and Chinamen. The original farmhouse, dating from 1877, is now the inn's reception lobby, dining room, and kitchen—a yellow clapboard building, with carriage lamps and a red door with bronze doorknobs, a refuge from New England; in fact, the whole setting looks like a picture of Maine that's been reversed, with the sun setting where it should be rising.

The Dennens spotted the old house in 1949, and decided to turn it into an inn (which is only fair, since it was built originally by Dennen's grandfather). Since then, they've added some more cottages to their hillside, and what they have now is not so much an inn as a village. The "village green" is a duck pond surrounded by alders; the gardens burgeon with azaleas, daffodils, nasturtiums, or wild blackberries; red lichen highlights the cliffs, and the Albion buoy gongs away steadily offshore.

APPLE HOUSE AND WATER TOWER. Some of the inn's sixty rooms are in new villas, but most of them are in buildings imported from other farms and sites along the coast—some of them with ingenious twists. An old apple-storage house has become the inn's lounge, a clubby room with walk-in fireplace, card tables, and a bar. There are a few guest rooms upstairs—the most popular one being "Salem," mainly because of its seventeenth-century solid-cherry fourposter bed. The

most unusual room in the inn, maybe on the entire coast, is the Water Tower—a suite that once really was a water tower, with tall windows looking across the duck pond to the ocean. The only problem with the Water Tower is that other guests are so intrigued, and envious, they want to take a peek inside, and you may find yourself spending the day giving guided tours. The Firehouse Room has lamps made from old fire hydrants; and the headboard in the Schoolhouse is the original sign for Greenwood School 1898, and the bedside tables are old classroom desks. No pool, no TV, no room phones—just good innkeeping. (Since all the rooms are different, ask to see the album with pictures of each room when you check in—it may help you decide, assuming there is still a choice.)

The presiding genius behind this inn-village, Don Dennen, learned his trade at the Clift Hotel in San Francisco. He has since built up a loyal staff; most of them have been with him for years, and seem to share his ideal—"Old-fashioned hospitality," he explains, as he slides behind the wheel of his sleek Ferrari. His special brand of old-fashioned hospitality includes nice little touches like having the waitress let the housekeeper know when you sit down to breakfast so that the maid can dash off to your room and fix the bed. "Just having the bed tidied up makes the place look so much neater when you get back to your room." It may not sound like much, but it makes all the difference between an average inn and a place where people care.

FRESH RHUBARB, GRANOLA, AND HOTCAKES. And when you see the gargantuan breakfast table, you might get the impression that it was created to give the maids plenty of time. Here you don't so much break your fast as shatter it. The meal begins with a buffet table groaning under a selection of juices; a choice of six fresh fruits (including rhubarb and figs); granola, porridge; followed by a choice of eggs, hotcakes, ham, and bacon. You don't even have to wait for your coffee and toast: the coffee is on your table almost as soon as you sit down, and many tables have their own toasters so you can make your own toast to your own taste, from a choice of three types of bread.

All of which prepares you for a day in the open air—that walk around the cove, or a picnic in the forest where you can kiss beneath a giant redwood tree. Or ride "The Skunk," an old logging train that follows Pudding Creek and Noyo River for three hours and forty miles through the redwood forests.

Name: Heritage House

Owner/Manager: L. D. Dennen

Address: 5200 N. Highway 1, Little River, Calif. 95456

Directions: On Coast Highway 1, 5 miles south of Mendocino. From Bay
    Area (3½ hours drive) take 101 north to Cloverdale, 128 to Coast 1, then
    5 miles north. From Eureka (3½ hours drive) take 101 to Leggett,
    Highway 1 to Coast, continue south to Heritage House.

Telephone: (707) 937–5885

Cables/Telex: None

Credit Cards: None

Rooms: 60, including 7 suites.

Meals: Breakfast 8:00–10:00, no lunch, dinner 6:00–8:00; no room service;
    jacket and tie requested at dinner.

Diversions: Fresh air.

Sightseeing: Pudding Creek, the Noyo River, the artists' colony at Mendoci-
    no, including the Art Center, numerous galleries and gardens, the old
    Masonic Hall, the lighthouses of Point Cabrillo, Point Arena and Cas-
    par, and the State Park at Russian Gulch, "The Skunk" train tour.

P.S. Closed December and January; no groups over 8; no pets; for weekends
    reserve well in advance, for Thanksgiving 3 *years* in advance.

THE HEADLANDS INN

Mendocino, Calif.

$

This may be the finest of the intimate little bed-and-breakfast inns on
the North Coast of California. It has every creature comfort (including private baths for all but three of its seven rooms) but its 110-year-
old shell and interiors have been restored with a taste and crafts-
manship that probably exceed by far the original building. Its looks
and its setting in the midst of Mendocino would make it suitable for
the most romantic Victorian novel.

    From the Coast Highway, drive only three blocks to Albion
Street where the inn's freshly painted buff siding shows warm in the
soft haze rising from the Pacific, two hundred yards away.

    Inside, there is no front desk, but the front hall leads naturally to
the guest pantry and kitchen where you might find Kathy Casper
baking lemon bread for breakfast the next morning. This cordial,

Very Special Places

hospitable young lady was, apparently, first lured to Mendocino by the description of Heritage House in an earlier edition of this guide, coming up from the blazing Mojave Desert where she was a junior high school teacher, to join the growing band of souls in search of peace along the North Coast. Kathy and her partners took over the building in late 1979, finished renovations and opened in 1980. They had no experience in hotels other than as guests, but they had superb ideas about what comforts they ought to offer. (The Headlands Inn is one of the few places in America, regardless of size, which has in every closet those evermore rare pieces of hardware called *clothes hooks*.) They also had the good fortune to find in Mendocino that winter an extraordinary itinerant craftsman named Rory Patrick Cleworth who installed exquisitely carved redwood mantels, oak frames and lintels over all the doors, and pure copper sheathing on the hearths in the three bedrooms which have fireplaces. Room 6, in what was once the attic, has windows on three sides and a window seat from which you can see the Pacific or read—perhaps a slim volume of Robinson Jeffers, the laureate of the California coast. The quilted down bedcovers, the flowers cut fresh from Kathy's garden, and a small Seth Thomas alarm clock make the room feel like a place where you could happily settle into. Room 2, on the second floor, is the prime nest—king-size bed, fireplace, bay window, and a spacious sitting area, probably one of the coziest rooms along the coast.

Guests serve themselves breakfast in the sunny kitchen where a new built-in microwave oven stands ready to reheat the lemon breads or coffee cake which Kathy has baked fresh the afternoon before. Or better yet, have it served in your room, on tastefully arrayed trays, in attractive chinaware.

For ideas on how to spend the rest of the day, she has an ample list, and if you want a tennis court or a table for dinner, she is glad to pick up the phone and make the reservations. But unless you're really ravenous, our suggestion would be to nip around the corner to the gourmet shop, buy up some cheese and bread and wine, take them back to your room, light the redwood logs in the fireplace, and settle down for a picnic.

A.M.

Name: The Headlands Inn
Owner/Manager: Kathy Casper

Address: P.O. Box 132, Mendocino, Calif. 95460

Directions: On Albion Street, three blocks from Route 1, 5 minutes north of Heritage House.

Telephone: (707) 937-4431

Cables/Telex: None

Credit Cards: None

Rooms: 7, with 3 sharing bathrooms.

Meals: Continental breakfast only, anytime.

Diversions: None in the inn; tennis, golf, and other sports nearby (see "Heritage House").

Sightseeing: See "Heritage House."

P.S. "The Inn does not have proper accommodations for children under sixteen"; 2-night minimum stay on weekends in summer, 3 on holiday weekends (when you have to get your reservation in 4 to 6 weeks in advance).

SALISHAN LODGE
Gleneden Beach, Ore.

$$

How many hotels do you know that print their own botanical guides? And tide tables? Or where every room has a leaflet extolling the habits of seagulls because the manager's favorite pastime is photographing gulls (and had been for many years before Jonathan Livingston flew on to the best-seller lists)?

Salishan is that kind of special place.

It was built by a wealthy Oregon manufacturer, John D. Gray, who used to vacation on this part of the coast and decided to build a hotel here. Something that would be a credit to Oregon, something that might also make some money. He picked a serene setting—a hill that looks over a lagoon and a promontory of beach to the ocean (but, unfortunately, across the highway); there he built what one architect has called "one of the most beautiful hotels in the world," and filled it with works of art, landscaped the grounds, tagged the plants, and hired one of the best managers in the country.

CERAMIC WALLS, TWO-HUNDRED-POUND RED OAK DOORS. John Gray and his team created a lovely lair for lovers. Ceramic walls decorate

garden courtyards. Thirteen sculptured teak panels gleam on the walls of the dining room. Driftwood "sculptures" guard the driveway, and the red oak doors that welcome you weigh two hundred pounds each. Even the therapy pool has a Japanese-style garden with Oregon grape, huckleberry, and vine maple. All very seductive. Enough to make you forgive any shortcomings. But you won't have to—Alex Murphy runs a tight ship, and even a faulty nozzle in the therapy pool doesn't escape his eagle eye.

Salishan's 150 guest rooms are in fifteen villas, linked by covered walkways and bridges, and constructed of Douglas fir, hemlock, and cedar. The woodsy character is retained in the close-to-luxurious interiors. All rooms have picture windows and every window faces a treescape. But the trees have tough competition from the interiors: open fireplaces (with a well-stocked supply of, alas, Prest-o-logs, not real timber), king-size or double-double beds, club armchairs, hand-woven light fixtures, floorboard electric heaters, soundproofing, TV, FM radio, individual heat controls.

INDEXED WINE LISTS. The Salishan's dining room is arranged on three levels and has lots of windows so that everyone can get a good view of Siletz Bay and the Pacific, once they've feasted their eyes on the teak sculptures. A handsome dining room is one thing, but how about the food? Chef Franz Buck, who joined the lodge in 1977, offers a seven-page menu ranging from local Tillamook Bay oysters on the half shell or salmon mousse en gelée, through a choice of nine salads to Dungeness crabmeat Pompadour and *grenadines de boeuf aux morilles* with cognac. (In Oregon? In Oregon.) The new Cedar Tree Room specializes in seafood and steaks cooked over "chunk charcoal processed from the mesquite tree and roots by the Yaqui Indian tribe." But wait until you see cellarmaster Phil de Vito's two wine lists. They're so comprehensive they need indexes, for scores of vintages from modest Bordeaux for $6 a bottle to a '55 Paulliac Château Lafite Rothschild for $175; a rare and welcome feature of the Salishan cellar is the range of *half*-bottles, including a Latour '64 and a La Ville Haut-Brion '62.

How do you fill your Oregon days between grapefruit juice and Haut-Brion? For starters, there are all the sports listed below (with indoor tennis and pool, Salishan is a first-rate winter choice, despite the reputation of Oregon weather). You can wander over to the beach, three miles of strand decorated with forestfuls of driftwood weathered and worn into grotesque and gruesome shapes. Or follow the old logging road up into the hills and forests, but don't forget to take along your botanical guide—here a kinnikinnick, there a salmonberry, everywhere a juniper.

Name: Salishan Lodge
Manager: Alex Murphy
Address: P.O. Box 118, Gleneden Beach, Ore. 97388
Directions: On U.S. 101, 20 miles north of Newport, 90 miles south of Portland; by private or charter plane to the 3,000-foot runway half a mile south of the lodge.
Telephone: (503) 764–2371
Cables/Telex: None
Credit Cards: American Express, MasterCard, Visa
Rooms: 150, 2 suites.
Meals: Coffee shop from 7:00 A.M. to 10:00 P.M., dinner 6:00–11:00 in Gourmet Dining Room, 8:00–1:30 A.M. in the Cedar Tree Restaurant (anywhere from $5 to $50 for 2); room service; dress optional; live music in the lounge year round, dancing in the Cedar Tree in summer.
Diversions: Indoor pool (with hydrostatically controlled humidity to eliminate the usual damp smells), 12-nozzle therapy pool, sauna, exercise

room, art gallery, billiard room, hiking trails; tennis (3 indoor with indirect lighting and a spectator's lounge with fireplace, 1 outdoor, $6 per court per 1 ¼ hour); golf (18 holes, $10 per round), bicycles for rent, horseback riding and deep-sea fishing nearby.

Sightseeing: Coastal scenery, forest preserves, and state parks.

P.S. Special tennis and midwinter escape packages available.

SUNRIVER LODGE
Sunriver, Ore.

This is one of the few hotels in the country with an ecologist-in-residence and an Ecologium—a mini-natural-history museum where ecologist Jay Bowerman interprets the surrounding wildlife and nature.

And there's plenty of both. Sunriver's thousands of acres, a lake basin formed some two thousand years ago by a lava flow, are surrounded on three sides by a national forest with 156 lakes. This is the country of black bear, elk, and pronghorn antelope, of bald eagles and China pheasants, where German brown and rainbow trout outsparkle the crystal water of mountain streams. It's a place to fill your lungs with clean air and enjoy the wide open spaces: seventeen miles of cycle tracks (and more bikes than cars), three dozen horses champing at the bit in the stables, waiting to trot you around the meadows and forests (this is one place where twosomes can go cantering off on their own), championship golf courses. You can go canoeing on the river, birdwatching in the meadow, or rock hunting among the lava beds. You never have to wear a jacket or tie. Which doesn't mean you're going to rough it: in a setting like this, most people would settle for a log shack, but up at Sunriver you enjoy wall-to-wall comfort. *You're* spoiled, not the countryside.

Sunriver is a planned community—but it looks as much like the average real estate blotch as a Rolls-Royce looks like a bulldozer. No more than one family per acre; *no* buildings on the banks of the river; all utilities underground, and so on. The man behind the project is the same John Gray who gave you Salishan Lodge, which means that

the surroundings are respected and little details of design are in impeccable taste (note the direction signs, or the "sculptured" inclined sun terraces around the swimming pool).

The main lodge is an unusual timber-and-lava-stone building, a creation of the Pacific in its blend of Oregon and oriental; and the lodge condominiums dotted around the fairways have pitched roofs, sundecks, fireplaces, color TV, and in some cases kitchens. Over in the lodge you'll find sauna baths, a rumpus room to keep the teenagers out of your hair, a coffee shop, and a handsome restaurant where you can enjoy veal Cordon Bleu or chicken à la Kiev with a view of the six-hundred-acre meadow, a Japanese bridge, and the Fuji-like cone of Mount Bachelor. It's an unpolluted setting—and Jay Bowerman's there to help keep it that way.

Name: Sunriver Lodge
Manager: Michael Derrig
Address: Sunriver, Ore. 97701
Directions: 15 miles south of Bend and 2 miles west of U.S. 97; by scheduled air service to Redmond (33 miles north of Sunriver), or by private or charter flights to Sunriver's own 4,500-foot strip, which is also served daily by Air Oregon scheduled flights.

Telephone: (503) 593–1221
Cables/Telex: None
Credit Cards: American Express, Diners, MasterCard, Visa
Rooms: 300-plus in a variety of lodge condominiums.
Meals: Breakfast 7:00–11:00, lunch 11:30–3:00, Sunday brunch 9:30–1:00,
     dinner 6:30–9:30/10 (approx. $18 to $25 for 2); no room service; informal
     dress; live music and dancing in the Owl's Nest.
Diversions: Sauna, game room, movies; heated outdoor pool, boating, nature
     program, canoeing, hiking trails, fishing, ice skating, sleigh riding in
     winter; bicycles (200 for rent, 17 miles of trails), tennis (18 courts, no
     lights, $6 per hour for doubles, pro shop, clinics), golf (18 holes, $12 per
     round), horseback riding, cross-country skiing (rentals), downhill at
     nearby Mt. Bachelor.
Sightseeing: Mountains, lakes, forests, in Bend: Sunriver art gallery, Des-
     chutes County Pioneer Museum.
P.S. Small seminar-type groups throughout the year (accommodations for up
     to 350).

TIMBERLINE LODGE
Mount Hood, Ore.

$$

The main door wouldn't look out of place in a medieval castle (a
thousand pounds of hand-adzed planks with iron hinges and a mas-
sive iron knocker); the hexagonal lobby/lounge revolves around a
ninety-six-foot-tall chimney constructed of volcanic rocks, with three
huge fireplaces, flanked by six massive pillars, each one the trunk of a
Ponderosa pine sculptured by one man with a broad-blade axe. Look
around you, at the stair newels handcarved from old telephone poles
and the andirons hand-wrought from old railroads, and you know
you're in no ordinary inn.

In fact, there is no other hotel in the country like Timberline
Lodge, a gray stone-and-cedar V with a soaring roofline to match the
mountain peak five thousand feet above; and for anyone who enjoys
unusual hotels, the good news from Mount Hood is that this splendid
specimen of Americana is being renovated, and by the time you get
there, most of the woodwork will be sanded and varnished, the

unique furnishings (strap-iron construction in true pioneer style) will be almost like new. Most of the rooms you're likely to prefer (they're known as standard, deluxe standard, corner, or deluxe fireplace) are one of a kind, with carved headboards, patchwork quilts, hooked rugs. (Deluxe in the context of Timberline means not so much plushness as extra floor space and a television set in the room; and you should also remember if you are here in winter to reserve a room on the upper floors, otherwise you might find yourselves looking out at a solid bank of snow.)

One of the deluxe rooms, the Roosevelt Suite, is named for the man who is usually credited with getting the lodge off the ground in the first place. This was one of FDR's WPA projects, built by some five hundred unemployed men and women during the Depression; they performed so beautifully their handiwork is now a National Historic Monument. But is it *romantic?* Even a Howard Johnson's could be romantic in such a setting—on the timberline, six thousand feet up a rugged mountain, with glacier-covered peaks above you, rolling pine-clad hills disappearing into the haze a hundred miles to the south.

Name: Timberline Lodge
Manager: Dawson T. Hubert
Address: Timberline, Ore. 97082
Directions: 60 miles east of Portland, 6,000 feet up Mt. Hood. Go east on Highway 80N from Portland, turn right at Wood Village, then go east on Highway 26; an hour later you'll see the signs for Timberline.
Telephone: (503) 226–7979
Cables/Telex: None
Credit Cards: American Express, MasterCard, Visa
Rooms: 60 (including 8 with fireplaces).
Meals: Breakfast 8:00–9:30, lunch 12:00–2:00 (snackbar to 5:00), dinner 6:30–8:30 (approx. $25 to $30 for 2); no room service ("well, sort of"); informal; occasional musical events (folk, bluegrass, sometimes yodeling in the dining room at lunchtime).
Diversions: Heated pool and heated deck (open to 11:00 P.M.), hiking (up and down and around the mountain); skiing all year (instructions available), night skiing, fishing.
Sightseeing: Mt. Hood National Forest.
P.S. Minimum 2-day weekend bookings December 15 through April 15. Some groups. For your information: "Regrettably the builders of this

beautiful lodge had paid scant attention to soundproofing. The wooden walls are not paper-thin but they can seem so at times. Please be considerate of others."

THE ADMIRALTY RESORT
Port Ludlow (Olympic Peninsula), Wash.

$$

Admiralty Inlet is a mile-long cove covered with trees—forests of fir, pine, and alder reaching right down to the crystal-clear water. At the head of the inlet a great pile of logs waits to be floated out to Puget Sound, reminding us that this is lumber country. All this land, all these trees, have been chopped down and reseeded for the past hundred years by a company called Pope and Talbot, which has moved into the residential community and resort business (and who will assume direct management of the resort in 1981). To keep things in the family, most of the houses, condominiums, and the inn buildings are constructed from local timber—wood in all its forms from tree-trunk pillars to Prest-o-logs in the fireplaces. The resort consists of trees and clusters of condominiums, each with a view of greenery or water, each with a private entrance. The most romantic rooms are the Loft Suites, with bed and bath on a gallery above a luxurious sitting room with a tall stone fireplace and floor-to-ceiling windows leading to a sun deck. The Beach Club (beside "shoreline" rather than a sandy beach) is a complex of Olympic-size pool, sauna, hydrotherapy pool, games room, and two of the development's seven courts, and if you follow the shore a hundred yards or so you come to the marina and lagoon. The Harbormaster Restaurant, focal point of the resort, has cathedral ceilings trailing chandeliers borne on iron chains, and panoramic windows looking beyond the marina to the spiky peaks of Mount Olympus. The Harbormaster features local seafood in original forms—like tournedos Dungeness (slices of filet mignon with Dungeness crab) and tournedos Ludlow (slices of filet mignon with Canterbury oysters).

With such hearty fare awaiting you, The Admiralty Resort is an ideal winter hideaway (winter temperatures seldom fall below freezing, and the rainfall, they're quick to point out in these parts, is considerably less than in Seattle), and a perfect base for touring the Olympic Peninsula and Puget Sound at any time of the year.

Name: The Admiralty Resort
Owners/Managers: Pope & Talbot Development Corp.
Address: Port Ludlow, Wash. 98365
Directions: Port Ludlow is on the northeast tip of the Olympic Peninsula, an hour's drive from Port Angeles, 2 hours by car and ferry from Seattle; signposts on Highway 101 will guide you for the last few miles.
Telephone: (206) 437–2222
Cables/Telex: None
Credit Cards: American Express, Carte Blanche, Diners, MasterCard, Visa
Rooms: 212, including 66 suites (all with fireplaces).
Meals: Breakfast 7:00–11:00, lunch 11:00–3:00, dinner 5:00–10:00 (approx. $15 to $25 for 2); no room service; informal dress; live music in the lounge (beneath the restaurant) 5 nights a week in the summer.
Diversions: Saunas, pool table, table tennis, heated Olympic-sized pool, saltwater lagoon, tennis (7 courts, no lights, in various locations on the estate)—all without charge; 18-hole golf course ($12 weekdays, $14 weekends, free transportation from the hotel, open all year); bicycles, sailboats, and ketch with crew for rent.
Sightseeing: Mount Olympus, the Olympic Peninsula, including the Olympic National Park and Forest, Puget Sound.

CAPTAIN WHIDBEY INN
Coupeville, Whidbey Island, Wash.

Captain Whidbey sailed with Captain George Vancouver, RN, when they scouted the Pacific Northwest at the end of the eighteenth century, but the inn bearing his name was built by a judge at the beginning of the twentieth. Its two stories of rugged madrona logs stand watch by the edge of Penn Cove, in a grove of fir trees. Across the choppy water, you can see the hamlet of San de Fuca, and off in the distance the snowy tip of Mount Baker. The entrance to the log cabin is guarded by Barney the golden Labrador, and once you get his sleepy nod of approval you enter a friendly lobby with armchairs and sofas pulled up around a big beachstone fireplace; beyond that is a rustic dining room decorated with nautical antiques, then a rustic bar festooned with empty bottles and calling cards, in honor of some seventy years of conviviality. The nine guest rooms on the second floor are mini-log-cabins, each with its own washbasin and sharing a couple of bathrooms in the hallway. They're the most popular rooms in the inn (especially the rooms on either end), although the newer wing beside the lagoon (rooms have private baths and occasional antiques) probably offer more quiet and privacy.

Peace and quiet are presumably what you have come here for, because other than a few excursions through the San Juan Islands and maybe a shopping trip to tiny Coupeville, there's little to do here. There is one bonus, and as good a reason as any for spending an extra day here—the Captain Whidbey wine list, pride and joy of young John Stone, who has taken over day-to-day operations from his father. Your choices include Puligny Montrachet "Clavoillon" 1974, Vosne Romanée Larronde Freres 1971, Pauillac Château Mouton Rothschild 1967, to say nothing of a collection of moderately priced California and Beaujolais vintages. Drain the bottle, and leave it hanging from the rafters as a souvenir of your idyll.

Name: Captain Whidbey Inn
Managers: John and Geoff Stone
Address: Route 1, Box 43, Coupeville, Wash. 98239
Directions: About 90 miles from Seattle, 3 miles north of Coupeville on Whidbey Island, via ferry from Mukilteo to Columbia Beach; by air (Harbor Airlines) from Seattle to Whidbey Island airport, 30–45 minutes from the inn (free ride, if you let them know in advance).
Telephone: (206) OR 8–4097
Cables/Telex: None
Credit Cards: MasterCard, Visa
Rooms: 25, including 9 upstairs (sharing bathrooms), 4 in cabins, and 12 overlooking a lagoon.
Meals: Breakfast 8:00–11:00, lunch 12:00–2:00, dinner 5:00–10:00, summer, 6:00–8:00 winter (approx. $15 to $22 for 2); no room service; informal dress.
Diversions: Tennis, golf, 2 rowboats, bicycles for rent; walking trails through woods; sailboats and scuba diving nearby.
Sightseeing: Coupeville, Whidbey Island.

EMPRESS HOTEL
Victoria, B. C., Canada

$$

Empress by name and Empress by nature. Majestically she domi-
nates the harbor, her venerable ivy-covered walls rising to an array of
Victorian pinnacles and turrets. The oak-paneled Library Lounge is a
clublike bar with armorial ceiling, and the main dining room could
well be an exile from Buckingham Palace. Upstairs, the corridors are
almost wide enough to accommodate the railroad cars of its owner,
Canadian Pacific; the rooms have lofty ceilings, brass door fittings,
and, in some cases, period bath fixtures, but the decor is gracious
and, in the case of the Vice-Regal Suite, palatial. If you decide to
forgo the Vice-Regal Suite, ask for one of the rooms facing the harbor,
the interior transformed into a tiny bower by the sunlight filtering
through the ivy that frames the windows.

Like any empress, however, this one is plagued by celebrity
seekers and the inquisitive, especially on weekends in summer. One
of the famed attractions here is afternoon tea ($4.50 for scones,
muffins, cakes, and tea served in large silver pots on silver trays), a
normally genteel ritual, but here the muffin masses turn the elegant
lobby/lounge into a company cafeteria. It's as if you went to Lord's for
a cricket match and found a baseball game instead. No problem, of
course, if you have checked into the Empress: just nip off to your
room and have your tea and scones served in your ivy-framed bower.

Name: Empress Hotel
Manager: E. G. Balderson
Address: 721 Government Street, Victoria, B.C. V8W 1W5
Directions: The easiest route is by ferry from Port Angeles, Washington,
    which deposits you almost at the Empress's feet.
Telephone: (604) 384–8111
Cables/Telex: 049–7121
Credit Cards: American Express, Carte Blanche, Diners, MasterCard, Visa
Rooms: 416.

Meals: Breakfast 7:30–11:30, lunch 11:30–2:30, afternoon tea 2:00–5:00, dinner 5:30–10:00 (approx. $16 to $30 for 2 in the main dining room); room service to 11:00 P.M.; jackets "recommended" at dinner; pianist at teatime, disco in the basement.

Diversions: None at the hotel.

Sightseeing: Victoria.

P.S. Special packages available.

For more suggestions in this area
turn to Added Attractions, page 375.

Hawaii

Kāua i ka huahuaʻi,
E ʻuhene la i pili koʻolua

HAWAIIAN LOVE SONG

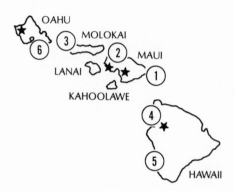

1. Hotel Hana-Maui
2. Kapalua Bay Hotel
3. Sheraton-Molokai Resort
4. Mauna Kea Beach Hotel
5. Kona Village Resort
6. Kahala Hilton
7. Coco Palms Resort Hotel
★ Added Attractions

HOTEL HANA-MAUI
Maui, Hawaii

You can get here by car—a laborious drive that winds and wanders around coves and headlands, through forests, past waterfalls. You can also get here by air, a twenty-minute flight from Kahului Airport aboard a six-passenger Cessna that skims around the mountains, along the coast. You land at a lonely clifftop airstrip with one small terminal building. It's for all the world like landing on an islet in the Grenadines, and when the Cessna takes off again without you, it's like saying good-bye to the rest of the world. When the hotel bus arrives to pick you up, it turns out to be an eight-seater, fire-engine red safari wagon like a twenties Packard. As it lumbers along the road past bamboo and wildflowers, kukui and koa, you begin to understand why islanders are always telling us Hana is the way Hawaii used to be.

The village consists of just over 1,500 souls—a cove, a jetty, a couple of churches, a couple of general stores. And the Hotel Hana-Maui, a one-story ranch house with cedar shake roofs, set among twenty acres of croton and plumeria, ti and pua. There's an eighteen-hole pitch-and-putt course, a swimming pool, a tennis court, and that's just about it. Jim Nabors and Richard Pryor have homes nearby, and Friday night brings the villagers and guests together for the dance at the nearby Ranch Steak House.

How did such a place come to be here? Back in the twenties a wealthy mainlander bought up the entire ranch, 13,500 acres of grazing land at the base of Haleakula. Later, he decided he ought to have a lodge for entertaining his friends, and opened the basis of the present inn in 1953. Over the years it has attracted a devoted clientele, and its guest list has included Charles Lindbergh (who is buried nearby), James Michener, and more recently, Lilli Palmer and a sultan or two. Many of the inn's guests have been coming back every year since they honeymooned here, and now their sons and daughters are honeymooning here. At times, especially in the winter months, when 80 percent of the guests are repeats, it almost seems like a club, as new arrivals greet the long-serving staff like old friends. A sort of L'Année Dernière à Hana-Maui quality. You needn't feel shut out—you can mingle if you wish, stay a twosome if you prefer. It has that kind of casual, take-it-as-it-is attitude. Hana-Maui is a place that grows on you. At first you might be disappointed with the rooms—having heard so much about this hideaway of the well-to-do you probably expect a little more flair in the furnishings, something more indigenous, perhaps. They're comfortable enough, and all come with ceiling fans, refrigerators, showers or tubs, and patios or lanais. The guest rooms are spread over a dozen bungalows in the garden, with a few more really isolated nooks in a separate garden up on the hill.

This is essentially a place to wind down. Relax. Lock your watch in your luggage. When the sun rises, you rise; when the sun sets you have a shower, put on your casual but dressy togs, and head for the Gun Room Lounge for a Mai-Tai ($4.25, unfortunately).

The attractions of Hana-Maui are mostly out of doors. Tennis is free. Pitch-and-putt before lunch. A picnic at the scenic Seven Pools, at the far tip of the island. A day on the beach—not the one in town, which is only so-so—but *the* beach a few miles away. It's called Hamoa. Michener once described it as one of the most beautiful untamed Pacific beaches he had ever seen. Usually a comment like that is guaranteed to destroy the untamed character, but Hamoa's half-moon of sand and pandanus is too far from the main tourist stream. The hotel will drive you over by wagon in the morning, then send over your picnic basket on the noon wagon.

All of which may sound close to idyllic, and the hotel itself is not reticent about tossing around the word *paradise* in its literature. Which makes it all the more dismaying, then, to walk into the lobby and have one's ears assaulted by the big color telly in the adjoining lounge blasting out a hockey game to an audience of one. And if you enjoy Hawaiian music, you may find it disappointing to discover that the postdinner trio includes an electric double bass (yikes!) and electric autoharp (double yikes!).

These caveats aside, think of the pluses—no highrises, no pollution, no traffic other than the hardy trippers willing to negotiate that laborious road.

Name: Hotel Hana-Maui
Manager: Tony R. de Jetley

Address: Hana, Maui, Hawaii 96713

Directions: On the southeastern tip of Maui, a scenic but laborious 3- to
3½-hour drive from Kahuliu Airport; but only 20 minutes away by Royal
Hawaiian Cessna, probably with a sightseeing commentary thrown in
(and there are 5 flights a day). The inn is 10 minutes from the airport, $4
per person each way on the red safari wagon.

Telephone: (808) 536–7522, toll free (800) 223–6625

Cables/Telex: HANAHO

Credit Cards: American Express, MasterCard, Visa

Rooms: 61 in a dozen lodges and cottages.

Meals: Breakfast 7:30–10:00, lunch 12:00–2:00, dinner 6:30–8:00; informal;
room service for continental breakfast only; Hawaiian combo or show
twice a week, luaus.

Diversions: Freshwater pool, tennis (2 courts, no lights, racquets for rent),
walking trails, croquet, par-3 pitch-and-putt, horseback riding (with
guide, or registered quarterhorses); beach nearby, shuttle bus.

Sightseeing: Trips by safari wagon through ranch country to Seven Pools,
waterfalls, ruins of sugar mills, remains of *heiaus* (Hawaiian temples).

P.S. Quiet time between Thanksgiving and Christmas; this is the wet corner
of the island, so expect rain anytime.

KAPALUA BAY HOTEL
Maui, Hawaii

$$$

"Arms embracing the sea"—Kapalua. It has a nice romantic ring
about it and it doesn't let you down. Where the two lava promonto-
ries embrace the sparkling sea, in a lush setting of lawns and palm
trees, masterly architects have created a terraced edifice of slender
concrete columns and three-story cubes with tops on. A lofty lobby
opens to the breezes. Wild flowers grow indoors. Fountains trickle.
Louvered hardwood shutters filter the sun. Rare feather *leis* adorn
the walls.

Kapalua is located beyond the old whaling port of Lahaina (now a
stomping ground for tour groups) and the beach at Kaanapali (now a
cluttered strip of lobby-to-lobby hotels and condos). Kapalua is the
end of the trail, a restful, uncrowded place, although it's only part of a

larger 750-acre resort estate, surrounded in turn by twenty-three thousand acres of private plantation. Across the street, the "Tennis Garden" pairs off courts and screens each pair with redwood fencing rather than wire and aluminum. Arnold Palmer's fairways amble through pineapple fields, past stands of Cook pine and ironwood skirting beaches and coves and making the most of the panoramas.

Kapalua's guest nests are everything you might expect—decked out with natural woods and lithographs, equipped with oversized beds, refrigerators, mahogany paddle fans, private lanais, and his-and-her dressing rooms with separate bathtub and shower so that everyone can be spiffed up in time for dinner. Of the resort's three dining rooms, The Veranda, emulating an island plantation of bygone days, is the specialty restaurant. Anywhere else it might be *the* place to dine; but we prefer one of the two open-to-the-breezes restaurants—the Bay Club, on a rocky promontory at the end of the beach, or, most romantic of all, the multilevel Dining Room, with comfy rattan seating, gleaming mahogany banisters, candlelight, and glimpses of stars through the palm trees.

Kapalua opened as a Rockresort operation, but the mantle has now passed to Regent International Hotels. The staff, matching guests almost one for one, is efficient and courteous, the place is impeccable. If you have any reservations, they may involve the music. Even the guitarist in The Veranda and the native trio in the lounge are amplified. Instead of sipping your sundown Mai-Tais serenaded by the riffle of palm fronds and the trickling of the fountain over the lava rocks, all you hear is the *thump-thump* of a rhythm section.

Linger in your room, order up room service, sip your Mai-Tais on your quiet lanai, and embrace your partner where the lava arms embrace the sea.

Name: Kapalua Bay Hotel
Manager: Hans D. Turnovsky
Address: 1 Bay Drive, Kapalua, Maui, Hawaii 96761
Directions: On the northwest coast, 35 to 40 minutes from Kahului Airport (jets), 10 to 15 from Kaanapali (Cessnas); taxi from Kaanapali, by request—about $9 to $10.
Telephone: (808) 669-5656, toll free (800) 421-0530
Cables/Telex: KABATEL/6696515
Credit Cards: American Express, Carte Blanche, Diners, MasterCard, Visa
Rooms: 196, including 3 suites.

Meals: Breakfast 6:30–10:30, lunch 11:30–4:00, afternoon tea in lounge, dinner 6:00–10:00 (in several dining rooms, air-conditioned or breeze-cooled, approx. $50–$55 for 2); jackets requested; full room service during dining-room hours; guitarists, Hawaiian trios, combos (all amplified), dancing in bar/lounge.

Diversions: 3 beaches, freshwater pool, body surfing; tennis (10 courts, some lighted, $4 per person per *day*), golf (36 holes), sailing, windsurfing, scuba, Mai-Tai cruises, whale-watching cruises; nearby, horseback riding (maximum 6 per group) through pineapple fields.

Sightseeing: Scenery—volcanoes, ranches, rain forests, seascapes; old whaling port of Lahaina (now awash with day trippers), helicopter tours, rides on Sugar Train.

P.S. Some groups, never more than 50 rooms.

P.P.S. Kapalua is a "total resort" with two extensive but tasteful condominium villages, if you want to be completely on your own: Gulf Villas (on the hill), Bay Villas (above the beach), the latter with sexy "garden baths"—sunken tub, skylights, potted plants. Rates from $77 per day, with special packages for longer stays.

SHERATON-MOLOKAI HOTEL

Molokai, Hawaii

$$

Turn right at the airstrip and drive for fifteen minutes through open ranchland and over the bare mountain. Your first sign of any kind of civilization will be a neat fieldstone gate with a sign saying "Kalua Koi." From here you still have a four-mile drive downhill, through open country that was once a vast pineapple plantation. It all looks ripe for carving up into a housing development but all that's there right now is the golf course and hotel.

The result is that Sheraton's outpost on Molokai is one of the most secluded resorts on the islands, with miles of beach, rocky headlands, and Oahu as a backdrop twenty-six miles away. It's a place of breezes, surf, spray, fresh air, sun, flowers. No planes, no cars, no noise other than the occasional whirr of a golf cart.

The developers (the Louisiana Land and Exploration Company "plus 800 Hawaiians," Sheraton is the operator) wisely settled for low-profile architecture, derived from traditional Polynesian styles by architects Wimberly, Whisenand, Allison, Tongg and Goo. The main lodge and the thirty-four cottages are designed to be cooled by the breezes—hence, lots of cedar louvers, sliding doors, and ceiling fans rather than air conditioning. Furniture is mostly variations on rattan. It adds up to a pleasantly island atmosphere without sacrificing anything in comfort (the big color TV sets are there only because some guests grumbled about not having them).

There are 290 such rooms, including several attractive suites. All of them have lanais or balconies, and what distinguishes the higher-priced rooms is what you see from your lanai or balcony. Some overlook the golf course rather than the beach and the sea, but the steady surf is so exhilarating you really should have a view of the sea. For the best views, ask for a room on the second floor, especially in one of the cottages numbered 31/36, 41/44, 51/54, 61/64. Best of all are the one-story Cottage Suites—particularly those numbered simply 1, 2, and 3, closest to the beach.

That 290 might seem like a lot of rooms, but in fact there seems to be space to spare and you never feel hemmed in. With three miles or so of beach you'll have no problem finding quiet spots and quiet coves. And that's without even leaving the resort. If you hop into a car and drive off to other parts of the island, you can have entire beaches to yourselves. There are various scenic spots worth seeing, too, but with such reasonable rates (compare them with Sheraton rates on Waikiki!), tennis on the house, and virtually free golf (one round for every night's lodging), you may never drive back up that lonely road until it's time to return to the airstrip.

Name: Sheraton-Molokai Resort
Manager: Charldon Thomas
Address: Molokai, Hawaii 96770
Directions: On Kepuli Beach, on the northwest coast, 12 miles or 20 minutes from the airport; Molokai is 20 minutes by Hawaiian Airline jets or 35 by Royal Hawaiian Cessnas from Honolulu.
Telephone: (808) 552–2555, toll free (800) 325–3535
Cables/Telex: None
Credit Cards: American Express, Barclaycard, Carte Blanche, Diners, Eurocard, MasterCard, Visa
Rooms: 292, in 32 bungalows, including 8 Cottage Suites and 24 one-bedroom suites.
Meals: Breakfast 7:00–11:00, lunch 12:00–2:30 (plus snack bar to 6:00),

dinner 6:30–9:00 (indoors, approx. $24 to $28); informal; room service for drinks only; combo and dancing in lounge after dinner.

Diversions: Beach (miles of it, but not good swimming in *winter*), freshwater pool, tennis (4 lighted courts, no charge), walking trails, golf (18 holes, 5 beside the sea, no charge); horseback riding a mile away.

Sightseeing: Scenery mostly—unspoiled rain forest, waterfalls, valleys, a mule trip to the historic leper colony of Father Damien (careful—it's 2½ hours down, 2½ hours back), Molokai Ranch Wildlife Park (aoudads, elands, oyxes, greater kudos, and other exotica).

P.S. Some groups, up to 100.

KAHALA HILTON HOTEL
Honolulu, Oahu, Hawaii

$$$$

Have breakfast served on your balcony, beside a wedge-shaped lagoon. Dolphins do the cetacean equivalent of an early-morning jog. Turtles and reef fish swim around in their private ponds. Walkways wander through gardens of hala, hau, and fiddleleaf. And a few yards from your room there's a quiet beach—yes, quiet, although you're only fifteen minutes from the thigh-to-thigh masses of that Coney Island called Waikiki. This Hilton is detached from all that, on the *other* side of Diamond Head, surrounded by sea and golf course rather than concrete. It's both a high rise and low rise, two stories in the lagoon-side wing, ten stories in the other, with slender concrete columns to add a touch of lightness, with fifteen types of bougainvillaea draped over the balconies to soften the mass. It's a very spacious, elegant Hilton, with 30-foot ceilings in the lobby and enormous chandeliers of Italian glass. You can dine indoors or out, dress up or stay casual. The formal Maile Restaurant (lace tablecloths, European crystal, that sort of thing) serves some of the finest cuisine on the island; if you dine in the beachside pavilion, you may want to time your meal to avoid the Hawaiian floor show, considered one of the best in Honolulu, but too "show biz" for our taste.

The Kahala is operated, by the way, by Hilton *International,* which means that service and comfort are world class. All rooms come with refrigerator, stocked minibar, TV and radio, air conditioning, plenty of sliding windows and louvered shutters for letting in the breeze while keeping out the sun. The suites (fifty-six of them!) are rather grand, but readers of this guide may prefer rooms in the two-story Lagoon Terrace, preferably one of the four spanking-new-in-1980 junior suites, or one of the ten beachside rooms with patios or balconies, just paces from the water, and screened from the main hotel by the hau and hala.

Name: Kahala Hilton Hotel
Manager: Jan Ouderdijk
Address: 5000 Kahala Avenue, Honolulu, Oahu, Hawaii 96816
Directions: It's in the Kahala residential district, 15 minutes beyond Waikiki, 30 from the airport.
Telephone: (808) 734–2211
Cables/Telex: KAHILTON/8456
Credit Cards: American Express, Carte Blanche, Diners, Eurocard, Master-Card, Visa
Rooms: 370, including 56 suites and junior suites.
Meals: Breakfast 6:30–11:00, lunch 11:00–3:00 (on the terrace), dinner 6:00–9:00, indoors or outdoors (approx. $60 to $65 for 2 in the main dining room, less on the terrace); jackets required in the dining room, informal on the terrace; full room service 6:30 A.M. to 11:00 P.M.; combo in the lounge, Hawaiian show on the terrace 6 nights a week.
Diversions: Beach (more or less private), freshwater pool; pedal boats, kayaks for rent; golf next door, tennis, horseback riding and water sports nearby.
Sightseeing: Diamond Head, the beaches, the mountains; in Honolulu, Waikiki, Pearl Harbor, Mission House Museum, restored Iolani Palace, Bishop Museum, "Falls of Clyde" sailing ship.
P.S. Some groups, but only up to 50 rooms, and mostly in early June or early September.

For detailed rate, turn to page 413.

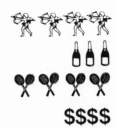

MAUNA KEA BEACH HOTEL
Kamuela, Hawaii

$$$$

The site was handpicked by Laurance Rockefeller himself when he decided to set up an outpost of his Rockresort fiefdom in the fiftieth state. He chose, as ever, with the eye of a true romantic.

For miles around there's nothing but space—open ranchland as far as the eye can see. On one side, rolling grassland climbs into the foothills of the Kohala Mountains; on the other a sweep of beautiful beach links twin lava headlands. Surf rolls across Kaunoa Bay. Palm fronds glisten in the sun. Hibiscus and bougainvillaea dangle from balconies. Half-a-million plants were shipped in to garland the terraced gardens, fairways were carved through lava flows. Rockresorts has since picked up and left (although one of their alumni is still in charge) and Westin (formerly Western International Hotels) has taken over, but Mauna Kea reigns serene in its isolation, splendid in its style.

Not enough that you should have the beauties of nature to soften the eye, Mauna Kea fills its corridors and hallways with the art of the Pacific and Orient, the kind of collection most curators would give their souls to acquire. Step through the lobby past two bronze *mokala* from Bangkok and three-legged brass *chamlas* from India. Stroll to dinner past a Buddhist altar and Fijian kava bowls. Step from the elevator and you come face-to-face with a wooden Thai goat or Sepik River ceremonial mask. On the way to your room, walls are lined tapestry-style with custom-crafted tapa cloths and traditional Hawaiian quilts. Even the Batik Room (one of *five* dining spots) is embellished with authentic antiques—batik tapestries, a Ceylonese phoenix, Buddhist stupas—and guests dine from brass service plates and stoneware candleholders. Since this elongated linerlike resort is designed with three inner courtyards, with lakes and greenery, waterfalls and breezes, guests enjoy the best of both worlds—candle-lit sophistication in the evening, casual beachy pleasures by day.

Guest rooms are fitted out with cane-and-willow furniture, tiled floors with fluffy scatter rugs, refrigerator, balconies with sliding louvered doors leading to private lanais. Island accents are supplied by framed clusters of seashells and numbered lithographs of tropical flowers. No television, no radio—just the bed, the lanai, and the view.

Settle for a room with mountain view and you can save enough for a few rounds of Mai-Tais (less expensive here than in most deluxe hotels). Even so, Mauna Kea's comforts do not come cheap. But where else will you find a hotel that tempts you with a menu that includes *lilikoi* juice and banana buttermilk cakes, Scottish banger sausages and *mahi-mahi meunière*, pecan rolls and Lehune raw honey—for breakfast? Or a hotel that pampers its guests by spending $100,000 a year just on yummy macadamia nuts?

Name: Mauna Kea Beach Hotel

Manager: Adi Kohler

Address: Kamuela, Hawaii 96743

Directions: On the sunny Kohala Coast, the northwest corner of the Big Island, about 30 minutes by car from Hilo or Kona airports (both jets) or Kamuela (Royal Hawaiian Cessnas); shuttle or taxi by arrangement.

Telephone: (808) 882–7222, toll free (800) 228–3000, or any Westin (Western International) Hotel

Cables/Telex: 882–7090

Credit Cards: None

Rooms: 310, including 8 suites.

Meals: Breakfast 7:00–10:00, lunch 11:30–4:30, (including lavish buffet on the terrace), dinner 6:30–10:00 (in one of 3 indoor dining rooms, approx. $55 for 2); jackets; full room service during dining-room hours; trios in lounge, dancing in Dining Pavilion; some luaus.

Diversions: Beach (more or less private), freshwater swimming pool, sauna; tennis (9 courts, no light, pro shop), massage, golf (18 holes), windsurfing, snorkeling, scuba, sunset cruises; horseback riding nearby.

Sightseeing: World's only drive-in volcano in Hawaii Volcanoes National Park, Akaka Falls, Lapakahi State Historical Park, various historical sites, Kailua-Kona village, the town of Hilo, Danken Ranch, Captain Coole's Monument.

P.S. Some high-class groups and seminars (no more than 110 rooms) in off-season.

KONA VILLAGE RESORT
Kaupulehu-Kona, Hawaii

$$$$

Some of the original Polynesian voyagers came ashore here, and you can still see the petroglyphs and fish ponds of their ancient settlement; and when the lava flow of 1801 rumbled and tumbled into the sea, this tiny oasis (or *kipuke*) somehow survived. Now, among palm trees and casuarinas, surrounded by twelve thousand acres of outlandish lavascape, you'll find one of the most unusual resorts in the islands: ninety-five thatched bungalows, built in the styles of different Polynesian islands—Samoa, Tahiti, Fiji, the Marquesas, and so on. When the resort opened fifteen years ago, the only way to get here was by boat, or by private plane to the resort's lava airstrip; but the new Queen Kaahumana Highway (only two lanes, with respects to her majesty) makes the village more accessible. To retain its early cherished privacy there's a gatehouse (thatched and flower-decked) near the highway, and a winding two-mile track through the lava flows.

An occasional chartered Cessna may touch down on the airstrip, but otherwise the only noises you hear are the waves surfing across the lava rocks, or the doves and chukkars. No traffic, no television, no radios, no jangly room phones to disturb your siesta. ("Do Not Disturb" signs are decorative coconuts placed outside the door of your *hale*.)

This is not to say that you'll be completely deprived of the amenities. Each *hale* has a ceiling fan and louvers for cooling you off, modern bathroom, colorful fabrics, private lanai.

You'll dine well, too. Cuisine is basically continental (*escalopes de veau aux chanterelles*, tournedos of beef stroganoff) with native touches like poi puff croquettes or *papio Kawaikae*, which is filets of *ulua* with sesame seeds. At the weekly luau the piglet is prepared in the authentic *imu* oven, and after tucking into the lunch buffet there's little option but to toddle back to your *hale* and put the coconut outside the door.

Kona Village is the sort of place that lures Hollywood escapists—Natalie Wood, Sidney Poitier, Arte Johnson, and Sandy Dennis, to name a few. Brando came here several times before putting down roots in Tetiaroa, and if you ever get to that Polynesian hideaway you may detect a few ideas picked up in Kona.

Days here drift by in a haze of sunning and swimming, snorkeling and surfing, eating, imbibing, playing tennis, dozing in a hammock, idling on your shaded lanai with a volume of Maugham or Michener. You might drive off for a spot of touring, but chances are you'll be eager to get back to your private oasis, grateful to that protective cloak of spooky, silent, surreal lava for shutting out that other world out there.

Name: Kona Village Resort

Manager: Fred Duerr

Address: P.O. Box 1299, Kaupulelu-Kona, Hawaii 96740

Directions: On the Big Island's west coast, about 10 minutes from Keahole Airport (served by Hawaiian Air jets), 20 from Kailua-Kona's shops and hotels.

Telephone: (808) 325–5555

Cables/Telex: COCONUT

Credit Cards: American Express, Carte Blanche, Diners, MasterCard, Visa

Rooms: 95, all individual *hales* (traditional Polynesian bungalows).

Meals: Breakfast 7:45–9:45, lunch 12:30–2:00 (outdoors), dinner 6:30–8:45 (approx. $45 for 2); "Our own strict dress code forbids coats and ties at dinner; on the other hand, no shorts or tank tops, please." No room service; various luaus and buffets with music; trio in lounge.

Diversions: Beach (200 yards at resort, additional mile beyond the point), freshwater pool, walking trails, tennis (3 courts, with lights, no charge, tennis pro), Sunfishes (no charge), snorkeling, outrigger canoes, glass-bottom boat; scuba and sailing on request; golf, horseback riding nearby.

Sightseeing: See "Mauna Kea."

P.S. Closed November 29 to December 15; very few groups off-season, never more than 50 people; lots of children in August; weather ideal anytime, but best months—May through July, September through November; packages available.

COCO PALMS RESORT HOTEL
Kauai, Hawaii

$$

First, the good points. The setting is a grove of very tall coconut palms. Two thousand palms, forty-five acres of grounds. Plenty of space. This was once the site of the summer home of Hawaii's last queen, and the lagoon in the middle was fashioned from the royal fish ponds. Somewhere among these coco palms is a score of thatch-roofed, louver-sided bungalows, furnished with rattan, decorated with hand-stitched quilts, their walls of *lauhala*—pandanus leaves woven with coconut fronds. Some of the *hales* have private open-air patios with sunken lava rock bathtubs, some with whirlpools. Pohuehe, pohinahina, pauohiaka and native shrubbery add an extra touch of privacy. Across the street there's a beautiful expanse of beach, Wailua, which seems to have no more than half-a-dozen sun lovers on it most of the time. And behind the coco palms, and raucous private zoo, there are nine tennis courts.

Now, the drawbacks. When this almost-legendary resort opened back in 1953 there were just the coco palms and a dozen *hales*. Over the years it became so popular that there are now more than four hundred rooms (with more in the offing)—the twenty-two *hales* and the remainder in two-story, standard motel-style wings. The nightly ceremony of the lighting of the torches (surprisingly impressive, first time around) attracts scores of day trippers, who may also sit down to early dinner in the lagoon-side restaurant. You can avoid them by trotting off through the palms to the air-conditioned Coconut Palace, or crossing the street to the resort's beachside Sea Shell, open to the breezes and the surf.

At four-hundred-plus rooms, Coco Palms is really too large for this guidebook (moreover, some of the decor will bedazzle your eyes), yet Grace Guslander and her hospitable crew make a real effort to extend the kind of warm, friendly reception one expects in an inn of much more modest proportions.

In any case, Kauai is such a beautiful island you ought to visit it at some point (the sooner the better, before the bulldozers take over completely) and this is as convenient a place to stay as any.

Beat the honeymooners to the bungalows. Sink into your lava rock tub. Listen to the drums during the torch ceremony. Peek at the stars between the coco palms, all silver in the moonlight. Forget everyone else.

Name: Coco Palms Resort Hotel

Manager: Grace Guslander

Address: Lihue, Kauai, Hawaii 96766

Directions: About 20 minutes from the airport, which is 30 minutes by Hawaiian Air jet from Honolulu.

Telephone: (808) 822–4921, toll free (800) 227–0848 (or 800–652–1000 in N. California, 800–252–9163 in S. California)

Cables/Telex: 7430178

Credit Cards: American Express, Barclaycard, Carte Blanche, Diners, Eurocard, MasterCard, Visa

Rooms: 416, including 11 suites and 22 bungalows.

Meals: Breakfast 6:00–10:00, lunch 10:00–2:00 (outdoors), dinner 6:00–10:00 (indoors or outdoors, approx. $30 to $35 for 2); informal ("no ties, ever"); room service during dining-room hours: live music in lounge and dining room, taped music in lobby.

Diversions: Beach, freshwater swimming pool, walking trails, snorkeling; tennis (9 courts, lights, video, $4 per person per day), surfboards; free shuttles to golf and horseback riding.

Sightseeing: Scenery (Fern Grotto, Wainer Canyon) and the spectacular, inaccessible north coast—helicopters will take you on tour, or drop you, with a bottle of wine, on an isolated beach.

P.S. Some groups all year (up to one-third of the house).

Added Attractions

Herewith a few hotels, inns, and resorts that did not, due mainly to reasons of deadlines, make the guide proper; plus a few others that were in the first edition but have now been relegated to these pages because a) they no longer quite measure up, or b) they were too tardy in supplying updated data. However, they may fill in a few gaps in your itineraries. They're arranged alphabetically by state, with peak-season double rates for 1981.

ARIZONA

CANYON RANCH, TUCSON

Make no mistake: Canyon Ranch is no ranch, nor is it a typical Arizona sport resort. This is a spanking-new, $6.5-million coed spa and weight-control center that the management prefers to call "America's first vacation/fitness resort." The hope is that the new description will remove stigmas of feminine narcissism and geriatric therapy, thereby luring men to its exercise mats, Cam II machines, and squash-ball courts with the same enthusiasm they usually reserve for putting greens and tennis clinics. The ploy may work; Canyon Ranch is an attractive, twenty-eight-acre oasis that resembles a freshly stuccoed Mexican village as it rambles over a quiet corner of the Sabino Canyon northeast of Tucson. There's a jogging trail on the desert; two heated outdoor swimming pools, and an indoor-outdoor aquatic exercise pool with retractable roof; six tennis courts (four lighted); and "gourmet" menus that espouse birdlike portions for weight watchers only rather than foisting bird-food ingredients on all comers. (L.E.B.) 70 rooms, from $200 in winter, $150 in summer AP. *Canyon Ranch, 8600 E. Rockcliff Road, Tucson, Ariz. 85715 (telephone 602–749–9000).*

HERMOSA INN, PARADISE VALLEY

Here it is—the desert equivalent of a small country inn in New England. Just twenty-eight rooms, hidden away somewhere between the Arizona Biltmore's estate and Camelback Mountain, across a canal, near a small white church with a big black cross, surrounded by cactus—and silence.

The Hermosa is a low white hacienda—a paella of Spanish, Mexican, and Indian. The tiny lobby has a pair of open fires that fill the cool desert evenings with the smell of burning mesquite. An archway leads through a quiet courtyard to a colorful dining room, all beams and gleaming table linen. The guest rooms are brick pueblos, nestled among seven acres of trees and cactus, decorated in what's usually called "Mediterranean style," with bare brick walls, soft light, wooden furniture, boldly patterned spreads and carpets. All rooms have radio, TV, and individual controls for heat and air conditioning. The inn's seven acres of grounds include a small heated pool, five tennis courts, professional instructors, and shuffleboard. *Hermosa:* beautiful, handsome. Hermosa it is. 24 rooms and suites in four villas, EP $54 to $165 in spring, $40 to $135 in fall. *Hermosa Inn, 5532 North Palo Cristi Road, Paradise Valley, Ariz. 85253 (telephone 602–955–8660).*

POCO DIABLO RESORT, SEDONA

When a shoot-'em-up is being shot in the nearby gullies of Oak Creek Canyon, stars such as Chuck Conners and Lee Marvin come here to rest their saddle-weary bones; and Jane Russell, it seems, is a regular on the Poco Diablo's trim little executive golf course (nine holes; par three). If you only drive past the place, however, you may wonder what these Hollywood biggies see in the little devil. From the road the Poco Diablo looks ordinary and from the main pool area it still looks ordinary. But if you bother to trek beyond the fairways, you come upon two neat rows of "villa" rooms and begin to understand why film crews have taken a shine to this little resort. It's there that you have the best view of the encircling red rock cliffs that have made Sedona famous and for years have exerted their colorful influence on artists, photographers, and movie makers. It's also there that you'll sleep like babies after a whirling wash-up in your private, in-room Jacuzzi, with the gently gurgling sounds of Oak Creek flowing over the rocks beneath your back patio. (L.E.B.) 56 rooms, 33 villa rooms, from $56 to $85 (January–March); $60 to $90 (April–December) EP. *Poco Diablo Resort, P.O. Box 1709, Sedona, Ariz. 86336 (telephone 602–282–7333; toll free through Best Western Motels).*

RIO RICO RESORT, RIO RICO

From the Santa Cruz Valley it looks promising, shimmering in the sun high on a mesa, a white pueblo with modern lines. On closer inspection, it turns out to be another cluster of terrace townhouses around a plaza and pool. The rooms are comfortable (some are equipped with kitchens); the dining room has a sweeping view of the countryside and the Robert Trent Jones golf course. There are also tennis courts on the mesatop and stables in the valley.

If you're bound for Mexico, keep Rio Rico in mind: it's only twelve miles from Nogales, and the most interesting stopover for miles around. 160 rooms, EP $48 to $55. *Rio Rico, P.O. Box 2050, Nogales, Ariz. 85621 (telephone 602–287–5601).*

CALIFORNIA

ALISAL GUEST RANCH, SOLVANG

Solvang, of course, is that Danish-type village with windmills and tourists, bakeries and tourists, cheese shops and tourists, but if you come to The Alisal you won't be stampeded, because the ranch is three miles farther along the valley—one of the greenest, serenest valleys in these parts.

The ranch itself is part of a real working cattle ranch, lying in the bottom of the valley surrounded by sycamores, giant oaks, a river, a golf course, and stables. It's first and foremost a place for horseback riding, but even if you just want someplace placid and an occasional game of tennis or golf, you'll find it worth the shuffle through Solvang.

But it's really the riding that corrals the guests, and ten thousand acres sprawling over the Santa Ynez Mountains, with sixty beautiful trails winding through the mountains (but you can ride only in the company of the wrangler).

The guest rooms are in small cottages scattered among the flower beds and lawns; they're not luxurious, but much more comfortable than you might expect on a ranch. No roughing it here. And when the sun goes down and the cattle come home, the ranch has two handsome restaurants serving Western food to take care of ranch-size appetites.

A real escape. A place to lie on the grass and look up at the sky until it's time to take a moonlight hayride and look up at the stars. $48 to $70 MAP. *The Alisal Guest Ranch, P.O. Box 26, Solvang, Calif. 93463 (telephone 805–688–6411).*

ALTA MIRA HOTEL, SAUSALITO

Translated, Alta Mira means the High View. You'll find it halfway up the precipitous hill behind Sausalito—a town that likes to think of itself as very Mediterranean. Up here on the terrace, beneath the sun umbrellas with their floral print, surrounded by vivacious people enjoying life, you could almost be on the Mediterranean. But Sausalito's high view is probably more dramatic—across the bay to Alcatraz, the Bay Bridge, and the skyline of San Francisco.

This hotel is popular with visiting advertising and television types, which says a lot for it because staying there means they have to drive twenty minutes to and from their appointments across the Golden Gate Bridge, or take the ferryboat across the Bay. The Alta Mira is a combination Spanish villa and Swiss chalet, a group of cottages in a hilly garden. Fourteen of its thirty-five rooms are in the main lodge. No two rooms are alike. Rooms 11 and 8 are probably your best bets; #22 is a cottage all to itself, with two bedrooms, if you want to splurge in the interests of privacy; #26 has a fireplace and porch, and #16 is a suite with fire, kitchen, and a view of Alcatraz. No air conditioning (you don't need it), no television. The most popular feature of the inn, though, is the terrace restaurant with its sun umbrellas. It has an adjectival menu—"sumptuous," "colossal," "sensational"—but you can enjoy a fine dinner of abalone steak, veal parmigiana, butterfly prawns, and so on. The prices are almost as steep as the hill up to the inn. But then, someone has to pay for the adjectives—and the *alta mira*. 35 rooms and cottages, $40 to $75 EP. *Alta Mira Hotel, 125 Bulkley, P.O. Box 706, Sausalito, Calif. 94965 (telephone 415–332–1350).*

BEVERLY WILSHIRE HOTEL, BEVERLY HILLS

You enter through iron portals that seem grander than the Great Gate of Kiev. And if you're driving anything humbler than a Mercedes, you can be made to feel like an absolute rube. Even the doormen here have class—and they want you to know it.

It's right smack on the main drag in Beverly Hills, not one but two hotels, in fact, divided by a cobbled street named El Camino Real. The beautiful people (or however they think of themselves these days) are on the go all day and all night. Which is not to say the place is noisy. It isn't. And yes, it is expensive. But if you're the kind who flushes with pleasure at the very thought of rolling out of bed and into Tiffany or Gucci, the Beverly Wilshire is the place for you.

The rooms are quite nice in terms of size and decor, the suites are stunning (in some cases even startling), but if you write home about anything, it will be the bathrooms. They are marvels—cunningly designed into three staging areas so each of you can go about your morning *toilette* in privacy. No secrets unexpectedly exposed. Bravo for the bathrooms.

Room service is swift. The breakfast table arrives about fifteen minutes after your call. (Juice, coffee, croissants, butter, and jam for two: $9.22. Not very thrifty, but convenient if one of you is still trying to find his or her way around the bathroom.) The breakfast tray is accompanied by one perfect rose. Or perfect tulip. Or perfect whatever.

The toniest shops in this most tony of neighborhoods are right at the front door of the Beverly Wilshire. And if you still enjoy star gazing, just linger by the cobblestones to see who's driving through the Great Gate of Kiev in all those Rolls-Royces, Lotuses, Alfas, and Mercedes-Benzes. *Mooo*vie people, that's who. They seem to have money to burn. And so must you—but you'll probably enjoy every glamorous minute of it. 450 rooms and suites, $135 to $180 EP. (R.E.S.) *Beverly Wilshire Hotel, 9500 Wilshire Boulevard, Beverly Hills, Calif. 90212 (telephone 213–275–4282; toll free 800–323–7500; 800–942–7400 in Illinois; 800–261–6353 in Canada).*

THE CASA MADRONA HOTEL, SAUSALITO

Looking like a genteel lady of a certain age and with certain secrets she'd rather not discuss at tea, thank you, the old Casa remains one of the few worthwhile remnants of a Sausalito that really was a simple fishing village once. Several billion tourists ago. Skirts held high above the hurly-burly, she sits on her eucalyptus-shaded hillside, no longer a lumber baron's manor house but now a guesthouse and candlelit restaurant. Beyond her windows and terraces twinkles one of the world's most spectacular harbors. Every room has been restored to a Victorian fare-thee-well with canopied brass beds, wood-burning fireplaces, and all the rest. There's also a tiny gatehouse in the garden, offering living room, bedroom, bath, and sunporch. When we were there, the restoration was just in the finishing stages, and a few wrinkles and rickety corners remained. But never mind. She's still by far the *grandest dame* in Sausalito. 20 rooms, from $35 to $75 EP. (C.P.) *The Casa Madrona Hotel, Sausalito, Calif. 94965 (telephone 415–332–0502)*.

HOTEL DEL CORONADO, CORONADO

Further proof, if we needed it, that the rich *are* different from you and me. Or, at least, were. Built on its own island with its own bridge to San Diego as one of the last truly grand resorts in America's turn-of-the-century heyday, the Del is a California landmark where the Astors met the Vanderbilts and the Prince of Wales met Mrs. Simpson. Today, it's where tour group meets tour group. But somehow that doesn't take the fun out of it, if you consider it more museum than resort. The original hotel—miles of red-roofed turrets, cupolas, and Victorian gingerbread—still stands as a masterpiece of architectural nose-thumbing. Even the *lesser* of its ballrooms is as wide and high as the Astrodome, and was constructed without a single nail or post or steel beam. Today the Del is actually three hotels. One consists of the original 399 rooms, as airy and high-ceilinged as ever but entirely renovated. Another is a graceful post-war addition nearer the beach. And the third is a new glass-walled annex right on the Pacific. There may be quieter, more romantic hideaways, but the Del is like the Grand Canyon and the Empire State Building. Everybody should experience it once. 683 rooms, from $49 to $89 EP. (C.P.) *Hotel del Coronado, Coronado, Calif. 92118 (telephone 714–435–6611)*.

HOTEL LÉGER, MOKELUMNE HILL

It looks exactly like an authentic hotel of the Wild West, with a two-storied pillar-and-rail veranda for pushing bandits over, and when it began life as a tent beer hall in 1851, the Léger had its share of authentic fisticuffs and gunfights. (In its heyday, "Moke Hill" managed to squeeze seventeen murders into one hell-bent weekend.)

The place is never that boisterous these days, even with all the saloon's amplifying equipment going full tilt. The saloon/restaurant is the most interesting part of the hotel, a medley of potted plants, striped wallpapers, and Franklin stoves—Gold Rush days with a dash of Greenwich Village. You won't find motel-modern conveniences upstairs, but the guest rooms have all been refurbished in more or less the manner of the days when Forty-niners came to town to whoop it up—or be wiped out. If the panning was good, they splurged on one of the parlor suites (now $42); if they blew their nuggets on a poker game, they had to settle for a room with semiprivate bath (now an inexpensive $25 double). There's a swimming pool in a grove of orange trees at the rear of the hotel. 13 rooms, $25 to $42 EP. *Hotel Léger, P.O. Box 50, Mokelumne Hill, Calif. 95245 (telephone 209–286–1401).*

LITTLE RIVER INN, LITTLE RIVER

Silas Coombs built this Maine-style mansion when he settled in these parts a hundred years ago and made a fortune in lumber and shipbuilding. Now his great-grandson and his wife run the old home as an inn, but its Victorian lobby still looks like the entrance to a prosperous home. The most interesting rooms are the attics, brightly decorated in early Californian style, with shower stalls added. Unfortunately, there are only four of these rooms, and the remaining forty-four are in a motel-like wing and cottages behind the eucalyptus trees—clean, comfy, but nothing special. There's a dining room serving steaks, seafoods, and home-baked breads; and the wood-paneled bar keeps special hours "for the benefit of early morning risers and golfers." Inexpensive-to-moderate rates ($40 to $56). The Inn is closed in January. *Little River Inn, Little River, Calif. 95456 (telephone 707–937–5942).*

THE MINE HOUSE, AMADOR CITY

The Old Keystone Consolidated Mining Company put up this building a hundred years ago to house its head office. Now the office is one of the oddest little hotels in California.

Its eight rooms have preserved as many as possible of the original fixtures. The Retort Room, for example, has a shower stall in the arch that supports the bullion vault above (over the years, more than $23.5 million worth of the stuff); the Keystone Room still has a dumbwaiter that used to carry the bullion to the vault; and the Vault Room still has the big safe that stored the bullion before it was shipped by Wells Fargo to San Francisco. The orthodox bedroom fixtures are genuine Victorian. The hotel has a small pool, but no coffee shop or restaurant; when you wake up in the morning and feel like breakfast, simply press a button and the Daubenspecks will bring over your complimentary tray of orange juice and coffee. It may not be the *plushest* spot around, but there are not too many inns in these parts that offer Victorian antiques, air conditoning, a pool, *and* coffee and juice served in your room every morning. EP rates $36 to $41. *The Mine House, P.O. Box 226, Amador City, Calif. 95601 (telephone 209–267–5900).*

RANCHO LA COSTA RESORT HOTEL & SPA, RANCHO LA COSTA

This must be the Cecil B. De Mille of resorts: four swimming pools, thirteen tennis courts, twenty-one miles of riding trails, a visiting palmist, its own post office, a movie theater, three restaurants, two snackbars, and a health spa with rock steam baths, sitz baths, colonic baths, roman baths, salt glows, and a Swiss shower with seventeen shower heads that zap alternating hot and cold water on your tingling flesh. It's not the coziest or the friendliest place, but you'd be surprised at the number of renowned anatomies that have suffered through that fiendish Swiss shower. Rancho La Costa is only sixty miles by limousine from Los Angeles and thirty from San Diego, so it's a convenient place for the beautiful people to nip off to for a few days to make themselves more beautiful between movies, tournaments, and big deals. The guest rooms are plush (pile carpeting, double drapes, color TV with bedside controls); some have wet bars, others bookshelves stacked with reading material, pullman kitchens, and electric beds that disappear into the wall. If you want to get away from the mainstream, ask for a room in one of the cottages facing the fairways. The ranch covers something like five thousand acres, most of which seem to be taken up with new or about-to-be-built homes and condominiums, and you really have to work at solitude here, unless you do what most of the movie biggies do: check into the health spa and stay there. From $90 to $260 FAP. *Rancho La Costa Resort Hotel & Spa, Costa del Mar Road, Carlsbad, Calif. 92008 (telephone 714–438–9111).*

SAUSALITO HOTEL, SAUSALITO

Feeling heroic? Spend a night in General Grant's bed—a hulking construction with a victoriously carved headboard so tall it would go right through the roof of a motel. But this is a rather unusual inn. You enter through a modest enough doorway and climb a narrow stairway to a tiny lobby with bold blue wallpaper and potted plants. There are only fifteen rooms, all different, but each one a valentine of Victoriana: the prizes are the Marquess of Queensberry (Grant's bed, a corner fireplace, velvet sofas and chairs, campaign chests) and the Queen Victoria (corner room, bay window, golden drapes, potted plants). Both the Marquess and the Queen rate private bathrooms, some of the others have washbasins only, and you have to walk down the hallway to the toilet. But why not? The charm of Sausalito is said to be its "European-ness." The hotel is right smack in the middle of town, between the main street and the waterfront. EP, with continental breakfast, $35 (no bath) to $95. *Sausalito Hotel, 16 El Portal, Sausalito, Calif. 94965 (telephone 415–332–4155).*

TIMBER COVE INN, NEAR JENNER

The shower stalls here (or at least some of them) have floor-to-ceiling windows looking out to the ocean, and you can stand and scrub each other's backs while you watch the gulls and surf and, maybe, the whales. Timber Cove is about as close as you'll ever come to the perfect matching of inn and setting: on one side the ocean and bluffs, on the other the forests, and between them, on the edge of the ocean an inn that looks as if Paul Bunyan's son had built a matchstick house. The redwood timbers still look like *trees*, and the inn seems to grow naturally out of a Japanese garden and pool. The lobby is a cavernous hall of glass with redwood pillars, a walk-in fireplace, art gallery, bar/lounge, and down a few steps, a dining room with views of the ocean. The forty-seven guest rooms maintain the rustic atmosphere (even the bases of the bedside lamps are rough-hewn timber, the decorations are hunks of driftwood), and about half of them have Franklin stoves. But no TV or telephone—"consistent with the Timber Cove philosophy." A new owner is renovating like crazy—installing new windows and furnishings, sharpening maintenance, improving the cuisine with a chef imported from the posh Lodge at Pebble Beach farther down the coast. He has also installed a new suite which must be one of the most romantic and dramatic nests in California—sunken bathtub with Jacuzzi and a sauna with ocean view, among other attractions. If all goes to plan, Timber Cove can reclaim its place as one of California's most romantic hideaways. 47 rooms, from $39 to $85 EP ($200 for the suite). *Timber Cove Inn, North Coast Highway 1, Jenner, Calif. 95450 (telephone 707–847–3231).*

COLORADO

ASPEN SKI LODGE, ASPEN

This is the fashionable new hostelry that rose like the phoenix on the site of the old Smuggler's Lodge. Nothing but a fireplace remains from the old place. The new designers simply dreamed up a dashing contemporary building to go around it. The decor here is very much of the moment—lean, spare, and very handsome. Co-owner Andy Williams has contributed some Indian rugs and artifacts from his personal collection. These make a smashing wall accent here, a simple mantel centerpiece there. While all rooms are pleasant, one in particular is a standout. If there's the slightest bit of the hedonist in you, treat yourself to a stay in Room #28. The Jacuzzi here is big enough for an *intime* orgy. And there are more mirrors in the place than you'll ever need—no erogenous zone could possibly go unnoticed. (R.E.S.) 34 rooms from $52 to $110 EP. *Aspen Ski Lodge, 101 West Main Street, Aspen, Colo. 81611 (telephone 303–925–3434).*

FAR VIEW LODGE, MESA VERDE NATIONAL PARK

You can scout high and low but you'll be hard pressed to find a love nest in a more dramatic location: on top of the mesa, a tortuous forty-five-minute drive from the park entrance, on an elevation looking across 125 miles of wilderness to Shiprock, the Carrizo Mountains, and most of the thirty-two canyons that slice the mesa. This is nature at its most shuddery spectacular; by day, it's mellowed by gardens of serviceberry and rabbit brush, but in the evening, when the day trippers have wiggled their way back to the highway, you're on top of the world, alone with the stars and the coyotes that holler at each other across the canyons, and you'd better be in love with each other. The main lodge is inspired by an Indian *kiva*, or ceremonial chamber, and decorated with Navajo sand paintings and rugs. The tri-level dining room has acres of windows so that you don't have to forgo the view when you settle down to dine. The menu tries to reflect the Indian heritage, but with the Food and Drug Administration and the Department of Health breathing down the chefs' necks, this is more of a token gesture. From $31 to $40 EP. *Far View Lodge, Mesa Verde Company, Box 277, Mancos, Colo. 81328 (telephone 303–529–4421).*

MEADOW RIDGE RESORT CONDOMINIUMS, WINTER PARK

Drive two miles north of Winter Park and your eye will be caught by some cliff-hanging buildings off to the right. They dazzle by their site and their architecture alone. Walk into one and be awed by the triple-level view: the sky above, the Rockies straight ahead, the Fraser River in the valley below— all from one spot. The accommodations themselves are pretty impressive, as well: big wood-burning fireplace (with all the free wood you want), fully equipped kitchen, and more space than any couple could ever need. You can revel in it—or bring friends. You pay for all the space and the spectacle, naturally.

You must specify location. Say you want to be *on* the ridge—in the Needle's Eye, Rail Bender, Derailer, Arrowhead, or Prospector condos. These are three-bedroom condos; smaller and cheaper condos are available without the spectacular view. (R.E.S.) $100 to $200 per day EP in ski season. *Meadow Ridge Resort Condominiums, Box 203, Winter Park, Colo. 80482 (telephone 303–726–5701).*

RAMS-HORN LODGE, VAIL

Many of the inns in this picturesque village get a bit too flounced up in their effort to resemble Swiss chalets. The Rams-Horn stands out because it doesn't even try. It is plain and simple and very nice. There are only thirty rooms here, twenty of them with mountain views. If your Achilles' tendons refuse to endure another day of skiing, simply stay in your room and watch everyone else overstretch theirs. Come spring, there's the Rams-Horn pool and its outdoor Jacuzzi. Beyond are some nearby golf courses, tennis courts, riding stables, or aerial trams. Rooms are spacious and comfortable—well done but very restrained. If you don't appreciate simplicity and understatement, you might not like the Rams-Horn. Morning coffee, tea, or hot chocolate are on the house. Continental breakfast is $3.50. No other meals.

Location couldn't be better: walk to the slopes, shops, and restaurants. (R.E.S.) 30 balconied rooms, from $48 to $80 EP. *Rams-Horn Lodge, Box 1068, Vail, Colo. 81657 (telephone 303-476-5646).*

SKY VALLEY LODGE, STEAMBOAT SPRINGS

It's quiet enough to hear a snowflake touch ground here, yet you're only fifteen minutes from the heavy ground action in and around Steamboat. There are only twenty-four guest rooms in the pair of lodges that make up Sky Valley (look for the sign soon after you get through Rabbit Ears Pass on U.S. 40). Big rock-and-timber affairs with lots of plate glass to show off the spectacular views. (Ask for #101 for the very best of these views.) Guest rooms are rustic but not primitive—bare cedar walls, homey furnishings. (R.E.S.) 24 rooms, from $34 in summer, many MAP packages available. *Sky Valley Lodge, Box 2153, Steamboat Springs, Colo. 80477 (telephone 303-879-5158).*

CONNECTICUT

BEE & THISTLE, OLD LYME

The village is a well-preserved collection of white clapboard houses behind trim lawns, beneath tall elms, and the inn will lend you a couple of bikes so that you can tour it in a leisurely way. The Bee & Thistle is a yellow-and-white structure with hip roof, set well back from the street behind lawns and trees, yet conveniently close to Exit 70 on the Connecticut Turnpike for impatient lovers. The public rooms are just what you hope to find in a simple, unpretentious country inn (the dining rooms are prettiest), the guest rooms are neat and tidy but lack flair, and some of them have an extra bed that detracts from the romantic ambiance. The talents of the owners seem to be directed elsewhere—Gene Bellows in the kitchen (the restaurant has a fine reputation), Barbara entertaining guests with folk songs to her own accompaniment on dulcimer, guitar, or bowed psaltery. 10 rooms, 8 with private baths, from $42 to $54 EP. Dining room closed on Tuesdays. *Bee & Thistle Inn, 100 Lyme Street, Old Lyme, Conn. 06371 (telephone 203-434-1667).*

THE INN AT LAKE WARAMAUG, NEW PRESTON

The house itself goes back to 1795. In the 1890s, its hilltop setting and wide shady lawns looking across the lake and the surrounding Litchfield hills prompted New Yorkers to endure a two-day horse and carriage trip to vacation here. That's when it was known as Lake View Inn and owned by William Henry Bonynge, grandfather of the present innkeeper. When Richard and Bobbie Combs took over in 1951, they changed the name and began to remove Victorian "improvements" to the building, returning it to its original Colonial heritage. The handsome paneled walls and old fireplaces were restored, the rooms filled with pine and cherry antiques and heirloom collections of pewter, copper, silver, and early Americana.

The dining-room color scheme changes with the seasons, as does the view from the big windows, but the traditional American menu is a constant: roast beef buffet is the Saturday-night special, Early American–style clam and lobster bakes over stones in an outdoor pit in summer.

Upstairs in the inn are five rooms, Colonial style with striped papers, wing chairs, and rockers and scenic views, particularly in the bay-windowed front bedroom. The rest of the lodgings are in two motel-type units on the grounds, less distinctive but pleasant enough, and the six rooms here with private fireplaces are ideal winter hideaways.

During the week the inn attracts tour buses for lunch and small business meetings, but the numbers are kept small and weekends are placid. (E.B.) 25 rooms, from $84 to $108 MAP. *The Inn at Lake Waramaug, New Preston, Conn. 06777 (telephone 203–868–2168).*

INTERLAKEN INN, LAKEVILLE

The northeast corner of Connecticut has more than its share of country inns, but it also has more than its fair share of attractions and the inns can be crowded at certain times of the year. Here's a fall-back alternative. The main lodge may be too sleekly modern for some tastes, the decor too stark, the guest rooms too "motelly"; moreover, Interlaken caters to seminars and business meetings. *But* it has a pool, tennis courts, and access to the nine-hole course belonging to the Hotchkiss School next door; the rooms are comfortable and efficient; the dining facilities are adequate. And if you insist on an inn that looks like an inn, Interlaken has a garden annex, Sunnyside, with shingle facade and half-a-dozen rooms in contemporary colors and fabrics, but with a sprinkling of antiques and, in some cases, fireplaces. 55 rooms, $45 to $48 EP, $110 EP for townhouse suites with kitchen. *Interlaken Inn, Route 112, Lakeville, Conn. 06039 (telephone 203–435–9878).*

MAYFLOWER INN, WASHINGTON VILLAGE

The shingle-sided, steep-roofed Mayflower crowns a knoll on thirty acres of gardens and woodlands, a pleasant place to idle away a few days among maples and pines and beechnut trees. You have a choice of rooms in the main lodge or in a couple of cottages in the garden, all with period furniture and some private bathrooms. $40 (without bath) to $60 EP. *Mayflower Inn, Washington, Conn. 06793 (telephone 203–868–0515).*

STONEHENGE, RIDGEFIELD

A flotilla of swans patrols the pond, pathways lead off into the woods, and three pines as old as the U.S.A. stand guard at the front door of this trim white Colonial-style mansion. Swiss chef Ans Benderer reigns over the kitchen, smokehouse, and the trout tank under the waterfall. Stonehenge is for gourmets rather than lovers; the guest rooms (two in the inn, six in motel-style cabins) are less sumptuous than the dining, but there's a tray of wine and cheese and an apple to greet you when you check into your room. And after dinner, it's so much nicer to jump into bed than into a car. $48.50 to $58.50, with continental breakfast, served in the room. *Stonehenge, Route 7, Ridgefield, Conn. 06877 (telephone 203–438–6511).*

UNDER MOUNTAIN INN, SALISBURY

The Berkshires are the backdrop, looming in the distance almost like a movie set. The white shuttered homestead, shaded by towering locusts, birches, and maples, could easily pass any central casting call for a typical New England inn. It was the seventy-seventh place that owners Al and Lorraine Bard had looked at in their search for an inn, and it was enough to prompt the California couple to pull up stakes in 1978 and head for Connecticut. They've made themselves right at home and transformed their Under Mountain Inn into a major asset for Salisbury—which was already one of the nicest towns in one of the nicest corners of the state.

There are sitting rooms on either side of the entry, both decorated in elegant Colonial with oriental rugs setting off the wide original floorboards of the house. Beyond are three intimate dining rooms, each with its own ambiance and its own fireplace whose glow adds to the candlelight on cold winter nights.

There are only seven rooms, and they've also been done with a touch of elegance, with striped reproduction wallpapers and matching drapes and chairs, formal velvet wing chairs in some rooms, simpler American country pieces in others. (E.B.) 7 rooms, from $55 to $60 CP. *Under Mountain Inn, Under Mountain Road (Route 41), Salisbury, Conn. 06068 (telephone 203–435–0242).*

FLORIDA

CHEECA LODGE, ISLAMORADA

Where did George Bush escape to after he was elected vice-president? Where does golfer Jack Nicklaus escape to with his buddies when they want to get away from tournaments and fans? Answer: An unpretentious, architecturally undistinguished, twenty-year-old cinder-block lodge by the edge of the sea, on a virtually private beach on a Florida key. Cheeca Lodge is primarily a fishing resort (Bush caught a ten-pound bonefish), but its attractions for nontrawlers include four tennis courts and a nine-hole golf course (in the design of which the aforesaid Nicklaus had a hand); and while half the guests are bobbing around on the high seas, you can be relaxing in uncrowded bliss beneath a thatched bohio, watching the egrets and pelicans. Half the eighty-six rooms are in the lodge itself, and of these, half (the pick of the bunch) overlook the sea. Penthouse rooms on the fourth floor are smaller but compensate with big balconies. If you decide on a villa room, make sure you have one *on* the beach, otherwise you'll be looking into the *back* of the one on the beach, not a pleasing prospect. In the evening there's live music in an otherwise nautically apt lounge. 86 rooms, from $100 to $120 EP. *Cheeca Lodge, P.O. Box 527, Islamorada, Fla. 33036 (telephone 305–664–4651; 800–327–2888).*

MARRIOTTS' CASA MARINA RESORT, KEY WEST

"It can be reached by through train from New York City in 46 hours, coming across the famous oversea railway conceived by the master mind of Henry M. Flagler, and built by him alone." So proclaimed the original 1921 brochure for the hotel that Flagler built to cater to his passengers, who hitherto had come across the oversea railway solely to catch the ferry to Havana. Now that you can get to Key West by Air Florida jet in half an hour from Miami, the Marriott people have reopened, refurbished, and enlarged Flagler's Casa Marina. In the lobby, wooden floors and coffered wooden ceiling gleam, rattan furniture plays hide-and-seek with planters, tall arched windows look out to lawns, ceiling fans coax the breeze in from the sea. The designers must have had romance in mind when they put together the restaurant, Henry's, a softly lit world of wicker gazebos and canopied banquettes, floral drapes and arched mirrors. Half the guest rooms are in the renovated original wing, the others in a four-story extension. Seven acres of gardens are given over to pool, whirlpool, artificial beach, a pair of tennis courts, and a six-hundred-foot private pier for fishing, waterskiing, wind-surfing, snorkeling, and fishing. 251 rooms, from $90 to $110 EP. *Marriott's Casa Marina Resort, Reynolds Street, Key West, Fla. 33040. (telephone 305–296–3535; 800–228–9290).*

GEORGIA

ELIZA THOMPSON HOUSE, SAVANNAH

There was once an Eliza Thompson, back in the middle of the eighteenth century, and this is the elegant house she built, three stories high with a double stairway leading to the main entrance on the second floor. Now carefully restored, its heart pine floors, mellow bricks, and antiques re-create something of the gracious life-style of the Savannah of yore. Sherry in a crystal decanter awaits guests in their rooms, continental breakfast is served whenever guests ask for it. The guest rooms are small, but individually decorated, each with full bath; when it's time to relax in the shade, there's a wicker-furnished porch overlooking a brick courtyard and fountain. Savannah's historic district is just steps away, and a twenty-minute drive will take you to Savannah Beach. The inn has free parking for five cars. 13 rooms, 3 suites, $68 CP. *Eliza Thompson House, 5 West Jones Street, Savannah, Ga. 31401 (telephone 912–236–6320).*

HAWAII

HANALEI COLONY RESORT, KAUAI

White breakers skim across Wainika Bay. Palm trees curve along the sweep of sand. Lushly green mountains soar to craggy peaks. At the end of the cove there's an unspoiled authentic Hawaiian village, Hanalei, and beyond it, almost at the end of the civilization before the road peters out into wilderness, you come to the beachside grove which is the Hanalei Colony Resort. Considering the awe-inspiring setting, the resort looks fairly commonplace, but no matter: a cluster of two-story bungalows, each with four large two-bedroom suites and lanais, most of them overlooking the cove. With its restaurant, that's all there is for miles around, and it has the potential for being one of the most serene spots in Hawaii. This is strictly a place to unwind, get yourselves a suntan, spend an extra hour or two in bed; but if you want a dash of adventure, there's an airstrtip half an hour away with twin-engine planes and helicopters that take you on sight-seeing trips above the jungly mountains and along the uninhabited Napali Coast, the one you see in all the pictures. For more action you can head for Princeville (see below), but you'll enjoy the Colony more if you decide to be self-contained. 20 rooms (insist on one overlooking the beach); from $53 to $65 EP. *Hanalei Colony Resort, P.O. Box 206, Hanalei, Kauai, Hawaii 96714 (telephone 808–826–6235).*

HONOKEANA COVE, MAUI

This small two-story resort is close to the Napili Beach resorts, but set among foliage and flowers in its own tiny cove. The beach is skimpy, but there's a freeform pool on the lawn. And no crowds. Since the rooms and townhouse suites are condominiums, decor varies, but they are comfortable and efficient even when they lack style. The management is friendly and helpful, but there's no maid service except for long stays. 24 rooms, $60 EP (minimum stay of 3 nights). No credit cards. *Honokeana Cove Apartments, 5255 Lower Honoapiilani Road, Maui, Hawaii 96761 (telephone 808–669–6441).*

LAE NANI, KAUAI

This is a quiet, five-acre enclave on the otherwise multi-hoteled, but beautiful beach at Kapaa. The eighty-four deluxe suites have soft and soothing island decor, ceiling fans, color television, dishwashers, garbage disposals, and fully equipped lanais overlooking the lawns and beach. A freeform pool awaits guests who want to avoid the beach, but otherwise the only sports facility is a tennis court. Lae Nani has its own laundermat, but no restaurants—but you'll find a wide selection of eating places a few minutes away in the village of Kapaa. 84 rooms, $90 to $110 EP (slightly less in summer) with daily maid service. *Lae Nani, 410 Papaloa Road, Kapaa, Kauai, Hawaii 96746 (telephone 808–822–4938).* Note: Lae Nani is one of the resorts offering special package rates that include room, Hertz rental car, and flight on United Airlines, arranged by Creative Leisure in San Francisco—and worth looking into. For details, call 800–227–4290 or any United office.

MAKAHA RESORT, OAHU

Here's an alternative to Waikiki, yet less than an hour from the action. Makaha Valley is located on the western side of the island, behind the town of Waianae, between two four-thousand foot escarpments. The resort is primarily a golf course, with a hotel in the middle, among gardens of plumeria and o'hia. The timber-and-shingle, two-story architecture is in keeping with the location, the decor is stylish and tasteful. The centerpiece is a swimming pool fed by four fountains, with a beautiful view of the valley and the sea from the terrace (don't look to your right, where some unfeeling developer has built a wall of glassy high rises right under the mountain). The main clubhouse is attractively furnished with soft colors, rattan, and bamboo; the dining room would be more pleasant if the live music were toned down—or extinguished. The only other sports facilities are tennis courts, but there's also a shuttle bus to the beach, one of the great surfing beaches. But the most attractive feature, bearing in mind the standard of comfort, may be the rates—a good chunk less than the equivalent rooms in Waikiki. 200 rooms and suites, from $52 to $125 EP. *Makaha Resort, P.O. Box 896, Waianae, Oahu, Hawaii 96792 (telephone 808–695–9511).*

HOTEL MOLOKAI, MOLOKAI

It looks like a Polynesian village, with steep curved shingle roofs among the spindly palms, beside the beach. Each room has a lanai with Polynesian-style swing, wood, and rattan to enhance the South Seas feeling, and there are lots of louvres and sliding screens to make the most of the sea breezes. The best rooms are Ocean Front; and if you can't have one of them ask for a Superior Studio on the garden level. This is a very casual, barefoot place, with a breeze-cooled beachside restaurant, a big swimming pool—and few intrusions. It's a convenient base for side trips to Molokai's rain forests and waterfalls, the Phallic Rock and the Measuring Pit. Kaunakakai, the island capital (such as it is), is a five-minute drive away. 56 rooms, from $45 to $65 EP. *Hotel Molokai, P.O. Box 546, Kaunakakai, Molokai, Hawaii 96748 (telephone 808–533–5347).*

NAPILI KAI BEACH CLUB, MAUI

Napili Bay and Napili Beach are quintessential Hawaii, and if the Beach Club were the only hotel there, it would be idyllic. It's not, but it is at the *end* of the row, on a private promontory, and if you check into a room or suite in the bungalows known as Puna 11 and Puna Point, above the rocky shoreline, you need never know the other hotels are there until you go to the beach. You could even avoid that by sticking around the small private pools, each serving its group of half a dozen rooms (the club has five pools in all). Room decor is a combination of Hilton, Hawaiian, and Japanese, with *shoji* screens across windows and closets. 56 rooms, from $80 to $115 EP. No credit cards. *Napili Kai Beach Club, 5900 Honoapiiliani Highway, Napili Bay, Maui, Hawaii 96761 (telephone 808–669–6271).*

NAPILI POINT, MAUI

This bulwark of four-story condominiums is on the promontory at the other end of Napili Beach from the Beach Club (above), and again, the choice rooms are those facing out to sea, turning their backs on the rest of the property. These are one-bedroom suites (superior or deluxe), each with complete kitchen. Resort facilities include two pools and barbecues; the beach is two minutes away through the garden; golf and tennis are available at Kapalua, five minutes away by car. There are stores and restaurants nearby. 100 rooms and suites, $65 to $75 (less in winter). *Napili Point, Napili Bay, Maui, Hawaii 96791 (telephone 808–922–3368, or toll free, in a special package, through Creative Leisure in San Francisco, 800–227–4290).*

PRINCEVILLE, KAUAI

When you see how stunningly beautiful the scenery is around here you'll probably wish the developers had stayed in Waikiki. They didn't. But there's still a lot to enjoy at Princeville, and in the end it would probably take more than a few hundred condominiums to overwhelm the natural glory of Hanalei Bay. This former ranch perches on a bluff above the sea and surf, and there are so many facets to the development you can choose your favorite location: at the edge of the bluffs looking out to sea (stay at the *Sealodge* condominiums); in a secluded enclave surrounded by fairways (opt for the *Pali Uli* cottages, the most interesting interiors of the lot); or facing across Hanalei Bay—in which case you should check into a room or suit of the *Hanalei Bay Resort*. This cluster of four-story lodges has eleven tennis courts (three lighted) right on the doorstep, and an attractive restaurant, the Bali Hai, on the crest of the hill. Elsewhere at Princeville, you can play golf (twenty-seven championship holes), sail catamarans, ride horses, fish, dive, snorkel, swim in pools or the sea—or go sight-seeing in a helicopter from the small airport nearby. From $70 EP (less in summer). *Princeville Reservations Office, P.O. Box 121, Hanalei, Kauai, Hawaii 96714 (telephone 800–367–7090). Or direct to Hanalei Bay Resort, P.O. Box 220, Hanalei (telephone 808–826–6522).*

WAIKOLOA, HAWAII

From your window what you see is wall-to-wall blue sky and wall-to-wall blue sea, with a glistening strip of sand and surf and a fringe of coco palms. Between you and the sea is an eerie landscape of lava flows, and behind you a ring of four mountain peaks. At your doorstep you have a spectacular eighteen-hole golf course, a swimming pool, a pair of tennis courts (free play), and paddle tennis (free play). If you want to spend an hour or two at the beach, there are several secluded strands ten to twelve miles away. Here at Waikoloa, you're a thousand feet above the sea, on the *mauka*, or uplands, that were once part of the famed Parker Ranch. You can still follow the old trails of the *paniolos*, or cowboys, on escorted rides from the Waikoloa Stable, or canter downhill for a cookout by the beach. Accommodations are studios and suites in a ridge of condominiums between the fairways and the clubhouse, overlooking the sea. The studios are rather cramped (but a bargain, among the least expensive accommodations in the islands); but the panorama compensates for any shortcomings in the furnishings, so ask for a room on the top floor and enjoy the view all the way to Maui. 50 rooms and suites (plus private homes), $35 to $49 EP (2-night minimum, fresh linen and vacuuming every fourth day). *Waikoloa Village, P.O. Box 3048, Waikoloa Village Station, Kamuela, Hawaii 96743 (telephone 808–883–9671).*

ILLINOIS

THE MAYFAIR REGENT, CHICAGO

Chicago's newest luxury hotel opened in fall 1980, with what may be the best location in town, right next to the Drake on Lake Shore Drive, but even closer to the lake than its dowager neighbor. The morning view from the rooftop dining room nineteen floors up is enough to turn breakfast into your favorite meal, especially with the big help-yourself baskets of croissants and brioches set out for you. Instead of a lobby, there's a formal lounge full of murals, potted palms, and period furniture set around coffee tables so that you can take your cocktails or tea drawing room style—and even to the tune of piano music in the late afternoon. The rooms are large, most with lake views, traditionally furnished, with big marble bathrooms and every convenience, even bedside and bath *and* desk telephones. Perish the thought that you need ever have to hurry across the room!

The dinner restaurant here is The Palm, a name well known to New Yorkers or Los Angelans, especially those on hefty expense accounts. The Mayfair Regent seems determined in every way to become *the* luxury small hotel in a city that has more than its share of contenders, but it's too soon to call the race. (E.B.) 224 rooms, from $135 to $165 EP. *The Mayfair Regent, 181 East Lake Shore Drive, Chicago, Ill. 60611 (telephone 312–787–8500).*

MAINE

BETHEL INN & COUNTRY CLUB, BETHEL

The town of Bethel lies on the edge of the White Mountain National Park, close to the New Hampshire line and seventy-odd miles northwest of Portland. A backwoods location, you might think, but the center of the town, and the Common, is a National Historic District where, if you can see beyond the ornate utility poles and cables, you will find some handsome old Federal and Colonial houses. Five of these structures are part of the Bethel Inn—the large inn itself and four of the former homes or carriage houses. Guest rooms (sixty-five in all) standard country inn style, with Hitchcock furniture, private bathrooms, and reasonable space. The dining room is large enough to accommodate coach parties and meetings (of which there may be too many for your taste). Outdoors, nine-hole golf course, tennis court, heated pool, beach clubhouse nearby, canoes and kayacks, cross-country skiing in winter. Just keep your fingers crossed there won't be a tour group in the house when you go. 65 rooms, from $75 to $100 MAP in season (EP available). *Bethel Inn & Country Club, Bethel, Me. 04217 (telephone 207–824–2175).*

BLUE HILL INN, BLUE HILL

There are several reasons to come here. One is Blue Hill itself, a placid village of white-clapboard homes and lawns, picket fences, and sheltering elm trees. Another is the surrounding countryside—coves and harbors, pine forests, Acadia National Park, artisans' workshops, and a chamber music festival in summer. A third is guest privileges (tennis and golf) at the nearby country club, which has one of the loveliest golf courses in Maine, winding along the edge of Blue Hill harbor. Finally there's the inn itself. Especially the home cooking. Jean Wakelin, the innkeeper's wife, prepares the meals (fixed menu, served at seven) always interesting, always tasty. The inn is cozy and homey, relaxed and friendly; the eight guest rooms are comfortable (each has private bathroom) but undistinguished, and the plastic chairs and paper napkins in the dining alcove that's been tacked on to the regular (and charming) dining room does no credit to Jean Wakelin's peach cheesecake. On the other hand, the rates are certainly reasonable. Dinner is $20 a couple (bring your own wine). 8 rooms, from $28 to $34 EP. *Blue Hill Inn, Blue Hill, Me. 04614 (telephone 207–374–2844).*

OLD FORT INN, KENNEBUNKPORT

The former fort, in this case, being a hotel rather than a fortress. It's located in a garden on the edge of town (not at the beach), an old shingle house that serves as reception, antiques store, and guests' lounge in a barnlike gallery; the other guest rooms are in a two-story stone-and-timber structure beside the trees. The place has just been taken over by a San Francisco couple, who plan to tone down the present slap-happy decor, and judging by their collection of antiques, they'll do a fine job. The nice attraction of the Old Fort, however, is that each room has a kitchenette, and it's the only inn in the neighborhood with a tennis court and a heated pool. 13 rooms, $50 to $65 EP. *Old Fort Inn, Old Fort Avenue, Kennebunkport, Me. 04046 (telephone 207–967–5353).*

PENTAGÖET INN, CASTINE

"The place where the waters meet," Pentagöet, the Indians called it, and if you walk down to the end of Castine's elm-and-clapboard-lined main street and board a boat, you can lose yourselves in scores of inlets and coves. The guesthouse is a newcomer, although the house itself was erected in 1894; the veranda and potted plants re-create its Victorian ancestry, and the fourteen dainty and spotless rooms (four with private bath) are decorated with pencil post beds and hooked rugs. Since innkeeper Natalie Saunders took over in spring 1980, you can now have dinner here, with wine selected from a commendable list for a small inn. Dinner, 5 courses, is by reservation, for guests and public, and costs about $25 for two. 9 rooms, some sharing bathroom. $26 to $36 EP. *Pentagöet Inn, Castine, Me. 04421 (telephone 207–326–8616).*

SEACREST INN, KENNEBUNKPORT

This is a place to be in a gale, by the window, a roaring fire at your back, a roaring sea outside, hands clasped around a mug of mulled cider. Rocking chairs on the big veranda and picture windows in the dining room make sure you never miss a single wave.

The old seafarer's home, a green-timbered house with a steep red roof, overlooks a rocky garden, the rocky shore and the rocky sea; a skinny road runs between the garden and the shore, and there's nothing else around but private summer houses.

The inn proper has seven rooms all with private baths. Try to get one of the two big rooms facing the sea, painted in soft pastel shades with turn-of-the-century Maine furniture. All the bedrooms have an ocean view—slightly angled in some cases, but an ocean view nonetheless.

If you can't get a room in the inn, settle for the small motel in the garden. These rooms are compact, but you can always pretend they're cabins on a yacht; they all have balconies facing the ocean, and such unnautical equipment as "noiseless mercury switches" and "hydronic radiant heating," and they're "scientifically constructed against sound-conduction." The attraction of the dining room, besides the view, is the price—a lobster dinner costs only about $7, depending on the day's catch. You'll find golf, tennis, riding, boating, and fishing nearby; Kennebunk Beach is within walking distance, or you can swim in the natural rock pools right in front of the inn.

Basically, a place for wave watching. 17 rooms and apartment, EP $33 to $43. *Seacrest Inn, Ocean Avenue, Kennebunkport, Me. 04046 (telephone 207–967–2125).*

MASSACHUSETTS

BRADFORD GARDENS, PROVINCETOWN

Say it's the dead of winter and there's no Caribbean escape in sight. Here's another kind of warming getaway: to arty Provincetown, where you'll have the galleries, shops, and restaurants almost to yourself, where you can don your woolies and walk the beach for a wintry seascape that may tempt you to get out a paintbrush yourself.

Six of the rooms in this 1820s inn have a working fireplace and a supply of firewood waiting for you. All have been furnished with affection using period pieces of all kinds—brass beds, old hat racks, pitchers and basins, unusual chests and chairs. On the more mundane side, each also has a color TV and private bath. The rooms have distinctive names that reflect their personalities. The Chimney Nook on the first floor has garden views and, literally, a fireplace nook; the Jenny Lind room is filled with early spool (Jenny Lind) furnishings; the Alcove has (you guessed it) alcoves, overlooking garden and sea; and the Honeymoon Suite has its own sitting room and an original Franklin stove. People reserve a whole year ahead to get the Cherry Tree Room for May, when the famous tree outside bursts into bloom. (E.B.) 11 rooms, from $44 to $49 CP. *Bradford Gardens Inn, 178 Bradford Street, Provincetown, Mass. 02657 (telephone 617–487–1616).*

BRAMBLE INN, BREWSTER

What could be nicer than dining in an art gallery filled with works in every medium done by talented artists from the Cape to the Pacific coast? That's the unique ambiance Karen Etsell and Elaine Brennan have established at the Bramble Inn. They've lavished obvious love on every detail—from the wheelbarrow full of petunias out front to the perfect pink-and-green color scheme inside, carried out right down to the hand-painted napkin rings and the pale green ferns hanging at the windows. They've taken equal care with their cuisine: their dessert, the "Bramble," a delicacy of chopped raisins and cranberries in a tender pastry, has become such a legend that the name has been legally trademarked and the pastries are on sale at a special takeout counter.

Upstairs there are just three simple bedrooms, sharing two baths in the hall. Each room has a different color scheme, a TV, and its own special touches—stencils, printed Colonial papers, original art, or perhaps a hand-weaving on the wall. Houseguests are served complimentary coffee and doughnuts each morning.

Bramble Inn is right on the main street of one of the Cape's most serene villages, within walking distance of beach and tennis. If you fancy the ambiance of a tiny inn, you won't find a nicer one. Just reserve early. (E.B.) 3 rooms, open late May to Columbus Day; $33 late June to Labor Day, $26 off-season, CP. No children under 12. *The Bramble Inn Gallery and Cafe, Route 6A, P.O. 159, Brewster, Mass. 02631 (telephone 617–896–7644).*

CHANTICLEER INN, SIASCONSET, NANTUCKET

'Sconset is another world, a beguiling village set between cranberry bogs and rose-grown bluffs about seven miles away from the town of Nantucket, with miniature cottages winding along lanes that date back to the seventeenth and eighteenth century. The picturesque charm of these onetime fisherman's shanties made the settlement an 1800s summer haven for theatrical luminaries like Lillian Russel and Joseph Jefferson. But once the actors' colony had drifted westward to Hollywood, 'Sconset's glorious beaches were left in peace and the only people who come to stay here are the lucky owners of those shingled cottages.

You can, however, rent a room in a cottage at the Chanticleer Inn. The Chanticleer is principally known for its food, universally acknowledged as the best on the island. Most of the guests don't even know that a few steps down the block, tucked away from the street, six rooms are for let in a little cottage complex abloom with hydrangeas and climbing roses. The cottage furnishings are a little disappointing considering the idyllic setting—nice and comfortable enough, but bland modern and not at all distinctive. Nevertheless, here you are ensconced in this never-never town, able to wander those winding lanes and stroll right over to a breathtaking beach, totally away from it all—except for the haute cuisine practically next door. There's a lot to be said for it. (E.B.) 6 rooms, $45 CP. *Chanticleer Inn, New Street, Siasconset, Nantucket, Mass. 02564 (telephone 617–257–6231).*

THE GATEWAYS INN AND RESTAURANT, LENOX

The Bicentennial was supposed to be *America's* big year but Czech-born Gerhard Schmid also came out of it smelling of roses. First he won four gold medals in the International Culinary Olympics in Frankfurt. Then he was invited to prepare a civic banquet for Queen Elizabeth in Boston's town hall—no mean feat when you consider the rudimentary kitchen facilities there, but it turned out to be a triumph, the queen polished off her dessert, and Prince Philip said his thank-you's in fluent German. To cap the year, the Schmids bought this country inn (with kitchens that are far from rudimentary) and now they are working happily ever after.

Their mansion (square, white, and flat-roofed, more London than Lenox) was built around the turn of the century for Harvey Procter of Procter & Gamble fame. A hugh mahogany-paneled hallway leads to a pair of elegant dining rooms and a large bar named, inexplicably, The Thistle; a flight of handsome mahogany stairs leads up to the dozen guest rooms on the second floor. Half of them, more or less, have private bathrooms, four have fireplaces (working, but only when lit by a member of the household). The two most in demand are the large corner chambers above the main portico, but Gateways regulars will settle for any room, just to be within reach of the dining tables. Cuisine, as you can imagine, is everything here, even to the point where the menu admonishes concertgoers to select from the list of special items ready to be served rather than rush the kitchen and try to gobble down a gourmet meal before dashing off to Tanglewood. 6 double rooms, 1 suite, from $30 to $145 EP. *Gateways Inn and Restaurant, 71 Walker Street, Lenox, Mass. 01240 (telephone 413–637–2532).*

WAUWINET HOUSE, WAUWINET, NANTUCKET

You don't come to Wauwinet House for the room decor, which frankly could be called "early tag sale." You do come, however, for a truly extraordinary solitary location on a spit of land between ocean and bay with beach on either side. It's one of the loveliest and most secluded areas of Nantucket—just one hotel, a few dozen homes, and not another commercial establishment in sight.

The rambling gray shingled hotel just sort of grew. It opened for business in 1897 and when Robert and Barbara Bowman took over, the longtime guests begged them to leave the place as it was. So far the Bowmans have agreed to the requests. The downstairs rooms are pleasant enough—a roomy paneled living room with a fireplace, overstuffed sofas, and lots of books and games for guests; an airy dining room decorated with murals showing the early fishing history of the area; a rustic bar; and an outdoor deck to enjoy lunch or a drink with a view.

There's a tennis court here and Sunfish for rent, but above all this is the perfect place to do nothing—just stroll and sun and appreciate the rare tranquility, assured for years to come by the Backus family's grant of more than five hundred acres of surrounding land to a nature conservancy. It will be just the two of you, with only the gulls and the sea for company. (E.B.) 26 rooms. $50 EP. Closed November to May. *Wauwinet House, Wauwinet, Nantucket, Mass. 02554 (telephone 617–228–0145).*

THE WILDWOOD INN, WARE

Come in, sit down before the fire, have a cup of tea. Or hot chocolate. Or mulled cider, depending on the season. When you wake up next morning the country-fresh breakfast room beckons with the aroma of freshly baked herbal bread or apricot rum bread, muffins with homemade peach butter, your choice of coffee or any of six types of herbal tea. The Wildwood is the creation of Margaret and Geoffrey Lobenstine, a young California couple who moved east to open a New England inn, took over this verandaed Victorian mansion in 1979, and filled it with antiques, collectibles, ingenuity, and enthusiasm. The five (just five) guest rooms are enlivened with custom-stitched quilts, eyelet pillowcases, Martex towels. Guests share two bathrooms, but none of them (doctors, lawyers, executives) seem to mind; even in the short time since Wildwood opened its doors, many guests have returned for extra vacations, others have enjoyed their visits so much they've sent the Lobenstines gifts—books, crewel work, things to hang on walls. It's a happy, convivial sort of place. And relaxing. There's a pile of parlor games in the old carpenter's chest in the lounge, piles of books to take out to the double swings on the veranda or the hammock under the trees. The two-acre garden is dotted with dogwood and wild blackberries, wisteria and apple trees, and beyond the stone wall there's a park with jogging paths and tennis courts.

Ware itself is nondescript (the inn is on a pleasant residential street), but it's a convenient center for touring western Massachusetts, which is worth touring. And who could overlook such bargain rates! 5 rooms, sharing bathrooms. $20 to $29 CP. *The Wildwood Inn, 121 Church Street, Ware, Mass. 01082 (telephone 413–967–7798).*

THE WILLIAMSVILLE INN, WEST STOCKBRIDGE

You come to these parts for peace and quiet and fresh air and this inn provides all three *plus* a ten-acre garden with a swimming pool and a clay tennis court. When you've swum, sniffed, and snoozed, you prepare yourselves for a leisurely dinner in one of the attractive dining rooms or, in summer, the patio. The eight guests rooms in the inn proper are fitted out in country style (plank floors, rag rugs, Victoriana), all with private bathrooms. Of these, two have fireplaces, most have air conditioning.

New owners took over in spring of 1980, but the members of the staff remained. Two-day weekends are required in summer, three-day minimums on holiday weekends, but this is one of the few inns in the area that doesn't jack up the prices for Tanglewood weekends, or any other weekend for that matter. 8 rooms, $50 to $60 EP. *The Williamsville Inn, Route 41, West Stockbridge, Mass. 01266 (telephone 413–274–6580).*

MINNESOTA

LOWELL INN, STILLWATER

Stillwater is a small town outside Minneapolis–St. Paul, and the Lowell is a place to keep in mind if you're driving cross-country on Interstate 94. Its thirteen-pillared veranda gives it something of the air of Mount Vernon, and the George Washington dining room carries the image one stage further with Williamsburg ladderback chairs, Dresden china, Capo di Monte porcelain, and other items from the Palmer family's private collection. The Matterhorn Room, on the other hand, honors the Palmers' Swiss ancestry with custom-carved woodwork that includes a life-size eagle. The twenty-five guest rooms, on the two upper floors, feature mostly Williamsburg reproductions. EP $59 to $139. *Lowell Inn, 102 North Second Street, Stillwater, Minn. 55082 (telephone 612–439–1100).*

NEW HAMPSHIRE

CHRISTMAS FARM INN, JACKSON

Sydna and Bill Zeliff from Pennsylvania took over this small inn a few years ago, and their friendly welcome makes it Christmas all year round. You'll find a hillside setting with panoramas of the White Mountains almost every way you turn, a large swimming pool on the grounds, and all the sports attractions of the area a short drive away. The main lodge dates from the eighteenth century, and it's been added to ever since (including an abandoned church that was eased down the hill and ingeniously transformed into deluxe guest rooms). Rooms vary considerably in size and comforts, depending on whether you're in the Log Cabin, the Sugar House, the newly renovated barn, the main house, or the church. The pleasant dining room is in Colonial style. 29 rooms, from $64 MAP (without private bath) to $90 MAP (with private bath). *Christmas Farm Inn, Route 16B, Box 176, Jackson, N.H. 03846 (telephone 603–383–4313).*

THE DANA PLACE INN, PINKHAM NOTCH

The forte here is food, served in a rustic-chic garden patio with floor-to-ceiling windows, but having come so far you might as well stay the night. Originally a farmhouse, the inn dates from the late 1800s, and for the past four years it's been owned and upgraded by Mal and Betty Jennings. Rooms vary in size, style, and decor, but put in a bid for numbers 6 or 17 or the Honeymoon Suite, a frilly, dainty room on the second floor. The swimming pool is screened by the apple orchard, the tennis courts are a short walk through the trees, and there's plenty of lawn for lounging and listening to the birds. (That is, if the traffic will allow, because Highway 16, though narrow and winding, is a popular route for Canada-bound tourists.) 14 rooms, EP $31 to $39 (sharing bath), $39 to $40 (private bath), all with full country breakfast. *The Dana Place Inn, 25 Pinkham Notch Road, Jackson, N.H. 03846 (telephone 603–383–6822).*

DEXTER'S INN & TENNIS CLUB, SUNAPEE

The panoramas of lakes and wooded hills, the three tennis courts, and the cross-country ski trails will keep you busy all day. In the evening, you can draw up a chair beside the fireplace in the library and browse among some of the inn's five hundred books. Dexter's has been an inn only since 1948, but its trim rooms are decorated in traditional country style. 17 rooms, 2 full housekeeping suites ¼ mile from the inn, MAP $62 to $78 in summer, no credit cards. *Dexter's Inn, Stagecoach Road, Sunapee, N.H. 03782 (telephone 603–763–5571).*

FRANCONIA INN, FRANCONIA

Old Zebedee Applebee, they say, was the first innkeeper in these parts, building his Colonial-era tavern on the same spot where the Franconia stands today; and although this particular inn was built in the thirties, as a farmhouse, it exudes something of the atmosphere of a Colonial tavern. In any case, how often do you find a country inn with indoor tennis courts?

The Franconia has been through some up-and-down years recently, and gone through several twentieth-century Zebedees, but is now owned and operated by Arman and Susan DeLorenz, who work hard to provide a comfortable stay for their guests. The most interesting nooks, on the second floor, have knotty pine walls throughout, even in the shower stalls and closets, which gives them the look of cabins on a nice old-fashioned yacht. The inn's dining room serves up French cuisine in a relaxed, softly lit atmosphere, decorated with antiques and hanging planters. When there's a chill in the New Hampshire air, guests can gather around the big old fireplace dating from 1862, a reminder at least of the inn's heritage. 29 rooms, EP only, $28 to $30. *Franconia Inn, Route 116, Franconia, N.H. 03580 (telephone 603–823–5542).*

THE INN AT CROTCHED MOUNTAIN, FRANCESTOWN

It's a nice old inn, about 150 years old and covered with ivy. The rooms are modest, the lounge hospitable, the home cooking pleasant, but what you really come here for is the outdoor life. The inn sits on the side of the hill, miles from civilization, with views fanning out for forty miles across the meadows and forests of the Piscataquog Valley. In addition to walks and hikes through forest and up mountain, there are two clay tennis courts and a pool at the inn, golf nearby, and skiing in winter. You'll find Crotched Mountain just off Route 47, between Francestown and Bennington, just north of Peterborough. 12 rooms, some sharing bath. $30 to $40 EP. No credit cards. Closed first three weeks in November. *The Inn at Crotched Mountain, Mountain Road, Francestown, N.H. 03043 (telephone 603–588–6840).*

LYME INN, LYME

The village common sweeps up to it, past the white clapboard houses, the Civil War soldier, the white church with the tall spire. The inn itself is a tall Early American structure with a broad porch where white-and-yellow wicker rockers and chairs overlook the common. The pine-floored, beamed interior is furnished with Hitchcock-style furniture, hooked rugs, frilly curtains, and antiques—Currier & Ives samplers in the dining room, antique ice skates and farm implements on the tavern walls, hand-stitched quilts and tester beds in the guest rooms. Even the shared bathrooms are models of charming country inn style. Lyme is on the Connecticut River, about ten miles north of Hanover, so there are plenty of places to visit and events to attend—but avoid football weekends in Hanover. 18 rooms, some sharing bath. $28 to $42 EP. *Lyme Inn, Lyme, N.H. 03768 (telephone 603–795–2222).*

SUGAR HILL INN, FRANCONIA

Sugar, the hill, is a mere lump compared with the peaks all around; Sugar Hill, the inn, is a friendly little spot with fireplaces in the lounge and Pewter Tavern, and the cheerful dining room has views all the way across the valley to Franconia Notch and lofty Lafayette. There's skiing as well as tennis and golf nearby. 12 rooms (6 in the inn, 6 in a motel unit in the garden), $28 to $34 EP; $66 to $72 MAP. *Sugar Hill Inn, Franconia, N.H. 03580 (telephone 603-823-5621).*

NEW MEXICO

HOTEL EDELWEISS, TAOS SKI VALLEY

Taos Ski Valley is the brainchild of a champion called Ernie Blake, and it's reputed to have some of the toughest ski runs in the world. That may be; right now we're considering the valley as a nice place to go in summer and fall. It's tucked away, nineteen miles deep within a steep-sided canyon, and speckled with half a dozen hotels and lodges, pools, sauna, Jacuzzi, tennis courts, and a choice of hearty restaurants. The Edelweiss is a pleasant base camp for walks through the forest or hikes up the mountain (the hotel will supply box lunches). Dinner is served family style at 6:30, but stay on the EP and you can dine whenever you like at one of the restaurants in Taos itself. Occasional entertainment includes chamber music and folk singing. 16 rooms, EP $45 in summer, AP $75 in winter. *Hotel Edelweiss, Taos Ski Valley, N.M. 87571 (telephone 505-776-2301).*

THE INN OF THE MOUNTAIN GODS, MESCALERO

You're seven thousand feet up here, among the gods and bald eagles, on a 460,000-acre reservation belonging to the Mescalero Apache tribe. Owners and operators of this unique deluxe resort, the Apaches allow no billboards or neon to spoil the views of mountain peaks, forests, and man-made lake. The entrance, via a bridge, waterfall, and stream, leads to a lobby dominated by a three-story copper-sheathed fireplace and a "chandelier" with twenty-four hundred bulbs. Outdoors, there's boating on the lake, skiing at nearby Sierra Blanca, and tennis, golf, and swimming on the reservation. 134 rooms, EP $50 to $85. *The Inn of the Mountain Gods, Mescalero, N.M. 88340 (telephone 505-257-5141; toll free, 800-545-9011).*

TRES LAGUNAS GUEST RANCH, PECOS

Another side to New Mexico—a Maine-like setting of log cabins dwarfed by Ponderosa pines and firs, with a bubbly mountain stream, between Willow Creek and Holy Ghost Creek. Besides the natural glories of the Pecos Wilderness area, Tres Lagunas has a stable of quarterhorses (you can go riding off by yourselves); a heated pool; three trout-stocked lakes and a private mile-long stretch of the Pecos for fishing; and mile after mile of walking tracks, along the stream and up the road (it goes nowhere so it's never crowded).

The cabins look just rustic and right in this all-embracing greenery, but you don't have to rough it. They have stone fireplaces, bathtubs in wood-walled bathrooms, Navajo rugs, and porches. Socializing takes place in the main lodge, an oversized frontier cabin with a comfy lounge, library, and three oversize fireplaces; meals are served in the wonderfully woodsy Waterfall Room overlooking the Pecos River and the Ponderosa pines. 5 rooms, 10 cabins, $109.50 AP. *Tres Lagunas Guest Ranch, Route 2, P.O. Box 100, Pecos, N.M. 87552 (telephone 505–757–6194).*

NEW YORK

THE CLINTON HOUSE, CLINTON

Another handsome old inn in another handsome old Upstate town in Finger Lakes country. Though nudged by supermarkets and parking lots to the rear, Clinton House looks out on an elmy village green with nearly the same character it had 150 years ago when it was the grandest house in town. Survivor of various incarnations plus a serious fire a few years ago, it now offers five immaculate guest rooms, the nicest of which are the Franklin with rooftop balcony and the Madison with bay window and old oak parquet floor. Below are a bar and three small dining rooms running the gamut of Italian cooking from antipasto to ziti. (C.P.) 5 rooms, from $35 to $40 EP. *The Clinton House, Clinton, N.Y. 13323 (telephone 315–853–5555).*

COLGATE INN, HAMILTON

Village Green and Village Inn updated. The green, at least, remains vintage nineteenth century with bandstand and grand old mansions in mint condition. The inn, however, is a Dutch Colonial re-creation dating from the twenties, after the original burned down. Owned by Colgate University, which pretty much owns the town as well, it's a reasonable cross between sanitized modern hotel and ye olde hostelry. Color television, individual thermostats, telephones, etc., in every room remind you it's been a long time since Alexander Hamilton slept here. But the rooms are roomy and the view is pleasantly steepled and cupola'd. (C.P.) 50 rooms, from $40 to $44 EP. *Colgate Inn, Hamilton, N.Y. 13346 (telephone 315–824–2300).*

HOTEL SAGAMORE, LAKE GEORGE

It stands, a proud dinosaur of a hotel, on Green Island, near Bolton's Landing, overlooking one of the most breathtaking aspects of one of the country's most beautiful lakes. The nostalgic traveler who misses the *Queen Mary* and *Twentieth Century Limited* will probably relish the Sagamore. No television sets clutter the rooms. Showers have been added to the old-fashioned bathtubs as an afterthought. The toilet seat has not been sanitized and banded. Floorboards squeak. And there are real pitchers to hold the drinking water (which comes, incidentally, not from the lake but from an

Adirondack mountain stream). The original Sagamore was built in 1883, about a hundred years after Lord Jeffrey Amherst mopped up the French and Indians in these parts, and Gentleman Johnny Burgoyne surrendered to General Horatio Gates at nearby Ticonderoga; but the present hotel was put up just before the stock market tumbled in the twenties. Through the years it has hosted everyone from photographer Alfred Stieglitz to golfers Richard M. Nixon and Sherman Adams. The Sagamore is now strictly a summer resort, on the American Plan, with plenty of activities—indoor and out—gymnasium, exercise machines, indoor pool, outdoor pool, six clay tennis courts, the lake for swimming and sailing, eighteen holes of golf a mile away at the hotel's own course. Chef Francesco Laudrone prepares a varied cuisine—Italian, continental, New York West Side; and entertainment includes combos and comedians in the lounge. 200 rooms. $76 to $91 AP. Closed Labor Day to mid-May. *Hotel Sagamore, Bolton Landing, N.Y. 12814 (telephone 518–644–3121).*

L'HOSTELLERIE BRESSANE, HILLSDALE

This is the sort of place where you come to tuck into *poitrine et haut de cuisse de canard en feuilles de choux* and *truit fraiche braisée au citron, sauce crème aux ciboulettes,* topped off with *oeufs à la neige, sauce neige, sauce au Grand Marnier,* and *citrons givrés,* and one of the inn's selection of twenty cognacs and armagnacs. Owner/chef Jean Morel's masterworks will set you back $50 to $60 a couple, but if it's any consolation you'd have paid much more for his cuisine when he worked in one of Manhattan's classiest restaurants. His *hostellerie* is an eighteenth-century Dutch Colonial mansion, of scrubbed russet-colored brick with white trim, standing at the junction of two country roads (across the street, unfortunately, from a Gulf station). The ground floor is given over to four snug, candlelit dining rooms and a split-level Victorian cocktail lounge; the four large guest rooms on the second and third floors are furnished country inn style with Hanover headboards, Windsor rockers, candle stands, and share two bathrooms. They're a mite overpriced, but Chef Morel wants serious diners and not "people in off the highway looking for a cheap room." 4 rooms, $45 and $75 (with bath) CP. *L'Hostellerie Bressane, Hillsdale, N.Y. 12529 (telephone 518–325–3412).*

THE 1770 HOUSE, EAST HAMPTON

There are only seven rooms here, but enough antiques to fill a Vanderbilt mansion. The reception desk is an assemblage of bank teller's cage, English letter box, and church collection box; walls are lined with original art from magazines of the twenties; and if you want to follow the chimes and ticking you'll find thirty (count them!) antique clocks, eight of them in the dining room alone. The original house is, of course, eighteenth century, but only in 1977 did it find its true métier, when the Perle family moved in with their antiques and talents. Sidney Perle is official greeter/host/bookkeeper, wife Miriam (who used to run a cookery school in Great Neck) supervises the kitchen. So popular is the dining room here that there are three sittings for dinner (6:30, 8:00, and 9:15, $36 to $40 for two). A typical evening may begin with scalloped oysters or pasta salad with crabmeat, continue with cassoulet or oriental lamb kebob, end with apricot mousse and whipped cream. Predinner drinks are served around the fireplace in the library, Mozart playing quietly in the background, or in the lively Tap Room downstairs, with its old hickory beams and Dutch fireplace.

East Hampton is one of the prettiest villages on Long Island, with a village pond where there should be a village green, a summer stock theater across the street from the inn, and acres of beautiful beach nearby. 6 rooms, 1 suite, from $69 to $100 CP. Reservations necessary for dinner; served only on Friday and Saturday in winter. *The 1770 House, 143 Main Street, East Hampton, N.Y. 11937 (telephone 516–324–1770).*

SWISS HUTTE INN, HILLSDALE

Behind the lodge, a steep hill struggles up to the highway; facing the lodge, across the meadow, is Catamount. The view is everything: you see it from the balcony of your room, when you're dining on the patio or outdoor terrace, when you're relaxing in the two wooden armchairs on the jetty by the pond. Even the Rode Gluckel Bar has its windows angled to take in the mountain view.

The Swiss Hutte lodge was a farm before the Breens converted it into a lodge and tacked on a motel wing. There's nothing grand about the Hutte; it's rustic in a yodelly sort of way, a pleasant, friendly place in a sheltered setting. You can swim in the spring-fed pond by the edge of the meadow, or in the heated pool (by the side of the lodge but actually in Massachusetts); walking trails wind up into the forest and lead you miles away from everyone. In winter you can skate on the pond, ski cross-country along the trails you hiked in winter, or ski the slopes of Catamount.

The rooms are so-so (all with TV, private bath/shower, individually controlled heating or air conditioning, balcony but no phone), but the lodge itself has a piney, flowery atmosphere that puts you in the mood for a hearty meal—the inn's specialty: scampi Dijonnaise, *roulade de porc Cordon Bleu,* that sort of thing, with a few items such as schnitzels, sauerbraten, and steaks in the $8 to $12 bracket. Any of the Swiss Hutte's dishes tastes more scrumptious on the terrace surrounded by pine, crabapple, and honey locust trees, with the stars over Catamount and the brook trickling by beyond the pond. 20 rooms, 1 suite, MAP rates $84 to $96. *Swiss Hutte Inn, Route 23, Hillsdale, N.Y. 12529 (telephone 518–325–3333).*

THREE VILLAGE INN, STONY BROOK

The inn is best known as a restaurant, an hour and a half drive from Manhattan, but you can stretch the evening into a night because there are a few guest rooms upstairs. Storybook Stony Brook is one of the oldest settlements on Long Island (it was founded sometime in the 1660s), a seafaring town where men built ships and then put to sea in them. The inn was built in

1785 by one of these versatile seafarers, Jonas Smith, who also happened to be Long Island's first millionaire; it stands at the end of the village green, down by the harbor, a white clapboard building sheltered by locust trees and surrounded by shrubbery.

Drive out here and stuff yourself on Stony Brook Harbor clams on the half shell, New England codfish cakes, sautéed Long Island bay scallops, or roast turkey with chestnut dressing; but it's the inn's dessert list that will make you thankful you had the foresight to book a room for the night— Colonial nut layer cake, steamed fruit pudding with rum hard sauce, ginger sundae, fresh persimmon with cream, Concord grape fluff with soft custard sauce, New England mince pie. Etcetera.

The alternatives to the Long Island Expressway turn out to be seven pretty little Colonial-style rooms above the Tap Room, all with private bath, air conditioning, wall-to-wall carpeting, and television.

There are also a few motel rooms in cottages around the corner, overlooking the yacht marina and a few yards from a stretch of sandy beach where you can rest up before dinner. 22 rooms, from $45 to $60 EP. *Three Village Inn, Stony Brook, Long Island, N.Y. (telephone 516–751–0555).*

NORTH CAROLINA

FAIRFIELD INN, SAPPHIRE

The setting alone is worth a visit—a huge, gracious, turn-of-the-century inn surrounded by stately pines, with a graceful, manicured back lawn sweeping down to a mirrored lake abutting a sheer rock precipice. If the setting is a dazzling gem, the inn could be, too, but it isn't. The rooms are small and unimaginatively decorated, and some of the public areas need repairs. But worse, the management is pushing real estate—even in the guest rooms. However, as of October 1980, Fairfield Inn came under new management, the Fairfield Community of Arkansas, which owns six other resorts. Improvements, they say, are forthcoming. In any case you can enjoy the splendors of the valley by skipping the inn and checking into the well-kept rustic cottage or luxury villas nestled among the trees, still close to the inn. The sports facilities are outstanding—the resort is also the Country Club of Sapphire Valley. Here you can play eighteen holes of challenging golf; play tennis, night or day, on one of ten courts; ride horses on miles of winding wooded bridle trails; swim in cool Fairfield Lake or in one of two heated swimming pools; boat in the lake in a canoe or rowboat; fish for bream and bass in the lake in the lake or mountain trout in the streams; take walks along mountain trails, around the lake, or under waterfalls. At night the inn and club have dancing and live cloggers and mountain music (but bring your own liquor, you're in a dry county). (S.H.) 55 inn rooms, from $42 to $46; condominiums from $55 to $70; 9 cottages $60 EP. *Fairfield Inn, Sapphire Valley Resort, Star Route 70, Box 80, Sapphire, N.C. 28774 (telephone 704–743–3441).*

OHIO

THE GOLDEN LAMB, LEBANON

This is Ohio's oldest. Since it opened its doors, The Golden Lamb has hosted ten presidents (including U. S. Grant and John Quincy Adams), several writers (Charles Dickens for one), and statesmen (DeWitt Clinton and Henry Clay, among others). But when *they* stayed here they didn't have great trucks growling past the window at three o'clock in the morning. If the Lamb were out in the fields, it would be an ideal nook for lovers; as it is it's right smack in the middle of town, so it can only be recommended as a pleasant place to spend a night on the way to somewhere else. The rooms are charmers—all done in period furniture, all of them with private bathrooms, some with big fourposter beds and rag rugs, all with TV and air conditioning. Beware: people who drop in for dinner are invited to take a look at the guest rooms when the doors are open, so remember to keep yours closed (and to be on the safe side, keep it *locked* when you're using it). All the rooms are named for notables who've visited the inn, and even if you've never heard of Ormsby Mitchell, ask for his room; it's pink and pretty with a pencil post bed, and it's on the quiet side away from the main street.

Diners at the Golden Lamb seem to outnumber staying guests by a thousand to one, and dining used to be a hassle, but now overnight guests get priority dinner reservations. The dining rooms are attractive in a ye-olde-tavern sort of way (apart from the intrusive piped music that does nothing to enhance the nineteenth-century atmosphere); the food is hearty and tasty, and the menus feature curiosities like Shaker sugar pie and prune and butternut fudge pie.

Right inn, wrong place. 18 rooms, EP rates $36 to $45. *The Golden Lamb, 27 S. Broadway, Lebanon, Ohio 45036 (telephone 513–932–5065).*

OREGON

THE INN AT OTTER CREST, OTTER ROCK

The inspiration for the inn is one of those teetering pastel villages that decorate hillsides along Italy's Amalfi Drive. Here it's been translated into the setting of an Oregon pine forest, with weathered cedar replacing the pastel stucco, and a restless ocean replacing the placid sea.

The inn's two-story lodges are stacked higgledy-piggledy with covered walkways and stairways, with the undergrowth and tumbled timbers lying around undisturbed for a natural look. A self-operated lift takes you from the top of the inn down the hill to the top of the cliff, where you can admire the dramatic seascape.

There are 272 rooms in all, almost half of them with fireplaces; the decor is modern, fairly subdued, and the occasional dreary painting is over-whelmed by the cedar interiors and picture windows. Ask for one of the suites with a loft—bedroom and bathroom upstairs, kitchen and lounge downstairs. Where the cliff juts out into the sea there's a restaurant vaguely (very vaguely) modeled on the dining room of an ocean liner. It's a red-and-lilac room called The Flying Dutchman, with a wide-ranging cuisine—including seafood Wellington.

A few steps from the restaurant there's a heated pool, with therapy pool, sauna (all open all year) and glass-enclosed sun terrace; another few steps brings you to a pathway leading down to the beach and a state-owned marine garden. 272 rooms, from $48 to $115 EP. *The Inn at Otter Crest, P.O. Box 50, Otter Rock, Ore. 97369 (telephone 503–765–2111).*

THE INN OF THE 7TH MOUNTAIN, BEND

The name is romantic enough. Ditto the setting: among the tall pines, red-barked manzanitas and blue sage of Oregon's High Country, surrounded by forest trails, rivers, and waterfalls, with Mount Bachelor popping its almost-perfect cone above the pines. In winter, 7th Mountain is a ski resort; for the remainder of the year it's a mountain playground with tennis, iceskating, outdoor chess with handcarved three-foot-high pieces, raft trips down the rapids, sailing and rowing on the lake; two heated pools, a therapeutic pool, two saunas, horseback riding, hiking, bicycles, golf. The two hundred guest rooms are in rows of cedar-sided villas around the perimeter, so that *all* the picture windows look out onto views of lake, forest, and mountain; they all have fireplaces, contemporary decor and furniture, color TV, tiled bathrooms, and thermostatically controlled temperatures. 200 condominiums, $34 to $86 EP. *The Inn of the 7th Mountain, P.O. Box 1207, Bend, Ore. 97701 (telephone 503–382–8711).*

PENNSYLVANIA

TULPEHOCKEN MANOR PLANTATION AND INN, MYERSTOWN

Go easy as you drive around the big barn because the geese may be sitting in the middle of the road. And if no one answers the doorbell, it's probably because Jim Henry is out mending the east fence; he'll be back soon, so just pull up one of the fourteen chairs on the veranda and enjoy the shade of the two tall maple trees.

Tulpehocken is a working farm that also takes in a few tourists and sight-seers because it's old, unique, and historic (it's now listed in the National Register of Historic Sites); it was built about the same time as the Republic, by a German settler who quarried his own limestone and cut the timber from the family's own groves of walnut trees. The original two-story building has had several additions, including a mansard roof, a third story, and an ornate two-story veranda. The other buildings on the property are unique for this part of the world—they're built Swiss-style over a ground-floor walk-through archway.

The farm was bought in 1960 by the Nissly family and Jim Henry, who've restored it and filled the bedrooms with furnishings of the period. Filled? Stuffed. Clogged. Like the creation of a benign Charles Addams. You squeeze your way to bed past a jumble of Victoriana, Belgian glass doors, handcarved walnut banisters, painted slate mantels, handcarved yellow pine doors, brass table lamps, Hitchcock chairs, Windsor chairs. One of the rooms has a fourposter bed and matching chest of drawers, another a bed with a headboard over eight feet tall and weighing between five-hundred and six-hundred pounds. The farm has thirty-one rooms in all; nine of them are in the adjoining old stone houses (with kitchenettes and private baths, but with nothing like the personality of the manor rooms). The thirteen rooms in the manor house share three bathrooms (a fact that didn't faze some multimillionaires who stayed there a few months ago).

Tulpehocken is a lazy place, a place to lie on the grass, chew a blade of grass, and dream dreams, or in winter a cozy place to curl up with a good book or something. It would be the ideal hideaway if you didn't have to leave the place every time you want a coffee, Coke, or chocolate chip cookie, though breakfast juices are served in the front foyer. If the geese don't get out of the way and let you drive to the local diner, you may not get breakfast at all. 31 rooms, from $30 to $40 EP. *Tulpehocken Manor Inn and Plantation, R.D. 2, Myerstown, Pa. 17067 (telephone 717–866–4926)*.

SOUTH CAROLINA

FRIPP ISLAND RESORT, FRIPP ISLAND

The full title incudes the ominous words *and Executive Conference Center*, but with three thousand acres of resort you can probably escape any crowds. Most of those three thousand acres are given over to natural terrain, typical Low Country landscape of salt marshes, live oaks, palm ferns; the remainder is a carefully designed resort of condominiums, anything from comfortable one-bedroom to three-bedroom suites and houses, weaving among an Olympian array of sports facilities—beach (three miles), tennis (pro shop, fourteen courts, with lights), golf (eighteen holes, with another thirty-six fifteen miles away), swimming pools (five in all), sport fishing, bicycling, fourteen-foot Aqua Cat sailboats, Parcourse for joggers (one and a half miles, eighteen exercise stations). There are four restaurants or snack bars right on the island, several more nearby, and two cocktail lounges for the evenings. Groceries can be picked up at the Island Grocery Store if you want to do your own cooking and have dinner in bed. The resort is now owned and managed by a company called Brandermill, from North Carolina and Virginia; they still have some organizational problems to straighten out, but they've made progress, so keep Fripp in mind because it's less crowded than its neighbor, Hilton Head. 123 rooms (the best best for lovers are the 1-bedroom Ocean

Front and Ocean View units). $50 to $220 EP (lower in winter). *Fripp Island Beach Club, Fripp Island, S.C. 29920 (telephone 803–838–2411).*

VERMONT

ARLINGTON INN, ARLINGTON

The bulky wine list would be the envy of many Manhattan bistros, and many big-city restaurateurs might also admire the *intime* Country Chic dining room, tastefully decorated in autumnal colors accented with brass candlesticks and Wedgwood. The Deming Tavern next door is a nice old pine-paneled snuggery, with a veranda sporting some of the most massive, chunkiest Quebeçoise rocking chairs you've ever seen. A lawn and tall maples screen the traffic from the inn, a late nineteenth-century structure in Greek Revival wedding cake style. The seven guest rooms in the main house are named for members of the Deming family, who built the mansion and lived there for years; of these Chloe's Room is most romantic, Pamela's Room the most spacious, Mary's Room the smallest (and least expensive). Arlington, the town, is a pretty backwater on the western flanks of the Green Mountains, just across the New York line. 7 rooms, $35 to $60 EP. *Arlington Inn, Route 7, Arlington, Vt. 05250 (telephone 802–375–6532).*

CHESTER INN, CHESTER

After a while it gets to be like a movie scenario: young couple gets fed up with life in big city, moves to country, buys old inn, lives happily, but busily, ever after. In this case the big city was Cleveland, the couple Betsy and Tom Guido, a former insurance executive, and the inn the nineteenth-century Chester Inn in southern Vermont.

It's colored beige trimmed with brown, a stubby three-story building sitting well back from the main street on the village green, its facade dominated by verandas and porches where you can sit and rock and watch a day in the life of a small Vermont town. The spacious lounge has generous supplies of magazines, armchairs, and sofas grouped around a big wood-burning fireplace; the walls are lined with original paintings by friends of the Guidos, the furnishings are country primitive. Pride of the place among the guest rooms goes to the Victorian Suite with authentic brocade swag draperies and a volume of Victorian poetry on the marble-topped night stand. Step through the doors of the cocktail lounge and you're insulated from the village green, on a patio with a heated pool surrounded by pink geraniums in pots; farther down the backyard there are two tennis courts and a garden growing fresh vegetables, herbs, and flowers for the inn dining room. Cleveland is light years away. 33 rooms, including 3 suites, EP (including breakfast) $31 to $45. *Chester Inn, Main Street, Chester, Vt. 05143 (telephone 802–875–2444).*

NEWFANE INN, NEWFANE

This is the less famous of the two inns in this pretty Vermont village. The Four Columns (see elsewhere in this guide) attracts attention with its superior kitchen, but the Old Newfane, as it's sometimes called, is more authentic—white clapboard with a long veranda and wicker rocking chairs facing the meetinghouse on the common. The dining room is the main reason to stay here, especially some of the continental dishes (the owners are European, trained at some of *the* grand hotels), and a meal will cost less here than at the Four Columns. However, on three recent visits we've been to see only one room ("Oh no, not *another* guidebook . . . " was the response last time around). A suite, presumably one of the best, but not very exciting. 10 rooms. $40–$50 EP. *Newfane Inn, Newfane, Vt. 05345 (telephone 802–365–4427).*

SAXTONS RIVER INN, SAXTONS RIVER

The rooms are named for the theme of the decor and give you an idea of the free-ranging, almost whimsical styling—the Cat Room, the Jonquil Suite, the Daisy Room. If you feel like slipping between Bill Blass sheets, you know which room to ask for; if you prefer a bed with iron-and-brass frame, ask for the Iron Room. A sleigh bed? The Sleigh Room. The inn's twenty guest chambers are spread over two floors of the three-story inn, and an annex across the street, the Colvin House, where the prime nest is the Major Angus Suite. Some of the rooms have private bath or shower, others share the bathroom down the hall, but the inn's rate sheet lists all the details, room by cheerful room. Innkeeper Averill Larsen's main responsibility is the kitchen, where she prepares dishes not usually found on country inn menus—*sambal goreng* (chicken livers pan-fried in a soy sauce, Indonesian-style); Greek *spanakopeta*; chicken breasts Savoyarde (with artichoke hearts and white cheese sauce). 20 rooms, half with private bath or shower. $30 to $45 CP. No credit cards. Closed January, and open only weekends in February and March. *Saxtons River Inn, Main Street, Saxtons River, Vt. 05154 (telephone 802–869–2110).*

SUGARBUSH INN, WARREN

The main attraction here, of course, is sports. Skiing in winter (downhill and cross-country), the Ken Rosewall/Jack Gardiner Tennis Ranch (sixteen courts) in summer. To say nothing of the soaring, riding, golfing, and hiking nearby. The inn itself, despite its traditional white clapboard style, is relatively new, poised on the crest of a hill, just before the road dips down to Sugarbush Village. Tall hedgerows protect it from the traffic; a glass-enclosed, plant-draped porch lets you enjoy your lunch while you enjoy the sun. Decor is a sort of Contemporary Colonial—comfortable and carpeted but undistinguished. If you want accommodations with more flair, check into one of the new (but more expensive) condominium units across the road. 70 rooms, $60 to $90 EP (lower in summer). *Sugarbush Inn, Warren, Vt. 05674 (telephone 802–583–2301).*

WESTON INN, WESTON

If ratings were awarded solely for friendliness and enthusiasm, the Weston would score well. It's a small, green clapboard village inn, once a farmhouse; the hayloft is now a bar, the dining room is lined with timbers from an old woodshed. The only way to get from the dining room to the Lilliputian lounge is through the kitchen, but this is one case where too many cooks never seem to spoil the broth. Or chowder. Or Chinese roast tenderloin of pork, or blueberry torte, or sour cream apple pie. The guest rooms are cramped, but most of them manage to tuck in a private bath or shower, and the decorations and furnishings have an unpretentious charm. The charm is enhanced by judiciously placed antiques, assorted wood-burning stoves, and hand-thrown pottery. But it's the easygoing, unformulated hospitality of owners Sue and Stu Douglas that gives the Weston its special appeal. They're young, eager-to-please ex–New Yorkers. They learned the business, we've been told, from a correspondence course; now their school should take a correspondence course from the Douglases. Weston is a pretty village with an octagonal bandstand on the village green, a classic country store, a few crafts shops and workshops, and the Weston Theater, which puts on some of the best summer stock in New England. In winter the inn is popular with cross-country skiers, for whom the Douglases provide hot spiced cider and homemade cookies. 11 rooms, from $35 to $40 CP. No credit cards; may be closed for a few weeks in November. *Weston Inn, Route 100, Weston, Vt. 05161 (telephone 802–824–5804).*

WASHINGTON

LAKE QUINAULT LODGE, QUINAULT

Turn off the highway at the signs for South Shore Recreation area and drive *east* for half an hour (mostly unpaved road) through tall stands of fir and pine and spruce until you come to an authentic rain forest. The lodge, the only country inn along this coast, is the nicest place in these parts for an overnight stop. It was built in 1925, in the shape of a cedar-shingled U, shrouded by spruce and cedar, above a vast lawn that sweeps down to the lake, with the tree-clad hills of the Olympic National Park rising from the far shore. In the cavernous lobby/lounge the rafters have hand-painted and hand-carved beams, the massive fireplace is native stone, the dining room is decorated with Indian artifacts, but the guest rooms upstairs in the main lodge (about half the total) are the kind of clean, comfortable country inn rooms you would find anywhere. Rooms in the adjoining Lakeside Inn have the rustic feel you'd hope to find in a setting like this, but be careful when choosing a room here because the kiddies' playground is right at the door, the parking lot at the rear. The Fireplace Rooms, in a new wing facing lawn and lake, are more spacious, more comfortable, with gas-powered fires and unrustic, uncountry inn, brown-orange-gold decor—but the view through the sliding glass doors makes up for it. Lake Quinault Lodge, then, is the kind of place you come to enjoy the outdoors rather than the indoors. It's also very moderately priced. 54 rooms, from $37 to $52 EP. *Lake Quinault Lodge, P.O. Box 7, Quinault, Wash. 98575 (telephone 206–288–2571).*

WEST VIRGINIA

PIPESTEM STATE PARK RESORT, HINTON

This is the poor man's Greenbrier. However, if you're looking for a room with a view, you'll see more trees and more mountains from the lodge at Pipestem than you could see if you climbed the flagpole at Greenbrier. Pipestem is a state park high in the Appalachians. It gets its name from *spiraea alba*, a hollow-stemmed plant that the Indians used for making peace pipes. The hills around here are covered with this *spiraea alba*, as well as forsythia and dogwood and blooming redbud, and pines and firs.

The main lodge is an overpowering seven-story timber-and-stone lodge perched on the edge of the hill. Its rooms are motelly, but who cares with that magnificent view out there beyond your balcony. All 113 rooms in the lodge have private bathrooms, room telephones, television, and individually controlled heating. There are also cottages snuggled among the trees, but even with fireplaces and porches they're more suitable for families than lovers.

The most unusual feature of Pipestem is Mountain Creek Lodge. This is a two-story complex of thirty guest rooms one-thousand feet down in Bluestone Canyon, at the edge of a winding mountain stream. The only way you can get down to the pleasant, comfortable motel-type rooms is by a thirty-six-hundred-foot aerial tramway (it's free, and runs more or less at your convenience). There's also a café/restaurant down there, so you have no reason to surface.

All the facilities of the lodge take advantage of the superb view—even the indoor swimming pool has windows two floors high, so you can frolic around in the pool even in winter and enjoy the layers of mountains covered with snowlike mounds of whipped cream. As a guest of the resort you have access to the state park's sporting facilities—miles of walking and riding trails, a nine-hole and an eighteen-hole golf course, tennis courts, archery ranges, and an outdoor theater. But nothing they perform there can be as dramatic as that view. 1980 EP rates $29 to $32. *Pipestem State Park Resort, Pipestem, W.Va. 25979 (telephone 304–466–1800).*

WISCONSIN

BAY SHORE INN, STURGEON BAY

Come on in, past the rail fence, the apple trees and the garden, and make yourself at home on one of the most scenic spots along Sturgeon Bay. The original inn here dates back to 1922 and still has the same owners, the Hanson family, who've kept things up to date, adding rooms and giving every room a private bath. Besides the white frame inn there are two motel-type units with rustic paneled pine rooms and porches, and another half a dozen A-frame cottages hidden in the trees along the grounds.

Down the path at the sandy small beach, guests can swim, waterski, sail, take a boat ride, or row their own boats. Above, there are tennis courts, hiking trails, and bikes for guests—all included in the rates. There's also a recreation room with Ping-Pong and such, and archery, shuffleboard, horseshoes, and basketball. If that sounds like something for everyone in the family, it is—and during the summer season the place is filled with families enjoying it all. Come spring or fall, however, when the kids are safely in school, here's a quiet getaway in an idyllic spot with everything you'd ever want to do—and hardly anyone around to watch you do it. (E.B.) From $86 to $90 MAP (July 1–September 1); $56 to $76 EP off-season. *Bay Shore Inn, Sturgeon Bay, Wisc. 54235 (telephone 414–743–4551).*

WHITE GULL INN, FISH CREEK

This is probably the closest you'll find to a Cape Cod inn west of Detroit. Nothing fancy, mind you; and small. But cozy, clean, and very American.

On the front porch are two settees, an old cider press, and a bulletin board covered with local notices. Out back is a flagstone patio where any Monday or Thursday you can mingle with Fish Creekers at the Early American Buffet, sampling such old-fashioned fare as turkey dumpling soup, corn and clam pie, maple-baked carrots, glazed ham, and scalloped potatoes. Or join the throngs who book weeks in advance for the Door County Fish Boil dinners featuring Lake Michigan catch-of-the-day, boiled potatoes, home-made coleslaw, and homebaked cherry pie. Top that off with a frothy Milwaukee beer and you've had yourself a good helping of old Wisconsin hospitality.

After a pleasant meal in the coolness of a Door County evening, take a stroll around the trim little village of Fish Creek, down to the dock, or over to Sunset Park. Sit by the fire in the parlor or retire to your little room that opens onto the second-story porch. Come winter, the inn opens weekends and you can fill up on homemade buttermilk pancakes and real maple syrup, then head for the excellent cross-country skiing in two nearby state parks. A glowing fire and hot cider will be waiting when you return. There's a simplicity and quiet about Door County, and Fish Creek, and the White Gull Inn in particular. Let the rest of the world drift away on the evening breeze while you cuddle up together in a white iron bedstead like Grandma and Grandpa used to have. (L.E.B.) 15 rooms, from $30 to $65 EP. *White Gull Inn, Box 175, Fish Creek, Wisc. 54212 (telephone 414–868–3517).*

The Rates –
AND HOW TO FIGURE THEM OUT

Hotels have different ways, often unfathomable, of establishing their rates, and what you're going to pay depends on a tangle of variables. Twin beds versus double beds. With bath, without bath. Lower floor, upper floor. On beach, off beach. And so on. I wish I could spell out all the variations for each hotel, but if I were to try, the seasons would be over before I managed to get halfway through. In any case, I assume that you like each other so much that tiresome trivia and a few dollars won't come between you and a glorious time.

A lot of letter writing, telephone calls, interrogations, and other travail have gone into acquiring accurate and up-to-date rates for this edition. The bulk of the research took place in the fall of 1980 and the first few months of 1981, so the rates printed in these pages are, to the best of my knowledge, accurate for the peak season of 1981. I stress these dates because some readers complain about inaccurate rates two or three *years* after the guidebook is published. It's almost impossible for innkeepers (especially in smaller inns without computers and economists) to forecast their costs accurately, and they may have to make additional price hikes as the season progresses. Therefore, as innkeepers always stress:

ALL RATES IN THIS GUIDEBOOK ARE SUBJECT TO CHANGE WITHOUT NOTICE, DUE TO MATTERS BEYOND THE INNKEEPERS' CONTROL AND THE AUTHOR'S CONTROL.

The best we can hope to do here is give you, as accurately as possible, the rates in effect at the beginning of 1981. This way you can use them for *comparative* purposes, by comparing how much it will cost you to stay at Hotel A compared with Hotel B. Supposedly, if rates go up for Hotel A, they will also climb at Hotel B, presumably in proportion. Always confirm the specific rate you will pay with the innkeeper when you make your reservation. If you have time, get the confirmation in writing, so that you have a record of precisely what has been agreed upon.

Remember also to check in the text and the data listed at the end of each hotel in this guide to see which activities are offered to guests without extra charge. Tennis, for example, is free at some resorts but costs a packet at others; it is impossible for us to keep track of and record all these variations, but we have, wherever practical, noted the differences. For example, the rate quoted in the listing that follows for Tanque Verde Ranch in Tucson, Arizona, includes horseback riding; the rate for Tides Inn in Irvington, Virginia, includes dinner cruises on a 128-foot yacht.

Categories of rates

EP	European Plan	You pay for the room only, no meals, not even breakfast.
CP	Continental Plan	You get bed and breakfast, usually a "continental" breakfast of croissant, muffins, or rolls, with juice and coffee.
MAP	Modified American Plan	You get room with breakfast plus dinner (which in some cases may be exchanged for lunch).
FAP	Full American Plan	You get room plus breakfast, lunch, and dinner, and sometimes also afternoon tea.

MAP and FAP oblige you to order your meals from a fixed menu, usually with a choice of dishes, and often with additional dishes available for a small surcharge (usually the dishes you really want—like lobster in Maine).

Which rate should you choose? Each has its advantages. MAP and FAP sometimes work out to be less expensive than the combined EP rate plus the à la carte cost of meals; in many cases, too, you may be staying in a hotel mainly because of the reputation of its dining room and you will be intending to dine there anyway; in some cases the hotel may be the only or the best restaurant for miles around. However, it's nice to have the *option*, so choose EP or CP rates so that you can take advantage of good restaurants in the surrounding countryside.

Meals that are served *family style*, standard practice in a few small inns, do not involve dining with the family, (although that *may* be the case, and often is a real pleasure); it simply means that dinner will be served at a fixed hour, with little or no choice of menu (unless you have a word with the cook in advance and have sound dietary or religious reasons for wanting a change).

In the table that follows: 1) tax and service charge apply to the total bill unless noted: 2) X means that off-season rates are available; 3) * means special inclusive packages are available—"weekend," "honeymoon," "tennis," etc.; 4) + means there is a minimum stay required for advance reservations.

PLEASE NOTE: All rates are for double rooms, peak season.

HOTEL	PEAK-SEASON RATES	TYPE OF RATE	SERVICE CHARGE (%)	TAX (%)	OFF-SEASON RATES	NOTES

THE NEW ENGLAND COAST AND LONG ISLAND

HOTEL	PEAK-SEASON RATES	TYPE OF RATE	SERVICE CHARGE (%)	TAX (%)	OFF-SEASON RATES	NOTES
GURNEY'S INN Montauk, N.Y.	136–176	MAP	15	7	X	+
MONTAUK YACHT CLUB & INN Montauk, N.Y.	190	MAP	Opt.	7		
THE GRISWOLD INN Essex, Conn.	28–42	EP	Opt.	7.5	X	
THE INN AT CASTLE HILL Newport, R.I.	33–75 300–420 (cottages, weekly)	CP	Opt.	6	X	
NEW SEABURY RESORT New Seabury, Mass.	95–125	EP	15 (f/b)	5.7	X	
CHATHAM BARS INN Chatham, Mass.	120–140	AP	Opt.	5.7		
SHIP'S KNEES INN E. Orleans, Mass.	18–46	CP	Opt.	5.7	X	
NAUSET HOUSE INN Orleans, Mass.	25–40	EP	Opt.	5.7		
JARED COFFIN HOUSE Nantucket, Mass.	40–55	EP	Opt.	5.7		
THE WHITE ELEPHANT HOTEL Nantucket, Mass.	95–125 110–295 (cottages)	CP	$2 (daily)	5.7	X	
SHIPS INN Nantucket, Mass.	28–34	CP	Opt.	5.7	X	
WESTMOOR INN Nantucket, Mass.	40–56	EP	Opt.	5.7	X	
CHARLOTTE INN Martha's Vineyard, Mass.	52–65	CP	Opt.	5.7	X	
DAGGETT HOUSE Martha's Vineyard, Mass.	38–55	CP	Opt.	5.7	X	
SEACREST MANOR Rockport, Mass.	40–54	CP	Opt.	5.7	X	
WENTWORTH-BY-THE-SEA Portsmouth, N.H.	90–120	MAP	15	6		
STAGE NECK INN York Harbor, Me.	65–80	EP	Opt.	5		
DOCKSIDE GUEST QUARTERS York Harbor, Me.	36.50–39.75	EP	Opt.	5	X	
THE CAPTAIN LORD MANSION Kennebunkport, Me.	49–69	CP	5	5		
BLACK POINT INN Prouts Neck, Me.	110–160	FAP	12	5		
THE SQUIRE TARBOX INN Westport Island, Me.	40	EP	15 (f/b)	5		
SPRUCE POINT INN Boothbay Harbor, Me.	94–106	MAP	12	5	X	
SAMOSET RESORT Rockport, Me.	58–62	EP	Opt	5	X	
PILGRIM'S INN Deer Isle, Me.	96 600 (weekly)	MAP	12	5		

HOTEL	PEAK-SEASON RATES	TYPE OF RATE	SERVICE CHARGE (%)	TAX (%)	OFF-SEASON RATES	NOTES

GREEN MOUNTAINS, WHITE MOUNTAINS

HOTEL	PEAK-SEASON RATES	TYPE OF RATE	SERVICE CHARGE (%)	TAX (%)	OFF-SEASON RATES	NOTES
THE INN AT SAWMILL FARM West Dover, Vt.	110–170	MAP	Opt.	5	X	
THE FOUR COLUMNS INN Newfane, Vt.	35–50	EP	Opt.	5		
THE OLD TAVERN AT GRAFTON Grafton, Vt.	30–60	EP	Opt.	5		
WOODSTOCK INN Woodstock, Vt.	49–73	EP	Opt.	5	X	
RELUCTANT PANTHER INN Manchester Village, Vt.	27–45	EP	15	5		
BARROWS HOUSE Dorset, Vt.	82–100	MAP	15	5		
HAWK MOUNTAIN Pittsfield, Vt.	94–104	EP	10	5	X	
TOPNOTCH AT STOWE Stowe, Vt.	75–100	EP	Opt.	5		
STOWEHOF INN Stowe, Vt.	53–85	MAP	15	5	X	
THE INN ON THE COMMON Craftsbury Common, Vt.	80–110	MAP	15	5		+
LOVETT'S INN Franconia, N.H.	46–50	EP	Opt.	6		*
SNOWY OWL INN Waterville Valley, N.H.	42–54	EP	Opt.	6	X	
STAFFORD'S-IN-THE-FIELD Chocorua, N.H.	84–90	MAP	15	6		+
THE JOHN HANCOCK INN Hancock, N.H.	35	EP	Opt.	Incl.		

IN AND AROUND THE BOSKY BERKSHIRES

HOTEL	PEAK-SEASON RATES	TYPE OF RATE	SERVICE CHARGE (%)	TAX (%)	OFF-SEASON RATES	NOTES
WHEATLEIGH Lenox, Mass.	145–175 (Thurs.–Sun.) 70–85 (Mon.–Wed.)	AP MAP	Opt.	6	X	+
THE RED LION INN Stockbridge, Mass.	36–62	EP	Opt.	5.7	X	+
THE PUBLICK HOUSE Sturbridge, Mass.	43–70	EP	Opt.	5.7 (room) 6 (f/b)	X	
LONGFELLOW'S WAYSIDE INN South Sudbury, Mass.	30	EP	Opt.	Incl.		
HARRISON INN AND CONFERENCE CENTER Southbury, Conn.	56–68 110–125 (suite)	EP	Opt.	7.5		*
WEST LANE INN Ridgefield, Conn.	65–75	CP	Opt.	7.5		

FROM THE ADIRONDACKS TO BUCKS COUNTY

HOTEL	PEAK-SEASON RATES	TYPE OF RATE	SERVICE CHARGE (%)	TAX (%)	OFF-SEASON RATES	NOTES
THE POINT Upper Saranac Lake, N.Y.	150–300	FAP (EP avail.)	Opt.	7		

HOTEL	PEAK-SEASON RATES	TYPE OF RATE	SERVICE CHARGE (%)	TAX (%)	OFF-SEASON RATES	NOTES
THE SPRINGSIDE INN Auburn, N.Y.	34.25	CP	Opt.	7		*
MOHONK MOUNTAIN HOUSE Mohonk Lake, N.Y.	132–146	FAP	$6 (daily)	7	X	+
AUBERGE DES QUATRE SAISONS Shandaken, N.Y.	58–70	MAP	Opt.	7		
SHERWOOD INN Skaneateles, N.Y.	30–50	EP	Opt.	7		
1740 HOUSE Lumberville, Pa.	46.60–53	CP	Incl.	Incl		+
BRAE LOCH VIEW Cazenovia, N.Y.	38	EP	6	7		
THE SIGN OF THE SORREL HORSE Quakertown, Pa.	34–36	CP	Opt.	6		

EAST SIDE, WEST SIDE

HOTEL	PEAK-SEASON RATES	TYPE OF RATE	SERVICE CHARGE (%)	TAX (%)	OFF-SEASON RATES	NOTES
THE UNITED NATIONS PLAZA HOTEL New York, N.Y.	125–205 275–595 (suite)	EP	Opt.	$2 (daily) 8		*
HOTEL ALGONQUIN New York, N.Y.	69–82 130–140 (suite)	EP	Opt.	$2 (daily) 8		
THE WYNDHAM HOTEL New York, N.Y.	66–75 100–130 (suite)	EP	Opt.	$2 (daily) 8		
THE MAYFAIR REGENT New York, N.Y.	115–220 (suite)	EP	Opt.	$2 (daily) 8		*
HOTEL CARLYLE New York, N.Y.	145–170 275–500 (suite)	EP		8		

AROUND THE CHESAPEAKE BAY

HOTEL	PEAK-SEASON RATES	TYPE OF RATE	SERVICE CHARGE (%)	TAX (%)	OFF-SEASON RATES	NOTES
ROBERT MORRIS INN Oxford, Md.	22–62	EP	Opt.	5		
THE MAINSTAY INN Cape May, N.J.	36–55	MAP	Opt.	5	X	
THE TIDES INN Irvington, Va.	124–160	FAP	Opt.	4	X	+
THE TIDES LODGE Irvington, Va.	91–108	MAP	Opt.	4	X	
COLONIAL HOUSES WILLIAMSBURG INN Williamsburg, Va.	65–105	EP	Opt.	4		
THE FAIRFAX HOTEL Washington, D.C.	120–150	EP	Opt.	10		*

UP HILL AND DOWN DALE—THE SHENANDOAH VALLEY AND BLUE RIDGE MOUNTAINS

HOTEL	PEAK-SEASON RATES	TYPE OF RATE	SERVICE CHARGE (%)	TAX (%)	OFF-SEASON RATES	NOTES
WAYSIDE INN Middletown, Va.	30–60	EP	Opt.	4		
SKYLAND LODGE Shenandoah Nat. Pk., Va.	35–65	EP	Opt.	4		

HOTEL	PEAK-SEASON RATES	TYPE OF RATE	SERVICE CHARGE (%)	TAX (%)	OFF-SEASON RATES	NOTES
BIG MEADOWS LODGE Shenandoah Nat. Pk., Va.	35–65	EP	Opt	4		
WINTERGREEN Wintergreen, Va.	72–90	EP	15	4		*
PEAKS OF OTTER LODGE Bedford, Va.	38	EP	Opt.	4		
THE HOMESTEAD Hot Springs, Va.	166–204	FAP	$6 (daily)	4	X	
BOAR'S HEAD INN Charlottesville, Va.	47–50	EP	Opt.	6		
THE GREENBRIER White Sulphur Springs, W.Va.	130–175	MAP	$11 (daily)	3	X	*
HOUND EARS LODGE AND CLUB Blowing Rock, N.C.	136–148	MAP	15	4	X	*
PISGAH INN Waynesville, N.C.	34.32 64.48 (suite)	EP	Opt.	4		
HIGH HAMPTON INN AND COUNTRY CLUB Cashiers, N.C.	70.50–78	FAP	10	4	X	

FROM THE CAROLINAS TO THE KEYS

HOTEL	PEAK-SEASON RATES	TYPE OF RATE	SERVICE CHARGE (%)	TAX (%)	OFF-SEASON RATES	NOTES
PINEHURST HOTEL AND COUNTRY CLUB Pinehurst, N.C.	75–90	EP	15	4	X	*
MILLS HOUSE Charleston, S.C.	70–85	EP	Opt.	4	X	
BATTERY CARRIAGE HOUSE Charleston, S. C.	58–63	CP	Opt.	4	X	
KIAWAH ISLAND INN AND RESORT Kiawah Island, S. C.	80–115	EP	15	4	X	*
SEABROOK ISLAND Seabrook Island, S. C.	60–90	EP	$2 (daily)	4	X	*
BEACH & RACQUET CLUB Isle of Palms, S. C.	75–100	EP	Opt.	4	X	*
HILTON HEAD INN AND SEA PINES RESORT Hilton Head Island, Ga.	85–100	EP	Opt.	4	X	*
17 HUNDRED 90 INN Savannah, Ga.	58–125	CP	Opt.	4 (state) 3 (room)		
THE CLOISTER Sea Island, Ga.	114–210	FAP	15	4	X	
THE KING AND PRINCE HOTEL St. Simons Island, Ga.	45–90	EP	Opt.	4 (state) 3 (room)	X	*
GREYFIELD INN Cumberland Island, Ga.	150	AP	15	4		
AMELIA ISLAND PLANTATION Amelia Island, Fla.	82–147	EP	15	4	X	
THE BREAKERS Palm Beach, Fla.	130–190	MAP	$14 (daily)	4	X	*

HOTEL	PEAK-SEASON RATES	TYPE OF RATE	SERVICE CHARGE (%)	TAX (%)	OFF-SEASON RATES	NOTES
PALM BEACH POLO AND COUNTRY CLUB West Palm Beach, Fla.	90	EP	Opt.	4	X	*
BOCA RATON HOTEL AND CLUB Boca Raton, Fla.	150–1,200	MAP	$7 (daily)	4	X	*
PIER HOUSE Key West, Fla.	90–175	EP	Opt.	4	X	+
FAR HORIZONS Longboat Key, Fla.	115–130	EP	Opt.	4	X	

FROM THE GREAT LAKES TO THE GULF

HOTEL	PEAK-SEASON RATES	TYPE OF RATE	SERVICE CHARGE (%)	TAX (%)	OFF-SEASON RATES	NOTES
GRAND HOTEL Mackinac Island, Mich.	120–200	FAP	18	4		*
HILTON SHANTY CREEK Bellaire, Mich.	43–73 75–120 (condominiums)	EP	Opt.	4	X	
DEARBORN INN COLONIAL HOMES AND MOTOR HOUSES Dearborn, Mich.	58–72	EP	Opt.	4		*
NATIONAL HOUSE Marshall, Mich.	35–50	CP	Opt.	4		
STAFFORD'S BAY VIEW INN Petoskey, Mich.	29–39	CP	Opt.	4		
THE HOMESTEAD Glen Arbor, Mich.	50–90	EP	Incl.	Incl.		+
THE RITZ CARLTON Chicago, Ill.	114–119 150–375 (suite)	EP	Opt.	8.1		*
THE WHITEHALL HOTEL Chicago, Ill.	110–140 170–450 (suite)	EP	Opt.	4		*
THE TREMONT HOTEL Chicago, Ill.	89–109 175–400 (suite)	EP	9.1	8.1		
THE PIONEER INN Oshkosh, Wisc.	45–49	EP	Opt.	8	X	
THE INN AT PLEASANT HILL Harrodsburg, Ky.	28–40	EP	Opt.	5 (state) 3 (room)		*
LODGE OF THE FOUR SEASONS Lake of the Ozarks, Mo.	125–165	FAP	15	5	X	*
HOTEL MAISON DE VILLE AND AUDUBON COTTAGES New Orleans, La.	70–96	EP	None	8		
THE SAINT LOUIS HOTEL New Orleans, La.	86–115	EP	Opt.	8		
GRAND HOTEL Point Clear, Ala.	45–62	MAP	15	4	X	*

IN AND AROUND THE ROCKIES

HOTEL	PEAK-SEASON RATES	TYPE OF RATE	SERVICE CHARGE (%)	TAX (%)	OFF-SEASON RATES	NOTES
TALL TIMBER Durango, Colo.	230 1,080 (weekly)	FAP	Opt.	5		

HOTEL	PEAK-SEASON RATES	TYPE OF RATE	SERVICE CHARGE (%)	TAX (%)	OFF-SEASON RATES	NOTES
STRATER HOTEL Durango, Colo.	38–45	EP	Opt.	8	X	*
KEYSTONE Keystone, Colo.	85–113	EP	Opt.	5		*
C LAZY U RANCH Granby, Colo.	970–1,100 (weekly)	FAP	Opt.	3	X	
THE HOME RANCH Clark, Colo.	950 (weekly)	FAP	Opt.	Incl.	X	
THE ASPEN CLUB CONDOMINIUMS Aspen, Colo.	400	EP	Opt.	7	X	
SUNDANCE Provo, Utah	150–225	EP	Opt.	4.75	X	
THE LODGE AT SNOWBIRD Snowbird, Utah	66–92	EP	Opt.	8 (room) 5 (food)	X	*
ALTA LODGE Alta, Utah	90–122	MAP	15	6.75	X	*
SUN VALLEY LODGE Sun Valley, Idaho	59–135	EP	Opt.	8	X	*
JENNY LAKE LODGE Grand Teton Nat. Pk., Wyo.	135	MAP	Opt.	4		
JACKSON LAKE LODGE Grand Teton Nat. Pk., Wyo.	92–136	EP	Opt.	4		

THE DESERT RESORTS OF THE GREAT SOUTHWEST

HOTEL	PEAK-SEASON RATES	TYPE OF RATE	SERVICE CHARGE (%)	TAX (%)	OFF-SEASON RATES	NOTES
THE BISHOP'S LODGE Santa Fe, N.M.	105–158	FAP	15	4.75	X	
RANCHO ENCANTADO Santa Fe, N.M.	75–135	MAP	Opt.	4	X	
SAGEBRUSH INN Taos, N.M.	28–36	EP	Opt.	4.75		*
ARIZONA INN Tucson, Ariz.	70–92	EP	16	7	X	
HACIENDA DEL SOL Tucson, Ariz.	100–120 150–175 (suite)	FAP	15	4		*
WESTWARD LOOK RESORT Tucson, Ariz.	71–91	EP	Opt.	3	X	*
TANQUE VERDE RANCH Tucson, Ariz.	100–160	FAP	15	4	X	*
THE LODGE ON THE DESERT Tucson, Ariz.	82 135	AP	Opt.	7 (room) 6 (f/b)	X	
SUNDANCER SADDLE AND SURREY RANCH RESORT Tucson, Ariz.	136–160	FAP	15	4		*
ARIZONA BILTMORE HOTEL Phoenix, Ariz.	125–145	EP	Opt.	5	X	*
MARRIOTT'S CAMELBACK INN Scottsdale, Ariz.	105–130	EP	Opt.	3	X	*
JOHN GARDINER'S TENNIS RANCH Scottsdale, Ariz.	120–175	MAP	15	4		*

HOTEL	PEAK-SEASON RATES	TYPE OF RATE	SERVICE CHARGE (%)	TAX (%)	OFF-SEASON RATES	NOTES
THE WIGWAM Litchfield Park, Ariz.	121–135	FAP	Opt.	4	X	*
WICKENBURG INN TENNIS AND GUEST RANCH Wickenburg, Ariz.	128–176	FAP	15	4	X	*
CAREFREE INN Carefree, Ariz.	80–90	EP	Opt.	3	X	*
GARLAND'S OAK CREEK LODGE Sedona, Ariz.	60–75	MAP	10	4		

SUNNY SOUTHERN CALIFORNIA

HOTEL	PEAK-SEASON RATES	TYPE OF RATE	SERVICE CHARGE (%)	TAX (%)	OFF-SEASON RATES	NOTES
INGLESIDE INN Palms Springs, Calif.	75–175	EP	Opt.	7	X	*
LA QUINTA HOTEL La Quinta, Calif.	80–125	EP	Opt.	8		
LA CASA DEL ZORRO Borrego Springs, Calif.	30–40 50 (house)	EP	Opt.	6	X	
FURNACE CREEK INN AND RANCH RESORT Death Valley, Calif.	110–130	MAP	Opt.	6		
RANCHO BERNARDO INN Rancho Bernardo, Calif.	85–93	EP	Opt.	8	X	*
LA VALENCIA HOTEL La Jolla, Calif.	42–54 60–100 (suite)	EP	Opt.	6	X	
THE INN AT RANCHO SANTA FE Rancho Santa Fe, Calif.	30–80	EP	Opt.	6		
BEVERLY HILLS HOTEL Beverly Hills, Calif.	85–140	EP	Opt.	7.5		
BEL-AIR HOTEL Los Angeles, Calif.	80–95	EP	Opt.	7.5		
WESTWOOD MARQUIS HOTEL Los Angeles, Calif.	100–140	EP	Opt.	7.5		
MARRIOTT'S SANTA BARBARA BILTMORE Santa Barbara, Calif.	70–115	EP	Opt.	8		

SAN FRANCISCO AND ITS NEIGHBORS

HOTEL	PEAK-SEASON RATES	TYPE OF RATE	SERVICE CHARGE (%)	TAX (%)	OFF-SEASON RATES	NOTES
VENTANA Big Sur, Calif.	115–135	CP	Opt.	8		+
HIGHLANDS INN Carmel Highlands, Calif.	96–190	MAP	Opt.	8 (room) 6 (sales)		
QUAIL LODGE Carmel Valley, Calif.	110–128	EP	Opt.	8		*+
THE SANDPIPER INN Carmel-by-the-Sea, Calif.	38–60	EP	Opt.	8	X	+
THE LODGE AT PEBBLE BEACH Pebble Beach, Calif.	125	EP	$12	8		+
MIYAKO HOTEL San Francisco, Calif.	84–106	EP	Opt.	9.75		
THE STANFORD COURT San Francisco, Calif.	127–161	EP	Opt.	9.75	X	

HOTEL	PEAK-SEASON RATES	TYPE OF RATE	SERVICE CHARGE (%)	TAX (%)	OFF-SEASON RATES	NOTES
THE MANSION San Francisco, Calif.	43–114	EP	Opt.	9.75		
THE PELICAN INN Muir Beach, Calif.	55–65	CP	Opt.	6		
SUTTER CREEK INN Sutter Creek, Calif.	40–65	CP	Opt.	6	X	
THE WINE COUNTRY INN St. Helena, Calif.	63–93	CP	Opt.	6		
THE MAGNOLIA HOTEL Yountville, Calif.	55–94	CP	Opt.	6		
BURGUNDY HOUSE Yountville, Calif.	53–68	CP	Opt.	6	X	
BORDEAUX HOUSE Yountville, Calif.	70	CP	Opt.	6	X	
SONOMA MISSION INN Boyes Hot Springs, Calif.	75–125	CP	Opt.	6		

THE PACIFIC NORTHWEST

HOTEL	PEAK-SEASON RATES	TYPE OF RATE	SERVICE CHARGE (%)	TAX (%)	OFF-SEASON RATES	NOTES
THE SEA RANCH LODGE Jenner, Calif.	47–65	EP	Opt.	6	X	
HERITAGE HOUSE Little River, Calif.	79–134	MAP	Opt.	6		
THE HEADLANDS INN Mendocino, Calif.	38–52	CP	Opt.	6		+
SALISHAN LODGE Gleneden Beach, Ore.	68–84	EP	Opt.	5	X	*+
SUNRIVER LODGE Sunriver, Ore.	64–82	EP	Opt.	6	X	*
TIMBERLINE LODGE Mount Hood, Ore.	38–79	EP	Opt.	6 (room)		
THE ADMIRALTY RESORT Port Ludlow, Wash.	42–52	EP	Opt.	5	X	
CAPTAIN WHIDBEY INN Whidbey Island, Wash.	25–50	EP	Opt.	5		*
EMPRESS HOTEL Victoria, B.C., Canada	62–80	EP	Opt.	5	X	*

HAWAII

HOTEL	PEAK-SEASON RATES	TYPE OF RATE	SERVICE CHARGE (%)	TAX (%)	OFF-SEASON RATES	NOTES
HOTEL HANA-MAUI Maui	139–178	FAP	Opt.	4		
KAPALUA BAY HOTEL Kapalua	156–204	MAP (EP avail.)	Opt.	4	X	
SHERATON-MOLOKAI RESORT Molokai	60–70 85–110 (suite)	EP	Opt.	4	X	
KAHALA HILTON Oahu, Honolulu	95–185 200–515 (suite)	CP	Opt.	4		
MAUNA KEA BEACH HOTEL Kamuela	185–230	MAP	15	4		*
KONA VILLAGE RESORT Kaupulehu-Kona	225	FAP	Opt.	4		
COCO PALMS RESORT HOTEL Kauai	59–95 100–205 (suite)	EP	Opt.	4	X	

POSTSCRIPT

If you'd like to share you experiences with other people who enjoy special places, please send me your comments, criticisms, and suggestions. Your reports can be invaluable in keeping track of the performance of individual inns. Also, if you'd be interested in subscribing to a quarterly newsletter featuring additional special places, in the U.S.A. and elsewhere, please let me know; if enough people are interested, I'll send you details at a later date.
Please address your letters:

Ian Keown
c/o Macmillan Publishing Company, Inc.
General Books Division, Adult Editorial
866 Third Avenue
New York, N.Y. 10022